PRESERVING
NEW YORK

NEW YORK PRESERVATION ARCHIVE PROJECT

PRESERVING NEW YORK

Winning the Right to Protect A City's Landmarks

ANTHONY C. WOOD

Routledge
Taylor & Francis Group
New York   London

Routledge
Taylor & Francis Group
270 Madison Avenue
New York, NY 10016

Routledge
Taylor & Francis Group
2 Park Square
Milton Park, Abingdon
Oxon OX14 4RN

Printed in the United States of America on acid-free paper
10 9 8 7 6 5 4 3 2 1

International Standard Book Number-13: 978-0-415-95284-2 (Hardcover)

Library of Congress Cataloging-in-Publication Data

Wood, Anthony C., 1954-
  Preserving New York : winning the right to protect a city's landmarks / Anthony C. Wood.
    p. cm.
  Includes bibliographical references and index.
  ISBN 978-0-415-95284-2 (cloth)
  1. Historic preservation--New York (State)--New York--History--20th century. 2. Historic buildings--Conservation and restoration--New York (State)--New York--History--20th century. 3. Architecture-- Conservation and restoration--New York (State)--New York--History--20th century. 4. New York (N.Y.)--Buildings, structures, etc. 5. New York (N.Y.)--Cultural policy. 6. New York (N.Y.)--History--20th century. I. Title.

  F128.37.W66 2007
  974.7'043--dc22
                                                    2007010037

Visit the Taylor & Francis Web site at
http://www.taylorandfrancis.com

and the Routledge Web site at
http://www.routledge.com

CONTENTS

To Anthony Badalamenti and in memory of my parents, Tanya and Leonard Wood

ACKNOWLEDGMENTS

Like the Landmarks Law itself, this book would not have been possible without the energy, excitement, and support of countless individuals and organizations. Over twenty years ago when I started to explore the story of how New York won the right to protect its landmarks, I had no idea it would ultimately take the form of a book. As a result, it is literally impossible to recall, let alone properly thank, everyone who has assisted me over these years. Many wonderful people have provided help, research assistance, encouragement, and suggestions. To all who played such a role but find themselves inadvertently omitted from those listed below, my sincere apologies and sincere thanks.

This book could not have been written without a six-month sabbatical provided by the Ittleson Foundation. For this I am indebted to all the foundation's trustees, particularly to H. Anthony Ittleson, Pam and Victor Syrmis, and Lionel Pincus.

A cadre of wonderful individuals and foundations provided essential funding for researchers, reproduction fees, and other costs associated with this book. Beyond their warm encouragement, the following generously financially supported this effort: Richard and Rosemary Vietor, R. Brandon Fradd, Constance and David Clapp, Christabel Gough, Henry Jordan, Arlene and Bruce Simon, Teri Slater, Jack Taylor, Suzanne Davis, Stephen Gross, Ruth Shuman, and Warrie Price. Foundations deserving great thanks are Furthermore: a program of the J. M. Kaplan Fund, the Ritter Foundation, the Norman and Rosita Winston Foundation, the Graham Foundation for Advanced Studies in the Fine Arts, the Felicia Fund, the Holbrook Family Foundation, and the Charina Foundation.

ACKNOWLEDGMENTS

x

Many individuals have provided encouragement, advice, information, and assistance essential to moving this project forward. Among them are J. Winthrop Aldrich, Eric and Mary Ann Allison, Simeon Bankoff, Kent Barwick, Laurie Beckelman, Bronson Binger, Maureen Bracken, Paul Byard, Nash Castro, Carol Clark, David Doheny, Stephen Facey, Margaret Ferguson, Amy Freitag, Ann Gaffney, Gregory Gilmartin, Roberta Brandes Gratz, Paul Gunther, Laura Hansen, Tony Hiss, Christopher Holbrook, Gordon Hyatt, John Jurayj, Ned Kaufman, Robert Kornfeld, Leah Krauss, Jeffrey Kroessler, Judy LaBelle, Steve Laise, David Lowe, George Martin, Randall Mason, Jerry Max, Felicia Mayro, David McBride, Tom Mellins, Richard Menschel, Pauline Metcalf, Dorothy Miner, Peg and Truman Moore, Charles Platt, Nicholas Platt, Rebecca Shanor, Carole and Richard Rifkind, David and Marie Ritter, Cricket Saurel, Claire Tankel, Anthony Tung, Vicki Weiner, Duane Watson, and Margot Wellington.

In researching a work like this, one makes the wonderful discovery that housed in a range of institutions from the likely, libraries and large institutions, to the unlikely, national fraternity offices and local civic groups, is a network of dedicated individuals as excited about the material they possess as the researcher who just discovered its existence. Archivists, researchers, and staffers in such places have helped ferret out informative documents and records. Thanks flow forth to such helpful institutions as the Manuscripts and Archives Division of the New York Public Library, the Central Office of the Chi Psi Fraternity, the Brooklyn Heights Association, the Municipal Art Society, New York City Department of Parks and Recreation, the Warwick Foundation, the Queens Borough Public Library, Long Island Division, the Century Association Archives Foundation, the Archives of American Art, the New York Community Trust, and Avery Architectural and Fine Arts Library. Particular individuals deserving recognition include Sam Bessey, James D. Birchfield, Russell A. Flinchum, Sally Forbes, Leonora Gidlund, Henrik Krogius, Michael Miscione, Kathy O'Callahan, Sony Onishi, Janet Parks, Laura Rosen, Judy Stanton, William Stingone, Sally Stokes, John Sutter, Judith Todman, and Melanie Yolles.

Of incredible value to this effort have been the memories that many protagonists in this story have shared. On the roster of those who have given generously of their time, memory, and patience are Seymour Boyers, Doris Diether, Marjorie Dunbar, Margot Gayle, Brendan Gill, Diana Goldstein, Harmon Goldstone, Carol Greitzer, Shirley Hayes, Ada Louise Huxtable, Robert Low, Otis Pratt Pearsall, Geoffrey Platt, Adolf Placzek, Henry Hope Reed, Norman Redlich, Whitney North (Mike) Seymour,

Jr., Henry Stern, members of the Switz Family, Elliot Willensky, Ruth Wittenberg, and Norval White.

Over the decades, I have benefited from the research assistance of an extremely talented brigade of historical detectives. Special kudos go to the ever resourceful and indefatigable Liz McEnaney, who not only served as research associate but also photo researcher extraordinaire. Others deserving thanks are Rudie Hurwitz, Susan De Vries, Richard Heaps, and Vanessa Norton.

For their extraordinary help, the following deserve special thanks. Joan Davidson's early belief in the project and her guidance were essential for making the book a reality. Lisa Ackerman and Andrew Dolkart provided invaluable critiques of the draft manuscript. The editorial assistance and strategic advice of Grace Friary were indispensable. To the entire team at Routledge/Taylor & Francis goes a very special thanks.

This book is an official project of the New York Preservation Archive Project. Many thanks to its board and staff for their help. The Archive Project receives generous support from the Samuel H. Kress Foundation and this project has particularly benefited from that assistance.

If despite the good efforts of all who have assisted in its creation, there are errors in the book, I alone am responsible. Though primarily an historic account, where opinions are expressed, they are solely those of the author.

In coming to a close, no words can express my thanks to Anthony Badalamenti. He lived with this project for years, made sacrifices for it, provided ongoing and essential support, contributed sage advice, assisted with research and analysis, and contributed invaluable insights. Without his constant encouragement, this book would not exist.

FOREWORD

It's ironic that preservationists, whose work is grounded in a respect for historic things, don't know much about the history of our own movement. The subject of this book is a case in point: Discussions of the history of preservation in New York generally begin with the demolition of Pennsylvania Station in the 1960s, an act so outrageous that it spurred New Yorkers to demand — and get — a law to protect their landmarks. It's a good story, but it isn't quite true.

As Tony Wood points out in this admirable book, the story of how New York's landmarks ordinance was enacted is a drama that played out over several decades, beginning long before Penn Station was flattened. It's a drama with a huge cast that included well-known names — Robert Moses, Jane Jacobs, and the National Trust, for instance — as well as many individuals and organizations unfamiliar to most of us: Albert Sprague Bard, the American Scenic and Historic Preservation Society, Francis Keally, and the Joint Emergency Committee to Close Washington Square Park to Traffic.

We know how the drama ended: eventually, New York got one of the strongest preservation ordinances in the country. And even if it didn't emerge directly from the rubble of Penn Station, what really matters is that the law was there to prevent the destruction of New York's other great terminal, Grand Central, and that it has since protected thousands of structures, districts, and interiors.

The history related here should inspire preservationists everywhere to be persistent in their determination to protect the places that matter. That makes it history worth knowing.

Richard Moe

President, National Trust for Historic Preservation

PREFACE

AS VICTOR LASZLO SAID IN *CASABLANCA*, WELCOME TO THE FIGHT.[1]

I arrived in New York City in 1978 energized by Lazlo's compelling greeting. It had been borrowed by the Municipal Art Society to serve as the closing line for their membership recruitment brochure. Fresh from graduate school with a degree in urban and regional planning, I was an enthusiastic recruit, eager to enlist in their army battling to make New York a more livable city. Specifically, I came in search of a job that would meaningfully engage me in the crusade to preserve New York's landmark treasures. Wanting to learn about the city's preservation history, I searched for the book that would tell me the story … only to discover it had not yet been written.

I soon learned that no serious effort had been made to research and preserve in words the intellectual capital of the preservation movement. There was no basic history of historic preservation efforts in New York City. There was no roster of New York's preservation heroes. The lessons they could teach from decades of inspired leadership had not yet been gathered. The wisdom to be mined from preservation's failures and the inspiration to be gained from its hard-won victories had never been brought together between two covers. There was hardly any indication that preservation in New York City had a history.

As I began my research for this book, it quickly became apparent to me that the defining event in the preservation story was the 1965 passage of New York City's Landmarks Law. That law represented a sea change. Before its passage, there was no process for formally identifying

FIGURE 0.1 New York preservationists have long turned adversity to their advantage. New resolve and ultimately success have sprung from the ruins of landmarks. Capturing this spirit of hope in the face of ruin is the iconic photograph of boa-wearing, jewelry-bedecked Gloria Swanson surrounded by the ruins of the Roxy Theatre, 50th Street and Seventh Avenue, memorialized in *Life* magazine, *November 7, 1960.* (Eliot Elisofon/Time & Life Pictures/Getty Images.)

and protecting the city's architectural and cultural heritage. While the law did not guarantee the preservation of every landmark, it created a legal process to ensure that none would be unnecessarily lost. Literally, the Landmarks Law of 1965 shaped the face of the city we know today.

Why was there no account of the origins of such a critically important piece of public policy? There is no mystery behind its absence. Passionately committed to saving the buildings, neighborhoods, and distinctive places that are the heart and soul of New York City, preservationists are like the firehouse Dalmatian. When the alarm sounds, off they race, and with good reason. In a city that worships the new, the preservation alarm rings with disturbing frequency—often signaling an impending loss. After all, demolition is the ultimate deadline. Those working to preserve New York's landmarks had been so busy trying to save the buildings telling New York's history that they failed to record their own story.

Not knowing my research would take over a quarter century and ultimately become a book, I decided to piece together the story of how New Yorkers won the right to protect their landmarks. I now realize I started my quest not a moment too soon. The actuarial imperative, the passage of time, was taking its toll. The lead players in key early preservation dramas, as well as those who witnessed them, had started to pass away. Preservation's oral history, the wisdom of its elders, was fading one obituary at a time. In addition, the personal papers of some of those involved in these preservation dramas had already gone to dumpsters rather than archives.

My research intensified with the growing realization that those currently involved in the field of historic preservation needed to know the history of the cause they embraced. Two thoughtful preservationists, Max Page and Randall Mason, posed the question, "How might preservation look different in the future if practitioners examined critically their movement's history?"[2] That history was largely missing, and with it the perspective and context history provides.

The Pulitzer Prize-winning author Arthur M. Schlesinger, Jr., observed: "It is useful to remember that history is to the nation as memory is to the individual. As persons deprived of memory become disoriented and lost . . . so a nation denied a conception of the past will be disabled in dealing with its present and its future."[3] New York's preservation movement has lacked documentation of where it has been. Those involved in saving our landmarks today are part of a long and grand tradition. It is one that inspires, instructs, and calls us to remember that preservation, like the very sites it seeks to save, exists in time. There is a continually changing context to preservation's work.[4]

I quickly discovered that though the full story of how New York came to have its nationally renowned Landmarks Law had never been told, pieces of the story had been recorded. These narratives often appear as a subplot in a much larger drama. Where such accounts exist, this work fully utilizes them. If a chapter in preservation's story has been well told elsewhere, it is only briefly recounted and the reader directed to the full narrative.

One source not extant when I started my quest in the early 1980s is Gregory Gilmartin's centennial history of the Municipal Art Society published in 1995. Because the history of the society and that of the Landmarks Law are so entwined, Gilmartin's *Shaping the City* deserves special recognition as an important source of information.[5]

During my research, I became fascinated with the idea that there might be an unbroken historic thread that would connect the city's earliest preservation efforts to the ultimate passage of the Landmarks Law. In discovering, unraveling, and reweaving the stories of the individuals, organizations, ideas, and sites involved with the law's history, the closest I came to finding that single elusive thread was in the person of the great, though largely forgotten, civic figure, Albert S. Bard (1866–1963). His passionate belief that aesthetic regulation was not only an appropriate but a necessary governmental function, and his long life of advocacy to achieve that end virtually spans the entire period of this narrative. While Bard's role in the creation of the law is singular, his is not the only story.

Although this is the first comprehensive effort to tell the story of how New York City won the right to protect its landmarks, the subject is far too rich and important for it to be the last. While this book is the story of the people, the places and the politics that created the city's Landmarks Law, it does not attempt to be a history of New York's preservation movement. That wonderfully intriguing and immensely complex story is a multivolume work awaiting another author.

If I had found the book I sought in 1978, I would have missed the excitement of interviewing some of the preservation giants who were still alive when my research began. Their recollections were the time machine that allowed me to see historic events through the eyes of those who made preservation history. My conversations with them brought me into virtual contact with a generation of colleagues who preceded them. The writer Tony Hiss uses the phrase "the Great Span" to capture the power of this type of connection over generations. He describes it as an "Appalachian Trail across time," a way for "adjacent generations to let ideas and goals move intact from one mind to another across a couple of hundred years or more."[6] The oral history aspect of my research literally granted me access to preservation's "Great Span."

Although critical to the success of this book, oral history has its limitations. When I interviewed the preservationist Margot Gayle in the early

1980s, she immediately brought one of them to my attention. She told me that some years earlier she had attended a Cooperstown, New York, program on the history of the National Trust. At the event was the eminent preservation historian, Charles B. Hosmer, Jr., who had researched the topic and Fred Rath, the nationally renowned preservation pioneer who was a major figure in the events being discussed. Because Hosmer had access to the written record, he found himself in the awkward position of having to correct Rath on dates and specifics of the events Rath had personally experienced.

Margot Gayle, aware of my research, reminded me of Hosmer's experience saying, "So you might find yourself in the same thing." Neither of us imagined that indeed this would be the case, and that it would involve *her* own memories. Gayle's often-repeated memory is that her efforts to save the Jefferson Market Courthouse began at a December 1959 Christmas cocktail party. This conflicts with a January 2, 1958 *Villager* article recording the formation by Gayle and others of "Neighbors to get the Jefferson Market courthouse clock started" at a Christmas party the previous month, December 1957.[7] So much for recording memories!

Considering that many of us have trouble remembering what we did last week, let alone last year, it is understandable that Gayle and others might err on the specifics of events transpiring over a quarter of a century ago. While oral histories paint a more vivid picture of events than we otherwise would have, one has to be cognizant of their limitations and seek to combine them with other available resources.

Another important "great span" providing a portal to the past is found in archival collections. Viewing the original documents penned decades ago by preservation greats was a thrill for me. By scouring these collections, I got to know these departed personalities on another level. During the many weeks spent going through the letters of Albert S. Bard, I gleaned essential information and gained equally invaluable insight into the life of a complicated and fascinating man. Spending afternoons reading Bard's papers, I felt I had visited with the man himself.

As with oral history, archives have their limitations. This story, as it has been pieced together from multiple sources, has been shaped perhaps equally by the records that were available as much as by those that were not. Fortunately, some collections of documents have survived in the most surprising ways. For example, because Albert Bard's papers were painstakingly saved by the wife of his "adopted" son, his extraordinary role in the civic life of New York City can be more fully told.[8]

Equally fortuitous was the preservation of the extensive papers of urbanist and dedicated Greenwich Village resident Robert C. Weinberg. Thanks in part to the efforts of Barry Benepe, the Vinmont Foundation, and Long Island University, this incredible resource is available to us today. In the same vein, twenty-first century preservation activists owe a double debt of gratitude to Otis Pratt Pearsall, first for his efforts to preserve Brooklyn Heights and second for his own archival instincts to preserve the history of that preservation struggle. Because of Pearsall's diligence, the campaign to landmark Brooklyn Heights is considered one of the best-documented preservation efforts on record.

Unfortunately, the papers and records of too many protagonists in this story, whether individuals or organizations, have been lost. To paraphrase an old saying, history is written from the papers that survived. There remains hope that more documents surface as research continues. In addition, with the passage of time, new collections of personal papers will become available to researchers. As this book was being written, the 181 boxes of papers in the archive of the influential lawyer, civic leader, and preservation champion Whitney North Seymour, Sr. were still unavailable to researchers.[9] It is exciting to imagine what they will contribute to our knowledge of the law's history when the public can access them.

Archives are treasure troves, oral histories gems. Where neither exists the loss to researchers is palpable. As I dug into preservation's past, it became clear to me that preserving the written and oral history of New York's preservation movement was imperative. To accomplish this, in the early 1990s, I recruited a handful of kindred spirits to found the New York Preservation Archive Project, a nonprofit organization devoted to documenting, preserving, and celebrating the history of preservation efforts in New York.[10]

The New York Preservation Archive Project works to secure the papers and capture the memories of significant participants in preservation's story. Many involved in preservation were citizens from walks of life whose notes, writings, and letters would not traditionally have been deposited in archives. The Archive Project serves as a matchmaker; we locate documents related to the history of preservation and then seek homes for them in appropriate collecting institutions. The Archive Project also functions as a clearinghouse connecting the preservation-curious with the collections and information they seek. Most importantly, the Archive Project seeks to raise the historical consciousness of New York City's preservation movement. When the idea for this book developed, the Archive Project was its logical nonprofit sponsor.

This account of how New Yorkers won the right to protect their cherished landmarks is told by a preservation advocate turned preservation historian. For this reason, it is more a "family" history than a detached clinical rendering. As such, its primary focus is on individuals and organizations and the landmarks they rallied to protect and the policies they fought to advance. Conducting oral histories with some of those intimately involved in preservation's story and getting to know others through their papers, turned what could have been detached and antiseptic research into an engaging, very personal adventure.

Today, we enjoy New York's landmarks and historic districts because yesterday someone fought to preserve them. Many New Yorkers are unaware of this as they walk by landmark treasures. Reminding New Yorkers of the high price paid for gaining the right to protect New York's landmarks is one antidote for taking this right for granted. Telling preservation's story is an act of preservation advocacy. Though the narrative of how New York got its Landmarks Law has an end, the story of how New York uses the law continues to be written. Knowing the former can only improve the outcome of the latter.

Anyone passionate about New York City could be the author of the next chapter in the city's continuing preservation story. The passage of the Landmarks Law did not end the battle to save the city's past; it just shaped the battlefield and defined the rules of engagement. As the *New York Times* editorialized when the law was passed: "It will take imagination, dedication, concern, citizen action, private financing and public cooperation to effect preservation under the new law. . . . The past is yet to be secured for the future. Celebration is premature until we can point to a safe and substantial legacy. New York is still the city that marks its history with gaping holes in the ground."[11]

Though much has been accomplished by many since those words were written in 1965, they still ring true. To all who may be inspired by this book to become advocates for preserving America's landmarks, I say, "Welcome to the fight."

ENDNOTES

1. "The Municipal Art Society the toughest street fighters in town," (New York: The Municipal Art Society, circa 1977). Margot Wellington, then the executive director of the Municipal Art Society at that time, recalls that Doyle Dane Bernbach, one of the great advertising firms of that time, created this membership brochure pro bono. Bill Bernbach, a member of the society's board, assigned two young associates to the account. Margot and others at the society felt their first effort missed the

mark. Margot then had the unenviable task of calling up Bernbach with this news. He "blew up" and Wellington remembers ending the call "shaking." After reviewing the material, Bernbach called her back the next morning and told her she was correct. He sent over two seasoned staffers, and they created the final brochure. Margot Wellington, email message to author, March 28, 2005. Fans of *Casablanca* will note that the brochure takes some liberty with the movie's dialogue.

2. Max Page and Randall Mason, eds., introduction to *Giving Preservation a History* (New York: Routledge, 2004), 13.

3. Arthur M. Schlesinger, Jr., "Folly's Antidote," *New York Times*, January 1, 2007.

4. Anthony C. Wood, "Celebrating Preservation's Story: 'It's your memory. It's our history. It's worth saving,'" *Forum Journal* 20, no. 2 (Winter 2006): 45–52.

5. Gregory F. Gilmartin, *Shaping the City: New York and the Municipal Art Society* (New York: Clarkson Potter, 1995).

6. Tony Hiss, *The View from Alger's Window* (New York: Knopf, 1999), 4–5.

7. Margot Gayle, interview by Anthony C. Wood, April 26, 1984, Anthony C. Wood Archive; "Neighbors Say Relight Old Clock," *Villager,* January 2, 1958.

8. When Bard died, his office of over fifty years had three long library tables piled high with papers, thirteen stuffed four-door file cabinets, a bookcase, and some fifteen piles of material on the floor. Over several months, Marjorie Dunbar, the widow of Robert Gordon Switz, the man Bard considered to be his "adopted" son, came down from upstate New York by bus one long day a week to organize the papers to the point that the bulk of them could be sent to the New York Public Library. Marjorie Dunbar, interview by Rudie Hurwitz, September 24, 2002, New York Preservation Archive Project.

9. The papers of Whitney North Seymour (1901–1983) were donated to the New York Public Library with the restriction that they would remain closed to the public until twenty-five years after his death. They will open to the public May 8, 2008. William Stingone, Charles J. Liebman curator of manuscripts, New York Public Library, email message to author, August 1, 2006.

10. The project began its work in 1992 as an all-volunteer effort. As with so many other preservation initiatives, it received early funding from the J. M. Kaplan Fund in the form of a grant to the project's fiscal agent, the Historic Districts Council. The project's efforts were sporadic at best in these early years. In the mid-1990s, it worked closely with the Greenwich Village Society for Historic Preservation on a series of events exploring the history of preservation in the Village and launching a Village oral history project. With its incorporation in the late 1990s, the project increased its level of activity.

11. "A Landmark Law," *New York Times*, April 27, 1965.

ONE

THE MYTH OF PENNSYLVANIA STATION

"In weekend stealth the vulture-like work of destroying another New York landmark has begun. . . . 'We ain't breaking no laws,' said an anonymous spokesman for the anonymous wreckers. There are no laws to break, and—at the rate the city is moving on passage of its pending landmarks legislation—there will be no landmarks to save. Just new monuments to ugliness." It was February 1965. New York City was as lawless as the legendary Wild West when it came to preserving its landmarks. Under the blazing headline of its scorching editorial, "Rape of the Brokaw Mansion," the *New York Times* decried the continuing despoiling of the city.[1]

The lamented buildings under assault that February were the Brokaw mansions. One could not have found better poster children for the preservation cause. Helping frame the East 79th Street entrance to the Upper East Side from Central Park, their style and opulence lived up to their prominent address. Of them, the noted architecture critic of the *New York Times* Ada Louise Huxtable wrote, "They were among the city's finest examples of the baronial and classical homes of New York's kingly merchants and bankers. . . . They were extravagant, luxurious constructions designed with pride and pardonable ostentation."[2]

The corner mansion, 1 East 79th Street, a partial replica of the sixteenth-century chateau Chenonceaux in the Loire Valley, had been built by the manufacturer, Isaac Brokaw, starting in 1887. Its neighbor to the north, 984 Fifth Avenue, was one of two twin "flamboyant gothic" houses modeled after the late-fifteenth-century Palace of Justice at Rouen, built for his sons after the turn of the century. To the east, 7 East 79th Street, designed in a "more chaste classical manner," was the home Isaac had

FIGURE 1.1 For more than half a century, the Isaac Brokaw mansion anchored the northeast corner of Fifth Avenue and East 79th Street. It was flanked to the north and the east by equally distinguished town houses that Brokaw had constructed for his children. The fate of this prominent corner would play a major role in advancing the passage of New York's Landmarks Law.

constructed a few years later for his daughter.[3] The Brokaw mansions were just the latest landmarks to be consumed in the city's building frenzy.

Months before on the streets of Manhattan's usually genteel Upper East Side, a placard-waving demonstration followed the public announcement of the plans to demolish the buildings. On Saturday, September 26, 1964, a crowd of some 125 people rallied in front of the threatened mansions to hear a cadre of speakers, mostly politicians, call for the preservation of the buildings. One of those at the megaphone calling for preservation was then leader of the Village Independent Democrats, future mayor of New York, Edward I. Koch.[4]

The demonstrators were not alone in their call for preservation. The city's Landmarks Preservation Commission, at this time a mayoral agency lacking the force of law, had already "designated" 1 East 79th Street as "worthy of being saved." Coming with no legal authority or protection, that designation was virtually worthless. The newspapers also sounded the call to arms. The *New York Times* asked "Will there be any historic

FIGURE 1.2 When the news broke that the Brokaw mansion was to be demolished for the construction of a high-rise apartment building, citizens took to the streets in protest. On Saturday, September 26, 1964, future mayor Edward Koch addressed over one hundred concerned New Yorkers as they rallied to save this unprotected landmark. The event was captured in *Park East*, the neighborhood paper then serving the "Silk Stocking" district.

landmarks left in New York City by the time a proposed law to save them sees the light of day? Hardly a week passes when doom is not pronounced for an admired old building. The latest marked for replacement is the fabulous Brokaw mansion."[5] The *New York World-Telegram* proclaimed, "If City Hall is serious about preserving landmarks, it had better wake up and take firm legislative action before they're all gone."[6] The *Herald-Tribune* logged in: "We have plundered and wrecked our heritage, to what end purpose? Who can truthfully say that this destruction of links with the past, this callous disregard for beauty and variety, produces a finer New York?"[7] The print media was not alone and editorials echoing the same sentiments were voiced on WCBS-TV.[8]

There were eleventh-hour efforts to intervene. A foundation considered buying the building for its offices. The city itself had considered acquiring the houses for a variety of possible uses, including a guesthouse for visiting dignitaries.[9] Even after the demolition had begun, there were frantic efforts at the highest level. Recalled Geoffrey Platt, first chair of the Landmarks Preservation Commission, "The Mayor's office tried to do something about that. One of the secretaries called me and said that we can hold things up until Monday, if you can think of what to do, you know, but nobody could think of anything to do. There was no mechanism. The mechanism wasn't there."[10]

Despite the passion of the people, the efforts of the politicians, and the cries of the press, nothing could save the Brokaw mansions. Anger and frustration abounded. The people, the press, and the politicians were all powerless. These were not the first buildings New Yorkers had fought to save and lost. Unknown to their defenders, they would be the last buildings New Yorkers would have to sacrifice to win the right to protect their landmarks.

The passage of New York's Landmarks Law was a sea change for New York City. Prior to the law, efforts to save the past were isolated, episodic, and often, as with the Brokaw mansion, failures. With the law came a defined governmental process through which preservation could be advanced. Since its passage, the law has created the playing field where competing forces battle over conflicting visions for pieces of New York's past. The law fundamentally changed the process of how New York City manages change.

To fully grasp the impact it has had on the face of the city, imagine for one frightful moment New York City without its landmarks. Conjure up your favorite New York image. Is it a quaint block in Greenwich Village, a soaring Art Deco skyscraper, a row of Greek Revival houses in Brooklyn Heights, a quiet corner of Central Park, a gracious old estate on Staten

FIGURE 1.3 Accompanying a feature article, "The Wreck of the Brokaw Mansions," in the April 11, 1965 issue of the *New York Herald-Tribune,* this stark image dramatizes the extreme vulnerability of New York's architectural treasures prior to the passage of New York's Landmarks Law. The demolition of the Brokaw mansions would be the last major loss the city would have to endure before Mayor Wagner signed the landmarks legislation into law on April 19, 1965.

Island, a remnant of the World's Fair in Queens, a bejeweled Broadway theatre, a tree-lined street in Riverdale? Odds are good that the special place you envisioned is either under the protection of the Landmarks Law or that some person or group is seeking such protection for it.

It is remarkable that the origins of a law so dramatically impacting the cityscape of one of the greatest cities in the world has generated so little curiosity. The law has now been in place so long and served the city so well that its very existence is only rarely questioned—and if it is, only by the most extreme political elements. Today, it is not whether the city should protect its landmarks that is debated, but what those landmarks should be and how they should be treated.

To most, it seems unremarkable that New York City has both the desire and the legal means to protect its past. Yet, looking at the city's history, this is not only remarkable, but extraordinary. The Landmarks Law contradicts one of the city's most chronic characteristic traits: its bullish pride in the new. How the city tempered its raging lust for the new, traditionally at the expense of the old, is an amazing yet largely unappreciated story.

Historically, it has been change, not preservation, that has been the constant in New York City. In the 1840s, Philip Hone wrote in his famous diaries: "Overturn! Overturn! Overturn! is the maxim of New York . . . one generation of men seem studious to remove all relics of those which preceded them."[11] Walt Whitman identified it in an 1845 essay as the city's "Pull-down-and-build-over again spirit." In more recent times, former landmarks commissioner Barbaralee Diamonstein-Spielvogel eloquently summed it up: "New York's quintessential characteristic is its quicksilver quality, its ability to transform itself not just from year to year, but almost from day to day."[12]

Time magazine captured these conflicting emotions when it wrote in 1950, "Nothing makes a New Yorker happier than the sight of an old building rich in memories of the past—unless it is tearing the damn thing down and replacing it with something in chromium and plate glass, with no traditions at all."[13] How did preservation grow to become such a strong civic emotion in a city whose favorite pasttime is real estate development? How did the instinct to preserve become so much a part of the city's persona? Was it always latent in the city's genes or was it a latter mutation? Seen in this context, one not only has to marvel that the law ever came into being, but also wonder how it came to triumph over that other, seemingly more dominant New York trait.

From a perspective colored by the rising dust of the stunningly beautiful and historically important buildings New York City was regularly destroying until 1965, one sees the question differently. Knowing also that other American cities were well ahead of New York in efforts to preserve their heritage, one instead inquires: Why did it take New Yorkers so long to win the right to protect their landmarks?

However framed, for years the question of how New Yorkers won the right to protect their landmarks (to the extent that anyone inquired) received the standard answer: the law was the result of the monumental and shocking loss of the legendary Pennsylvania Station. Indeed, Pennsylvania Station has become a preservation icon. In New York, its demolition is seen as the defining event of the movement's history and the genesis of the Landmarks Law. So prevalent is this imagery of preservation policy

FIGURE 1.4 For those who never experienced historic Pennsylvania Station, it is hard to imagine just how vast a structure it actually was. Occupying two full city blocks, over 500 buildings were cleared for its construction. Its demolition would take three years.

emerging from such a spectacular loss that preservationists in other cities often talk of their "Pennsylvania Station," the great loss their community had to endure to shock it into taking action to preserve their past.

The Pennsylvania Station explanation for the birth of New York City's Landmarks Law is a captivating one. Consider the powerful imagery of the building itself. Thomas Wolfe's famous passage lyrically captures its romance as the place where "the voice of time remained aloof and unperturbed, a drowsy and eternal murmur below the immense and distant roof."[14] Physically, it was massive: "nine acres of travertine and granite, 84 Doric columns, a vaulted concourse of extravagant, weighty grandeur, classical splendor modeled after royal Roman baths, rich detail in solid stone, architectural quality in precious materials that set the stamp of excellence on a city."[15] It more than achieved "its psychological purpose . . . to serve as an outward and visible sign of the prosperity of the new great corporation that commissioned it."[16]

Disguised and disfigured by poor maintenance and tasteless alterations, the beauty and value of the station had almost become invisible to the stream of countless commuters flowing through it every day. When the impending demolition of the station finally penetrated the public consciousness, only several hundred New Yorkers were moved to action. The

FIGURE 1.5   AGBANY, the Action Group for Better Architecture in New York, organized the now famous August 2, 1962 protest rally against the demolition of Pennsylvania Station. Front right is the architect Philip Johnson. He would go on to become a preservation champion, joining in efforts to save Grand Central Terminal, St. Bartholomew's Church, and defend the Landmarks Law.

most visible protest, the picketing of the station, was famously described as "one of the city's strangest and most heartening picket lines," and has become legend in the annals of preservation.[17] Today, those few who marched that August day in 1962 are saluted as preservation heroes.

And then, there was the demolition itself. Starting on October 28, 1963, it took three years to complete. The *New York Times* editorial on the subject, penned by Ada Louise Huxtable, has become perhaps the most famous piece of preservation prose ever composed: "Until the first blow fell no one was convinced that Penn Station really would be demolished or that New York would permit this monumental act of vandalism against one of the largest and finest landmarks of its age of Roman elegance. Somehow someone would surely find a way to prevent it at the last minute—not-so-little Nell rescued by the hero. . . . Any city gets what it admires, will pay for, and ultimately, deserves. Even when we had Penn

Station, we couldn't afford to keep it clean. We want and deserve tin-can architecture in a tin-horn culture. And we will probably be judged not by the monuments we built but by those we have destroyed."[18]

As the Pennsylvania Station story goes, Phoenix-like from the ruins of the great station, propelled by the growing public awakening, the city's landmarks law emerged. From this bitter defeat, sweet victory would soon ensue. The station was the ultimate sacrifice ensuring no such loss would ever be endured again. Could one wish for a more heroic history for New York's Landmarks Law? Beauty, loss, villains, heroes, tragedy—and ultimately, redemption. A civic morality play. What a story!

The power and romance of this straightforward explanation of how New York City won the right to protect its landmarks is hard to resist. As the answer to the question "How did New York get its Landmarks Law?" it suffers from just one fundamental problem. It is a myth. If the "first blow" fell on Penn Station in October of 1963 and that tragedy is what brought forth the Landmarks Law, why was New York City still powerless to save the Brokaw mansions in February of 1965? Since the passage of legislation does take time, perhaps this is understandable. Then again, it might suggest that there is more to the story than the demolition of Pennsylvania Station.

Harder to dismiss are numerous actions to advance some form of landmarks protection that predate the demolition of the station. In June of 1961, Mayor Robert Wagner appointed a Committee for the Preservation of Structures of Historic and Esthetic Importance to advise him on a course of action for the city to take on landmarks preservation. This was well before any signs of serious public protest over the plans to demolish Penn Station. What led Mayor Wagner, a man not known for quick and decisive independent action, to take this step? Also, what of that Landmarks Preservation Commission whose landmark designation was unable to save the Brokaw mansions? What had led to its creation over a year before the loss of the station?

Further suggesting that the Penn Station explanation of the law is more legendary than factual are even earlier events that transpired in Brooklyn Heights and Greenwich Village. On April 21, 1959, over four hundred residents of Brooklyn Heights attended a town meeting in the Bossert Hotel ballroom. The headline announcing the meeting in that morning's *New York Times* read "Brooklynites Set Action on Heights; Residents Meet Tonight to Discuss How to Preserve Community's Charm; Seek to Use State Law; Ask City to Invoke Measure to Protect Area's Historic and Esthetic Values."[19] Five years earlier in the spring of 1954, Frederick Rath

FIGURE 1.6   For many, Washington Square Park and the rows of townhouses that define it are the heart and soul of historic Greenwich Village. Threats to the houses on Washington Square North, seen here flanking both sides of the Washington Square Arch, helped stoke efforts to find a way to protect the Village. The park itself would be the focus of another major battle with Robert Moses.

Jr., executive director of the National Trust for Historic Preservation, was the featured guest at the meeting of the Greenwich Village Association. The association's president, James Kirk, describes the meeting as the "opening gun in the campaign for adequate laws to safeguard the Village for the future."[20] What is stirring up the residents of Brooklyn Heights and Greenwich Village in the 1950s? What is behind their demands for legal protection for their historic neighborhoods? Certainly not the demolition of Pennsylvania Station.

The headline on the Brooklyn Heights story references a state law and notes the public cry that it be invoked to save Brooklyn Heights. That state law is the Bard Act, a 1956 piece of enabling legislation giving municipalities in New York State the legal authority to enact local landmark laws. Ultimately, it provided what had been the missing legal basis for New York City to adopt a landmarks law. Who was this Bard behind the Bard Act? What prompted him to advance this idea in 1956? Even more curious, if New York City had the ability to enact a law to protect its landmarks as early as 1956, why did it wait until 1965 to do so?

■　■　■　■　■　■　■　■

FIGURE 1.7 Dying during the newspaper strike of 1963, prominent civic figure Albert Sprague Bard was denied the substantial *New York Times* obituary such a distinguished citizen deserved. He fared much better in *Purple and Gold,* the magazine of Chi Psi, the fraternity to which Bard was dedicated his entire adult life. This, his favorite portrait, was taken in 1936, two weeks prior to his seventieth birthday.

Albert Sprague Bard, the Bard of the Bard Act, died in 1963. For over fifty years, he was a major player on New York's civic scene. After he died, some eighty-five cartons of his papers were given to the New York Public Library. They not only reflect the richness and depth of his many decades of multiple civic involvements, but raise even more questions about the origins of the Landmarks Law. Bard's papers reveal that as early as 1946, he was in correspondence with the secretary of the Vieux Carré Commission of New Orleans inquiring about the legal methods used in New Orleans to preserve its historic French Quarter. Why, a decade before the Bard Act, was Bard exploring the applicability of the legal methods used

FIGURE 1.8 As New Yorkers sought a way to protect their historic neighborhoods, time and again their attention would turn to the example of the Vieux Carré in New Orleans. Though it would not provide the needed legal model, the Vieux Carré would inspire New York preservationists and provide them a compelling example of the future they sought for places like Greenwich Village and Brooklyn Heights.

to protect the Vieux Carré to the preservation of the "special character of the Greenwich Village section of New York City"?[21]

One person in a position to shed light on these events was the architect Geoffrey Platt. An active member of the Municipal Art Society of New York, a civic group long immersed with issues of the physical city, he was very much on the scene in the 1950s and 1960s. He knew Albert Bard and was the chair of the 1961 Mayoral Committee mentioned above. He was also the first chair of the Landmarks Preservation Commission. Platt was a key player in the landmarks drama and might be able to make things clear.

Platt's recollections further debunk the Pennsylvania Station story. In a 1984 oral history, he suggests the origins of the law lie elsewhere. "The Municipal Art Society started the ball rolling in 1954 with a forty-page mimeographed list of noteworthy buildings in New York City." What was the motivation behind this and related society actions leading up to the law? According to Platt, it "was Robert Moses, really, who had more effect than anybody else."[22] Since Moses was not a lead player in the Pennsylvania Station drama, rather the protagonist in earlier preservation battles, had Platt's memory become the victim of his age? Not in the least. What was at fault was not Platt's memory, but the Pennsylvania station paradigm as the explanation for the Landmarks Law. It just fails to accommodate the facts.

Reinforcing Platt's pointing of the finger toward Robert Moses is a 1941 newspaper article reporting on a meeting called by the New York Historical Society and the American Scenic and Historic Preservation Society on the subject of the preservation of historic sites and buildings in the City of New York. A resolution passed at the meeting called for the exploration of the creation of a

FIGURE 1.9   Geoffrey Platt would be prominent in any preservation hall of fame. An architect active in the Municipal Art Society, he chaired Mayor Wagner's 1961 Committee for the Preservation of Stuctures of Historic and Esthetic Importance and was intimately involved in the creation of the Landmarks Law. He served as the first chair of the Landmarks Preservation Commission.

Love for all and lots for Gertrude
from Cousin Marion.

No. 68 -View of the Battery and New York Harbor.

J. KOEHLER, N.Y

FIGURE 1.10   The eleven-year battle between New York's civic leaders and Robert Moses over the fate of the historic Battery and Castle Clinton at the tip of Manhattan would fundamentally influence New York's preservation movement. The rich history of the Battery, with its links to the very origins of New York, made it sacred soil. Seeing it so vulnerable to the whims of one man demonstrated the need for some form of landmarks protection.

permanent board to seek "means to prevent demolition" in such cases in the future. The likely trigger for that meeting was the threat to historic Castle Clinton in Manhattan's Battery Park. The man behind that threat was Robert Moses.[23]

Having traced back the date of interest in creating a formal process to protect the city's landmarks to at least the 1940s, the demolition of Pennsylvania Station as the defining explanation for the origin of the Landmarks Law loses any credibility. That story is a powerful and cherished myth, but legend it is. There is no question that the loss of Pennsylvania Station is a key chapter in the history of the creation of the law, but for it to be seen as either the entire or primary story of the law is to rob New York City of the richer, more complex, and inspiring true story of how New Yorkers won the right to protect their landmarks. Instead of the Penn Station myth being recognized as a type of historic "shorthand," it has been mistaken as the entire story. As such, it denies New Yorkers and preservationists in particular their full legacy.

If the origins of the Landmarks Law are not to be found in the debris of Pennsylvania Station, where are they to be found? The answer lies entwined in the larger, and still largely unwritten, history of New York's preservation movement. To find the law's story it must be teased out of this larger, even more complex narrative. Where does it begin? With countless variables shaping events, history is not so neat as to provide us with a "begin here" sign. Nevertheless, a starting point is necessary, a first action that, when followed through an unbroken series of events, leads us to the passage of the Landmarks Law. From that beginning, a narrative unfolds revealing the people and places, the buildings and battles, and the politics and processes that ultimately produced the law. The thread of events flowing from that first step, woven together with other relevant, contributing historic strands discovered along the way, creates the rich tapestry that is the history of the law. The story is full of starts and stops. It circles back on itself and then moves forward again.

A few chapters in the story of the law, like the battle over Pennsylvania Station, are well known. Other key pieces of the puzzle have been revealed, but remain largely overshadowed by the larger stories of which they are only contributing sidebars.[24] Still other information reflects new discoveries. Combined here, they offer the most complete narrative yet available on the origins of the law. As the first comprehensive attempt to compile a coherent and complete history of the law, new ground is being ploughed. As future scholarship evolves, our knowledge of this intriguing and important story will only deepen and become more complete.

Where does the story of the Landmarks Law begin? What might be that first action that put New York on the path that ultimately led to the law? In the law itself are the clues to its origins. In the period before the law, there were numerous successful preservation efforts. However, these efforts were ad hoc. A legal system for landmark protection was missing. If there was governmental intervention, it was apt to involve emergency funding to save a particular threatened site. It was the Landmarks Law that established governmental regulation as the predominant tool for landmark protection and did so, remarkably enough, on aesthetic grounds.

The law created a formal governmental process to identify, designate, and regulate sites "thirty years old or older," which have "a special character or special historical or aesthetic interest or value as part of the development, heritage or cultural characteristics of the city, state, or nation."[25] At the heart of this work is the city agency the Landmarks Preservation Commission. Created by the law, appointed by the mayor, and representing a variety of expertise mandated in the law, this Landmarks Preservation Commission of eleven members, supported by a professional staff, is the entity that brings the law to life.

■ ■ ■ ■ ■ ■ ■ ■

The origin and evolution of these key aspects of the law (an orderly public process, a governmental review body, a systematic identification of important sites, and the ability for government to regulate private property largely grounded in aesthetics) suggest where to look for its origins.

To provide the context for exploring the emergence of these key elements found in New York's law, a short overview of preservation's history is essential. Indeed, the story of the law is only one narrative in the larger story of preservation in New York. Though impulses for a landmarks law can be traced back to at least the early civic community battles with Robert Moses, the history of preservation itself well predates Moses. From a national perspective, efforts in preservation begin with a narrow focus on sites associated with the nation's early heroic leaders and with the formative events in the early history of our country. These early, well-known efforts with their patriotic flavor set the tone for much of what would follow.

An acclaimed preservation "first" was the 1850 purchase of Washington's headquarters in Newburgh by New York State. This is recognized as a first for several reasons. It is regarded both as the "the first success of the preservation movement" as well as the first historic house museum in the United States.[26] The patriotic nature of the site and its preservation through public purchase would set the tone for successful preservation efforts to come in the nineteenth and early-twentieth century.

The other significant "first" for preservation was the successful campaign to save Washington's home, Mount Vernon, by Anne Pamela Cunningham and her Mount Vernon Ladies' Association of the Union. This effort, dating from 1853, set the standard for private efforts reaching out to citizens to help finance the acquisition and restoration of such patriotic shrines. Private, meaning nongovernmental, preservation organizations would soon emerge focused not only on single sites but on the historic resources of entire regions. The Association for the Preservation of Virginia Antiquities was founded in 1888 and William Sumner Appleton incorporated his Society for the Preservation of New England Antiquities in 1910.[27]

When it comes to contemporary preservation efforts in New York City, the movement finds its roots in the confluence of two streams of thought, interest and energy: the historic, with its patriotic motivation, and the aesthetic. One side of New York City's preservation's lineage can be traced back to the type of early efforts mentioned above that focused on the preservation of patriotic and historic sites. Whether buildings, statues, battlefields, or open spaces, the concern was with what preservation scholar Randy Mason has called "totems of civic memory."[28]

There were a number of patriotic preservation organizations at work. Most were focused on particular sites. Leading the charge, however, was the American Scenic and Historic Preservation Society. Founded in 1895, it was originally named the Trustees of Scenic and Historic Places and Objects in the State of New York. Notwithstanding the national ambitions reflected in its renaming, its primary focus remained New York State.

The American Scenic and Historic Preservation Society was the creation of Andrew Haswell Green, a giant in New York City's history but today a still largely unsung New York civic hero.[29] Lawyer, reformer, public official, master planner, and visionary, according to historian Kenneth T. Jackson, Green is "arguably the most important leader in Gotham's long history, more important than Peter Stuyvesant, Alexander Hamilton, Frederick Law Olmsted, Robert Moses and Fiorello LaGuardia."[30] Even with a list of credits that include Central Park, the consolidation of the five boroughs into greater New York, and his involvement with the New York Public Library and the American Museum of Natural History, for preservationists it is Green's American Scenic and Historic Preservation Society that marks his greatest contribution. Though Green was killed in 1903 at the age of eighty-three in a case of mistaken identity, the American Scenic and Historic Preservation Society would live on well into the twentieth century as a major player in preservation.

The other half of preservation's intellectual parentage largely comes from the City Beautiful Movement. The influence of the World's Columbian Exposition of 1893 on New York City would be hard to overstate. To a great extent the product of New York talent, the Chicago World's Fair, vividly demonstrated what a city could look like if planning, art, architecture, and landscape design were given their due. The fair showed what could result if beauty was a civic priority. Having seen this vision come to life temporarily on the shore of Lake Michigan, New Yorkers returned home wanting to make it a permanent reality on the banks of the Hudson. For decades, many of these same New Yorkers had experienced this type of civic beauty on their European tours. Now they had seen it in their own land and wanted it for their own city. Born out of this energy and enthusiasm, the Municipal Art Society of New York came to life in 1893. It and sister art organizations, many created in that same heady moment, soon set to work to make New York the beautiful city their visionary members believed it could be.

The patriotic societies and the art societies were the intellectual parents of New York's preservation movement. Often seen today as two distinct civic movements, there was significant inbreeding between them. They

5c. Mrs. Tom L. Johnson's Thrilling Story of her Husband's First Speech
"THE KING CHAIR" - - GOV. ROOSEVELT AT HOME 5c.

SUCCESS

COPYRIGHT, 1899, BY THE SUCCESS COMPANY, NEW YORK

ORISON SWETT MARDEN, Editor
Cooper Union, New York

New York, Saturday, August 5, 1899

PRICE, $1.50 A YEAR
5 Cents a Copy

HON. ANDREW GREEN, THE FIRST CITIZEN OF NEW YORK

FIGURE 1.11 Andrew Haswell Green forever changed the physical and political landscape of New York City. In the words of New York historian Kenneth Jackson, Green is "arguably the most important leader in Gotham's long history." His American Scenic and Historic Preservation Society survived until the 1970s and played an important role in many New York landmark dramas.

often shared the same members and at times focused on the same concerns and the same sites. There was, however, a difference in motivation and emphasis between such organizations as the American Scenic and

Historic Preservation Society and the Municipal Art Society. "The Preservation Society cared more about history and patriotism; MAS cared more about architecture and the cityscape."[31] Though much is made of the distinctions between these groups, in the story of the Landmarks Law, their shared agenda is more important than their differences.

The protection of sites of historic value, particularly patriotic sites linked to the origins of the country, was a keen motivating force behind early preservation efforts in New York City. Despite this, it does not provide the starting point for our story. As has been observed by others, what these late-nineteenth century and early-twentieth century efforts at preservation did not achieve "was the kinds of public policy framework (laws, best-practice guidelines, financial incentives) and broad public support that are the measures of success today."[32]

Odd as it may at first appear, the beginning of the unbroken thread that can be followed over time to the passage of the Landmarks Law is not found in the work of the organizations seeking to save sites of historic importance, but rather in the actions of those more concerned with the concept of advancing civic beauty. It was this aesthetic concern for civic beauty that would, after a long journey, ultimately manifest itself in the Bard Act. The beginning of our story is to be found in the work of the art societies in the first decades of the twentieth century and more particularly, in the labors of one Albert Sprague Bard.

ENDNOTES

1. "Rape of the Brokaw Mansion," *New York Times*, February 8, 1965.
2. Ada Louise Huxtable, "Despair of Demolition," *New York Times*, September 17, 1964.
3. Ibid.; Thomas W. Ennis, "Landmark Mansion on 79th St. To Be Razed," *New York Times*, September 17, 1964; Daniel Selznick, "The Wreck of The Brokaw Mansions," *New York Herald-Tribune*, April 11, 1965; Christopher Gray, "Streetscapes," *New York Times*, December 3, 2006.
4. "Rally at the Brokaw," *Park East News*, October 1, 1964.
5. "The Disappearing Landmarks," *New York Times*, September 18, 1964.
6. "Vanishing Landmarks," *New York World-Telegram*, September 18, 1964.
7. "The Wreckers at Work," *New York Herald-Tribune*, September 21, 1964.
8. "City Landmarks," editorial broadcast on WCBS-TV, November 18, 1964.
9. Thomas W. Ennis, "City Hoped to Buy Brokaw Mansions," *New York Times*, February 15, 1965.
10. Anthony C. Wood, "Pioneers of Preservation: An Interview with the Late Geoffrey Platt, the First Chairman of the Landmarks Commission," *Village Views* 4, no. 1 (Winter 1987): 20.
11. So reads the entry for Monday April 7, 1845, *The Diary of Philip Hone*, 1828–1851 (New York: Dodd, Mead and Company, 1927).

■ ■ ■ ■ ■ ■ ■ ■

12. Barbaralee Diamonstein-Spielvogel, *Landmarks of New York* (New York: Monacelli, 2005), 7.

13. "Faceless Warrens," *Time*, January 23, 1950, 13.

14. Thomas Wolfe, *You Can't Go Home Again* (New York: Harper Perennial Classics, 1998), 46.

15. "Farewell to Penn Station," *New York Times*, October 30, 1963.

16. Brendan Gill, "McKim's Monuments," *The New Yorker*, March 14, 1994.

17. Editorial, "Saving Fine Architecture," *New York Times*, August 11, 1963.

18. "Farewell to Penn Station," *New York Times*, October 30, 1963. In a meeting with the author on March 13, 2006, Ada Louise Huxtable identified the editorials that she authored for the *New York Times*. This was one of them.

19. Charles Grutzner, "Brooklynites Set Action on Heights," *New York Times*, April 21, 1959.

20. "GVA Meeting Called for April 20 Authority on Historic Preservation will speak," *Villager*, April 1, 1954.

21. Albert S. Bard to Mr. William Boizelle, January 16, 1946, Albert S. Bard Papers, New York Public Library.

22. Wood, "Pioneers of Preservation: An Interview with the Late Geoffrey Platt," 34.

23. "Act to Save Landmarks: Historical and Scenic Groups Meet to Preserve Aquarium," *New York Times*, May 29, 1941.

24. Contributing to our knowledge of the origins of the law are two works dealing with much larger subjects. Particularly informative is Gregory Gilmartin's history of the Municipal Art Society, *Shaping the City* (New York: Clarkson Potter, 1995). Also of interest is the chapter on historic preservation in Robert A. M. Stern, Thomas Mellins, and David Fishman, *New York 1960* (New York: Monacelli Press, 1995), 1091–1153.

25. Definition of a "Landmark," Administrative Code of the City of New York, Title 25: Land use, Chapter 3, 25–302 Definitions, n.

26. Charles B. Hosmer Jr., *Presence of the Past* (New York: G.P. Putnam's Sons, 1965), 35–37. Hosmer is recognized as the historian of the national preservation movement. Those interested in the history of the preservation movement before Williamsburg will want to read this cover to cover. Those interested in the later history of the movement will want to study his two-volume work *Preservation Comes of Age: From Williamsburg to the National Trust 1926–1949* (Charlottesville: University Press of Virginia, 1981).

27. In addition to Hosmer's *Presence of the Past*, William J. Murtagh's *Keeping Time* (New York: Sterling, 1990) offers several chapters on the history of the preservation movement.

28. Mason's essay "Historic Preservation, Public Memory, and the Making of Modern New York City," in Page and Mason, *Giving Preservation a History* (New York: Routledge, 2004) covers this early chapter in the history of preservation in New York City.

29. Thanks to the work of Michael Miscione, Green is being rediscovered by more and more New Yorkers. Miscione's campaign to achieve greater public recognition for Green continues to introduce Green to a new and broad audience.

30. Editorial, "The Forgotten Giant," *Daily News*, November 13, 2003.

31. Gilmartin, *Shaping the City*, 332. Those with a particular interest in this subject should spend some time with Gilmartin's book.

32. Mason, "Historic Preservation, Public Memory, and the Making of Modern New York City," *Giving Preservation a History*, 133.

TWO

ALBERT BARD AND THE CITY BEAUTIFUL

ALBERT WHO? IT IS THE RARE NEW YORKER WHO can identify Albert Bard. If not for Bard, there would have been no Bard Act, and if not for the Bard Act, New York City would have had no legal basis for its Landmarks Law, and if not for the Landmarks Law, New York City would be diminished beyond recognition. What a twist of fate that the person so indispensable to the efforts that won New Yorkers the right to protect their landmarks has been so forgotten by the city forever transformed by his tireless labors.

Who was this unknown man and why is he of singular importance in the history of New York's Landmarks Law? Born in Norwich, Connecticut on December 19, 1866, and dying in East Orange, New Jersey, on March 25, 1963, his ninety-six years virtually overlap the entire span of events leading to the passage of the law. Time and again, whether out front, or more often laboring behind the scenes, Bard figures prominently in the key events that would ultimately shape preservation's future.

For more than a half century, Bard was a major figure and fixture in New York's civic community. Brilliant, dedicated, witty, and feisty, Bard served

ALBERT S. BARD, X'88

FIGURE 2.1 This photograph of a dapper Albert Bard appeared in *Purple and Gold,* the Chi Psi fraternity magazine, in 1922 along with a resolution thanking him for all his many contibutions to this national fraternity including serving as its President from 1919–1921. Close to fifty-five years of age at the time of this photograph, Bard had already completed his term as president of the Municipal Art Society and had likely only recently met the Switz Family, which he would treat as his own until his death in 1963. It is also in this same period that he would join forces with Elizabeth Lawton in what would become their decades-long crusade against the billboard industry.

for decades on the boards of numerous civic organizations, frequently chairing active committees and serving as an officer. His interests ranged from voting and political reform to parks and urban planning. His stature was such that Bard's ninetieth and ninety-fifth birthdays merited news stories in the *New York Times*. His ninetieth birthday in 1956 triggered the following *New York Times* editorial:

> Albert S. Bard, one of the oldest civic leaders in years lived and years served, observes his ninetieth birthday today, an occasion deserving salutation and appreciation. For a half-century or more he has been constructively and continuously active. . . . He has helped keep the public alert. . . . Long one of our most faithful and valued correspondents in the columns to the right of this page, he has been a guardian of the public interest in natural resources . . . and the esthetically sound development of our city.[1]

Son of a banker, Bard went to Amherst, where he became a member of Chi Psi Fraternity. This began his lifelong robust involvement in college fraternities. Until his death, many of his social interactions would have fraternal ties. He attended Harvard Law School and graduated in 1892. In the fall of that year, he became a clerk at the New York City law firm of Hornblower & Byrne. By 1901, he had launched his own law firm in partnership with another Harvard man, Leighton Calkins. Located at 25 Broad Street, Bard would work out of these offices until his death some sixty-two years later. Though a serious lawyer, it was in the civic realm that Bard would make his mark.

A bachelor of prodigious energy and financially comfortable for much of his life, Bard had character traits that well served a civic reformer. Whatever he got involved with, whether his fraternity or a reform effort, he stuck with it, not just for years, but literally, for decades. In 1897, he helped found the Citizen's Union and six decades later was still one of its officers, classic Bard behavior. He began serving as an officer of the Fine Arts Federation in 1917 and was still doing so at the time of is death. In 1917, he also became president of the Municipal Art Society. The architect Harmon Goldstone, a president of the society in 1960 and the second chair of the Landmarks Preservation Commission, would reminisce: "I discovered that Albert Bard had gone on the Board the year I was born! And that really gave me a certain perspective, because I thought, 'Every month since I was an infant, he's been coming to these meetings—and here he still is!' And of course he was terrific."[2]

His extraordinary length of service to such a variety of organizations not only earned him significant stature, but also infused him with an encyclopedic knowledge of issues as they had evolved over time. Though his own direct experience gave him an intimate knowledge of past events and actions, his personal focus was always on the future. The reporter doing the story on Bard's ninetieth birthday observed, "His is no world of fond and hazy memories. Mr. Bard is robust and alert, with firm flesh and steady hand, and he counts these the good old days."[3] Add to Bard's historical knowledge and personal stature an extensive network of contacts. Because he served on so many boards for such long periods of time, he was able to simultaneously advance his agendas using a variety of different organizations. Even on occasions when these groups might officially be at odds with each other, Bard would still have access because of his relationships.

Needless to say, Bard possessed a keen mind to back up his quick wit and his frequently caustic tongue and pen. Bard not only argued for reform, he also instituted it. He walked the talk. While Bard was a nationally recognized expert on legislation to control billboards, he would personally remove illegal posters from New York City lampposts. Bard lore is filled with story upon story of such personal interventions. As Bard said of his own behavior, "I operate on the theory that criticism is most effective when it is concrete."[4]

His energy, his attitude, his tenure, his status, and his contacts positioned him well to successfully move ideas from fringe status to public policy. As was the case with his belief that cities had the right to be beautiful, such a transformation in society would take decades. But Bard was in it for the long haul.

Though not trained in the arts, Bard was drawn to them. Like many of his contemporaries, he collected and wrote poetry, enjoyed music, and attended theatre. He did have a particular interest in architecture, having considered it as a career possibility before choosing the law.[5] He was a man who took the concept of beauty seriously and personally.

Bard was also well traveled. He had made trips to Europe in 1907, 1910, and 1922. His trip notes indicate visits to museums and include numerous commentaries on architecture. As usual, he had strong opinions and recorded them. Of Chartres, he notes: "Cathedral the most wonderful thing yet." In Rome, he observes: "Loyola tomb. This the culmination of the baroque. Perfectly dreadful," and of Saint Paul's Outside the Walls: "This is a beautiful and grand basilica. Not much spoiled by baroque—indeed little. But it would be much better, if simpler." After his visit to the Sistine Chapel he writes: "A very wonderful experience," but feels

■ ■ ■ ■ ■ ■ ■ ■

compelled to add: "I revised the judgments of the Baedecker somewhat," typical Bard.[6]

A particularly important trip was Bard's visit to the White City, the Chicago World's Fair of 1893, the Columbia Exposition. His papers are devoid of any account he might have written on his visit to the fair, but there are notes in his copy of Rand McNally's "A Week at the Fair." He made a list of ten sites and then underlined various passages of text. Statuary at the fair seems to have been a particular attraction for him.[7]

One can only imagine the impact the fair had on Bard, but if his reaction was anything like that of his fellow New Yorkers, he was in awe. It was the

FIGURE 2.2   It is hard to overstate the impact the Chicago World's Fair had on New York City. The fair's administration building and environs (shown here), like the entire fair, offered an exciting vision of what a city could be if architecture, planning, and the arts were harnessed for that purpose. Such a civic vision contrasted sharply with the reality of New York City at the turn of the century.

energy generated by the fair that had led to the creation of the Municipal
Art Society. The society, along with such preexisting organizations as the
Architectural League and ones that followed its creation, like the National
Society of Mural Painters, would become part of what had become by the
turn of the century an "elaborate network of art societies in New York."[8]
With Bard's interests and experiences, it is no surprise that he would be
drawn to their work and become enmeshed in their networks.

Bard joined the Municipal Art Society as a life member in 1901. That
year, the society reorganized and focused its energy away from presenting

FIGURE 2.3   Albert Bard was only one of a parade of New Yorkers who made the pilgrimage to Chicago to see the
"White City." This view of the fair's obelisk captures the power of the scene that greeted them. Many would return
home to help launch art societies and engage in other activities to make the dreams nourished by the fair a reality
for New York City.

the city specific works of art, and instead concentrated more broadly on the cause of making New York a more beautiful city.[9] Bard first served on the society's board in 1911, became its secretary in 1912, and became its president in 1917. Through the Municipal Art Society, the Fine Arts Federation, and his other affiliations, Bard became part of a family of organizations with a set of beliefs and goals to which he would dedicate himself for the rest of his life.

The art societies had their work cut out for them. New York at the turn of the century faced a host of problems. Visions of what New York could be, informed by European examples and inspired by the World's Fair, crashed up against the hard reality of what New York was. The challenges were many. The city was awash in a sea of political corruption, the lack of decent housing was a massive problem, and immigrants were inundating a city ill-equipped to address their needs. There was good reason that Bard, like others who cared about beautifying New York City, was involved in a wide range of civic causes. Bard's interests included reform politics and voting reform. Bard helped found the Honest Ballot Association that believed "poll-watchers were the only answer to honest elections in the city."[10]

In addition to larger social and societal issues, the art societies had plenty of challenges with which to be concerned. In the early-twentieth century, it "was accepted that government had the right, the 'police power,' to restrict property for the sake of public health and safety, or to bar 'nuisances,' but that was all."[11] What government lacked was the ability to control private property for aesthetic purposes. Time and again, efforts to advocate for the control of private property on the grounds of appearance ran up against questions of constitutionality.

In writing about New York City in this period, Gregory Gilmartin calls it the "The Laissez-Faire City," succinctly capturing the spirit of the time. He describes one of the Municipal Art Society's failed efforts to place modest limitations on the use of private property, in this case an effort to prohibit the placement of billboards on the roof of buildings, as being "a bit like trying to pass a gun control law in Texas."[12]

Indeed, the proliferation of billboards in New York City was one aesthetic issue that the Municipal Art Society and other organizations had been trying to tackle since the turn of the century. They saw this, as the historian Christopher Gray has written, as "a sort of advertising anarchy swamping their dreams for the city Beautiful."[13] Their efforts to control this spreading visual anarchy were largely unsuccessful, but in these failed attempts we find the progenitor of the Bard Act and plausibly the beginning of the story of the Landmarks Law.

■ ■ ■ ■ ■ ■ ■

Particularly troubled by the billboard blight was the Fifth Avenue Association. In 1912, because of growing complaints "in relation to nuisances in connection with billboards and signs used for advertising purposes," Raymond B. Fosdick, New York City's commissioner of accounts, issued "A Report on an Investigation of Billboard Advertising in New York City."[14] This report led the Avenue Association's president Robert Grier Cooke to write Mayor Gaynor urging the appointment of a commission to further study this growing problem. The mayor told Cooke to select a committee and he would appoint them. He named Cooke its chair.[15] One of the seven members of the commission and its secretary was Albert Bard.

Not wanting to wait for public funds to be made available to support its work, the Commission took up a subscription from civic organizations and raised $150. Among those contributing were the Municipal Art

Fifth Avenue, 89th and 90th Streets, Opposite Central Park, Adjoining the Residence of Andrew Carnegie

FIGURE 2.4   In the early-twentieth century, the billboard blight attacking New York City became so severe that the mayor appointed a special commission to advise him on how to deal with the issue. This photograph is one of many that appeared in the report the commission issued in 1913. Immensely influential in shaping this report and the committee's recommendations to advance aesthetic regulation was its secretary, Albert Bard.

Society and the American Scenic and Historic Preservation Society.[16] In 1913, after holding a series of public hearings, Cooke's committee issued its "Report of The Mayor's Billboard Advertising Commission of the City of New York." The report noted that "One important conclusion with respect to outdoor advertising in New York City to which our investigation has led us is that the fullest and most satisfactory handling of the billboard situation cannot be attained until the State constitution has been so amended as to give unequivocal warrant to the legislature and the courts to regulate billboard advertising on the ground of public beauty." Again, the agenda of the City Beautiful movement clashed up against regulatory limitations. The report continues: "We believe that the time has arrived in this State when public sentiment will warrant writing the word 'beauty' into the constitution."[17]

That was indeed the solution they presented, a short but powerful amendment to New York State's constitution: "The promotion of beauty shall be deemed a public purpose, and any legislative authority having power to promote the public welfare may exercise such power to promote beauty in any matter or locality, or part thereof, subject to its jurisdiction. Private property exposed to public view shall be subject to such power."[18]

Though the subject at hand was billboards, the solution to control them could also advance many items on the agenda of the City Beautiful movement. For years, various efforts at improving the physical city ran up against constitutional limitations. As a 1909 court decision stated, "esthetic considerations are a matter of luxury and indulgence rather than necessity."[19] Not the first to recognize the constitutionality problem, the commission appears to be the first body to propose a concrete solution to it. Bard, who at this time was also serving as the secretary of the Municipal Art Society, is rightly credited as being the driving force behind the commission's work and recommendations. His files on the commission's work reveal his leadership in shaping and advancing its agendas, framing its discussions, and crafting its final report.[20]

It is obvious that the art societies would be major players in the effort to curtail the billboard nuisance. More surprising is the significant involvement of the American Scenic and Historic Preservation Society in the work of the commission. In addition to being one of only a handful of civic organizations helping to pay for this initiative, more importantly, one of the commission members was Colonel Henry W. Sackett, a lawyer and the vice president of the American Scenic and Historic Preservation Society. He was also the first vice president of the Fifth Avenue Association. Of even more interest is the role of Dr. Edward Hagaman Hall, the paid executive secretary of the American Scenic and Historic Preservation Society.

Initially, Hall was one of those who testified at one of the commission's several public hearings. He was regarded as somewhat of an expert on the subject, having written about it for the American Scenic and Historic Preservation Society and having researched European precedents.[21] Beyond this, he played a significant role in the preparation of the report. Hall was hired by the committee to help write the final report. After its publication, Bard wrote to Hall thanking him for "your great assistance in drafting the report." In Hall's response to Bard, he returns the compliment, confirming Bard's key role in the commission's work: "The Commission is largely indebted to you for the painstaking manner in which its labors have been summed up in the Report, for it is my impression that you have put in more work upon it than any of the others."[22]

Surviving records do not provide conclusive proof as to who was responsible for including the constitutional amendment in the commission's final recommendations. The possibility of such a recommendation was mentioned by Bard in an exchange with the Assistant Corporation Counsel in charge of Tenement House Departments and Bureaus of Buildings, during the Commission's March 24, 1913 hearing.[23]

Bard and Hall played the largest roles in the actual drafting of the report, with comments being submitted by other commission members. Regarding the amendment, Hall wrote to Bard, "You are a lawyer and can figure out the solution of the problem better than I can. But I doubt if a constitutional amendment is practicable or necessary."[24] Reviewing the papers that do survive from the commission's work, Bard clearly emerges as the most likely father of the amendment.[25] His efforts over the next years and the decades that followed further suggest his likely parentage of this idea.

It is important to note that both the Municipal Art Society and the American Scenic and Historic Preservation Society were involved with this effort to advance the notion that under the police power, New York City should have the ability to regulate on aesthetic grounds. Over forty years later, this would become a reality in the form of the Bard Act. The societies represented the two major schools of thought undergirding preservation: the historic, with its patriotic origins, and the aesthetic traditions. Ultimately, they would unite in the Landmarks Law.

The commission's proposed constitutional amendment was both timely and ahead of its time. A Constitutional Convention, a rare occasion in New York State, was scheduled for 1915, providing a readymade forum at which the commission's recommendation could be presented. Bard chaired a special committee of the Fine Arts Federation focusing on the 1915 convention. Among the three items proposed for their discussion was the commission's constitutional amendment.[26] Unfortunately, the proposed amendment made no headway at the convention. As the Municipal Art Society's bulletin reported, "The Constitutional Convention paid scant attention to the proposals before it opening the door to the recognition of purely aesthetic considerations in city planning."[27]

Unfortunately, the commission was wrong in its belief that "the time has arrived in this State when public sentiment will warrant writing the world 'beauty' into the constitution." Bard, however, would continue to beat this drum. In 1916, as secretary of the Municipal Art Society, he testified before the Commission on Building Districts and Restrictions [of The City of New York], "This Society greatly regrets that the present constitutional situation prevents the Commission from giving weight to aesthetic considerations." He ends with vintage Bard flourish, "Americans generally are far behind many other nations in realizing the value of beauty as a municipal asset expressible in dollars, to say nothing of its daily contribution to the happiness of the citizen."[28]

Over the course of his long life, Bard time and again demonstrated his capacity to bird-dog a cause over the decades. Many of Bard's beliefs were well ahead of their day. For Bard, the passage of time was an ally, gradually changing attitudes, shifting politics, and constantly creating new opportunities to move his ideas forward.

In 1938, at the age of seventy-one, Bard saw yet another opportunity to advance the cause of aesthetic regulation. The every-twenty-year question of whether there should be a Constitutional Convention in New York had received a positive answer and the big event had been scheduled for that summer. Bard went to work writing and promoting a proposed new clause for the constitution. His efforts were remarkable, not just because of his age, but because of events overshadowing his personal life.

Since the 1920s, the emotional focus of Bard's private life had been the young man Robert Gordon Switz.[29] Gordon, as he was known, was the middle of three sons who grew up with their widowed mother in East Orange, New Jersey. Though never legally adopted, Bard regarded Gordon as his adopted son and was "absolutely devoted" to him.[30] In 1933, with Bard's blessing, Gordon married Marjorie Tilley. Bard had known her since she was a little girl. Marjorie had grown up in the rooming house where Bard kept rooms and her mother worked. The newlyweds went to live in Paris where they were promptly arrested as communist spies in December of that year.

Bard came to their rescue. What was left of his fortune, which had received a major body blow because of the depression, was now committed to helping his "son" through the crisis. For the next several years, his considerable talents would largely be focused on Gordon and Marjorie's predicament. After confessing and then cooperating with the French authorities, Gordon and Marjorie were released in the spring of 1935. Bard went to Paris to help them pick up the pieces of their lives With his financial and emotional support, the couple stayed in Europe to avoid further scandal at home.

By 1938, Gordon and Marjorie Switz were living in Salzburg, then Deutsche Ostmark, Germany. The situation in Europe was disintegrating around them. Back home, Bard and the Switz family were greatly concerned for the couple's safety in a Europe on the brink of war. Worry was even greater with the arrival of a child, Albert Bard Switz. It is in the midst of this uncertainty about their safety and Bard's efforts to orchestrate their safe passage home that New York's Constitutional Convention opened. Despite the pressing demands his personal life was placing on his time and emotions, Bard had the stamina to pursue his civic agenda.

Bard's constant correspondence with Gordon and Marjorie, though largely focusing on family news, occasionally notes his ongoing civic endeavors, and indeed his activities centered on the convention. He writes on Friday, May 27, 1938, "My dear dear Children . . . I have been terribly busy about a lot of civic matters, etc. We now have a Constitutional Convention in session revising the New York Constitution, and this amounts to a second legislative session. I have been studying and criticizing proposals submitted to the Convention and have drafted three."[31]

The main focus of Bard's efforts was the proposed amendment that he called the "patrimony of the people" clause (Intro 508, No. 535). Introduced into the Constitutional Convention by the Hon. O. Byron Brewster of Elizabethtown, New York at the request of the City Club of New York, the Citizens Union, and the Fine Arts Federation of New York, it read: "The natural beauty, historic associations, sightlines and physical good order of the state and its parts contribute to the general welfare and shall be conserved and developed as a part of the patrimony of the people, and to that end private property shall be subject to reasonable regulation and control."[32] The amendment's language is new, but its intellectual roots are in the proposed 1913 amendment. Bard was clearly the father of the 1938 amendment though he was not alone in his interest in this subject.[33]

■ ■ ■ ■ ■ ■ ■

Working through a variety of his civic organizations, Bard sought to build support for the amendment.[34] For the City Club of New York, Committee on Constitutional Convention, he authored a pamphlet, "The Next Step in Community Planning: Civic Design Versus Private Property," providing background on the evolution of governmental architectural controls. It ended with a plea for the proposed amendment: "We ought not wait for another constitutional convention twenty years hence. It would not be a mere matter of twenty years in any event. During those two decades thousands and thousands of incongruous, misplaced and damaging constructions would go up."[35] How right he was.

Despite Bard's considerable efforts on behalf of his bill, trips to Albany, talks to civic organizations, publications, and a radio broadcast, it failed.[36]

FIGURE 2.5 In pre-landmark law New York City, virtually anything was at risk, even city hall itself. Starting in 1888 and raging well into the next century, the controversy over the future of city hall has been called by historian Max Page, New York's "first and longest-running preservation battle." Though city hall was saved, the recognition of the need for a systematic way to protect the city's landmarks was still years away.

Bard had already tempered his expectations. On Tuesday, August 2, 1938, as point nine in his letter to Gordon and Marjorie Switz sent via the S.S. *Normandie* (he often numbered the various subjects he addressed in his lengthy letters), he observes: "The New York Constitutional Convention is drawing to a close and its work is getting reduced to concrete and specific proposals. The results will be meager. It has been a politician's convention."[37] Bard would not get his constitutional amendment in 1938, but the year would not be a total loss. On December 17, two days short of his seventy-second birthday, Bard received a wonderful present, the safe return to America of Gordon, Marjorie, and his namesake, their son "Bertie."[38]

The problem of finding a legal basis for regulation of private property on aesthetic grounds had not been solved. It would require almost another twenty years and a different set of circumstances for Bard to achieve this end. It is, however, in these earlier efforts that the intellectual origins of his 1956 success are found. In Bard's efforts to achieve the protection of the patrimony of the people through aesthetic regulation, the beginning of the unbroken chain of events that ultimately leads to the Landmarks Law is found.

With the failure of the patrimony of the people amendment, the effort to achieve protection through aesthetic regulation hit a wall. What was still missing was what Bard had been trying to provide and what architect and former Municipal Art Society president Electus D. Litchfield described as the "necessary foundation for planning and conservation legislation greatly to be desired, without which we are ever threatened with the loss of much that the people of New York hold dear."[39] In the "patrimony of the people clause," Bard had sought to attack the problem head on: "The trouble has been with the over-emphasis on private right in contravention of public interest."[40] As was often the case in his life, Bard's thinking was still well ahead of his time.

While Bard and the art societies were unsuccessfully advancing their aesthetic agenda, preservation was making some modest progress in another sphere. Patriotic societies and other organizations were at work saving individual sites associated with historic events and people. The early decades of the twentieth century saw the preservation of such New York City landmark sites of associative value as Washington's Headquarters, today known as the Morris–Jumel Mansion; Fraunces Tavern, where Washington bid farewell to his troops, and Hamilton Grange, the country house Alexander Hamilton had built for himself in Upper Manhattan. All three were preserved through purchase: Morris–Jumel by the city in 1903, Fraunces Tavern in 1904 by the Sons of the Revolution, and after initially being moved out of harm's way in 1889, the Grange was purchased for the American Scenic and Historic Preservation Society in 1924.[41]

If one were writing a history of New York's preservation movement, the chapter on this early period would include detailed accounts of several signature preservation controversies. Among them would be the city's "first and longest-running preservation battle," the struggle over city hall and its park, which, in one form or another, stretched from 1888 until the late 1930s.[42] That success would be counterbalanced by the failed efforts to save St. John's Chapel. Built on Varick Street by Trinity Parish, the chapel, designed by John McComb Jr., with its soaring spire, was the subject of a preservation drama that ran from 1908 to the chapel's demolition in 1918. There would also be a shorter account of the loss of the Madison Square Presbyterian Church in 1919.[43]

All of these efforts led to a public discourse about preservation, but none contributed in any clearly identifiable way to the ultimate chain of events leading to a regulatory system for the preservation of the city's landmarks. As Randy Mason, a student of this period of preservation's history, writes: "Instead of regulatory structures, preservationists sought to shape the city by creating actual sites of memory."[44]

In this period, there are several other preservation initiatives worthy of mention, although there is no evidence that they directly contribute to advancing landmark protection. They are of interest because of what they might have led to if events had transpired differently. The compiling of lists of important buildings has played a critical role in advancing the protection of historic sites. This should not be surprising because identifying what needs to be saved is an essential first step in building a constituency to become engaged in its preservation. Ultimately, it would be the development and refinement of such a list in the 1950s that would greatly assist in efforts leading to the Landmarks Law.

In 1913, the Art Commission of the City of New York, the charter-mandated agency charged with reviewing public art and the design of certain structures on city-owned lands, took a modest step toward developing such a list of important sites when it hired Frank Cousins and assigned him the task of photographing fifty "old buildings of historical as well as architectural interest." It is not clear how the list was compiled, but we know that buildings "were selected not only because of their interesting character and history, but a number of them because of their liability to be torn down soon."[45] Cousins was a photographer, a historian, and an expert on Colonial architecture.[46] It is likely he had some input into the shaping of the list. Some of the photographs and a paragraph on the

FIGURE 2.6 St. John's Chapel was at the center of a preservation struggle waged from 1908 through 1918. Captured here in a photograph by Frank Cousins, an early documenter of the city's threatened heritage, this 1803 Episcopal church stood on Varick Street below Canal until demolished in 1918. Preservation champion George McAneny, in his role as Manhattan borough president, was involved in the failed effort to save this architectural treasure designed by noted architect John McComb.

project were included in the Commission's 1913 published report, a copy of which is found in Bard's papers. There is no indication that this list of fifty buildings directly inspired or informed the 1950s list project that would play such a key role in advancing the cause of preservation.

More tantalizing in the category of "what could have been" are a series of ideas floated by Park Commissioner Francis Gallatin in January of 1923. Under the stirring headline "A City Beautiful Is Gallatin's Hope/ Park Commissioner Would Keep Landmarks and Harmonize Building Designs/Advocates New Laws," the article announces Gallatin's plan to talk to the mayor about his proposal to "enable the city to step in and save any building of antiquarian or sentimental interest or of architectural beauty." He was truly visionary, imagining the city would "possess

FIGURE 2.7   Concerned with the fate of New York's old buildings of architectural and historical interest, in 1913 the Art Commission of the City of New York hired the photographer Frank Cousins to document fifty buildings. One of them was Gracie Mansion. The project received some press attention and several of Cousins' photographs were used to illustrate the Art Commission's annual report for that year.

the power to preserve" not just a handful of buildings but "hundreds of historic landmarks, homes, and hostelries." His vision included a "commission" that would be established to designate buildings, "thereby preserving them against the future and from money-making demands." The article closes, noting that "in his conference with Mayor Hylan, Commissioner Gallatin will take up the feasibility of having the Legislature adopt measures for vesting power in either a special commission or the Municipal Art Commission for the naming of public monuments."[47]

Gallatin's concept was even more expansive. He wanted the Art Commission to have the power to "veto designs for buildings which would produce grotesque incongruities because of the conflict between their style and existing kinds of architecture." He talked of establishing "architectural zones" in which the "designs of each building's architecture would conform and harmonize with the neighboring buildings . . . an old, mellowed neighborhood could not be spoiled by a building that would belong in a modern, newly developed locality."[48]

Here, some forty years before the Landmarks Law, Gallatin, a city official, is advancing the concept of legislation to create a commission with the authority to protect scores of individual buildings of historical or architectural interest, as well as a system to protect the design integrity of historic neighborhoods. In at least broad strokes, Gallatin's vision resembles the Landmarks Law of 1965.

What was motivating Gallatin? He did not come to his position from the ranks of the art or patriotic societies. He was, however, as eloquent as some of their leaders in extolling the role of historic sites in the Americanization of immigrants. His background does not provide any real clues to why he took up the City Beautiful cause. He does note that his proposed design ordinance would never have "permitted the gloomy, foreboding Post Office to overshadow the charm of the colonial City Hall." At another point, he cites the lesson of the loss of St. John's Chapel as a reason for action to protect historic sites.[49]

Gallatin's remarks, though worthy of a few stories in the newspaper, do not seem to have received much notice. There is no indication that they were ever taken seriously. One person who paid attention was Albert Bard. A fervent clipper of articles, Bard's files include a copy of the above-cited *New York Times* article with the handwritten note "Charter Revision Munic. Art Society," indicating both where it was to be filed and how Bard thought Gallatin's ideas might be best directed. Gallatin had spelled out a framework to protect the city's landmarks: a law and a commission. He was not able to solve the more daunting problem that would continue

■ ■ ■ ■ ■ ■ ■

to stump preservationists for decades: finding a constitutional basis for such a law. Though it must have been heartening for Bard and others to see a city official publicly advancing a scheme to protect sites of historic and architectural importance, Bard, more than most, would have appreciated its true limitations.

All we know about the meeting at which Gallatin was to present his idea to Mayor Hylan is that nothing came out of it. Imagine for a moment that something had. If in the early 1920s, New York had authorized the commission Gallatin imagined, vested with the powers he described, today we would be living in a city that would look radically different.

By the close of 1938, neither episodic events like the Art Commission of the City of New York's photo documentation project, nor Gallatin's trial balloon, nor consistent efforts to advance aesthetic regulation by Bard and like-minded colleagues had achieved any level of protection for the city's landmarks. Events that would soon unfold would only underscore the desperate need for such protection.

ENDNOTES

1. Much of what we know about Bard comes from the Albert S. Bard Papers, New York Public Library. The New York Preservation Archive also has a collection of Bard's personal papers, The Albert Bard Archive, which shed considerable light on Bard the man. We also have learned much about Bard from interviews conducted with Marjorie (Switz) Dunbar. She met Bard when she was a little girl, when in 1916 he rented rooms in the house where her mother worked and they all lived. In 1933, she became the wife of Robert Gordon Switz, the young man Bard considered to be his unofficially adopted son. Even after the death of her husband in 1951, she remained close to Bard until he died in 1963. Her children considered Bard their grandfather. Bard's ninetieth birthday was reported on by McCandlish Phillips, "A. S. Bard, at 90, Sets Brisk Pace/Lawyer Continues Practice Here and Wages Private War on Illegal Posters," *New York Times*, December 19, 1956. Bard's ninetieth was noted in the editorial, "Albert S. Bard at 90," *New York Times*, December 19, 1956. His ninety-fifth generated two news stories in the *New York Times*, one by Charles Grutzner, "Outdoor Ad Foe Turns Strong 95/Hasn't Torn Down Poster in Months, but Isn't 'Soft,'" *New York Times*, December 20, 1961 and the other, author unknown, "Civic Group Hails Its Hothead at 95/Citizens Union Founder Says Bad Temper Got Results," *New York Times*, December 21, 1961. In some small way, the coverage of his ninety and ninety-fifth birthdays makes up for the fact that Bard only received a one-paragraph *New York Times* obituary, having died during the 114-day newspaper strike.

2. Anthony C. Wood, "Pioneers of Preservation: Part II: An Interview with Harmon Goldstone," *Village Views* 4, no. 3 (Summer 1987): 18. The sentiment expressed is appropriate, though technically not fully in accordance with the facts. Bard resigned from the society's board in 1923 in protest over its failure to defend the

Art Commission in the debate over the sculpture, Civic Virtue, Gilmartin, *Shaping the City*, 258. Though no longer on its board, Bard continued to work closely with the society and ultimately returned to its board in 1946.

3. Philips, "Albert S. Bard, at 90," *New York Times*, December 19, 1956.

4. "Civic Group Hails Its Hothead at 95," *New York Times*, December 21, 1961.

5. "Bar's Bard," *The New Yorker*, February 23, 1957, 25.

6. Bard's typed notes, "Trip to Europe—1922," Albert S. Bard Papers, New York Public Library.

7. Bard's copy of Rand McNally's "A Week at the Fair" is found in the Albert S. Bard Papers at the New York Public Library. His actual attendance at the fair was confirmed in an interview with Marjorie Dunbar at her home in Hurley, New York. Marjorie Dunbar, interview by Anthony C. Wood, May 30, 2003, New York Preservation Archive Project.

8. Gilmartin, *Shaping the City*, 13.

9. Ibid., 29–30.

10. "Albert Bard Dead at 96," *Newark Evening News*, March 26, 1963.

11. Gilmartin, *Shaping the City*, 138.

12. Ibid., 140.

13. Christopher Gray, "The Battles Over Outdoor Ads Go Back a Century," *New York Times*, June 17, 2001.

14. Raymond B. Fosdick, A Report on An Investigation of Billboard Advertising in the City of New York (City of New York, Office of The Commissioner of Accounts, 1912).

15. Robert Grier Cooke to Mayor Gaynor, September 23, 1912, Albert S. Bard Papers, New York Public Library.

16. Bard also served as treasurer of the Commission and his papers have documents covering its finances. Albert S. Bard Papers, New York Public Library.

17. City of New York, Report of The Mayor's Billboard Advertising Commission of the City of New York, August 1, 1913, 8.

18. Ibid., 95.

19. Ibid., 28.

20. Gilmartin, *Shaping the City*, 147, writes that Bard "dominated" the Mayor's Billboard Advertising Commission and Bard's files on his work on the commission reveal his leadership and intense involvement, Albert S. Bard Papers, New York Public Library.

21. Hall testified before the Mayor's Billboard Advertising Commission at the public hearing of January 24, 1913. Transcripts of all the commission's hearings are in the Albert S. Bard Papers, New York Public Library. In the American Scenic and Historic Preservation Society's Annual Report of 1905. Appendix F is an article by Hall: "The Poster Nuisance/An Argument Against the Abuses of Outdoor Advertising."

22. Bard to Edward Hagaman Hall, August 15, 1913, and Hall to Bard, August 15, 1913, Albert S. Bard Papers, New York Public Library.

23. Transcript of the Mayor's Billboard Advertising Commission's March 24, 1913 hearing, 357, Albert S. Bard Papers, New York Public Library.

24. Edward Hagaman Hall to Bard, undated, but Bard writes on the letter that it came with Hall's draft of the report. We know from a June 10, 1913 letter from Hall to Bard that he has just "cleared the decks of other matters" and expects to get "down to the work of your report now," so the first letter was written in the summer of 1913. In that letter he also states his belief that the proposed amendment needs "more careful consideration" and suggests the larger problem is with the Federal Constitution.

25. Gilmartin, *Shaping the City,* 147, refers to it as "Bard's proposal," and Hall's letters to Bard support this conclusion.

26. Bard to Members of the Special Committee of Five of the Fine Arts Federation, January 21, 1915, Albert S. Bard Papers, New York Public Library.

27. Municipal Art Society Bulletin, October 1915.

28. New York (N.Y.) Commission on Building Districts and Restrictions, Final Report, June 2, 1916 (City of New York, Board of Estimate and Apportionment, Committee on the City Plan, 1916), 82.

29. Bard's life and his over-forty-year relationship with the Switz family is the subject of a forthcoming work by the author. In addition to our knowledge of this aspect of Bard's life from interviews with Marjorie Switz Dunbar, Gordon's wife, extensive surviving correspondence and other personal papers provide rich detail on this aspect of Bard's private life. Albert Bard Archive, New York Preservation Archive Project.

30. Dunbar, by Wood, May 30, 2003.

31. Bard to Gordon and Marjorie Switz, May 27, 1938, Albert Bard Archive, New York Preservation Archive Project.

32. "Constitutional Amendment Proposed for New York," New York State Planning News 2, no. 6, (July 20, 1938); Albert S. Bard Papers, New York Public Library; Bill no. 535, int. 508, New York State Constitutional Convention 1938, Bills, 455–750.

33. The desire to get aesthetics into the constitution was shared by others. The architect Arthur Holden had drafted a clause with much more precise language that was being discussed by the Civic Design Committee of the New York Chapter of the AIA Gerald Holmes, the chair of that committee, in a letter to Bard (April 14, 1938, Albert S. Bard Papers, New York Public Library), sends Holden's text to Bard and notes: "Your more general statement of principle is probably a much better way of doing it, and I agree with you that the revised version is an improvement." In an April 14, 1938 letter to the editor of the *New York Times*, Electus D. Litchfield, himself a great citizen of the city, called out both Holmes of the AIA and Bard of the Fine Arts Federation as "each having proposed such a clause," and then cites the language of the patrimony of the people clause. In a June 28, 1938, letter to Gordon and Marjorie Switz, Albert Bard Archive, New York Preservation Archive Project, Bard writes: "I am speaking at a luncheon at the City Club tomorrow in connection with an amendment I drafted for the New York Constitution." He goes on to reference the "City Club pamphlet dealing with the subject," the subject being his patrimony of the people clause.

34. Bard was on the Citizens Union Committee on Constitutional Revision and served as the Chair of its subcommittee on State Planning and Conservation. Albert S. Bard Papers, New York Public Library.

35. In this pamphlet, Bard provides a brief account of the evolution of the doctrine governing the regulation of private property for aesthetic purposes. He focuses on the evolution of design controls referencing the "Shipstead–Luce Act" approved in 1930 dealing with Washington, D.C. and ordinances in California. He also discusses architectural control abroad. Though the patrimony of the people clause itself mentions historic associations, Bard does not reference controls in other cities specifically dealing with preservation. Bard certainly had a national knowledge base, so one can assume he was aware of the 1936 Amendment to Louisiana Constitution authorizing the new Vieux Carré Commission. Clearly, what Bard hoped

to achieve encompassed the protection of historic resources, but was much broader in its scope. He framed it in the larger context of architectural controls. Albert S. Bard, "The Next Step in Community Planning Civic Design Versus Private Property," The City Club of New York Committee on Constitutional Convention, May 1938, Albert S. Bard Papers, New York Public Library.

36. Bard's Office Diary for 1938 in the Albert Bard Archive at the New York Preservation Archive Project notes time devoted to working on the New York Constitution. His efforts included a one-day trip to Albany, taking the Empire State Express from Grand Central on May 23, 1938, to meet at the Fort Orange Club to discuss the constitutional amendment. The diary is supplemented with references in his correspondence of this period to Gordon and Majorie Switz. Albert Bard Archive, New York Preservation Archive Project.

37. Bard to Gordon and Marjorie Switz, August 2, 1938, Albert Bard Archive, New York Preservation Archive Project.

38. Because Gordon and Marjorie Switz were confessed spies, their return to the United States was of interest to the FBI. When the S.S. *Hansa* carrying them back to the United States docked in New York City, there to greet them, along with Bard, were two FBI agents. In their report, they talk of preliminarily interviewing Gordon and Marjorie at 8:00 a.m. in their "tourist class stateroom." They were described as being "quite cooperative in manner" and willing to accompany the agents to their office for an interview. It was noted that Gordon Switz "apparently regrets his former spying activities and states he desires to reinstate himself in good standing as American citizen." As for Bard, the report notes that "SWITZ stated that Mr. BARD is a lifelong friend of his family and has practically been a foster-father to him as long as he can remember; that Mr. BARD knew nothing whatever about his spying activities until he was arrested in Paris. . . . Mr. BARD stated that he has a very deep friendly interest in SWITZ and desires to assist him in every way possible." FBI Report, File No. 65-23, January 23, 1939, 2.

39. Electus D. Litchfield, letter to the editor, *New York Times,* April 17, 1938.

40. Bard to Charles C. Weinstein, Esq., Corp. Counsel, New York City, May 24, 1938, Albert S. Bard Papers, New York Public Library.

41. Randall Mason, "Memory Infrastructure: Preservation, 'Improvement' and Landscape in New York City, 1898–1925" (Unpublished Dissertation, Columbia University, 1999), 49–50.

42. Max Page, *The Creative Destruction of Manhattan 1900–1940* (University of Chicago Press: Chicago, 1999), 113. Bard, in both his role as Secretary of the Court House Site Committee of the Bar Association and as a member of the Citizen's Union, appeared at a 1910 Board of Estimate hearing at which Bard protested the size and location of the proposed new court house because of its impact on City Hall. He testified, "It doesn't take an architect to see that such a building in such a location as has been approved by the court House board will have the inevitable effect of ruining our little gem of a City Hall." He ended his testimony, "It is stupidity and shortsightedness and folly. Pardon me if I show too much heat, but we are hot about this thing." "Court Site Decision Held Up By Gaynor," *New York Times,* March 19, 1910.

43. For more on the efforts to save St. John's Chapel and City Hall, turn to Mason, "Memory Infrastructure: Preservation, 'Improvement' and Landscape in New York City," and to Page, *The Creative Destruction of Manhattan.*

44. Mason, "Memory Infrastructure," 44.

■ ■ ■ ■ ■ ■ ■

45. Art Commission of the City of New York, Annual Report, 1913, 16; "Plan to Preserve by Photograpy New York's Landmarks," *New York Sun*, June 29, 1913; "The Camera To Preserve New York's Old Buildings," *New York Times*, May 10, 1914. For a history of the Art Commission and the evolution of its powers, see Michele H. Bogart, The Politics of Urban Beauty: New York and Its Art Commission (Chicago: University of Chicago Press, 2006).

46. For more on Cousins, turn to Mason, see "Memory Infrastructure," and consult materials at both the Art Commission of the City of New York and the Peabody Essex Museum, Salem, Massachusetts.

47. "A City Beautiful Is Gallatin's Hope," *New York Times*, January 7, 1923.

48. Ibid.

49. Ibid.; "Gallatin Pleads for City Beauty," *New York Times*, February 18, 1923.

THREE

The Bridge, The Castle, and Moses

THIS BRIDGE, IF BUILT, WOULD DESTROY THE MOST NOBLE ASPECT OF THE ISLAND OF MANHAT-
TAN AND IN DOING THAT DESTROY ALSO THE MOST NOBLE ASPECT OF THE PRINCIPAL ENTRANCE
OF OUR COUNTRY. THE VIEW OF MANHATTAN AS WE APPROACH IT FROM EUROPE IS THRILLING.
THE PROW-LIKE END OF THE ISLAND WITH THE TALL MAST-LIKE BUILDINGS BACK OF IT EXCITES
OUR IMAGINATIONS TO SEE IT AS A GIGANTIC, GALLANT SHIP RIDING BETWEEN THE TWO BROAD
RIVERS. I, FOR ONE, SHALL NEVER WANT TO SEE IT AGAIN IF A LONG, SLANTING LINE OF A RAMP
TO A BRIDGE AT AN IRRELEVANT ANGLE, THROWING ASKEW ALL OF THE TALL PERPENDICULARS
AND BROAD HORIZONTALS, MUST WHOLLY DESTROY THIS EFFECT.[1]

Featured in a 1939 open letter to President Franklin D. Roosevelt, this
passionate plea against the proposed Brooklyn-Battery Bridge, written by
the sculptor Frances Grimes, vividly portrays what New York's civic community felt was at stake in its now legendary struggle with Robert Moses
over the future of New York's Battery. Moses, the great city planner and
master builder whose immense power was in part a tribute to his remarkable political acumen as well as his multiple governmental positions, was
proposing a bridge that many felt would forever violate the beauty and
integrity of this most historic part of New York City.

   The civic community's short, yet intense, skirmish with Moses over the
Brooklyn-Battery Bridge and the epic battle it would ignite over the future
of Castle Clinton at the foot of Manhattan created a shared set of experiences that would inspire and motivate a generation of New Yorkers. First
hand, they experienced New York City's dire need for a formal method
to protect the architectural treasures, historic relics, and civic beauty that
they so deeply cherished.

(101)   AIRVIEW OF LOWER MANHATTAN, NEW YORK CITY

FIGURE 3.1   Lower Manhattan was beloved by New York's civic leaders. Its southern tip, site of Battery Park and Castle Clinton, would have been forever changed by the proposed Brooklyn-Battery Bridge and its approaches. While Moses envisioned the bridge as a new monument, others saw it as a disfigurement of what sculptor Frances Grimes called "the most noble aspect of the Island of Manhattan."

It was January of 1939. At this point in his ascendancy, Robert Moses was well along in amassing power and brutally proficient it its application. He announced to New York City his next grand project, plans for the "Battery-Brooklyn link in the great chain of marginal arteries and parkways encircling Manhattan, Brooklyn, Queens and the Bronx."[2] For reasons of vision, power, finance, and ego, Moses unveiled a proposed bridge that would be under his control, instead of the expected tunnel that would not. After a decade of assuming this river crossing would be a tunnel, his announcement took New York by surprise since "the idea of a Battery-Brooklyn bridge never occurred to anyone before."[3]

The unveiling of the proposed bridge ignited a political firestorm that ranged from New York City to Albany and ultimately to the White House. This struggle between New York's civic community and Robert Moses was intensely fierce. Though it raged only from January through October of 1939, its repercussions would be felt for years. This contest of wills has been vividly captured in rich detail by Robert Caro in his monumental work, *The Power Broker*—the chronicle of the evolution of Robert Moses from civic reformer to brilliant tyrant. That book (or, at bare minimum,

AERIAL VIEW OF LOWER MANHATTAN AND BROOKLYN WITH BRIDGE INDICATED IN PROPER POSITION

FIGURE 3.2   This Triborough Bridge Authority photograph, courtesy of the MTA Bridges and Tunnels Special Archive, shows the revised plans for the Brooklyn-Battery Bridge submitted to the War Department on May 24, 1939. Though the modification located the bridge closer to Governor's Island, it did not in any way mitigate its visual or functional impacts on the Battery. In the end, it would be the War Department that stopped the bridge.

its chapters on the bridge and Castle Clinton) is essential reading for anyone interested in the history of preservation in New York.[4]

Leaving to Caro much of the play-by-play coverage of the conflicts, a truncated account provides us the understanding needed to appreciate their role in the larger story of the origins of New York's Landmarks Law. The bridge needed a variety of approvals from entities ranging from city agencies, such as the Art Commission of the City of New York and the City Planning Commission, to city governmental bodies, the city council and the Board of Estimate, to state governmental bodies and officials, and finally, because of its possible impact on a strategically important navigable body of water, a final approval by the War Department, whose decision could be appealed to the president of the United States.

Because of his popularity, his multiple power bases, and his impressive track record of accomplishments, Moses was well positioned to obtain these permissions. He entered the battle with immense political capital. Some of this flowed from his multiple official positions, most notably in this episode as chairman of the Triborough Bridge Authority (the entity seeking to build the bridge) and Park Commissioner for the City of New York (the agency responsible for Battery Park). As chair of the Authority, he commanded vast financial resources during a period when the city itself was financially strapped. Also, at this point in his ascension, his great public works still blinded most observers to the more questionable tactics he often employed to advance them.

Moses enjoyed a level of public support that made him a political threat as a potential candidate, as a king maker, or as a spoiler. And why shouldn't he? Already, he had built thousands of acres of parks in New York State and had constructed bridges and parkways. For New York City, he was delivering endless new playgrounds, stunning swimming pools, and such impressive new parks as Orchard Beach. He had mastered the New Deal to the great benefit of New Yorkers. Moses delivered public works in a way never seen before or since. As a result, Moses occupied a truly unique position.[5]

Contributing mightily to the success of Robert Moses was his willingness to play political hardball. In 1939, Albert Bard wrote, "There is more involved in Mr. Moses's campaign for the bridge than the merits or demerits of the project. Mr. Moses' tactics in this matter have been quite characteristic, but in this case have gone to lengths he has not always felt obliged to resort to. His perversions of fact, his intemperance of epithet, his back-stairs methods . . . have been quite outrageous but thoroughly typical of his methods."[6]

Moses relentlessly drove the project. He demanded speedy approvals and would entertain no compromises: "Either you want it or you don't want it, and either you want it now or you don't get it at all."[7] One after another, the review bodies fell before the Moses juggernaut. By March of 1939, Moses had demonstrated his ruthless ability to get approvals for the bridge. Additional approvals from these bodies would be needed, but his ability to acquire them was now proven. The only remaining uncertainty was what was assumed to be the rather perfunctory approval of the Department of War.

Architectural historian and Avery Librarian at Columbia University, Talbot F. Hamlin, wrote:

■ ■ ■ ■ ■ ■ ■

K

or

)

)E

ns

of
ith
yn
ay
ert
on-
est
ap-
re-
ted
ing
the
ns.
ion
the
and
ne-
ter

dso

Times Wide World

SANDHOGS DEMONSTRATE AGAINST PROPOSED BATTERY BRIDGE

A delegation in colonial costumes staging a protest parade in Battery Park yesterday. The sandhogs say the erection of the span to Brooklyn in place of a tunnel would deprive them of many hours of work.

FIGURE 3.3 One of the most colorful protests against Moses' bridge was captured in this *New York Times* photograph that appeared on March 21, 1939 with the following heading and caption: "SANDHOGS DEMONSTRATE AGAINST PROPOSED BATTERY BRIDGE. A delegation in colonial costumes staging a protest parade in Battery Park yesterday. The sandhogs say the erection of the span to Brooklyn in place of a tunnel would deprive them of many hours of work."

The steamroller so deftly put together by the supporters of the proposed Battery-Brooklyn bridge seems to be careering full-tilt, overcoming and crushing to the earth all of the opposition which has risen so persistently against it, only to be overwhelmed by the great weight of this enormous machine. . . . The whole mad, impetuous clamor for haste in this matter might almost seem to augur a fear that, if the merits of the problem were really examined carefully, the whole project would be seen to be the folly which many of the city's experts feel it is.[8]

Masterminding the opposition to Moses were four New York civic reformers: Stanley Isaacs, borough president of Manhattan, George McAneny, appearing in his role as the president of the Regional Plan Association, and bolstered by his status as a former borough president with a long and distinguished record of public service, Albert Bard, tireless advocate for civic beauty, and C. C. Burlingham, an admiralty lawyer and private citizen whose lifetime of civic involvement and behind-the-scenes access to those in power had earned him nearly legendary status as reflected in the moniker bestowed upon him by the press, "New York's First Citizen."[9] One could not have found a more impressive civic fearsome foursome to tackle Robert Moses.

Each played a key role. Stanley Isaacs, as a member of the Board of Estimate, was the only one of the three who could, and courageously did, fight the project from an elected position. He provided strategic advice to the opponents and managed their testimony at the infamous March 27, 1939, seven-hour city council committee hearing on the bridge. That drama has captured a place in the annals of municipal history because of the unbridled ferociousness of Moses' personal attacks on his opponents. That day Moses personally savaged both Isaacs and McAneny.[10]

It was in April after that brutal hearing that the opponents of the Brooklyn-Battery Bridge regrouped. With the War Department the only entity yet to fall before the Moses blitzkrieg, Caro stresses the apparent hopelessness of the opposition's situation. Their actions suggest they saw things differently. The opponents came together and formed the Central Committee of Organizations Opposing the Battery Bridge. Over seventeen groups strong, ranging from the Fine Arts Federation (itself representing sixteen groups) to the Real Estate Board of New York, its work was led by an Organizing Committee chaired by Albert Bard and closely advised by George McAneny. Bard pressed

Moses and Isaacs Clash Again At Hearing on Battery Bridge

Herald Tribune photo—Acme

Park Commissioner Robert Moses defending his proposal for a Battery-Brooklyn bridge yesterday at the City Council hearing

FIGURE 3.4   One of the most vicious encounters in the battle over the proposed bridge was a seven-hour city council committee hearing. At that hearing, Robert Moses brutally disparaged George McAneny, the elderly but feisty president of the Regional Plan Association, as an "extinct volcano."

FIGURE 3.5 Charles Culp Burlingham, almost universally known as C.C.B., is shown here on the right promenading up Fifth Avenue on Easter Day in 1930 with the noted educator Nicholas Murray Butler. In his early seventies at that time, for his extensive civic efforts C.C.B. had earned the moniker "New York's First Citizen." C.C.B. was instrumental in the successful effort to reach out to F.D.R. to block the Brooklyn-Battery Bridge and also played a role in saving Castle Clinton.

C. C. Burlingham to play a formal role with the Committee, but Burlingham felt he would be more effective working behind the scenes.[11]

The opponents of the bridge formulated a sophisticated strategy to wage a war of attrition against the project, preparing to fight it before

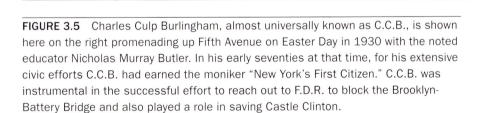

Crowds inspecting a model of the Battery-Brooklyn bridge after the Board of Estimate had voted contingent approval of the proposal

FIGURE 3.6 The controversy over the proposed Brooklyn-Battery Bridge was extensively covered in the press and attracted significant public interest. This photo, which appeared with the *New York Herald-Tribune*'s June 9, 1939 coverage of the Board of Estimate meeting at which the project received contingent approval, shows the "crowds inspecting a model of the Battery-Brooklyn bridge." Bard appeared at the hearing filing "the most complete argument against the structure."

every agency that it needed to return to as well as before each new tribunal it might face.[12] Bard coordinated and led the testimony at the April 25, 1939, hearing before the War Department and McAneny led the unsuccessful charge when the project was returned to the Board of Estimate in June. Moses' performance at that hearing led Stanley Isaacs to comment, "I've seen a number of versions of 'The Mikado' but the greatest Poo Bah of them all seems to be Mr. Moses."[13]

It was the War Department's surprising rejection of the project, affirmed by President Roosevelt in October of 1939, that killed the bridge. This victory was not a triumph of reason over force, but the trumping of one powerful man by an even more powerful one. It is Burlingham who gets the credit for activating this Hail Mary pass strategy, his relationship with President Roosevelt being so personal that he referred to him in his telegrams as "Skipper."[14]

Because of past political battles too legion to recount here, there was no love lost between F.D.R. and Moses.[15] The opponents of the bridge were able to skillfully use that dynamic to pave the way for their ultimate victory. Eleanor Roosevelt became a player with a brief but potent paragraph questioning the bridge in her syndicated national newspaper column. "In graveyard confidence," Burlingham used his access to the president to advance the opposition's case. Such behind-the-scenes efforts were complemented by such public efforts as the opposition's "An Open Letter to the President and His Advisers" laying out the case against the

Bridge.[16] Not pinning all their hopes on obtaining a negative ruling by the War Department, the Central Committee had been preparing to continue its struggle, identifying both potential future legal strategies and lobbying in Washington against a bill providing an easement over federal property required for the bridge's construction.[17]

There were many reasons for the extraordinary opposition to the bridge: its cost, its impact on real estate values in lower Manhattan, issues of navigation, and the danger it posed in times of war. High on the list was the negative aesthetic impact of the bridge, its ramps, and its terminus on Lower Manhattan. Speaking for the multiple arts societies it represented, the Fine Arts Federation eloquently nailed it: "A bridge with its terminus and approaches at the Battery will seriously disfigure perhaps the most thrillingly beautiful and world-renowned feature of this great city."[18]

Almost from day one, the opponents raised the aesthetic issue. Though unquestionably the rich history of Lower Manhattan underpinned their concern, it was the visual impact on the historic face and skyline of the city that was their greatest concern. Isaacs was quick to point out that the bridge's anchorage would "be a solid stone mass equal in size to a ten-story building, at the Battery."[19] Albert Bard raised the question of the impact of the bridge on the Battery's "waterscape," a term he coined for "the special factor created by the conformation of the lower end of Manhattan Island in its relation to the Upper Bay and the Hudson and East Rivers. Although created by nature, this waterscape has in it a certain element of design which has been emphasized by the architectural construction of man . . . are we prepared to sacrifice that municipal asset?"[20]

Opponents were eager to dramatize for the public the visual impact of the bridge. The views offered by Robert Moses showed the bridge from "high in the air or out at sea where only those who travel by boat or airplane could get such a view." The Central Committee produced and distributed a composite photograph prepared by three architects showing the visual impact of the bridge as seen at eye level.[21] At the Board of Estimate, Bard even challenged Moses to "erect in Battery Park a structure consisting of a few poles and some rope which would show where the bridge project would go and its size and height. Of course, the challenge passed unheeded."[22]

The art societies and Robert Moses possessed fundamentally different senses of aesthetics. As a builder of bridges, for Moses "there was nothing built these days more beautiful than a well designed suspension bridge."[23] The cultural chasm between these clashing worldviews is dramatically revealed in conflicting reactions to Chicago's 1893 World's Fair. Many

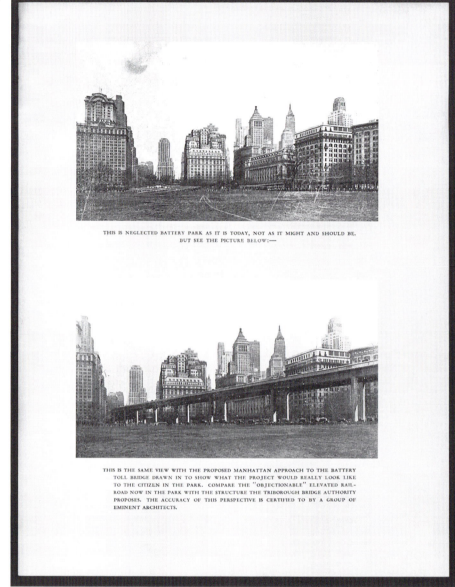

THIS IS NEGLECTED BATTERY PARK AS IT IS TODAY, NOT AS IT MIGHT AND SHOULD BE,
BUT SEE THE PICTURE BELOW:—

THIS IS THE SAME VIEW WITH THE PROPOSED MANHATTAN APPROACH TO THE BATTERY
TOLL BRIDGE DRAWN IN TO SHOW WHAT THE PROJECT WOULD REALLY LOOK LIKE
TO THE CITIZEN IN THE PARK. COMPARE THE "OBJECTIONABLE" ELEVATED RAIL-
ROAD NOW IN THE PARK WITH THE STRUCTURE THE TRIBOROUGH BRIDGE AUTHORITY
PROPOSES. THE ACCURACY OF THIS PERSPECTIVE IS CERTIFIED TO BY A GROUP OF
EMINENT ARCHITECTS.

FIGURE 3.7   As a precursor of today's more sophisticated visualization techniques, these two views helped New Yorkers appreciate the impact of the proposed bridge on lower Manhattan. Prepared by the architects Hugh Ferriss, Chester B. Price, and Schell Lewis, the photographs were circulated by Bard's Central Committee of Organizations Opposing the Battery Bridge and were included in its July 14, 1939 "Open Letter" to President Roosevelt and his advisers asking for further study of the bridge.

of the art societies had been founded by New Yorkers who had attended the fair and returned inspired and transformed. Moses, years after the bridge battle dismissed that very same fair, saying, "everything was Greek

Revival, a bunch of damned outhouses with a lot of white columns in front of them."[24]

The fight over Manhattan's Battery was itself a bridge linking that struggle to earlier preservation efforts. Prior to this episode, George McAneny had already earned impressive preservation credentials. Decades earlier, as borough president he had provided a temporary reprieve for St. John's Chapel and had played a role in the restoration of city hall. Even earlier, in 1913, he had helped rescue the Poe Cottage in the Bronx.[25] In his testimony against the bridge at the city council, McAneny placed the bridge battle within its preservation context, referencing the turn-of-the-century fight to save city hall: "I am in fact of the opinion that if the plans under discussion are seriously pressed, there will be an uprising of public opinion the like of which has not been known since, forty years ago, some well-intentioned gentleman in office proposed that the City Hall be torn down, to make way for something more modern in the skyscraping line."[26]

Through its protagonists, McAneny and Bard, the battle against the bridge is as clearly tied to preservation's past as its tactics and strategy link it to preservation's future. The organizing of diverse civic opposition into a coordinated coalition, the development and execution of a strategy systematically challenging every approval needed by a project (no matter how seemingly inconsequential), the visual simulation of the impact of a project, and the activation of complex political networks at all governmental levels, make the Brooklyn-Battery Bridge fight the clear forerunner of future preservation struggles. It also shares with contemporary preservation efforts the sentiments Bard expressed to his friend Felix Frankfurter, the then freshly minted Supreme Court Justice: "The whole thing is being railroaded through in an outrageous manner. Information is withheld and inquiries are obstructed. Even hearings have not been fairly conducted. . . . Can feeble little folk like me save the city from a serious blunder? I don't know. It is certainly uphill work."[27]

In this battle with Robert Moses, the civic community had confronted a new type of enemy. It found itself in a world where facts, reason, and logic held no sway. It had run up against a force so powerful that none of the traditional lines of defense held. It confronted a dawning world where despite its own considerable power, unity, and organization, it had been marginalized. In fact, as Albert Bard wrote on the welcomed action by the War Department, "By the grace of God and the War Department (the latter having the more limited control, as well as a more limited view) New York has been saved from a very serious planning blunder."[28]

The shared memory of the narrow defeat of the bridge would be part of the mental landscape of many of those involved in the effort to secure a system of landmark protection for New York City. Those memories would be augmented and reinforced by the seemingly endless nightmare of the even larger conflict with Moses that was born out of their defeat of the bridge project. Together, these events would set the stage for what would follow in the 1950s.

Unlike earlier preservation battles over individual buildings of historic importance, in the battle over the bridge, it was the scenic beauty, the aesthetics, of historic lower Manhattan that had been at risk. As Talbot F. Hamlin wrote, "I do not think the opponents of the bridge need be ashamed of stressing the aesthetic damage to lower Manhattan which the bridge would cause. Civic beauty is the product of generations; partly unconscious, it is the result of years of dreaming and effort. It belongs to all the people, and it belongs to our descendents as much as it belongs to us."[29] The iconic image of lower Manhattan would have been forever changed if the bridge had been constructed. With its defeat, the crossing of the East River would now be done by tunnel.

The construction of such a tunnel did not have to trigger another clash with the civic community and those who cherished historic and aesthetic values. Moses, however, had something else in mind. Stinging from his rare defeat, and one that he felt robbed New York City of a glorious new monument, Moses sought to use the construction of the Brooklyn-Battery Tunnel as a tool for revenge.

If the civic community had been shocked by the failure of reasoned argument to carry the day in the debate over the bridge, they must have been in total awe of what came next. In February 1941, New Yorkers learned that by fiat, parks commissioner Robert Moses was closing and demolishing the Aquarium, the latest in a long series of names and adaptive reuses for Castle Clinton, the old fort at the foot of the Battery. Because of its rich history, during the long struggle to save it, the site would interchangeably be called the Aquarium, Fort Clinton, and Castle Clinton.[30] By whatever name it was called, Moses' announcement of its fate was the first shot in a siege that he would relentlessly press until July of 1950, when the Secretary of the Interior announced the designation of Castle Clinton as a national monument.[31]

Moses' public reasons for his action were the obsolescence of the Aquarium and, more importantly, the assertion that Castle Clinton's demolition was necessitated by the construction of the new tunnel. As Robert Caro so convincingly establishes, those justifications failed to stand up to scrutiny,

FIGURE 3.8 Bitter at having to substitute a tunnel for his beloved bridge, Moses sought revenge by demolishing old Fort Clinton, known today as Castle Clinton, and at that time popularly known, because of its reuse, as the Aquarium. Disingenuously stating that Castle Clinton had to be demolished because of the tunnel, Moses also argued that the vastly popular Aquarium was obsolete. Though the walls of the old fort would ultimately survive, the McKim, Mead & White Aquarium structure was demolished.

then or now. Ultimately it is only revenge, Moses' desire to punish those who blocked his bridge by destroying something dear to them, that can adequately account for his decade-long, dogged determination to remove any trace of Castle Clinton from the isle of Manhattan.[32]

Why was Castle Clinton so important? Its past was so rich and varied that it was a living definition of adaptive reuse, years before preservationists ever coined the term. With each of its reincarnations, another layer of meaning was added to the site. As Burlingham wrote reassuringly in 1949 in response to yet another setback in his efforts to save the fort, "The

fort has as many lives as a cat. My father heard Jenny Lind sing there in the Fifties and I expect my youngest great-grandson will hear one of her successors warble from the same nest or perch." Time may well prove Burlingham's sentiment correct.[33]

Its importance began with its location, at one time only three hundred feet from the tip of Manhattan. It stood where New York's story began. Built near the site of the original Dutch fort, it was constructed between 1808 and 1811 as a harbor fortification known as the West Battery. Though a shot was never fired from it, its presence is credited with helping deter the British during the War of 1812. Renamed Castle Clinton in honor of Mayor De Witt Clinton, who served as New York's mayor during that war, it remained in military use until 1823 when it began the next phase of its life as Castle Garden. In that incarnation it was "the largest public assembly hall and entertainment center in the United States." Whether it was the adulation on Lafayette's sentimental return to America or the sensation of Jenny Lind's American debut, it happened at Castle Garden. Having added a roof in 1844, its next act opened in 1855 as the Castle Garden Emigrant Depot and by 1890, when the curtain came down on that drama, over eight million immigrants had passed through it. It was in its adaptive reuse as the New York Aquarium, a role it assumed in 1896 with a McKim, Mead & White makeover, that most New Yorkers knew it when the controversy began. With over 2.5 million visitors flocking to it every year, it was a major attraction—even by today's standards.[34] The Aquarium's attendance was larger than that which the "Giants, the Dodgers and the Yankees combined draw to their local ball games in a single season."[35]

Steeped in history and actively enjoyed by the masses, it is not a surprise that the announcement of the Aquarium's closing, its proposed relocation to the Bronx Zoo, and the complete demolition of Castle Clinton caused serious consternation. In a radio address on WOR-Mutual, A. J. Wall, the director of the New-York Historical Society, spoke to the nation:

> I want to talk to you about a famous old New York building—a building which is known from one end of the U.S.A. to the other and is one of the most popular tourist attractions in all the world— the Aquarium, located in Battery Park at the very tip of Manhattan Island. . . The aquarium building does not belong to the people of New York, or to its Park Department. It is part of the historical heritage of America and as such belongs to the nation as a whole. That is why the threat to demolish it—to take it down brick by brick and stone by stone so that it will be removed from the face of the earth

for ever more—concerns you out there as much as it does us here in New York City.[36]

The fact that the engineers of the Brooklyn-Battery Tunnel refuted the notion that its construction necessitated the removal of the castle only made the impending loss of the Aquarium building that much more painful.

Unlike the earlier battle over the Brooklyn-Battery Bridge, which involved both aesthetics and history, this fight was all about history. Robert Moses tried to introduce aesthetics into the debate, ridiculing the castle as a "half-sunken gas tank" and offering the assessment he attributed to an 1824 observer that it was "that red wart fixed on the fair face of our city." In addition, the old Fort blocked a vista his new plan for the park was creating for the viewing of the Statue of Liberty. [37] With equal gusto, Moses attacked the site's history: "Fort Clinton has no history; it never fired a shot. . . . The Barnum period, when the Aquarium was Castle Garden, has gone. And no one wants to dwell on the period when the structure was an immigration station—that was a disgrace."[38] Even if the building had a history, it was a bad one needing to be eradicated.

Willing to stand up for the fort in the face of certain ridicule by Moses were his old foes Isaacs, McAneny, Burlingham, and Bard. All took up arms to defend the castle. Ultimately, it is to McAneny that Castle Clinton is most in debt for its survival. Pulling together a "delegation of eighteen historical and architectural associations," he helped organize early opposition to the proposal and then, as president of the American Scenic and Historic Preservation Society, kept the issue alive until he achieved success in 1950, almost a decade late. Albert Bard, too, deserves significant credit. In response to his public salute to McAneny as the "head, the center, and at times the radii and periphery of the effort" that saved Castle Clinton, McAneny wrote of Bard "that in the whole period I have had no more resourceful co-operator—and certainly no more faithful friend."[39]

The civic coalition to save Castle Clinton was even broader than the one that had come together to battle the bridge. This time, the historical societies joined the fray. In fact, though this battle was of equal concern to the art societies, the staying power over the course of the struggle was provided by George McAneny and the American Scenic and Historic Preservation Society, which he came to chair.

Moses was in an ideal position to lay siege to Castle Clinton. Unlike the situation that had surrounded the failed bridge, as parks commissioner, Moses already controlled the entire site, Battery Park. He had complete authority to do what he wished. The only actions requiring the approval

■ ■ ■ ■ ■ ■ ■ ■

FIGURE 3.9 George McAneny, the champion of Castle Clinton, was a true preservation hero. For years, the American Scenic and Historic Preservation Society presented their historic preservation medal in his name. This photograph, taken at one of the society's award ceremonies in the 1960s, shows the plaque in Federal Hall honoring McAneny as "Pioneer in City Planning/Protector of Historic Places/Leader of a City/Friend Beyond Compare."

by others were budgetary matters dealing with such things as rehousing the Aquarium's fish and the actual demolition of the structure. Though the opportunities seeking those approvals created were fully used by the opposition, this was a battle that was going to have to be won in other forums.

The opponents took their cause to the press, to the courts, and in the second phase of the fight, to Washington, D.C. The battle would become the preservation story of its decade. Usually in agreement with such civic voices as those of Burlingham, McAneny, and Bard, this time the *New York Times* aggressively backed Moses in his efforts to destroy Castle

Clinton. The reformers chalked this up to the friendship between Robert

Moses and Iphigene (Mrs. Arthur Hays) Sulzberger, wife of the publisher of the paper. The rollercoaster story of the battle over Castle Clinton's fate was not only closely covered as news, but was partially waged in editorials and in letters to the editor. In addition to helping with the *New York Times*, Iphigene Sulzberger also was able to deliver to Moses the support of the Park Association of New York, of which she was president and on whose board he sat. That association was a lonely civic voice raging against the preservation of the castle.[40]

In the struggle, the courts were adroitly used by the civics to buy time, anything to keep the wrecker's ball at bay. The first challenge was brought in the fall of 1941 by Pierce Trowbridge Wetter, the treasurer of the Greenwich Village Historical Society, with Bard acting as one of the attorneys. Wetter sought an injunction to keep the Aquarium open. In the fall of 1942, he returned to the courts seeking an injunction to prevent Moses from actually demolishing the building.[41] Moses went personal, revealing to the press that Wetter, a pacifist and Quaker, had spent five years in jail for his opposition to the first world war. Not only was this irrelevant, but Moses omitted the fact that, in 1933, Wetter had received a full pardon from President Roosevelt.[42]

Though ultimately unsuccessful, Wetter's legal efforts helped buy the time needed to organize the civics and to build public awareness. The Fine Arts Federation sponsored a design competition to show that the park could be redesigned with Castle Clinton preserved and an exhibition of historical prints of the Battery and the building in its various incarnations was displayed at the Architectural League.[43] Thanks to delays, by the time demolition could move forward, the immense needs created by America's entry into World War II made it impossible to find the manpower and equipment needed to demolish the castle's walls, ranging in thickness from 8 to 12 feet.[44] Moses had been able to destroy the roof and demolish the McKim, Mead, and White Aquarium structure, but the historic walls of the old fort remained. He created the appearance of a demolition site and fenced it off from the public. The war had spared the fort's massive historic walls, but it appeared to many that Castle Clinton's epitaph had already been written.

Moses was smart enough to know his attack on Castle Clinton would incite New York's civic community to action. What he could not have known was that it would prod the civics to take nascent steps towards better securing the future of the city's landmarks. In fact, a strong case can be made that it was in response to the excesses of Robert Moses that the efforts toward landmarks preservation were launched.

FIGURE 3.10 Surrounded by the construction site for the new tunnel and with the Aquarium structure itself having been largely demolished, it was not surprising that many New Yorkers had given up hope that there was any of old Fort Clinton left to save. George McAneny, however, never gave up hope. Bolstered by the constant support of Albert Bard and other civic leaders, he kept the campaign to save the old fort going until he ultimately triumphed over Moses.

In May of 1941, just three months after the announcement of the Moses plan to terminate the castle, a one-page flyer announced a public meeting to discuss the question: "The Preservation of Historic Sites and Buildings in the City of New York." The meeting was jointly called by the American Scenic and Historic Preservation Society and the New-York Historical Society. Both organizations were heavily involved in battling Moses over Castle Clinton.[45] The meeting announcement notes the immediate cause for the meeting: the "threatened demolition of the Aquarium, the Schenck House in Highland Park, Brooklyn, and other historic properties owned

FIGURE 3.11 The Schenck House in Highland Park, Brooklyn, along with Castle Clinton, was one of the threatened buildings that led the New-York Historical Society and the American Scenic and Historic Preservation Society to call a special meeting in 1941 on the subject: "The Preservation of Historic Sites and Buildings in the City of New York." Though Robert Moses' plan to demolish this early-eighteenth century Dutch-style farmhouse was thwarted, only a few years later it was lost to fire.

by the City of New York and under the control of the Parks Department."[46] Which is to say, sites under the lion's paw of Robert Moses.

The Schenck house, "a charming old Dutch colonial farmhouse built in 1705, located in Highland Park in Brooklyn" had been in danger for several years. As parks commissioner and the person responsible for the care and management of such old structures in the parks, Moses had stated his opposition to preserving it in a 1940 letter printed in the journal of the American Society of Architectural Historians. In early April 1941, he had announced his intentions to demolish it.[47] The reference in the announcement to "other historic properties" likely refers to an unidentified early-nineteenth century "beautiful dwelling" located in the Bronx.[48]

At the meeting, the focus was not only on the immediately threatened landmarks, but on "any historic buildings in the City of New York which might be in danger of destruction in the future." To address this concern, a committee was created on the spot to "ensure immediate and effective protest should any landmark be threatened, and to organize cooperative efforts for its preservation." Among those on this new committee were representatives of the New-York Historical Society and the American Scenic and Historic Preservation Society. Its membership included architect Ely Jacques Kahn, George McAneny, Albert S. Bard, and the history-minded Gardner Osborn. The committee was also charged to "consider setting up a permanent board to act on such questions in future.[49] In November of 1941, the Municipal Art Society Minutes note that the society was approached by the American Scenic and the New-York Historical Society to be part of a "Standing Committee" of "leading civic, historic and patriotic groups, to meet bi-monthly and exchange ideas," most likely a further evolution of what had been set in motion in May.[50]

It appears that some immediate good did come from that May meeting. The effort to save the Schenck house from this threat was a success, though it was later lost to fire.[51] The Board of Estimate rejected park commissioner Moses' request for its demolition. Petitions with over three thousand signatures helped convince Brooklyn borough president Cashmore to "openly sponsor" this revolt against Moses at the Board of Estimate meeting.[52] This would be one of several instances where Cashmore intervened to prevent Moses from savaging a piece of Brooklyn's history. Those who knew Cashmore credit these preservation assists to his astute political instinct to be responsive to his constituents, not to any personal passion for preservation.[53] Also credited with helping achieve this solid victory over Moses, the Board of Estimate vote was thirteen for saving the house and three against, were the "reputable and respected organizations" that had rallied to the cause, among them the New-York Historical Society and the American Scenic and Historic Preservation Society.[54]

For our purposes, even more intriguing than this May public meeting are discussions on the need to protect the city's historic sites that unfolded at the Municipal Art Society. The society had been among those battling Moses on the bridge. By February 19, 1941, just days after his pronouncement on Castle Clinton, and having heard from the chief engineer of the New York Tunnel Authority that the castle's demolition was not required by the tunnel, the Municipal Art Society joined the ranks of the opposition.

■ ■ ■ ■ ■ ■ ■

Clearly, it was this threat to Castle Clinton that initiated the broader conversations at the society, though it was certainly informed by other factors. Among them, the society had already clashed with Moses over his plans to redesign Washington Square Park and had logged in against his rebuilding of the Bronx River Parkway.[55] In addition, New Yorkers had seen the growing war in Europe take its toll on foreign landmarks. Though an ocean away, such losses were on the minds of those who cared deeply about New York's landmarks, including A. J. Wall, who wrote in the fall of 1941:

> For nine months now—ever since the Nazis began to bomb Britain from the air—we have been shocked by the loss of England's famous old buildings. Our hearts have been sore and heavy and our minds stirred to indignation by the ruthless and indiscriminate destruction of these irreplaceable objects of beauty and historical significance. One by one they've been demolished by bombs or fire or both . . . at the very same time that we shudder at the loss of Europe's cherished antiquities—here in New York city our own cherished landmarks are threatened with demolition.[56]

It was under the leadership of the Municipal Art Society's new president, the architect Ely Jacques Kahn, that it started to explore what could be done to address the larger question of the preservation of the city's historic places. Kahn's ascension to the presidency of the society was itself the result of the world at war. Ralph Walker had just been elected the society's president in the spring of 1940, but only a year later he had to resign because of defense work, at which point Kahn was elected to succeed him.[57]

October 1, 1941, found the Aquarium closed and a high board fence keeping it from public view.[58] New York City was one step closer to losing Castle Clinton. At that month's board meeting, after an update on the society's latest actions to save the structure, Kahn reports that an "active committee" was being formed "for the purpose of endeavoring to protect and preserve New York's remaining historic buildings, as well as areas with architectural charm of the past." Kahn had been in contact with Talbot Hamlin and Carl Feiss, a professor at Columbia. Hamlin had agreed to "assist unofficially." Gardner Osborn would also serve on the committee.[59]

These men represented considerable talent. The fact that each of them were firmly at odds with Robert Moses only partially explains their willingness to help. It was under Hamlin's leadership that Columbia University's

FIGURE 3.12 Architect Ely Jacques Kahn is the man second to the left of the plaque at this unveiling ceremony at the Municipal Asphalt Plant on October 31, 1941. At the time Kahn was the president of the Municipal Art Society. Responding to growing threats to historic and architecturally important buildings, Kahn appointed a society committee to protect and preserve such buildings.

Avery Library became "the great library" it is known as today. Hamlin is also credited with writing the first "very great book on American architecture." He was a star in his field and a regular and respected voice for preservation. He also had an "absolutely ardent dislike" of Moses and felt personally insulted by his attacks on "do-gooders," of which Hamlin was the "epitome."[60] Hamlin brought his significant gravitas to the effort.

Carl Feiss had come to Columbia's Architecture program in 1938 to be the director of its housing and planning division. He arrived fresh from MIT with one of their first master's degrees in urban planning. Becoming involved in New York City issues, he had proposed that Castle Clinton be "restored to its original appearance and be converted into an historical museum of marine commerce and harbor relics pertaining to the Port of New York."[61]

In Gardner Osborn, Kahn had enlisted a passionate defender of lower Manhattan. Playing a major role in the preservation of Federal Hall, he was also a veteran of the battle with Moses over the Brooklyn-Battery Bridge. He was a stalwart member of the American Scenic and Historic Preservation Society. He was focused on trying to preserve, at least on film, the "old houses on lower Greenwich Street" condemned by the Battery-Brooklyn Tunnel. He would be the member of this active committee who reported at the Municipal Art Society's board meetings.[62]

Kahn also went about seeking advice on how the society could address this larger topic. He consulted with I. N. Phelps Stokes, the architect and historian renowned for his monumental work, *The Iconography of Manhattan*. Kahn reports on an interview he had with Stokes, "who urged that the study of the city's historic sites and buildings be carried on under the guidance of experienced and technical leadership."[63] The candidates for Kahn's committee certainly fit that bill.

The minutes of the next several Municipal Art Society board meetings show a growing engagement in the subject of preserving the city's landmarks. Osborn reported on his efforts to have the "old houses on lower Greenwich Street, which are of great historic significance," photographically documented, as they were "condemned" because of the construction of the Brooklyn-Battery Tunnel. Osborn states that "he has found interest and determination, rather than technical ability, to be vital factors in carrying out any efforts to preserve the city's historic landmarks."

At that meeting, the level of interest and excitement in preservation was such that it led to the suggestion that the society should consider it the topic for one of its major events. At that time in its history, the society regularly put on annual luncheons or dinners to focus on key subjects. Under Osborn's leadership, this idea developed further and at the January 21, 1942 meeting, plans were presented for a dinner in early April devoted to the discussion of the "Preservation of Historic Landmarks; the protection of these and other works of art; and the Historical Significance of

■ ■ ■ ■ ■ ■ ■ ■

these efforts viewed from the past and future. Mr. McAneny and important speakers from Washington are being invited to make the principal addresses."[64]

None of these discussions at the society were happening in a vacuum. On December 7, 1941, to the nation's shock, Pearl Harbor was bombed. America was plunged into war. At the Municipal Art Society's next board meeting, it was suggested that its "policy as related to the war situation might be featured at the luncheon together with the need for the preservation of the city's landmarks."[65]

Preservation was still receiving billing as a top priority for the society but the war had dislodged it from the top of the list. By the time of the February board meeting, the plans for the dinner—to be the celebration of the society's fiftieth anniversary—had changed. Now the focus was the society's "war-time objective," postwar planning. The evening's subject was cast as "New York City—Past, Present, Future." Its call to arms was: "We must prepare now for the realities of peace, for a better world and in this world a better city for all."[66] World events had pushed preservation off the center of the society's stage.

The role the bombs dropped at Pearl Harbor played in world history is well known. Lesser known is their impact on preservation in New York and in particular, on a different war, the one between Robert Moses and what Robert Caro described as the "Gotham Gentry," the leaders of New York's civic community. Ironically, just as those same bombs thwarted Moses in his desire to demolish what remained of Castle Clinton, they also delayed by a decade the Municipal Art Society's efforts to focus the city on the need to protect its landmarks. While the "protection and preservation of New York City's remaining historic buildings as well as areas with architectural charm of the past," would still receive lip service, being reported as a "society" endeavor at its 1942 Annual Meeting, by that fall the society found itself focused on such new concerns as "What is the Municipal Art Society? What is it doing? What can it do?" By 1943, facing the challenges of trying to function in a country at war, the society had suspended its bulletins and banquets. At the society, the momentum that had been building for a major preservation initiative had first been redirected and ultimately dissipated as America and the society entered the war years.[67]

Though undermined by the war, Municipal Art Society efforts may have helped generate a useful document whose rediscovery in the 1950s would help guide future preservation efforts. In reaching out to Talbot Hamlin, the society may well have prompted him to create a list of buildings that, over time, would be refined and ultimately guide the early work of the

■ ■ ■ ■ ■ ■ ■ ■

Landmarks Preservation Commission. The list's earliest known version is titled the "Tentative list of Old Buildings of Manhattan built in 1865 or earlier, and worthy of preservation. Annotated by Talbot Hamlin." As the head of Avery Library, and in 1940, one of the cofounders of the Society of Architectural Historians, Hamlin was singularly suited to promulgate such a list. The earliest date attributed to its existence is 1941. The earliest copy yet found dates to November 14, 1942. There is little information on how this first version of the list was compiled. It is not known whether it was solely the work of Hamlin or whether he sought input from others, either on the Kahn committee or beyond. It is also uncertain whether he created the list at the behest of the Municipal Art Society or whether he was already independently at work on it. The society's minutes for this period never specifically mention this list so its formal link to the society's efforts remains unknown.[68]

Any effort to address the larger issue of preserving the city's "remaining historic buildings as well as areas with architectural charm of the past" needed a way to make such a concept come alive to the people of the city. What better way than by compiling a list of what was at stake? A list of such sites would make it clear what it was the society and others wanted to protect. This preliminary effort, though leading to naught at the time, would be a seed that would grow and come into brilliant, full bloom in postwar New York.

For preservation, the fall of 1941 had been a season full of possibility. Bloodied by Moses, the civic community had united and organized. They had realized that the problem they faced was larger than any one threatened site. The talent and sophistication to address the problem was in place. A growing awareness among the civic community had been created by the furor over Castle Clinton. The creation of a list of important sites could put a face on the larger issue. Even with all of this in place, what was still missing was an articulated solution to the problem. A need for some entity to save buildings had been recognized, but that conversation had not evolved to the point of a proposed structure, nor had the legal basis for some form of protection been discussed. It seems likely that if the interest, momentum, and focus had been sustained, those issues would have been tackled next.

Enraged and engaged by Moses, yet thwarted by larger world events, this beginning of an effort by the civics to take on the larger question of the preservation of the city's landmarks went into hibernation. The seasonal change needed to awaken its slumber would be provided by the new spring born of the energy pulsating in postwar New York.

■ ■ ■ ■ ■ ■ ■

ENDNOTES

1. Frances Grimes, quoted in the Central Committee of Organizations Opposing the Battery Toll Bridge, "An Open Letter To the President and His Advisers Requesting Further Study of the Battery Toll Bridge Project," July 14, 1939.

2. Open letter from Robert Moses, chairman, Triborough Bridge Authority to Mayor Fiorello La Guardia, January 23, 1939, Albert S. Bard Papers, New York Public Library.

3. "Bridge at Battery Proposed by Moses," *New York Times*, January 23, 1939.

4. Robert A. Caro, *The Power Broker: Robert Moses and the Fall of New York* (New York: Random House, 1975). Chapter 29 "And When the Last Law Was Down" is the original and best account of the battle over the Brooklyn-Battery Bridge and provides much of the background material for this account of that struggle.

5. Those seeking a bit more on Moses should turn to Kenneth T. Jackson's *The Encyclopedia of New York City* (New Haven: Yale University Press, 1995) and read the entry on Moses. Those seeking a lot more should read Caro's *The Power Broker*. Those interested in recent works on Moses should go to Hilary Ballon and Kenneth T. Jackson, eds., *Robert Moses and the Modern City: The Transformation of New York* (New York: W.W. Norton, 2007).

6. Bard to Harold W. McGraw, president, West Side Association of Commerce, June 3, 1939, Albert S. Bard Papers, New York Public Library.

7. "Council Due to Back Bridge; Moses in Seven-Hour Clash," *New York Times*, March 28, 1939.

8. Talbot F. Hamlin, "Cheers and Tears," *Pencil Points*, July 1939, 451–454.

9. George Martin, *CCB: The Life and Century of Charles C. Burlingham, New York's First Citizen, 1858–1959* (New York: Hill and Wang, 2005), 3.

10. Caro, *The Power Broker*, 666–668; "Council Due to Back Bridge," *New York Times*, March 28, 1939. One unanswered question is why Bard was seemingly spared such a public attack by Moses. Bard's role leading the coalition put him in the public spotlight, and he certainly did not hide his criticism of Moses, which like most of the reformers was still mixed with occasional praise. Moses rabidly attacked Isaacs because Simon W. Gerson of his staff was a member of the communist party. Earlier in the 1930s, Bard had been linked in the New York press to Robert Gordon Switz, his "adopted son," who had pleaded guilty to being a communist spy in Paris. With Moses' pension for red-baiting, it is curious why he passed up such an opportunity to go after Bard who had been so publicly linked with Switz.

11. Bard pressed Burlingham to lend his name as the head of the General Committee opposing the bridge. He writes to Burlingham on July 5, 1939, "My dear Burlingham," continuing, "That you are old and deaf and want to spend a pleasant summer at your Sabine Farm on the Sound is quite irrelevant, because we shall not be asking you to do any work except now and then to sign a few letters." In a telegram to Bard on July 6 Burlingham responds, "Sorry but I am adamant thou art the man." Bard then writes back on July 7 asking Burlingham to consider being just a member of the committee. In a handwritten note written at the bottom of Bard's letter to him, Burlingham reveals his real reasons for saying no: "I have a notion that I can do more for our Cause by keeping off Committees. Now I write to anybody and everybody from F.D.R. down. This I couldn't do if I were a member of a Comm. Don't you think I am right. I couldn't in my telegram express my appreciation of your kindness in thinking of me for Chairman. One reason for declining was as above; the other that I should be useless at a meeting. Yours,

CCB." All correspondence in the Albert S. Bard Papers, New York Public Library. THE BRIDGE, THE CASTLE,
AND MOSES

69

Burlingham's handwritten note was transcribed by George Martin, author of the biography of Burlingham.

12. April 17, 1939 press release from the Central Committee of Organizations Opposing the Battery Bridge, "Minutes of Informal Conference Concerning Proposed Battery-Brooklyn Bridge held at Offices of Merchants' Association of New York," April 6, 1939; "Minutes of Meeting of Organizing Committee of Central Committee of Organizations Opposing the Battery Bridge," April 10, 1939, Albert S. Bard Papers, New York Public Library.

13. "New Bridge Plan Is Voted by Board," *New York Times*, June 9, 1939.

14. Martin, *CCB*, 419–429. Also a telegram from Burlingham to Marguerite A. LeHand, President Roosevelt's secretary, July 14, 1939, Albert S. Bard Papers, New York Public Library, opposing a transfer necessary for the bridge: "Kindly tell Skipper Moses Offers U.S. 105 foot slice battery park exchange for easement to run bridge over barge office. Bill reported by Lanham requiring unanimous consent preventible [sic] by jovian nod or wink. All objections still hold plus folly placing span within biscuit's or bomb's throw of military post. Regards C. C. Burlingham."

15. Caro's *The Power Broker* provides accounts of these for those who would like to explore them.

16. Caro, *The Power Broker*, 671–674; "An Open Letter To the President and His Advisers Requesting Further Study of the Battery Toll Bridge Project from the Central Committee of Organizations Opposing the Battery Toll Bridge," July 14, 1939, Albert S. Bard Papers, New York Public Library.

17. This is succinctly explained in the Minutes of Meeting of Central Committee of Organizations Opposing the Batter Toll Bridge, July 7, 1939, Albert S. Bard Papers, New York Public Library, "The Triborough Bridge Authority had had a bill introduced in the House of Representatives authorizing the Secretary of the Treasury to grant New York City an easement over the Barge Office site in exchange for a strip of land 105 feet wide to be taken from Battery park for a new Barge Office site." The Committee's position against S. 2662 and H.R. 6880 was advanced in Washington by Albert T. Reid.

18. "5 Groups Condemn Moses' Bridge Plan: Call it Ruinious to Skyline, Harmful to City and Harbor—'Same Old Tripe,' He Says," *New York Times*, March 27, 1939.

19. "Isaacs Sees Snag in Battery Bridge," *New York Times*, January 26, 1939.

20. Albert S. Bard, letter to the editor, *New York Times*, March 10, 1939.

21. The three architects were Hugh Ferriss, Chester B. Price, and Schell Lewis. Press release from the Central Committee of Organizations Opposing the Battery Bridge, May 20, 1939, Albert S. Bard Papers, New York Public Library.

22. Bard to William Hicks, June 19, 1939, Albert S. Bard Papers, New York Public Library.

23. "Moses and Isaacs Clash Again at Hearing on Battery Bridge; Commissioner Berates Critics, Calls McAneny 'Extinct Volcano'; Committee Finds Problem Too Hot, Passes It On to Full Council Today," *New York Herald-Tribune*, March 28, 1939.

24. Robert Moses quoted and broadcast, January 5, 1964, in "Reflections on the Fair," WCBS-TV, produced and written by Gordon Hyatt, Robert Trout, Correspondent.

25. As borough president, he had provided funding to rebuild the portico of St. John's Chapel, sparing it from the widening of Varick Street, sadly only prolonging the building's life by several years. Mason, "Memory Infrastructure," 149, 155; Gilmartin, *Shaping the City*, 335.

■ ■ ■ ■ ■ ■ ■

26. "Council Due to Back Bridge; Moses in Seven-Hour Clash," *New York Times*, March 28, 1939.

27. Bard to Felix Frankfurter, June 1, 1939, Albert S. Bard Papers, New York Public Library.

28. Bard to the Hon. Thomas Ball, July 19, 1939, Albert S. Bard Papers, New York Public Library.

29. Hamlin, "Cheers and Tears," 454.

30. Though many of its defenders over the years referred to the monument as Fort Clinton, today it is best known as Castle Clinton and that appellation is largely employed here.

31. "Aquarium Becomes a U.S. Monument," *New York Times*, July 19, 1950.

32. Caro, *The Power Broker*, 678–688.

33. C. C. Burlingham, letter to the editor, *New York Times*, April 11, 1949. The Battery Conservancy's conceptual plans for the future of Castle Clinton call for its reestablishment as a venue for the performing arts.

34. "From Greatness to Shame," Conservancy for Historic Battery Park; Diamonstein-Spielvogel, *Landmarks of New York*, 89; The Reminiscences of George McAneny 1949, in the Oral History Collection of Columbia University.

35. A. J. Wall, "Save The Aquarium Building" radio address, WOR-Mutual, June 26, 1941, 2:30–2:45 p.m.

36. Ibid.

37. "Moses Writes to 'Stuffed Shirts' Who Weep for the Aquarium. 'Not a Dry Eye at the Knickerbocker Club,' He Says, and Proposes Saving the Smell for the Sentimentalists After the Fish Are Gone," *New York Herald-Tribune*, February 25, 1941; "City Will Dedicate New Battery Park," *New York Times*, July 14, 1952.

38. "Votes to Demolish Aquarium," *New York Sun*, June 25, 1942.

39. Albert S. Bard, letter to the editor, *New York Times*, July 28, 1950; George McAneny to Bard, August 1, 1950, Albert S. Bard Papers, New York Public Library.

40. The Reminiscences of George McAneny 1949, 81; Hosmer, Preservation Comes of Age, 781–784; Susan E. Tifft and Alex S. Jones, *The Trust* (Little, Brown New York, 1999), 180; Gilmartin, *Shaping the City*, 326–330.

41. "Aquarium Safe Until Oct. 30," *New York Sun*, October 21, 1941; "Foes of Moses Institute Suit to Save Aquarium, Injunction Sought in Final Effort to Balk Razing of Battery Park Landmark," unattributed article, Fine Arts Federation Records, Archives of American Art. For more on Wetter, see chapter 7.

42. Again this raises the question mentioned in note ten, why did Moses not personally attack Bard, who had publicly been linked to a known communist spy? "Pierce T. Wetter, Engineer, 68, Dies, Tilted with Moses to Save Fort Clinton at Battery," *New York Times*, May 12, 1963; "President Gave Wetter Pardon," unattributed newspaper article in Fine Arts Federation Records, Archives of American Art.

43. "Competition Sponsored by the Fine Arts Federation of New York for the Selection of an Alternative Design for the Development of Battery Park, New York City," August 1941, Albert S. Bard Papers, New York Public Library; an invitation to a dinner at the Architectural League "upon the occasion of the Presentation of Prizes" of wining designs, Albert S. Bard Papers, New York Public Library.

44. Caro, *The Power Broker*, 683. Accounts of the wall's width vary from source to source. This information comes from the National Park Service via Warrie Price, the founder and president of the Battery Conservancy. Warrie Price, email to author, January 17, 2006.

■ ■ ■ ■ ■ ■ ■

45. "Report of the President," Municipal Art Society Annual Meeting, May 21, 1941; Municipal Art Society Board Meeting Minutes, June 18, 1941, Municipal Art Society of New York Records, Archives of American Art.

46. "Help to Preserve Our Historic Buildings!," One-page flyer, Anthony C. Wood Archive.

47. A. J. Wall, director New York Historical Society, "Aquarium Issue Excites National Interest to Action," *Manhattan Chronicle*, September 25, 1941, Albert S. Bard Papers, New York Public Library; Robert Moses to the New York City Board of Estimate, September 19, 1940, *Journal of the American Society of Architectural Historians* (July–October, 1941): 31–32; Henry D. Barmore, president, Cypress Hills Board of Trade, "Report on Movement to Save Schenck Homestead in Highland Park, Brooklyn, To All Participating Organizations and Individuals," June 25, 1941, American Scenic and Historic Preservation Society Records, 1895–1971, New York Public Library.

48. A. J. Wall, director New York Historical Society, "Aquarium Issue Excites National Interest to Action," September 25, 1941; Hosmer, *Preservation Comes of Age*, 781–782. Wall mentions the other property but does not name it.

49. "For Preservation," New-York Historical Society Quarterly Bulletin, 25, no. 3 (July, 1941).

50. Municipal Art Society Board Meeting Minutes, November 19, 1941, Municipal Art Society of New York Records, Archives of American Art; "Act to Save Landmarks," *New York Times*, May 29, 1941.

51. The particular Schenck house in question was the one known as the Cornell-Schenck house. It burned down in 1944. Kevin Stayton, *Dutch by Design: Tradition and Change in Two Historic Brooklyn Houses: The Schenck Houses at the Brooklyn Museum* (New York: Brooklyn Museum in association with Phaidon Universe, 1990), 86. In the photographic records of the New York City Department of Parks and Recreation, the house is referred to as the Johannes Schenck House.

52. Barmore, "Report on Movement to Save Schenck Homestead in Highland Park, Brooklyn, To All Participating Organizations and Individuals."

53. Anthony C. Wood conversation with Otis Pratt Pearsall, May 3, 2006.

54. Barmore, "Report on Movement to Save Schenck Homestead in Highland Park, Brooklyn, To All Participating Organizations and Individuals;" A. J. Wall, "Aquarium Issue Excites National Interest to Action," *Manhattan Chronicle*, September 25, 1941, Albert S. Bard Papers, New York Public Library; Wall.

55. For more on the redesign of Washington Square Park, see chapter 7; "Bulletin of November, 1939," Municipal Art Society of New York, Archives of American Art; Ely Jacques Kahn, letter to the editor, *New York Times*, May 10, 1941.

56. A. J. Wall, "Aquarium Issue Excites National Interest to Action," *Manhattan Chronicle*, September 25, 1941.

57. Municipal Art Society Board Meeting Minutes, May 15, 1940 and March 19, 1941, Municipal Art Society of New York Records, Archives of American Art.

58. Albert S. Bard, Report of the Committee on City Development, The Fine Arts Federation of New York, May 5, 1942, 1–4.

59. Municipal Art Society Board Meeting Minutes, October 22, 1941, Municipal Art Society of New York Records, Archives of American Art; Gilmartin, *Shaping the City*, 344; Anthony C. Wood, "At Dawn We Slept: Pearl Harbor and Preservation in New York," *The New York Chronicle* 2, no. 1, Winter 1999, 10–12.

■ ■ ■ ■ ■ ■ ■

60. Anthony C. Wood, "Pioneers of Preservation: Part III: Preservation's Scholarly Roots: Talbot Hamlin and the Avery Library; An Interview with Commissioner Adolf Placzek," *Village Views* 4, no. 4 (Fall 1987): 15.

61. "Carl Feiss, a Pioneer of Urban Preservation, Dies at 90," *New York Times*, October 27, 1997; Municipal Art Society Board Meeting Minutes, February 19, 1941, Municipal Art Society of New York Records, Archives of American Art. Feiss, who lived until 1997, would go on to become a major player on the national preservation scene. He played a major role in the effort that led to the creation of the Federal Historic Preservation Act of 1966 and a National Register of Historic Places.

62. Alfred E. Clark, "Gardner Osborn, Preservationist, 86," *New York Times*, July 8, 1979; "New Bridge Plan Is Voted by Board, "*New York Times*, June 9, 1939; Municipal Art Society Board Meeting Minutes, November 19, 1941, Municipal Art Society of New York Records, Archives of American Art.

63. Municipal Art Society Board Meeting Minutes, November 19, 1941, Municipal Art Society of New York Records, Archives of American Art.

64. Ibid.; Municipal Art Society Board Meeting Minutes, December 17, 1941 and January 21, 1942, Municipal Art Society of New York Records, Archives of American Art.

65. Municipal Art Society Board Meeting Minutes, December 17, 1941, Municipal Art Society of New York Records, Archives of American Art.

66. Municipal Art Society Board Meeting Minutes February 18, 1942, Municipal Art Society of New York Records, Archives of American Art; "Invitation to Fiftieth Anniversary of the Founding of the Society Dinner on April 8, 1942," Municipal Art Society of New York Records, Archives of American Art.

67. "Memorandum Annual Meeting," Ely Jacques Kahn letter to the Municipal Art Society Board, September 9, 1942; Municipal Art Society Board Meeting Minutes, October 20, 1942, November 17, 1942, January 19, 1943; June 10, 1943 letter to the Membership of the Municipal Art Society from Ely Jacques Kahn, Municipal Art Society of New York Records, Archives of American Art.

68. Foreword by L. Bancel LaFarge, president, "Buildings in Manhattan Built Before World War I Designated as Worthy of Protection," Municipal Art Society, January 1955 provides the earliest date attributed to the original list. In Gilmartin, *Shaping the City*, 344, he refers to Hamlin's list as his "contribution" to the work of the Kahn committee. Certainly, the date of the early Hamlin list supports such a conclusion. This connection between Hamlin's early list and the Kahn efforts has been accepted. It is, however, worth noting that we lack any solid documentation of the connection. There were other list-making activities going on at the time. The "Historic American Buildings Survey Catalog of Measured Drawings and Photographs of the Survey in the Library of Congress, March 1, 1941" includes a shorter list of New York City sites. Another possible motivation for listing and documenting landmark sites was the fear of America's possible entanglement in a war that was already taking a heavy toll on the world's landmarks.

FOUR

Postwar as Prelude

Located on Madison Avenue between 46th and 47th Streets, it seemed a permanent fixture in the social swirl of New York's life. Woolworth heiress Barbara Hutton, "America's Poor Little Rich Girl," surrounded by California eucalyptus trees, had debuted in its famed ballroom in 1930. Countless magical evenings, including a jungle theme party with biting monkeys and an orangutan, played out under its roof.[1]

It was the great Ritz-Carlton Hotel.

As *Time* magazine would report, "Princes, Premiers and the wealthiest wanderers of the world flocked to the Ritz. So did New York Society." It was at the Ritz that the Organizing Committee of the Central Committee of Organizations Opposing the Brooklyn Battery Bridge gathered on April 10, 1939, to plan their campaign to stop Robert Moses. Invited for dinner and discussion by George McAneny and joined by Albert Bard, these civic warriors convened in the famous hotel, elected the committee's temporary officers, chose its name, and developed the opposition's strategy.[2]

A dozen years later, suffering no "obvious signs of decrepitude," the Ritz-Carlton Hotel would close its doors forever. It was to be replaced by an office building. Having been built in 1910 and designed by Warren and Wetmore, the architects who gave New York the Grand Central Terminal and the New York Yacht Club, the hotel faced what many felt was a shockingly premature rendezvous with the wrecker's ball. On that spring evening in 1939, as the group of civic warriors gathered at the Ritz to plan their defense of historic lower Manhattan, perhaps they strolled through the hotel's majestic Palm Court or wandered in its magical Japanese tea garden. The one thing they certainly did not do that night was imagine

FIGURE 4.1   It was in the spring of 1939 at the famed Ritz-Carlton Hotel, gathering
place for world travelers and New Yorkers alike, that George McAneny convened the
leaders of the effort to stop Robert Moses' Brooklyn-Battery Bridge. At that time,
none of them could have imaged that only twelve years later, the hotel itself would be
demolished and its loss would help ignite a new wave of preservation advocacy.

that the Ritz itself, such a seemingly secure piece of their New York world,
would so soon be overwhelmed by the forces of change.[3]

The loss of what many believed to be "the finest of all New York hotels"
was one of several events in the early 1950s that would revive the interest

in preservation that had started to grow at the Municipal Art Society just before World War II.[4] Witnessing the postwar destruction of substantial and important buildings that had been erected during their own lifetimes only contributed to a growing realization among a number of New Yorkers that something had to be done.

The pace of change was accelerating beyond control. It was as if the very ground was being rudely yanked out from under the feet of those who cared passionately about their city. In April of 1949, a crowd of three hundred gathered at the Brevoort Hotel, long a Greenwich Village landmark, to show their concern for the future of Washington Square North. Five years later, the Brevoort itself would be demolished. Whether it was the Ritz-Carlton uptown, or the Brevoort downtown, the very places where New Yorkers gathered to come to grips with change were themselves becoming victims of it.[5] As the 1950s unfolded, the growing sense among some civic leaders that something had to be done would translate into action.

Postwar events of the 1940s set the stage for the preservation activities that would soon come forth from the Municipal Art Society and other civic organizations. The continuing saga of Castle Clinton provided the preservation leitmotif of this postwar period. As America went to war, Castle Clinton's fate appeared sealed. As soon as equipment and personnel could be spared, the structure was to be leveled and its remains hauled away. Time and again, however, the history of preservation has proven true the immortal words of the great Yogi Berra, "It ain't over till it's over." Such would be the case with Castle Clinton.

The ink was hardly dry on the formal Japanese surrender documents ending World War II before George McAneny launched a new offensive in his campaign to save Castle Clinton. Taking the form of a letter to the editor of the *New York Times*, it appeared on September 20, 1945 under the signature of sixteen prominent New Yorkers. This preservation broadside evoked the recent war as it sought to refocus New York's attention on the plight of the castle.

As civilization takes stock, now that active warfare on every front is ended, we of the New World can feel deeply relieved that our historic shrines have been spared the devastation which has seared so much of Europe and the Far East. Yet one of our most priceless heritages—one which stands both as a special symbol of the nation's growth and an outstanding landmark of our own metropolis—is at this moment threatened with destruction, not by a chance bomb in the heat of war, but as a deliberate and wholly unnecessary sacrifice.

It concludes by suggesting that the only thing needed to save the Castle is "a vote by the Board of Estimate, withdrawing any permission it may have given to demolish Castle Clinton."[6]

Still very much in power, Robert Moses successfully deflected McAneny's thrust by having the motion defeated when it was advanced at the Board of Estimate's October meeting. Moses reiterated that Castle Clinton needed to be demolished because of its proximity to the approaches of the Brooklyn-Battery Tunnel. He also pushed aside an offer by McAneny, now president of the American Scenic and Historic Preservation Society, to have the historical organizations concerned with saving Castle Clinton

FIGURE 4.2 At the end of World War II, Castle Clinton looked like a war zone. Fortunately, enough of the castle had survived the onslaught of Robert Moses that as the war ended, its defenders renewed their efforts to seek the castle's preservation. This is how the castle looked in 1950, the year it was transferred to the federal government, declared a national monument, and was finally out of harm's way.

raise the funds needed to restore it, commenting that there was "little or nothing of Fort Clinton" left to be restored.[7]

In this first skirmish in the renewed warfare over Castle Clinton, both sides gave hints of their future battle plans. For Moses, it was to reinforce the misperception that the preservationists had already lost the war. Castle Clinton was gone. There was nothing to save, nothing to restore, nothing left to fight for. Hidden for years behind a high fence, surrounded by piles of debris and an active construction site described as a "battlefield," the remains of the old fort had become largely invisible.[8]

Knowing that Moses had stacked the deck against him, McAneny sought a change of venue. In their letter to the *New York Times*, McAneny and his followers cited the role of Castle Clinton in the nation's history. Robert Moses' New York political allies might not cherish their past, but what about the keepers of the nation's history? Thwarted in New York, McAneny sought a more receptive audience for his message. He took his case to Washington, D.C. and found open ears there.

At this point, local and national preservation politics come together. Charles Hosmer, the historian of the national preservation movement, has recounted this fascinating confluence of concerns in rich detail in his classic *Preservation Comes of Age*.[9] McAneny's efforts on behalf of Castle Clinton were well received by key players at the National Park Service. However, their interest and commitment to the fort went beyond what was merited by its historical significance. Though Castle Clinton itself was important to them, more important was the good will of its patron saint, George McAneny, and the impact the Castle Clinton cause could have on the national preservation scene.

His national allies saw in McAneny and his crusade "a means for uniting preservationists into an organization that could combine the strength and fervor of the private historical and preservation field with the professional skills developed by the National Park Service."[10] The organization envisioned would ultimately become the National Trust for Historic Preservation.

McAneny's preservation activities had earned him respect and recognition among like-minded individuals. His imprimatur would help bring gravitas and validation to a fledgling national organization.

Perhaps the key strategist in advancing the idea of a national organization to centralize "the private sector of the preservation community" was Ronald Lee, the National Park Service's chief historian.[11] To succeed, he knew he needed to enlist McAneny as an ally and active supporter. Further earning the Ritz-Carlton Hotel a place in preservation's history, it was there over dinner on October 28, 1946, that Lee pitched McAneny two ideas that could advance his goal of solidifying the efforts of preservationists across the country. The first option was to restructure the American Scenic and Historic Preservation Society to play that role. The other option was to create a new entity. For legal reasons, the second option was chosen.[12]

McAneny played a major leadership role in creating the new national organization. He became deeply involved in its formation and launch, even helping draft its constitution. When it came into being on April 15, 1947, as the National Council for Historic Sites and Buildings, he was elected the chairman of its board. Other New Yorkers were also present

FIGURE 4.3 New York preservationists were active on the national preservation scene helping launch the National Council for Historic Sites and Buildings. This April 15, 1947 photograph shows the delegates, including George McAneny, who helped draft its constitution, at the council's organizing meeting. The council, and its successor group, the National Trust for Historic Preservation, would time and again support New York preservation efforts.

at its birth. Horace M. Albright, the former director of the National Park Service and long interested in a national preservation program, as well as a fellow signer of the 1945 Castle Clinton letter, was joined by Gardner Osborn, Eric Gugler, and Alexander Hamilton.[13] Albert Bard, an astute observer of events, clipped a press story on the creation of the National Council and noted that it should be filed with his Fort Clinton–Aquarium materials.[14] The strategic relationship being forged between New York City and a growing national preservation movement was not lost on Bard.

One of the National Council's top priorities was to create another new organization, described as McAneny's "dreamchild." It would "receive donations of money and property." For an organization to have the stature to do this it needed a Congressional Charter. The organization that emerged, the National Trust for Historic Preservation, inspired by the British National Trust, came into being in the fall of 1949. In 1953, to alleviate confusion, the National Council merged with it.[15]

McAneny's investment of energy in bolstering a national preservation movement would pay immediate dividends in the form of essential behind-the-scenes federal support for saving Castle Clinton. Over the years, that relationship would continue to benefit New York City handsomely. How appropriate that New Yorkers were heavily invested in the creation of the National Council and the National Trust. Both organizations would become supporting players in future preservation efforts culminating in the creation of New York's Landmarks Law.

By late summer of 1946, McAneny's Washington efforts bore fruit. After being carefully shepherded through the House and Senate, a bill establishing Castle Clinton as a national monument was signed by President Truman on August 14, 1946. One might think this was the fairy tale ending of the Castle Clinton story. Instead, it was just another act in a preservation drama. The legislation was an essential step toward victory, but not the definitive one. The bill was only an enabling act. It provided no actual funds to restore the fort, nor did it compel New York State to relinquish the site. It recognized that New York State would have to voluntarily "re-cede" the site to the federal government.[16] Still needed from Washington was the appropriation of restoration funds and from Albany a decision to give the site back to the national government.

By this point in the controversy, at least one issue had been resolved: enough of the historic site had survived so that there was a physical entity to restore and to do battle over. The claim that the remains of the fort had already been demolished was proven false. At McAneny's urging, the *New York Herald-Tribune* had arranged for an aerial photo of the site. When

it was published there was no longer any doubt that Castle Clinton was very much still there.[17]

In 1947, Castle Clinton was again commanding headlines. The struggle over its fate had become a virtual civic soap opera. In April, over a lunch in Fraunces Tavern organized by the American Scenic and Historic Preservation Society and attended by "twenty-eight representatives of educational institutions and historical and other bodies," Ronald Lee of the Park Service stated the willingness of the Interior Department to accept Castle Clinton and to approach Congress for an appropriation for its restoration.

The purpose of the luncheon was to convince Mayor O'Dwyer to support the return of Castle Clinton to the Federal government for its restoration. Among the many noted speakers at the event was Carl Van Doren, the historian, author, and a signatory of the postwar letter to the *New York Times* that had reinvigorated the campaign to save Castle Clinton. He argued eloquently, "Castle Clinton is for Americans of the nineteenth century what Plymouth Rock was for the Americans of the seventeenth. To destroy Castle Clinton seems to me an act of civilized vandalism. Shall the proud city of New York make it possible for posterity to say that the people of the city in 1947 did not cherish so important a monument enough to preserve it?"[18] Others at the meeting included McAneny, Burlingham, Robert W. Dowling, a lay member of the Art Commission, Gardner Osborn, Stephen H. P. Pell, the man who restored Fort Ticonderoga, Peter Grimm, president of the Chamber of Commerce of the State of New York who would go on to play a critical role in a 1960s preservation drama, Alexander Hamilton, treasurer of the American Scenic and Historic Preservation Society, and eighty-year-old Albert Bard.[19]

At lunch the mayor, who "had been promised not to be called upon to speak," volunteered that he "emphatically favored the preservation of the old fort as a national monument, rather than merely as a city relic, and favored its cession to the federal government for preservation and use as such."[20] Over the ensuing months the mayor, as well as others, would vacillate on their position, as the likelihood and timeliness of federal funding for restoration was debated. Headlines over the next year would swing from "City Votes Death of Old Aquarium," to "Aquarium Razing Stayed for Year As City Waits for U.S. to Rebuild It," to "Estimate Board Votes to Complete Demolition of Old Aquarium Here."[21]

As the political pendulum swung back and forth, the defenders of the castle strategically returned to the courts. The Art Commission of the City of New York had long maintained that the fort was a monument and that its demolition would require their approval. The Act of Congress signed by President Truman, though lacking in some things, had clearly proclaimed and indeed labeled the site a monument. Bolstered by this, the Art Commission reminded the Board of Estimate of its position.[22] Albert Bard, as treasurer of the Fine Arts Federation, strongly affirmed the correctness of the Art Commission's position in a letter to the editor of the *New York Times*."[23]

Robert Moses dismissed Bard's claim as having already been settled in the earlier litigation over Castle Clinton. This opinion was not shared by the American Scenic and Historic Preservation Society or the courts. Under the prestigious name of one its officers, Alexander Hamilton, the American Scenic and Historic Preservation Society filed suit in June of 1948. In December, Castle Clinton received a reprieve in the form of an injunction issued by Supreme Court Justice Samuel Null. He warned that: "A people indifferent to the landmarks and monuments of its past will not long retain its capacity to achieve an honored future." Though his decision would be overturned in the spring of 1949, his sentiments still ring true today.[24]

The suit had achieved its purpose, it had bought Castle Clinton's defenders much needed time and they used it well. By the time of the court's final decision, the assembly and the state senate in Albany had passed the legislation required to recede the property to the Federal government. Because of Robert Moses' objections, it had taken two attempts to get the bill through the New York Assembly, but McAneny's efforts ultimately triumphed. The bill was sent to Governor Dewey on March 22, 1949. A week later, the Courts ruled against Hamilton and the American Scenic and Historic Preservation Society. Worried that Moses would seek to use that decision to influence Governor Dewey, the American Scenic and Historic Preservation Society unleashed a telegram campaign on the governor. It was successful and he signed the bill on April 29, 1949.[25] It was the perfect eightieth birthday present for George McAneny.

What remained missing was the formal commitment of federal funds to restore the site. In October of 1949, President Truman signed the appropriation bill with $167,750 allocated for Castle Clinton's restoration. With approval by the New York State Attorney General, the deed conveying the site to the Federal government was executed and in July of 1950, Oscar Chapman, Secretary of the Interior, announced the designation of Castle Clinton as a national monument.[26] After almost a decade, with ownership of the castle now firmly in Federal hands, Robert Moses' siege of the castle had been lifted.

New Yorkers had lived with this preservation crisis through the entire decade of the 1940s. The public debate over preservation had commanded endless headlines, filled numerous column inches, and resounded in edi-torials and letter-to-the-editor columns alike. As Hosmer observed, the battle over Castle Clinton "was a protracted conflict that transformed Castle Clinton into a symbol of the opposition of preservationists to the high-handed tactics of city planners."[27]

As with the battle over the Brooklyn-Battery Bridge, the campaign to preserve Castle Clinton previewed key elements of future preservation efforts. Led by a passionate, almost all-consumed individual, George McAneny, marshalling a cadre of citizen leaders, and assembling a wide coalition of groups, the campaign demonstrated the deft use of the courts and an astute sense of public relations. Highly strategic, it utilized political networking at all levels of government. It embraced a never-say-die attitude and drew from a seemingly bottomless well of energy and creativity.

The role of the press was so important to the success of the effort that the American Scenic and Historic Preservation Society presented one of its prestigious McAneny medals for "outstanding effort in historic preserva-tion" to Geoffrey Parsons, chief editorial writer of the *New York Herald-Tribune*. An account of the presentation of the award to Parsons, and also of one given to Burlingham at the same ceremony, noted that it was the "consensus of the society" that the two recipients "had done more in the effort to preserve the old fort at the Battery than any one else outside the immediate circle of the 'Fort Clinton Boys.'"[28]

The saving of Castle Clinton was a personal victory for George McAneny. For nearly a decade, he had shouldered the heavy lifting of the campaign year in and year out. He is the reason Castle Clinton still sits today overlooking New York Harbor. Gracious to a fault, in victory McAneny thanked his allies, including the National Park Service and Mayor O'Dwyer. With typical flourish, Albert Bard corrected this, "In apportioning praise for the happy consummation of the struggle, Mr. McAneny omits Hamlet. To George McAneny himself should go the main credit for the result."[29]

The effort to save Castle Clinton had engaged and touched numerous civic organizations, their leaders, and their members. It imparted them a shared set of experiences providing the context for the preservation activi-ties that would emerge in the 1950s. Castle Clinton was clearly the preser-vation story of the 1940s, but it would not be the only event of the decade to leave its mark and influence the shape of preservation efforts that would follow.

One action, having no known impact but worth noting in the category of what might have been, is a suggestion that came forward late in 1948 after Judge Samuel Null's hopeful decision on Castle Clinton and before its reversal. A person signed J.O.G. wrote to the *New York Times* noting that with all the new interest in the city kindled by that year's Golden Jubilee celebration of the consolidation of Greater New York, perhaps the time was right for the mayor to appoint "a special commission to make a survey and report on the scenic and historic sites still left and worthy of preservation in our city?" Though the suggestion triggered an immediate hostile response from Robert Moses, it otherwise landed with a thud.[30] "J.O.G." was well ahead of his time. It would take more than a dozen years of preservation Sturm und Drang before a future mayor would take that step.

As the fate of Castle Clinton was played out in Albany, Washington, the courts, and at New York City's city hall, other beloved landmarks were also hanging in the balance. This was no coincidence. New York had emerged from World War II as the capital of the world. The Depression had ended the last period of significant private building in the city. Now New Yorkers were ready to build again. Apartment houses and office buildings were on the drawing boards. Nineteen forty-nine witnessed the dawn of what would blossom into a full-blown building boom transforming New York City.[31] These new buildings had to go somewhere. With growing frequency, that "somewhere" would be sites already occupied by buildings that at least some New Yorkers were not yet ready to let go without a fight.

One of these buildings was St. Nicholas Church. Located at the northwest corner of Fifth Avenue and 48th Street, the Collegiate Reformed Church of St. Nicholas was threatened with replacement by "Fifth Avenue's largest post-war skyscraper."[32] Called by the press a "famous landmark," this Gothic structure designed by W. Wheeler Smith featured a "lofty spire . . . considered one of the most beautiful in the world."[33]

Dedicated in 1872, it was steeped in history. Its congregation was the oldest in Manhattan and it was reported to be "not only the oldest church in the city, but the oldest Protestant church with a continuous history in the United States." Its steeple housed the 1731 bell from the Netherlands called "New York's Liberty Bell." Formerly hanging in the Old Middle Collegiate Reformed Church on Nassau Street, it was said to be the first bell to ring in New York City announcing the signing of the Declaration of Independence. In its pews once sat Theodore Roosevelt and its basement was home to three millstones dating to the first settlement of New Netherland.[34]

St. Nicholas already had several broken dates with the wreckers. In 1929, it almost became part of an assemblage for Rockefeller Center. At

FIGURE 4.4   Noted photographer Berenice Abbott preserved on film what New York City failed to preserve in bricks and mortar, the Collegiate Reformed Church of St. Nicholas at the northwest corner of Fifth Avenue and 48th Street. The demolition of this "famous landmark" for a skyscraper was one of several postwar loses that helped reignite the Municipal Art Society's interest in finding a way to protect such structures.

that time, its pastor observed, "There are some things money cannot buy and I think the Collegiate Reformed church is one of them."[35] In 1949, the controversy that had been ignited three years earlier by the announcement of plans to sell the church (which had resulted in the departure of the pastor who opposed the sale and the dissolution of its congregation) finally

ended, sealing the building's fate. Money could buy the church, and it did.
When the president of the wrecking company encountered his date, he
acknowledged the building's beauty, but commented, "No different from
any other church I've wrecked."[36] Not all agreed.

If new office towers were the harbingers of change for midtown, it was
the apartment building and the growth of New York University that would
play similar roles in one of New York's most cherished neighborhoods:
Greenwich Village. These threats to the Village would draw the attention
of the larger civic community. In the shared consciousness of New York,
the Village has always occupied a special place and Washington Square

FIGURE 4.5 Under the heading, "Collegiate Reformed Church of St. Nicholas Is Stripped for Site of Skyscraper,"
this graphic image accompanied the September 16, 1949 *New York Times* story, "Old St. Nicholas Goes to
Wrecker." Such headlines and photographs would appear with greater frequency as the postwar building boom
would begin to transform the face of the city.

has long been its sentimental heart. As novelist and former Village resident Fannie Hurst once proclaimed, "Boston and baked beans are no more closely related than New York and Washington Square." Of all of New York City's neighborhoods, perhaps none has been as closely tied to preservation for as long as has Greenwich Village.[37]

The late 1940s brought serious threats to Washington Square North. A beloved and defining feature of Washington Square, the street at the northern edge of the park, divided by Fifth Avenue, was lined with a row of buildings that virtually exuded history and civility. "There is nothing left in our city comparable in beauty and dignity with the two rows of houses on the north side of Washington Square East and West. To demolish these would be like tearing down the Crescent in Bath or the granite row on George Street, Edinburgh." These sentiments, expressed in 1949 by such luminaries as Hamilton Fish Armstrong, Eleanor Roosevelt, and Carl Van Doren, and also embraced by such preservation stalwarts as C. C. Burlingham and George McAneny, were triggered by New York University's negotiations to acquire a portion of the eastern part of the row on Washington Square North.[38]

The goal of these writers was to have Sailors' Snug Harbor, the owner of the site in question, insert into the long-term lease it was negotiating with NYU a "clause obligating the lessee to preserve the façades of the houses on the north side of the Square." In their words, "Does not this modest request seem reasonable?"[39] Apparently, to the university, it did not. Of the many decades-long debates raging in Greenwich Village, one of the fiercest has been over whether New York University

FIGURE 4.6   It would be the assault of new development on the historic fabric of old Greenwich Village that would in 1950 prompt Francis Keally, president of the Municipal Art Society, to call for a law to protect the "aesthetic character of private structures." In particular, it was the plan to demolish this stretch of Fifth Avenue from Washington Square North to West 8th Street, including the Rhinelander houses and the Marble house, that sparked a controversy that received national attention.

contributes as much to the Village as it consumes. Fortunately, in this case, the Village dodged a bullet. At the announcement of the signing of the lease, the chancellor assured the public that the university "expects to maintain the residential character of this important block, which is one of the finest architectural developments in the country." He and the sellers also went out of their way to point out that the deal had saved the site from sprouting a "huge apartment house" which would otherwise be under negotiation.[40]

New York City would not fare as well when it came to the fate of the western stretch of Washington Square North. World War II had not yet officially ended before this block was under assault. In December of 1944, the parcel, which included the "ancestral home" of the Rhinelander Family, was sold by the Rhinelander Real Estate Company to a syndicate planning to build a nineteen-story apartment building. The controversy led to a debate at the City Planning Commission over proposals for special restrictions limiting the height of buildings facing public parks and for rezoning "almost the entire Greenwich Village area" to limit building height throughout the Village.[41] Robert Moses, always more responsive to external threats to the city's parks than to the threats posed by his own actions, was able to use his position as a city planning commissioner to advocate the special parks protective zoning proposal. The threat to the site was so real that George McAneny, immersed as he was in his campaign to save Castle Clinton, devoted time to finding a way to save the Rhinelander houses.[42] In the fall of 1945, demolition began and one building was lost, but because of all the objections to the project, it was abandoned before any greater damage was done.[43]

This provided only a temporary reprieve. In January of 1950, a different syndicate, one headed by builder Sam Rudin, bought the site for "one of Manhattan's largest private apartment projects." Twelve stories tall and housing three hundred families, the building would be "Colonial in style, in keeping with the neighborhood."[44] Rudin's proposal unleashed a firestorm and for good reasons.

The site he was planning to clear was occupied by a lively assortment of buildings that were as quintessentially Greenwich Village as one could imagine. Anchoring the northwest corner of Washington Square North and Fifth Avenue were the Greek Revival Rhinelander Homes (at least one attributed to Upjohn of Trinity Church fame and dating from 1839) that had been "converted" into an apartment house in the twenties.[45] Also on the development site as one moved up Fifth Avenue, "partly hidden behind a fence of brick-and-iron grilles" was a private garden and two old stables

turned into multiple dwellings, then housing the Women's Engineering Club among others.[46]

At the southwest corner of Fifth Avenue and Eighth Street stood the Marble House, the "city's first marble mansion," built in 1856 for John Taylor Johnston, a railroad executive and a founder of the Metropolitan Museum of Art. On occasion, it was opened to the public for viewings of his art collection. By this time, it had become the home of New York University's Center for Safety Education with tenants on the upper floors. Turning onto west Eighth Street, the site picked up the Clay Club at 4 West Eighth Street, Johnston's former stables, which provided studio space to such artists as Issamu Noguchi.[47]

Rudin acknowledged the "old-time atmosphere" of the setting, volunteering that his project, designed by Emory Roth & Sons, was in keeping with it, but he aggressively fought the "wholly mythical claim" that there was anything historic about the site. He had an uphill battle on that front. Even before there was organized opposition to his project, the word "historic" was just naturally ascribed to the threatened buildings.[48] Though no patriotic greats were known to have slumbered in them, the Rhinelander buildings had seemingly framed the northern edge of the park forever and had witnessed enough history as backdrop to the Washington Square, the Arch, and Lower Fifth Avenue to seem part of that history.[49] Most importantly, they were a critical piece of what Talbot Hamlin called the "community picture."[50]

Opposition to the project took many forms. The tenants in the threatened buildings formed the "Washington Square Committee, to preserve historic Rhinelander House and the beauty and atmosphere of the Square and Washington Arch." Advancing the cause of the site's history they "considered a nation-wide fund campaign" to purchase the plot as a "national historical area." This notion was further advanced when legislation was introduced in Washington to have the Federal Government step in to save the houses as a "precious historical heritage" for "all the people throughout the land."[51]

There was national interest in saving the buildings. In his role as president of the National Council for Historic Sites and Buildings, Major General Ulysses S. Grant III (retired) pledged the council's support for "any move" to preserve Washington Square as "a cultural heritage." This sentiment was echoed by David Finley, the chair of the newly formed National Trust for Historic Preservation, now congressionally chartered to hold such properties. He sent the American Scenic and Historic Preservation Society and George McAneny, who was still at work trying to save the buildings, his best wishes for success and an offer to have a representative of the trust come to New York if hearings were called.[52]

The controversy reached such a point that the City Planning Commission, "in response to widespread demand on the part of the press, civic organizations, residents and property owners for the protection of Washington Square," brought forth for public debate three amendments to the city's Zoning Resolution.[53] The commission resurrected the idea of special zoning for the perimeter of city parks. That proposal was dear to the heart of the Municipal Art Society and they joined in the fray. Their leadership in promoting that proposal set the stage for the society's serious reengagement in the cause of historic preservation. The society organized the civic community in a campaign to support the proposed zoning in order to protect not only Washington Square, "but every other small park in the city against the encroachment of tall buildings." The zoning amendment would limit buildings surrounding such parks to five or six stories. The zoning amendments ignited even further debate.[54]

In the midst of this escalating controversy, the City Planning Commission suggested that the developer sit down with a committee of citizens to see if a compromise could be hammered out. Key among those citizens was the architect Harvey Wiley Corbett, a board member of the Municipal Art Society. He was in charge of the committee the society had formed of the organizations concerned with the protection of small parks. In May, the City Planning Commission announced that a "compromise" had been reached to "preserve the esthetic value of the Square."[55] With the immediate problem solved, the commission could avoid addressing the larger policy concerns.

In its newsletter, the Municipal Art Society described the compromise solution as one "designed to preserve the aesthetic values of the Square" by keeping the frontage of the new building on the square to the height of the existing structures. The society acclaimed the success of this "design by persuasion" and felt that because of "Mr. Corbett's success in these negotiations, it is believed that the Municipal Art Society will gain prestige in the affairs of the City."[56]

However, unhappiness over the compromise remained. Subsequently, there would be debate over whether the builder fully honored the details of the compromise. About this, Corbett would later comment, "While the restyling may not make all the critics of the project happy, it may make some of them less unhappy."[57] One who was not made less unhappy was the architectural historian Talbot Hamlin. As he wrote to the planner and Greenwich Village advocate Robert C. Weinberg, "The Roth monstrosity

■ ■ ■ ■ ■ ■ ■

certainly is as bad in its Washington Square section as it is enormous in its other parts. They certainly put one over! To conceive that what they have done on Washington Square is in harmony with the square seems impossible. . . . The whole thing is a great tragedy and I cannot conceive how anybody in his senses would consider they had fulfilled their part of their agreement."[58]

The compromise did not end the efforts of those trying to save the old buildings themselves. That fall, they took their efforts to another level of government, the New York City Council. A resolution was introduced authorizing the city to acquire the buildings as "historic monuments."[59] Albert Bard was among those not settling for the design compromise. He introduced, and the Municipal Art Society passed, a motion supporting the city council resolution calling on the mayor, the Board of Estimate, and the City Planning Commission to acquire the Rhinelander apartments and No. 2 Fifth Avenue for either "appropriate use" by the city or for transfer to the National Trust. This, and all other efforts, failed to save the threatened buildings, and by February of 1951, demolition was underway.[60]

The loss of the Rhinelander houses was keenly felt. Later that year, when the Municipal Art Society unveiled a major preservation campaign to its members, it would explain its reasons as follows:

> The accumulated evidence that New York's architectural and historic monuments must be protected by direct action suggests that the Municipal Art Society take the lead in nominating structures for preservation. The controversy over Castle Clinton made many civic-minded citizens aware of the need for intelligent protection of such monuments, and more recently the destruction of the Rhinelander houses, St. Nicolas' church and the Ritz-Carlton building have emphasized the desirability of an immediate expression of opinion on this important subject.[61]

Of all the controversies referenced by the society, it was the society's involvement in the struggle over the Rhinelander houses that propelled it to raise the preservation banner it had dropped at the start of the World War II. Though the battle over Castle Clinton provided context for the Municipal Art Society's growing preservation interest, for years the society had only lent its name to that effort, letting others do the real work. It is also clear that although the demolition of St. Nicholas Church and the Ritz-Carlton had caught the society's attention and ultimately helped prod it to action, in both instances the society was no more than just another witness to their demise.[62]

FIGURE 4.7 The effort to save the Rhinelander houses at the northwest corner of Washington Square North and Fifth Avenue ultimately failed. As seen in this January 19, 1951 photograph, the buildings were demolished despite an effort to have the city acquire them and turn them over to the National Trust for Historic Preservation. The apartment house to replace them was redesigned to "preserve the esthetic value of the Square," but in the eyes of many, failed in that effort.

It was in the heat of the Rhinelander affair that the society confronted head-on the bigger preservation problem facing the city: the absence of a mechanism to protect landmark buildings and historic neighborhoods. In his report at the May 1950 board meeting, Francis Keally, the society's president, "outlined the need of legislation at Albany for some kind of guidance or control over the aesthetic character of private structures through appropriate zoning, such as has been accomplished in Alexandria, Virginia; Charleston, South Carolina; and New Orleans, Louisiana. Mr. Bard was asked to consult with Mr. Cannon in the development of a bill to be placed before the Legislature."[63] Events had led the society to the inevitable conclusion that legal protection for landmarks was needed. The subject of how to go about getting it would be on the society's agenda for the next fifteen years.

It is interesting to note that it was aesthetics that drew the Municipal Art Society to the Rhinelander issue. The society's stated concern was the aesthetic value of the Washington Square area, not the history of the individual threatened buildings. The solutions advanced by the society were design solutions like the proposed special zoning to protect the scale and ambiance of streets surrounding all small parks, and particularly Washington Square. The redesign of the proposed new building for the site was also a design solution.

On the heels of the Rhinelander battle, the society decided to approach the mayoral candidates to learn their position on whether "aesthetic and historic zoning" should be included in the rezoning of the city then under discussion.[64] The society's mindset is seen in a later board discussion noting that "the tearing down of the Ritz-Carlton, a well designed building, and replacing it with a mediocre substitute in Carlton House on Madison Avenue, might well be viewed with alarm."[65] The loss of good design, not the loss of history itself, was their stronger lament.

At the Municipal Art Society, the Rhinelander controversy continued to trigger broader conversations about the state of preservation in New York. When it came to the protection of existing monuments, the society still felt things were under control. At its September 1950 board meeting, the society dropped its own Committee on the Preservation of Existing Sites and Monuments because "this activity is carried on by the American Scenic and Historic Preservation Society which will seek the aid of the Municipal Art Society when needed on special projects." Even though the art societies and the historical organizations often shared members and indeed frequently worked side-by-side to save the same sites, the perceived division of duties between the groups still existed. At this point, the Municipal Art Society

was largely content to leave the matter of existing historic monuments to the leadership of the American Scenic and Historic Preservation Society.[66]

As the Rhinelander buildings were vacated and demolition drew near, the Municipal Art Society continued to discuss the state of preservation in New York City. This discussion brought forth the news that the Metropolitan Museum of Art was studying the "English manner of preserving monuments and historic buildings" and elicited the news that Georgetown had a new ordinance that could make it a "second Williamsburg." It also raised the question, "Does the American Scenic and Historic Preservation Society possess a survey of early New York buildings worthy of preservation?" Clearly the Municipal Art Society was trying to get a better understanding of the preservation landscape. Who was actually doing what? Were things under control? What role should the society play?

As the discussion evolved, it was suggested that the society "direct its efforts towards the enactment of legislation which would empower the City to take over and maintain historic landmarks." Importantly, the outcome of the conversation was an agreement on "the desirability of entrusting to the Municipal Art Society the directing power in the preservation of buildings considered essential to the prestige of the city." The society's interest in the cause was clearly growing.[67]

In February 1951, it all came together. President Keally's earlier recognition of the need for legislation in Albany, the society's questioning of the state of preservation, and the growing realization that the society needed to assume a leadership role, led Edgar Williams, Francis Keally's successor as the society's president, to take action. He turned to the architect William Hamilton Russell to take on the leadership of this effort.

Williams reported to the board that Russell had agreed to "take under consideration a study of what is being done in various cities with respect to preserving buildings and sites of historic or esthetic importance. The recent difficulty encountered at Washington Square exemplifies the need for legislation and it is hoped that the Society can present definite suggestions towards this end in the future." It was also suggested that Russell form a committee and make up a "list of twenty to fifty items in the city which should be preserved."[68]

The die was cast. Almost a decade had passed since the fall of 1941 when Ely Jacques Kahn had appointed his committee "for the purpose of endeavoring to protect and preserve New York's remaining historic buildings, as well as areas with architectural charm of the past." The war had intervened. Peace returned, but did not bring tranquility to the streets of New York. Postwar pressures had again made preservation a top priority for the Municipal Art Society and not a moment too soon.

ENDNOTES

1. "Society Showcase Closes its Doors And a Story of 37 Fabulous Years," *New York Times*, February 17, 1951.

2. "Last Days of the Ritz," *Time*, May 14, 1951, 27; "Minutes of Meeting of Organizing Committee of Central Committee of Organizations Opposing the Battery Bridge," April 10, 1939, Albert S. Bard Papers, New York Public Library.

3. Lee E. Graham, "The Passing of the Potted Palm," *New York Times*, February 4, 1951; Stern, *New York 1960*, 1105.

4. Nathan Silver, *Lost New York* (New York: Shocken Books, 1971), 71; Municipal Art Society Board Meeting Minutes, May 21, 1951, Municipal Art Society of New York Records, Archives of American Art.

5. "Lease Widens Hold of NYU in 'Square,'" *New York Times*, April 2, 1949.

6. R.W.G. Vail, George McAneny, et al., letter to the editor, *New York Times*, September 20, 1945.

7. "Board Acts to Get Land for Center," *New York Times*, October 12, 1945.

8. Caro, *The Power Broker*, quoting Walter Binger, 683.

9. Hosmer, *Preservation Comes of Age*, 779–795.

10. Ibid., 794.

11. Ibid., 819, 832.

12. Ibid., 786, 819.

13. Ibid., 822, 813–814, 816, 823. In addition to working with McAneny on the Castle Clinton campaign, Albright also assisted him in efforts to preserve the Rhinelander houses on Washington Square.

14. "National Preservation Council Duly Organized in Washington," *New York Sun*, October 24, 1947, Albert S. Bard Papers, New York Public Library.

15. Hosmer, *Preservation Comes of Age*, 822, 861–863; Charles Messer Stow, "National Trust is Established To Aid Historic Preservation," *New York Sun*, April 18, 1947.

16. "Aquarium Block Made a Monument," *New York Times*, August 13, 1946. Not surprisingly, among those urging the president to take this action was Bard. Bard to President Truman, July 31, 1946, Albert S. Bard Papers, New York Public Library; "'Saving' Fort Clinton," *New York Times*, August 14, 1946. After the fort had ceased to serve a military purpose, it had been given to New York City. To convey the property back to the federal government required legislation in Albany.

17. Caro, *The Power Broker*, 684–885.

18. Carl Van Dorn as quoted in Gardner Osborn, letter to the editor, *New York Times*, April 5, 1947.

19. Minutes of the Meeting of the Board of Directors of the Fine Arts Federation of New York, April 3, 1947 with a special "Report on Fort Clinton Luncheon," submitted by Bard, Fine Arts Federation Records, Archives of American Art.

20. Ibid.; The Fine Arts Federation of New York, Report of Committee on City Development, April 24, 1947, Fine Arts Federation Records, Archives of American Art.

21. "City Votes Death of Old Aquarium," *New York Times*, July 25, 1947; "Aquarium Razing Stayed for Years As City Waits for U.S. to Rebuild It," *New York Times*, August 29, 1947; "Estimate Board Votes to Complete Demolition of Old Aquarium Here," *New York Times*, May 28, 1948.

22. "Delay Asked in Aquarium Razing; Art Board Says It Must Approve," *New York Times*, August 1, 1947.

23. Albert S. Bard, letter to the editor, *New York Times*, August 7, 1947.

24. "Ancient Aquarium Wins New Chance," *New York Times*, December 24, 1948; Hamilton v. Moses, Supreme Court: New York County Special Term: Part I, December 10, 1948; "Moses Wins Plea on Castle Clinton," *New York Times*, March 30, 1949.

25. "City's Plan for Aquarium as Shrine Faces Battle Before Legislature," *New York Times*, January 29, 1948; "Society to Continue Battery Park Fight," *New York Times*, March 16, 1948; "Bill Revives Fight to Save Aquarium," *New York Times*, February 19, 1949; "Assembly Passes Fort Clinton Bill," *New York Times*, March 22, 1949; "Fort Clinton Bill Sent to Governor," *New York Times*, March 23, 1949; Hosmer, *Preservation Comes of Age*, 793; "Fort Clinton Bill Signed by Dewey," *New York Times*, April 29, 1949.

26. "Work will Start Soon on Castle Clinton Park," *New York Times*, October 14, 1949; "Aquarium Becomes a U.S. Monument," *New York Times*, July 19, 1950.

27. Hosmer, *Presence of the Past*, 781.

28. Charles Messer Stow, "Medals Given Two For Service To Fort Clinton," *New York Sun*, June 10, 1949.

29. "Aquarium Becomes a U.S. Monument," *New York Times*, Albert S. Bard, letter to the editor, *New York Times*, July 28, 1950.

30. J.O.G., letter to the editor, *New York Times*, December 20, 1948. This letter unleashed a ten-paragraph response by Moses, in which, among other things, he again dismissed Castle Clinton as a "sunken gas tank at the Battery." Robert Moses, letter to the editor, *New York Times*, December 31, 1948. In response to Moses, Walter Binger turns to Gilbert and Sullivan, noting that in "standing four-square behind himself with practically no support," Moses is like the Duke of Plaza Toro in Gilbert and Sullivan's *Gondoliers*, who "led his regiment from behind, he found it more exciting." Walter D. Binger, letter to the editor, *New York Times*, January 3, 1949. There certainly was something about Moses that brought the Gilbert and Sullivan out in people.

31. For an encyclopedic account of building in the postwar period, turn to Stern, *New York*, 1960.

32. Lee Cooper, "St. Nicholas Church Again Plans Sale," *New York Times*, February 5, 1949.

33. Austin Stevens, "Old St. Nicholas Goes to Wrecker," *New York Times*, September 16, 1949; John A. Bradley, "St. Nicholas Church to Be Razed to Make Way for Office Building," *New York Times*, April 1, 1949.

34. John A. Bradley, "St. Nicholas Church to Be Razed to Make Way for Office Building," *New York Times*, April 1, 1949; Austin Stevens, "Old St. Nicholas Goes to Wrecker," *New York Times*, September 16, 1949.

35. "Plan to Sell St. Nicholas Church for $3,000,000 Stirs Conflict," *New York Times*, January 28, 1946; John A. Bradley, "St. Nicholas Church to Be Razed to Make Way for Office Building," *New York Times*, April 1, 1949.

36. Austin Stevens, "Old St. Nicholas Goes to Wrecker," *New York Times*, September 16, 1949.

37. "Opposition to Law Center Mounts," *Villager*, Nov. 20, 1947. See chapter 7 for more on the tradition of preservation in the Village and its intersection with city-wide preservation efforts.

38. Hamilton Fish Armstrong, C. C. Burlingham et al., letter to the editor, *New York Times*, March 23, 1949.

39. Ibid.

40. "Lease Widens Hold of NYU in 'Square' College to Rent Most of block from Sailors' Snug Harbor for Two Centuries," *New York Times*, April 2, 1949.

41. "Rhinelanders Will Stay in Realty Despite Sale of Old Home Site, Company Owns 200 Parcels in Manhattan and is Preparing to Expand—Washington Square Property Held 120 Years," *New York Times*, December 24, 1944; "Rezoning Project For City Put Off," *New York Times*, May 10, 1945.

42. Hosmer, *Presence of the Past*, 816.

43. "Wreckers Start Razing Rhinelander Buildings," *New York Times*, November 1, 1945; "Apartment Project to Replace Historic Washington Sq. Homes," *New York Times*, January 4, 1950.

44. "Apartment Project to Replace Historic Washington Sq. Homes," *New York Times*, January 4, 1950.

45. In her book *It Happened on Washington Square* (Baltimore: Johns Hopkins University Press, 2002), 273, Emily Kies Folpe notes that in the conversion the architects, Maynicke and Franke, "preserved most of the red-brick shells of the buildings and reused other materials—marble flooring, iron balconies—in a manner that anticipated the adaptive reuse more common to the later twentieth century." In addition, she notes that the "distinctive granite doorway with two Corinthian columns from the corner Rhinelander house was reused at the central entrance of the low-rise apartment building." In his "Memorandum on the buildings along Washington Square North" sent by Robert C. Weinberg to Talbot Hamlin in 1951, he reports that the conversion was less sensitive. "In 1923 the Rhinelander Estate demolished all but the bearing walls of these three houses and built in their place a five-story red brick, non-fireproof tenement of undistinguished but inoffensive design. Its cornice line was higher than that of the original Row." The Talbot F. Hamlin Collection, Avery Architectural & Fine Arts Library, Columbia University.

46. Lee Cooper, "Apartment Project to Replace Historic Washington Sq. Homes," *New York Times*, January 4, 1950.

47. Folpe, *It Happened on Washington Square*, 273; "Villagers Regret Loss of Old Homes," *New York Times*, January 5, 1950; "Apartment Project to Replace Historic Washington Sq. Homes," *New York Times*, January 4, 1950.

48. The first *New York Times* story was headlined "Apartment Project to Replace Historic Washington Sq. Homes," January 4, 1950 and the follow-up story the next day read, "Villagers Regret Loss of Old Homes/Historic Rhinelander, Johnson Houses to Be Torn Down for Apartment Building."

49. "Rhinelander Unit Held Not Historic," *New York Times*, April 10, 1950. Even the first *Times* story on the project was captioned, "Apartment Project to Replace Historic Washington Sq. Homes," *New York Times*, January 4, 1950. Robert C. Weinberg, architect, planner, villager, and astute observer, felt differently about the Rhinelander houses. He stressed that the original houses had been demolished in 1922 and been "replaced by a six-story structure of indifferent design." Robert C. Weinberg to Edward Steese, April 19, 1955, Professional Papers of Robert C. Weinberg, Long Island University.

50. Edward Steese refers to this phrase of Hamlin's in a series of correspondence he has with Weinberg. Steese to Weinberg, April 16 and April 23, 1955, box 54, folder 111, Professional Papers of Robert C. Weinberg, Long Island University.

51. "Group Seeks to save Rhinelander Mansion," *New York Times*, January 25, 1950; "Rhinelander Tenants Map a Drive to Buy Property As Historic Area," *New York*

Times, April 2, 1950. The legislation was introduced in the House by Frederic R. Coudert Jr., Republican and Senator Herbert H. Lehman, Democrat. "Limit on Buildings Backed by Moses," *New York Times*, April 12, 1950.

52. "6-Story Top Sought Around All Parks," *New York Times*, April 7, 1950; David Finley to George McAneny, June 15, 1950, Records of the National Trust for Historic Preservation, National Archives at College Park, Maryland.

53. "Zone Shift Urged for Washington Square," *New York Times*, March 23, 1950.

54. "6-Story Top Sought Around All Parks," *New York Times*, April 7, 1950; "Limit on Buildings Backed by Moses," *New York Times*, April 12, 1950; "Square Rezoning Opposed," *New York Times*, April 24, 1950; "'Ceiling' Opposed on Washington Sq.," *New York Times*, April 26, 1950.

55. "City Asked to Get Historic Houses," *New York Times*, November 22, 1950.

56. Municipal Art Society Newsletter, June 1950, Municipal Art Society of New York Records, Archives of American Art.

57. John Bradley, "New 19-Story Village Apartment to Have Old-Style Front on Square," *New York Times*, March 4, 1951.

58. Hamlin to Weinberg, December 18, 1951, Talbot F. Hamlin Collection, Avery Architectural and Fine Arts Library, Columbia University.

59. The resolution was introduced by Councilman Robert Weisberger, Manhattan Democrat. "City Asked to Get Historic Houses," *New York Times*, November 22, 1950.

60. Ibid.; Municipal Art Society Board Meeting Minutes, October 23, 1950, Municipal Art Society of New York Records, Archives of American Art.

61. Edgar I. Williams, president, letter "To All Members of the Municipal Art Society," November 1, 1951, Municipal Art Society of New York Records, Archives of American Art.

62. At the Society's January 28, 1952, Board Meeting it was noted that the "demolition of the Ritz-Carlton had aroused people and awakened interest in such things." Municipal Art Society of New York Records, Archives of American Art.

63. Municipal Art Society Board Meeting Minutes, May 15, 1950, Municipal Art Society of New York Records, Archives of American Art.

64. Ibid., January 15, 1951.

65. Ibid., May 21, 1951.

66. Ibid., September 25, 1950. Even when the decision was made for the society to compile its list of buildings, it was felt that "The historical societies take care of architectural historic structures whereas those buildings of artistic importance should be guarded also." Steese at the September 24, 1951 Municipal Art Society Board Meeting Minutes, Municipal Art Society of New York Records, Archives of American Art.

67. Municipal Art Society Board Meeting Minutes, January 15, 1951, Municipal Art Society of New York Records, Archives of American Art.

68. Ibid., February 19, 1951.

FIVE

THE CIVICS ENGAGE

LOOKING BACK THROUGH A CONTEMPORARY LENS AT THE PRESERVATION efforts that would unfold in the early 1950s, one can find all the components of a brilliant master plan. Having concluded that a legal mechanism to preserve their architectural and historical treasures was needed, New Yorkers sought inspiration and knowledge from the experiences of other cities. A roster of important New York City sites worthy of preservation was carefully created and documented. This list of architectural and historical treasures provided the raw material for exhibitions, publications, and a range of other efforts that would begin to engage the citizenry. As civic consciousness was gradually raised, a constituency for preservation emerged. The legal mechanism needed to create a process to protect the city's heritage began to take shape. Growing public support found its voice and organized behind the legislative proposal. The rest is history.

Was the creation of New York City's 1965 Landmarks Law the final outcome of a finely tuned and well-executed master plan? Or, is the appearance of such a thoughtful strategy merely a mirage?

When asked, Geoffrey Platt, the first chair of the Landmarks Preservation Commission who came on the scene at the Municipal Art Society in the mid 1950s, responded: "There was no master plan, just a lot of activity, and then circumstances that finally brought progress. 1961 was the pivotal year. There were many things that had gone on before which laid the groundwork for what happened in 1961 and thereafter."[1] Indeed, there is nothing that suggests the existence of a highly detailed, finely honed plan that was subsequently executed. What did seem to exist was a guiding vision of what it would take to obtain meaningful landmark protection. That guiding vision provided the conceptual framework for the "activity" remembered by Platt.

William Hamilton Russell, the man asked in 1951 to chair the Municipal Art Society committee studying how other cities had protected their landmarks, understood the larger challenge the society faced. Concluding that the protection of the city's "architectural and historical structures" would require legislation, the preservation experience of other countries and cities would need to be studied and an appropriate solution devised for New York City. Russell, however, understood devising legislation alone would not be enough. The society would have to "ascertain what it wants to have preserved and then get public opinion behind it." He knew that no matter the form legislation might ultimately take, its passage would require "the backing of a large number of citizens."[2]

Simply put, those seeking legal protection for New York's landmarks were faced with two challenges: to develop the legislation needed to protect landmarks and to build the constituency needed to get such legislation passed into law. The future preservation activities of the Municipal Art Society and allied civic organizations can be seen as advancing these objectives. Both would be pursued in tandem. Neither would be easily achieved. Of the two, finding the legal solution to protect the city's landmarks would prove to be the more elusive.

It was in the midst of the controversy surrounding the Rhinelander houses that the Municipal Art Society reached the conclusion that a landmarks law was needed. The society was not the first to reach such a conclusion, nor was it the first to seek precedents for such a course of action.

Albert Bard was far ahead. Despite the lack of success of Bard's 1938 "patrimony of the people'" amendment, he never gave up on his belief that government should have some regulatory say on the subject of beauty. In the course of his work, Bard had become a recognized national expert on the subject of aesthetic regulation. The extent to which government could regulate the appearance of private property was a subject he studied and monitored for decades. His early-twentieth century work to control billboards in New York City demonstrated his passion for aesthetic regulation, a concept that would provide the foundation for the Landmarks Law.

As early as the 1920s, Bard joined forces with Mrs. Walter L. Lawton, a tireless campaigner against the blight of roadside advertising. A housewife, Elizabeth Lawton began battling billboards in her own backyard, the scenic Lake George area of upper New York State. Her interests grew and she became the sparkplug driving a national movement to restrict outdoor advertising. Bard served as counsel to both Lawton's National

FIGURE 5.1 In the early 1950s, when the Municipal Art Society focused its attention on the question of how to protect landmarks, it turned to Albert Bard for help. By this time, Bard, pictured here on the left on June 23, 1952 receiving an award on behalf of the National Roadside Council, was eighty-five years old. Fortunately for the cause of historic preservation, he would live almost another eleven very active and productive years.

Committee for the Restriction of Outdoor Advertising and her National Roadside Council for the Protection and Development of Roadside Beauty. The goal of the council was "to promote the picturesque simplicity of rural scenery with special reference to the abuses of outdoor advertising, and to promote a similar regard for dignity and amenity in our towns." Endorsing her efforts were national organizations ranging from the Garden Clubs of America to the National Grange to historical societies and state planning boards. By the time of her death in 1952, the council had affiliate organizations in "nearly every state."[3]

Together, Lawton and Bard battled the billboard industry for almost thirty years in classic David vs. Goliath style. Women were both generals and foot soldiers in the billboard wars. Their billboard adversaries dubbed them the "scenic sisters."[4] Bard and his scenic sister Lawton were true comrades in arms though frequently in disagreement over tactics. Bard characteristically opted for a more adversarial advocacy approach.

As he wrote Lawton, "I know that I am inclined to shout where you whisper. Thank you for shushing me from time to time. But I also know that a lot of people are deaf, and that the gladiators did not go to afternoon teas in the coliseum."[5]

Bard's anti-billboard activities earned him a national reputation. A 1938 *Reader's Digest* article on Lawton and efforts to control billboards described Bard as her "veteran counsel, shrewd as any billboard lawyer, who for years has donated his legal skill."[6] Bard published frequently on billboard control and the larger issue of aesthetic regulation. He was a regular contributor to *The American City*, a professional journal addressing municipal issues, providing readers updates on legal developments across the nation. Whether writing or speaking about new ordinances, recent court decisions, or emerging concepts such as "Highway Zoning," he was one of the most informed persons on the subject in the nation. His dedication to this issue brought him in regular contact with citizen advocates, lawyers, public officials, planners, and press from all across the country. He would remain a national leader and expert on aesthetic regulations until his death.[7]

Because of his considerable expertise and passion, it is no surprise that Albert Bard was well ahead of the Municipal Art Society at that time it recommitted itself to a preservation agenda. He surely approved of the society's renewed interest. In 1946, approaching his eightieth birthday, a still passionate Bard returned to the society's board on which he had last served in 1923. His ongoing role representing the society on the Fine Arts Federation had kept him close to the organization. By this point in his life, Bard was virtually an institution in his own right. Though still actively involved with multiple civic organizations, his stature was such that he could function as a free agent working any and all channels to advance causes to which he was committed. Bard did not need the imprimatur of any organization. Strategically brilliant, he was a master at utilizing his organizational affiliations to beat his favorite civic drums, aesthetic regulation being high on that list.

Before the Municipal Art Society formed William Hamilton Russell's committee to investigate how other cities protected important historic sites and architectural treasures, Bard was already researching the subject. In 1946 he was in communication with the City of New Orleans regarding the preservation of the historic French Quarter. That exchange grew out of a correspondence that had been initiated by activists in Greenwich Village. Likely motivated by threats to Washington Square North, the Greenwich Village Artists Gallery and Museum had written the mayor of

FIGURE 5.2 New Yorkers frequently looked to the Vieux Carré in New Orleans as an example of the protection they were seeking for New York's historic neighborhoods. Confronting increased threats to the Village, as early as 1945 villagers were in contact with officials in New Orleans to learn more. Assisting the villagers in their efforts was Albert Bard.

New Orleans asking to be "informed of the legal method whereby" that city was able to preserve its Vieux Carré.

The February 20, 1945, response from the Vieux Carré commission's secretary, Mr. William Boizelle, must have given the villagers great hope. "I believe that the City of New York, under its general police powers, can

pass an ordinance, along the lines of our ordinance, in the interest of the general or public welfare, as your Greenwich Village is known to be a valuable asset to the city, drawing tourists from all over the States which contribute to the wealth of your city in incalculable sums." Noting "the preservation of such localities involves legal questions and legislation," he ends inviting the Village group to have their "attorneys" communicate with him.[8] Sadly, despite Boizelle's optimism, New York's landmark law was still two decades away, and the eager villagers would have to wait until 1969 for the protection they sought for their beloved neighborhood.

The villagers turned to Bard. His status, interests, and existing relationships made him a logical choice to pursue the matter.[9] Bard was already well aware of the New Orleans ordinance that had created the Vieux Carré Commission and of the amendment to the Louisiana State Constitution on which it was based. Since New York State lacked such a constitutional amendment, Bard doubted that the Vieux Carré could serve as a "precedent in favor of the legality and constitutionality of such an effort." Lacking such a constitutional underpinning in New York State, legislative authority to protect the Village lacked a legal basis. Hoping to learn something that would change his mind, Bard wrote to Boizelle of his skepticism regarding the applicability of the Vieux Carré approach to New York City and asked for more information. To Bard, Boizelle's response was not convincing. Though New Yorkers would continue to look to the Vieux Carré as a model, unfortunately it could not provide New York City the answer it needed to address its preservation problems.[10]

Never daunted, Bard continued his search for applicable regulatory models. In the late 1940s, he looked to the west coast, contacting officials in Santa Barbara and San Diego. In 1949, he turned eastward and wrote to Paris, France, for information on that city's system of architectural review.[11] Bard was inexhaustible.

In the spring of 1950 when Municipal Art Society president Francis Keally went public with his call for a landmarks law, what did he have in mind? An architect who had worked for Cass Gilbert and Trowbridge and Livingston, Keally had launched his own firm, Keally & Patterson, in 1945.[12] In the midst of the Rhinelander crisis, he sounded his clarion call for a law in an address to the Greenwich Village Association. His talk generated a *New York Times* headline: "Law Urged to Save Landmarks of City."

First, Keally stressed that what was at stake "goes far beyond Washington Square and the Village." He asked his audience to imagine a New York where a skyscraper had been substituted for the Church of the Ascension,

FIGURE 5.3 As president of the Municipal Art Society in 1950, Francis Keally would set that organization on its long search to find a formal mechanism to protect the city's landmarks and historic neighborhoods. An architect, Keally is shown here second from the right at the 1937 signing of the contracts for the Central Library Building in Brooklyn that he designed with the architect Alfred Morton Githens. Keally, who would also serve as president of the New York Chapter of the American Institute of Architects, would continue his advocacy for legal protection of the city's landmarks into the 1960s.

or where the south side of Gramercy Square was built up "to smother the sky." Noting the loss of the Collegiate Church of St. Nicholas, he paints a picture of a New York where Trinity, St. Paul's, St. Bartholomew's, St. Patrick's, and St. Mark's-in-the-Bouwerie have all gone "the same way." The newspaper account of Keally's remarks goes on to provide some specifics of what he had in mind at this stage of his thinking.

Keally references the laws of Charleston, South Carolina, Alexandria, Virginia, and New Orleans. He then goes on to list "four categories of buildings and neighborhoods that should be preserved by subjecting to official scrutiny all changes in construction and occupany [sic]: Outstanding works of art; those possessing outstanding characteristics of the age in which they were built; structures whose attributes give a depth of time in an otherwise modern atmosphere; and buildings that were scenes of important events."

FIGURE 5.4   When Francis Keally issued his call for legislation to preserve New York City's historic buildings and neighborhoods, he cited as examples the laws of Charleston, South Carolina, Alexandria, Virginia, and New Orleans, Louisiana. This photograph of Charleston's South Battery near Meeting Street captures the distinct sense of place that particularly makes it "the Holy City" for preservationists. Over the years, New Yorkers would study Charleston as they worked to devise a preservation mechanism for their own city.

In what is one of the earliest and most detailed public calls for a New York Landmarks Law, Keally emphasized two important themes that would resound for years to come. First, echoing the Vieux Carré's Boizelle, he makes a case for the law in economic terms. "Mr. Keally declared that the value of such properties in inviting tourists far outweighed any putative gain in values from their displacement by skyscrapers." He imagines a day when "the City Hall, the University Club on Fifth Avenue, the Morgan Library, many others, may be as sought after by tourists here as the Coliseum in Rome."

■ ■ ■ ■ ■ ■ ■

Secondly, Keally seeks to assure mainstream interests that a landmarks law is not as threatening as some might imagine. He cautioned that "the monuments worthy of preservation must be judiciously chosen. Many places merely old . . . should yield to progress." Here, Keally is already at work to both ease the fears of those who might worry about the indiscriminate use of such a law and to dissuade those who might see in it a vehicle to save everything.[13]

The press account of Keally's remarks reports that "such legislation" is "now under consideration by New York authorities."[14] It seems likely the press was confused. Though Keally's talk does shed some light on what he felt should be contained in a New York City Landmarks Law, it is highly unlikely that any of his thoughts had taken the form of an actual proposal. Keally's public comments preceded both his declaration to the society's board that a law was needed and his request to Albert Bard to explore the possibility of such legislation. At this time, William Hamilton Russell's committee had yet to be created. Certainly, the society was not yet floating any formal proposals for a landmarks law. It seems possible that the press mention of legislation might have been a reference to the site-specific legislation that was being discussed at that time to save the Rhinelander property.

Keally and the Municipal Art Society were not alone in their conclusion that a law was needed. In the context of the City Planning Commission's hearing on the proposed zoning changes intended to save the Rhinelander buildings on Washington Square North, the noted architectural historian Talbot Hamlin weighed in on behalf of the New York Chapter of the Society of Architectural Historians. Again referencing the preservation successes of New Orleans and Charleston, South Carolina, Hamlin, though "heartily" supporting the zoning changes, cautioned that they are "but a single step in what should be a much wider attempt to discover and to arrange for the preservation of many other elements of old New York which still stand and which still preserve something of that sense of continuing tradition which makes a city a living entity."[15]

As one would imagine, Keally's call for a landmarks law was particularly well received in Greenwich Village. For obvious reasons, pro-landmark sentiments were running extremely high in the Village. That spring Albert Bard addressed the Friends of Democracy, Inc. at the Greenwich Village Center and was thanked for his "expert presentation on the legal aspects of factors controlling the preservation of beautiful buildings and beautiful and historic sites and areas."[16] When Owen Grundy of the *Villager* contacted the Society regarding the idea of developing some historic zoning to protect the Village, Keally put him in touch with Bard.[17]

FIGURE 5.5 Noted architectural historian, Pulitzer-Prize-winning author, and distinguished professor, Talbot Hamlin looked every inch all of the many roles he played. The preliminary list of important New York buildings that he compiled in the early 1940s laid the groundwork for the index compiled in the 1950s by the Municipal Art Socity and the Society of Architectural Historians. That index would guide the early work of the Landmarks Preservation Commission.

The public advocacy of a law to protect historic buildings and neighborhoods was indeed an important step. The more difficult step was drafting a law that could accomplish this goal and stand up to legal challenge. Bard and the society continued to look to other cities for examples. Reacting to an article in the December 1950 issue of *Planning and Civic Government*, Bard reached out to the National Council for Historic Sites and Buildings requesting copies of zoning ordinances from Charleston, New Orleans, Alexandria, Williamsburg, and Winston-Salem. He wrote to the council that "various organizations in New York City have shown an interest in the framing of provisions to protect historic sites and buildings in New York City, but the drafting of an appropriate law or laws remains to be done." Frederick L. Rath, the director of the National Council, responded with the requested information and also suggested Bard might want to look into an ordinance being put before the Philadelphia City

Council to protect sections of Germantown. Rath ended his letter asking to be kept abreast of the New York efforts in case the National Council could be of help.[18]

It was in 1951 that Russell's Municipal Art Society committee on the "Protection and Preservation of Important Buildings" joined the search for a legal basis for regulating sites of historic and aesthetic interest. The occasional accounts of its progress in the society's board minutes are sadly telling. At the March 1952 meeting, Bard cut to the chase by asking the committee the all-important question: "What principle can be invented that will cover the proposal of the right to take charge of private property?" Russell responded with an explanation of the French system, noting that owners are "excused from taxes and assessments" and then went on to suggest that "it will be necessary to find means to get some compensation for the owner" of protected properties. Despite these difficulties, Russell offers the positive note that at least one elected official, Frederic Coudert, is interested and "believes legislation to be possible."[19] It remains unknown whether Coudert's belief was based on anything more than just wishful thinking.

Bard's papers from this period indicate that he is seeking answers to two critically important questions: "1. May the legislative power (either of the State itself or delegated) constitutionally prohibit the destruction or alteration of a privately owned building without affording compensation? 2. If such a prohibition must be deemed a 'taking,' upon what principle or principles is the compensation to be computed?" There were no easy answers to these or other related difficult questions.[20]

In a subsequent society board discussion, the question was raised as to whether the society "should investigate the matter of the proper organization to introduce the bill for the preservation of worthy buildings." Russell, introducing some reality into the conversation, responded: "It will be necessary for the Society to decide on how definite legislation will be initiated to secure the protection of certain buildings—through the reduction of taxes or condemnation of the property."[21] This exchange is illustrative of the Municipal Art Society's growing desire to move forward with legislation and its inability to overcome the considerable legal hurdles in its path.

Russell became the president of the Municipal Art Society in 1952 and Edward R. Finch, Jr. took on the leadership of Russell's committee. There were still high hopes for the committee's work. A society memo requesting input in the list of buildings that was being compiled to be nominated for "preservation or protection by law" reflects these expectations. "No such law exists, but it is, we believe, possible to effect fair legislation—national, state, or civic—which will ensure the continued existence not only of recognized artistic monuments of the past but also such later structures as may be added to the roster from time to time in coming years."[22] Those hopeful words were in contrast to the legal realities the committee was confronting. The society board minutes became increasingly silent on the subject of the development of the proposed legislation for a landmarks law. What does appear on occasion are comments about how "extremely difficult" securing such legislation will be. A statement in the context of a conversation on architectural design controls nicely sums up the situation. The "control of aesthetics of private property in the city is a very difficult matter."[23]

So difficult was the matter that by the end of 1952, with no apparent official announcement to the society's board, the issue of drafting and advancing legislation to protect landmarks was put on the back burner. This would be explained in early 1954 when the Finch Committee, then being called the Legislation for Protection of Buildings Committee, explained that a "determined investigation had been made two years ago which had revealed that any legislation to protect and preserve buildings would deal with the right of private property and that it had been decided to drop the matter temporarily since nothing constructive could be done at this time."[24]

The society had not been able to find a legal basis for a system of protection for the city's landmarks. The lessons learned from other cities did not lead to a solution applicable to New York City's situation. A basis to regulate private property without compensation continued to be elusive. The one sure basis for a law was an amendment to the New York State constitution but the political realities of that solution ruled it out as a viable course of action.[25] In its efforts to draft a landmarks law, the Municipal Art Society had hit a wall.

Early on, the society had realized it faced a two-pronged challenge: drafting a law to protect landmarks and creating a constituency to support such legislation. The society took on both challenges simultaneously. Just as the society's legal aspirations were ahead of the legal realities of the day, its preservation ethic was equally out of sync with the public mindset of the fifties. Unlike the twenty-first century where history, architecture, and historic preservation have secured a place in the national consciousness, the gestalt of the 1950s was all about the "new." The goals of preservationists and the emerging ethos of the 1950s could not have been more at odds.

Having endured the depression and emerged victorious from World War II, America was enjoying a new prosperity. This was a decade where assembly line techniques would change society. Courtesy of GM and Detroit, flashy cars would hit the roads. Bill Levitt would show the way to quick and affordable new housing in Levittown on Long Island. The McDonald brothers would bring the assembly line concept to food preparation and Ray Kroc would bring the fast food it produced to the nation. New, instant, fast, and flashy were the adjectives of the fifties. The new American dream was about affluence and abundance, about what was "new" and "now." For many, the dream was to be realized in the suburbs.[26]

Many Americans had the ability to actually attain the dream—or at least buy a piece of it. Prosperity, new production techniques, and new social attitudes about spending made it possible for more and more people to live the dream. Promoting this dream was a new means of communication. A growing media industry capable of reaching and engaging more Americans than ever before was coming into its own. As David Halberstam has written, "America, it appeared, was slowly but surely learning to live with affluence, convincing itself that it had earned the right to its new appliances and cars. Each year seemed to take the country further from its old puritan restraints; each year, it was a little easier to sell than in the past. By the mid-fifties television portrayed a wonderfully anti-septic world of idealized homes in an idealized unflawed America."[27] The burgeoning field of advertising was rolling up its sleeves to promote a range of products heretofore unimagined, and all part and parcel of a new way of living.

The new American dream did not include old neighborhoods or old homes. It did not even include yesterday's hotels, apartments, or office buildings. Being out of style was just as much a death sentence as being inefficient. This sensibility, with huge advertising budgets helping drive it, was changing popular values. New styles, new expectations, new features were making even the not-so-old obsolete. New was better just because it was new. Like the auto companies who helped create it, American society "became caught in a vicious syndrome: a worship of the new at the expense of the old, even if on occasion, the old was better."[28] This new worldview, with energy, excitement, and the economy driving it, threatened historic buildings and neighborhoods. Its success dramatized the need to organize a countervailing force to save such buildings and special places while making the job of doing so even more challenging.

Selling preservation to New Yorkers in the 1950s would have been an uphill struggle even if it had been driven by a solid, well financed, highly developed and sophisticated organization. Instead, preservation's white knight and press agent was the Municipal Art Society. At that time, the society's base was described as "a handful of people—ladies with floppy hats and tennis shoes joined by a few crackpots." Unlikely as it seems, the Municipal Art Society, in partnership with other equally under-resourced organizations, would venture forth on this crusade and ultimately build a credible constituency for preservation.[29] It would, however, take years. In the 1950s, no rational person looking at the resources of the society and the enormity of the task it faced would have given the effort any chance of success. The challenge was no less than launching a cultural revolution in New York City. Fortunately, the Municipal Art Society rarely focused on the magnitude of the challenges it undertook. Instead, year after year, idea by idea, opportunity by opportunity, in seemingly Sisyphus-like fashion, it kept pushing the preservation rock up the hill. The ultimate success of these efforts is another example of the oft-observed phenomenon in social change that those who don't know that their goal is impossible are the ones who achieve it.

Today's concept of a civic nonprofit with a professional staff, a budget (even a modest one), a professional communications capability, a good-sized membership, and a powerful board of directors bears little if any resemblance to the Municipal Art Society of the 1950s. The society's primary asset in those days was its board. What it lacked in cash (and it certainly lacked that) it made up for in the creativity, connections, and commitment of its board.

The society was a "tiny little organization, without any money at all." Its staff consisted of a seemingly ageless secretary who since 1912 had kept the society's minutes. For that, historians are tremendously in her debt. Those minutes, even with their limitations, are the primary window available to view the society's work. Only partially in jest, the society's treasury has been described as residing in a "little cardboard box she kept in her desk drawer."[30] The society was driven by volunteer energy. It was organized into committees whose level of activity fluctuated, as did that of the society itself. Even when combined with the energy and assets of the other civic organizations with whom it would collaborate, the society's resources were dwarfed by the sheer magnitude of the challenge of educating New Yorkers to the value of their built heritage.

The society and its sister organizations were in no position to wage an all-out culture war against the trends of the time. They could, however, mount a series of rearguard actions. The late 1940s and early 1950s found the great preservation icons—McAneny, Grant, and Bard—receiving honors from their peers. Unlikely part of a conscious strategy, these accolades helped focus attention, at least within the civic sector, on the values and causes those recipients had championed. In 1951, over a dinner featuring Gumbo Creole, breast of duckling stuffed with bread and apples, and crowned with Baba au Rhum and demitasse, the Municipal Art Society saluted the hero of Castle Clinton, George McAneny, with its medal of honor. Two years earlier, McAneny had been feted with a testimonial dinner by his own American Scenic and Historic Preservation Society. In 1951, the American Scenic and Historic Preservation Society presented its George McAneny medal to Ulysses S. Grant III, of the National Council for Historic Sites and Buildings. The City Club of New York got into the act using its sixtieth Anniversary Dinner of May 27, 1952 to present to the "venerated citizens" Albert Bard, C. C. Burlingham, and George McAneny citations for their distinguished civic achievements. The 1950s would also see the Municipal Art Society Medal of Honor going to Bard and Burlingham.[31]

While these events could help keep preservation front and center within the narrow precincts of New York's civic organizations, real progress depended on reaching out beyond their own motivated though modest ranks to engage a larger audience. The foundation for such an effort was provided by a project that would grow into one of the most ambitious and influential educational initiatives ever undertaken in the history of the Municipal Art Society, the development of a roster of important New York buildings and sites. Ultimately published in book form in 1963 as Alan Burnham's *New York Landmarks*, this list of buildings proposed for preservation would provide the intellectual capital needed to fuel multiple outreach programs to the general public. It would be through the index and related projects that the society would begin to engage the public and in so doing experience the excitement such outreach could generate. The project also provided the raw data that would guide the early work of the Landmarks Preservation Commission itself.

Since its re-engagement with preservation, the society had been searching for a list of buildings and places in New York that should be protected. Not finding one, the society contemplated making one of its own. It would be under the leadership of the poetry-writing architect Edward Steese that this idea would come to life. Earlier in Steese's career, he had been the chief designer for the well-known architectural firm Carrere & Hastings. At this point, he was retired. Harmon Goldstone remembered him as "passionately interested in traditional architecture and conservation." Brendan Gill, the *New Yorker* writer and well-known preservationist, would later reminisce: "Ed Steese was a difficult, cranky man, as Chairman of

FIGURE 5.6   The architect Edward Steese was the driving force behind the all-important Index of Architecturally Notable Structures in New York City. This index guided the early work of the Landmarks Preservation Commission. Steese is seen here in 1969, six years after the index had been transformed into Alan Burnham's book *New York Landmarks*.

our Preservation Committee . . . he would insist that we do something. He hated glass box buildings . . . he called them megahyaline buildings. Megahyaline buildings were Ed Steese's enemy wherever he turned."[32]

At this point, the Municipal Art Society was in communication with the Society of Architectural Historians whose annual national meeting was coming to New York City in January of 1952. There was talk of the two organizations collaborating on an exhibit of "buildings and monuments of historic interest and architectural character, including those buildings that are considered worthy of preservation." Because such an exhibit would have to be based on something, it raised the still unaddressed need for a definitive list of buildings deemed worthy of preservation. The search for such a list turned up a preliminary one in the "hands of the Society of Architectural Historians" and also in the Avery Library. Steese reported these developments back to the society's board while continuing his dialogue with the Society of Architectural Historians. The Municipal Art Society's board was so intrigued by the possibility of collaborating with the architectural historians on the "preservation of historically important buildings of architectural value" that they immediately

decided to have the society become an institutional member of the Society of Architectural Historians.[33]

There is no doubt that the architectural historians' 1952 New York conference provided the impetus that jump-started serious work on the critically important inventory of significant New York buildings. If that opportunity had not presented itself, would the Municipal Art Society have been sufficiently motivated to create such a list? That we will never know, but we do know that the concrete reality of the impending national conference of the Society of Architectural Historians created the opportunity, energy, and urgency that turned talk to action. Edward Steese proposed the list project to the Municipal Art Society board, noting that the "directors have discussed at past meetings the need for a compilation of a list of buildings in New York that should be preserved." Unlike previous discussions, this one would lead to action.

Steese presented his plan. Working with the president of the New York Chapter of the Society for Architectural Historians, James Van Derpool, who would later become the first executive director of the New York Landmarks Preservation Commission, the two societies would collaborate to compile a list of New York City sites that should be preserved. The preliminary list was the one "compiled by Talbot Hamlin in 1941 of buildings of architectural value erected since 1865, some of which may have been demolished since." Hamlin agreed to update the list. It would then be circulated to the membership of both societies for additions and comments. With some luck, an exhibition and the list itself would greet the members of the Society of Architectural Historians on their arrival in New York on January 25, 1952.[34]

Fortuitously, the American Institute of Architects was having their convention in New York in June of 1952. In anticipation, they were also preparing a list of buildings to give to their attendees, but its focus was "only the more modern buildings." The Municipal Art Society and Society of Architectural Historians list could supplement that effort. Seeing the opportunity created by this confluence of events, the Municipal Art Society board "agreed on the value of the proposed list since it would advance the basic ideas that there are buildings in New York that should be saved" and they approved the "expenditure" for the activity.[35] If the society had fully appreciated what it was agreeing to undertake, it seems highly unlikely they would have approved such an ambitious, multi-year effort. However, with the list project being given the green light in September and facing the deadline of the arriving architectural historians

FIGURE 5.7 The fledging Landmarks Preservation Commission received a huge boost when James Grote Van Derpool became its first executive director in 1962. A former head of Avery Architectural Library at Columbia University and a past president of both the New York Chapter and the National Society of Architectural Historians, he brought unquestionable wisdom and expertise to the new agency. A board member of the American Scenic and Historic Preservation Society, he had important links to both the aesthetic and historic roots of the preservation movement.

the next January, Steese and his Committee on Historic Sites, Monuments and Structures were now in business and very much on the fast track.

The Municipal Art Society now had two committees advancing their preservation work: William H. Russell's Committee for Protection and Preservation of Important Buildings, primarily concerned with finding a legal mechanism for preservation (though also aware of the need to build a constituency for such a law) and Steese's Committee focusing on the development of the list of sites recommended for preservation. Both were equally committed to increasing the public's appreciation of the need to protect the city's landmarks. Because of their shared agendas, the boundary between the work of the two committees was not always clear. As a result, they cross-pollinated and reinforced each other's efforts. Those involved in compiling the list shared an awareness of the legal and political

hurdles that preservation faced and understood the role their effort could play in advancing the cause. As Talbot Hamlin, the birth father of the list noted, "It is only an aroused public opinion that can save New York's many worthwhile monuments."[36]

Curiously enough, there is no indication that either Steese or anyone else at the Municipal Art Society was aware of the Ely Jacques Kahn preservation initiative that had enlisted Talbot Hamlin in the Municipal Art Society's nascent efforts in 1941 to address the problem of preservation in New York City. Also missing is any recognition that Hamlin's preliminary list, the one serving as the basis for this new effort, had any ancestral link to that 1940s effort. It is conceivable that no one at the society remembered Kahn's preservation committee. (Why should the preservationists of the 1950s have had a greater awareness of their history than today's preservationists have of their own?) How much Hamlin's original list owes its existence to the society's 1941 preservation efforts or whether it was triggered by something else, remains a mystery. There is, however, no mystery when it comes to the singular role that Hamlin's early list played in shaping what would become *New York Landmarks: An Index of Architecturally Notable Structures in New York*, and ultimately, Alan Burnham's *New York Landmarks*.

Uncharacteristically, and no doubt the result of the impending January 1952 deadline, work on the list project moved forward with alacrity. Hamlin agreed to spruce up his original preliminary list and put it in a form that could be circulated for comment and additions. A system of codes explaining why buildings were on the list was created. Reasons for listing could include architectural importance, historical interest, the incorporation of sculpture in the structure, the use of stained glass, paintings, or mosaics.[37] What began life as Hamlin's 1940s "Old Buildings of Manhattan built in 1865 or earlier, and worthy of preservation" became a roster of "structures in Greater New York built prior to World War I and tentatively nominated for preservation as public monuments by civic, state, or national authority."[38]

By early November, Hamlin's preliminary roster of buildings with a questionnaire inviting additional nominations to the list was sent to the members of the Municipal Art Society and the Society for Architectural Historians. It was in this mailing that Edgar I. Williams, president of the Municipal Art Society, explained that this initiative was being prompted by such lost and threatened structures as Castle Clinton, the Rhinelander Houses, St. Nicholas' Church, and the Ritz-Carlton. He urged a "full and prompt response" to the questionnaire, noting that this will encourage the "cooperation of other artistic, civic and historical organizations, and it is our hope that thus a jointly supported list of monuments throughout the five boroughs will result."[39]

Williams closed his letter: "This is a major undertaking in its final scope and must be expedited to insure protection of venerated landmarks before any more of them are destroyed." The magnitude of the project was beginning to dawn. In a letter supporting a request to the Brunner Foundation for funds to help cover the direct costs of this volunteer effort, the partnership between the two societies and the importance of the project is stressed:

One of the basically important projects I would like to commend is that sponsored by the Municipal Art Society and the New York chapter of the Society of Architectural Historians. This is to build up a comprehensive list of significant New York buildings which are especially deserving of preservation. Our friend, the well-known historian Talbot Hamlin has well-begun the compilation and architect Edward Steese has agreed to spend the time needed to manage a general poll and the work incident to compiling the final descriptive lists. These will, of course, take a huge amount of work.[40]

As work moved forward, excitement grew at the Municipal Art Society. Its president reported that "the project is receiving popular interest and it is quite possible that strong arguments with public or private interests might lead to the preservation of buildings that are now unprotected."[41] Despite the short turnaround time given for responses to the questionnaire, twenty days at best, the preliminary version of the evolving list presented in January at the Society for Architectural Historians Conference had been shaped by "some 100 returns to the questionnaire, in many instances heavily annotated with valuable and detailed information about the structures nominated." Material relating to 296 buildings had been gathered and had been incorporated into a "Master Card Index" created by Steese's committee.[42] The result was "a far greater list of buildings than the original list furnished by Professor Hamlin."[43]

The gathering of the Society of Architectural Historians provided both the stimulus and partnership to generate the list and to create the initial opportunities to use it to begin to generate interest in preservation. The rich talent pool from which the Municipal Art Society could draw included not only those with the architectural knowledge to develop this list, but others with the abilities to use it to stimulate interest in preservation.[44] As a harbinger of things to come, when the Society of Architectural

Historians arrived in January, they were greeted by two exhibits generated from the preliminary list.[45]

Showing the synergy and coordination between the Municipal Art Society's two committees, it was William Hamilton Russell's Committee on Historic Sites, Monuments and Structures that partnered with the Museum of the City of New York to help prepare a "special panel show in the main lobby" of the Museum. "Thirty New York Buildings Most Worthy of Preservation" consisted of photographs of "some of the most interesting of the 'unprotected' buildings" on the list. Its purpose was to "enlist public support and understanding" of the society's preservation initiative. The public would be invited to vote for the buildings "they would like to see preserved." As briefly reported to the society's board, the results of voting for buildings in Manhattan were: "St. Marks in-the Bouwerie; Numbers 1 to 4 Gramercy Park and the Washington Square North houses receiving" the most votes "with various churches shown, the Plaza Hotel, Flatiron Building, MacDougal Alley, Wanamaker Store and others receiving a lesser number of votes."[46]

The second exhibit, in the Pine Room of the Architectural League, featured buildings of "historical and architectural note which are now fully protected." Of the two exhibits, Mr. Charles Magruder of *Progressive Architecture* "stated that he felt the activity had created considerable attention and awakened the interest of people who ordinarily would give the matter of the need for preservation of these buildings any thought."[47]

The list was beginning to provide the Municipal Art Society intellectual ammunition, and it knew how to use it. Plans were taking shape for the society's annual dinner and the focus would be historic preservation. In essence, the 1952 dinner turned out to be what the society had previously envisioned for its 1942 dinner before Pearl Harbor, and World War II had turned the society's attentions elsewhere. The guest speaker would be General Ulysses S. Grant III, president of the National Council for Historic Sites and Buildings. His topic: "The Preservation of Historically Important Buildings and Works of Art of New York City."[48] Further underscoring the theme of preservation, Albert Bard would receive the society's medal of honor at the dinner.

Ever savvy, the society would also use the occasion to unveil and present to General Grant a list of twenty buildings selected by the members of the Municipal Art Society and the Society of Architectural Historians from the list of three hundred nominated buildings as being of "national importance to be preserved at all cost." General Grant deemed the list "an important and essential part of the over-all list" of buildings in the nation

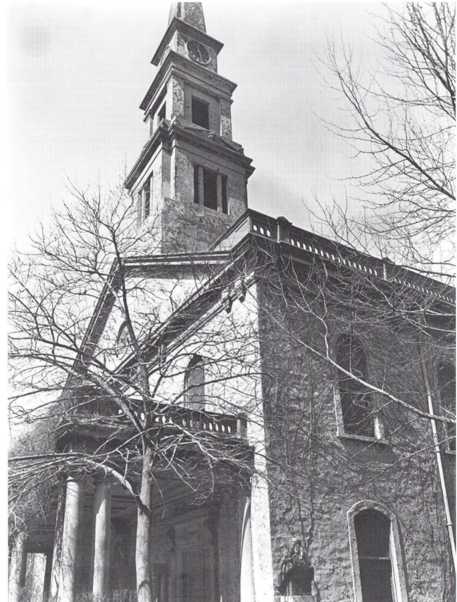

FIGURE 5.8 Captured here by photographer Berenice Abbott who documented so much of New York City, St. Mark's in-the-Bouwerie was long a landmark in the eyes of New Yorkers. In 1952 at a Municipal Art Society panel show held at the Museum of the City of New York titled, "Thirty New York Buildings Most Worthy of Preservation," the public was invited to vote on the buildings they most wanted to preserve. St. Mark's was among the sites receiving the most votes.

that should be preserved."[49] The list of twenty was published in the *Journal of the American Institute of Architects* that June. It was explained that the Municipal Art Society and Society of Architectural Historians were

dividing their roster of structures into three categories: "I—Structures of *national* importance which should be preserved at all costs; II—Structures of great *local* importance which should be preserved; III—Structures of importance which are designated for protection." It was further explained that famous New York buildings, of which other cities had better architectural examples, were omitted from the first category but would appear in the others.

The list of twenty was impressive:

- Bowne House, Flushing, c. 1655, Dutch
- Quaker Meeting House, Flushing, 1694–1695, Dutch Colonial
- Dyckman House, 18th century, Dutch
- St. Paul's Church, Eastchester, 1760, Colonial
- St. Paul's Chapel, Broadway and Vesey Street, McBean, 1764–1766, Georgian
- Erasmus Hall High School, Brooklyn, 1786, Dutch Colonial
- Flatbush Dutch Reformed Church, Brooklyn, 1793–1796, Dutch Colonial
- St. Mark's-in-the-Bouwerie, 1795, Georgian
- New York City Hall, McComb (Mangin & McComb), 1803–1812, Federal–French
- Bartow Manor, Bronx, R. O. Bolton, c. 1830, Greek Revival
- Trinity Church, Richard Upjohn, 1830–1840, Gothic Revival
- U.S. Sub-Treasury Building, Town & Davis, Ross & Frazee, 1834–1841, Greek Revival
- Church of the Ascension, Richard Upjohn, 1841, Gothic Revival
- Plymouth Church of the Pilgrims, Joseph C. Wells, 1847–1850, Classic Revival
- Litchfield House, Brooklyn, A. J. Davis, 1855, Italianate Villa
- Brooklyn Bridge, John A. & Washington A. Roebling, 1869–1884, Gothic Eclectic
- Sailors' Snug Harbor & Chapel, Richmond, Chapel by R.W. Gibson, 1831–1890, Classic Eclectic
- University Club, McKim, Mead & White, 1899, Renaissance Eclectic
- Morgan Library, McKim, Mead & White, 1905, Italian Renaissance
- Woolworth Building, Cass Gilbert, 1913, Gothic Eclectic[50]

In addition to devoting its 1952 annual dinner to the subject of preservation, the society's annual meeting, a separate event, was also largely devoted to the work of Edward Steese's committee. Though the society

FIGURE 5.9   At its 1952 annual dinner, the Municipal Art Society presented to
General Ulysses S. Grant III, the president of the National Council for Historic
Sites and Buildings, a list of twenty sites of "national importance to be preserved
at all cost." First on the list was the Bowne house in Flushing, Queens, seen
here being painted by Deputy Mayor Paul Screvane and Junior Hostesses as part
of a May 10, 1960 painting of the house's exterior in one day. Dating at least in
part to the 1660s and one of the oldest surviving structures in New York City,
Bowne is also a landmark of religious freedom.

was certainly generating interest and some degree of excitement in its
work, it was still on a very modest scale. At the society's annual dinner with Grant at the podium and Bard as the honoree, there were only

eighty-three members in attendance, eleven being guests, generating a deficit of $161. Though "the occasion of the dinner was deemed to have been most satisfactory," it was suggested that in the future the society might want to secure a "name speaker."[51] Despite his name, title, and importance in the rarified world of the national preservation movement, the cold reality was that even to members of the Municipal Art Society's own board, General Grant did not have the star power they sought.

Further putting these early preservation efforts in a larger context, although the society's dinner and the list of important buildings had generated some press attention, Steese noted "while anticipated articles in *Time*, *Life* and the *New York Times* Sunday Magazine Section have not appeared, the project is a long term one and publicity can keep."[52] The society was pleased later in the year with the "excellent publicity" the list received in a half-page photo story in the *New York World-Telegram and Sun*. [53]

If all this wasn't enough activity for 1952, in June, New York City hosted the national meeting of the American Institute of Architects. As promised, there was a publication created for the event, Huson Jackson's *A Guide to New York Architecture 1650–1952*. The guide was based on "selections and suggestions" from a variety of sources including the Municipal Art Society and the Society of Architectural Historians.[54]

The importance of this publication went beyond its value as an architectural guide for visiting architects. Several years later, it would help empower preservationists in Brooklyn Heights.

Cooperation between the civic organizations concerned with preservation continued to grow. There was an emerging sense of an actual preservation movement. In late 1953, both Steese and Williams were invited to join Talbot Hamlin's Committee on Preservation of Buildings of the NY Chapter of the American Institute of Architects. Not only did that forge an even closer link between the two groups, Hamlin was already closely tied to both the Society of Architectural Historians and the American Scenic and Historic Preservation Society.[55] In reporting on his invitation to serve on Hamlin's committee, Steese stressed "that there should be very close cooperation between the organizations interested in the preservation movement and that the Society's data and all materials collected will be made available to Mr. Hamlin's committee."[56] The use of the term "preservation movement" was a sign of something new. The heightened focus on preservation and the extensive energy devoted to it in the early years of the 1950s had begun to create the sense of a true movement.

The Municipal Art Society, through its two committees and in active partnership with other organizations, was advancing its preservation agenda. The committees, with their frequent board reports, had made preservation the "hot" issue at the society. The committees informed and fed off each other, strategically maximizing their accomplishments. The same can be said for the collaborating organizations. The individual activities and efforts of all the groups were magnified through their partnership. Singularly, these efforts would not have the same impact. The creation of the index of important buildings would have been particularly difficult for any one group to undertake in isolation.

As the Municipal Art Society became aware of more and more buildings through the ever evolving and expanding index project, it naturally found itself becoming involved in preservation advocacy on behalf of buildings facing immediate threats. Though seeking a systemic solution to the problem of landmark preservation, the society felt compelled to confront more site-specific skirmishes.

When the Chapel at Sailors' Snug Harbor was slated for demolition, a key structure of one of its Category 1 sites, the society reached out to the owner, the trustees of Sailors' Snug Harbor, for an explanation only to reluctantly concur with them that for financial and safety reasons, the chapel could not be saved.[57] The society also became concerned with the threat of a roadway that would "pass directly through" the Wyckoff House address, the "second oldest frame house in the United States and the oldest structure in New York State," which led Steese, as chair of the committee, to write the powers that be on its behalf.[58]

The Pieter Claesen Wyckoff House would survive to become the first landmark designated after the passage of New York's Landmarks Law.

As the society became more deeply involved in preservation struggles, it also began to discuss questions of preservation philosophy. It appreciated that in advancing a list of buildings recommended for preservation, it needed to assume a level of responsibility for such actions. Initially, there even was concern that by singling out buildings as worthy of preservation, the society might be putting itself in financial jeopardy. The fear was that a property owner might bring legal action against the society if its recommendation for "permanent preservation" of a site led owners to suffer a "pecuniary loss if . . . denied such possibility as alternation, demolition, or other conversion for profit." The issue was researched and though it was dismissed as a serious consideration, it did result in a legal disclaimer that would appear on the society's index of sites.[59]

The board discussions reflect some of the preservation issues beginning to face the society. In one such conversation, the opinion was "expressed that the society should be prepared to suggest a useful purpose for those

FIGURE 5.10 As the Index of Architecturally Notable Structures in New York City was being compiled by the Municipal Art Society and the Society of Architectural Historians, sites listed on it would become threatened. Early on, the Pieter Claesen Wyckoff House in Brooklyn, the oldest in New York State, was in danger of having a roadway run through it. The Municipal Art Society came to its defense and after the passage of the Landmarks Law, it would be designated as the first official city landmark.

buildings selected as worthy of preservation." Also articulated was the admonition advanced by Francis Keally in his headline-producing speech in Greenwich Village two years earlier: "No attempt should be made to save structures of questionable character. While there is need for practical judgment and persistence, the Society should devote its efforts to such structures as are outstanding in quality."[60]

The list project had stoked the fires burning for preservation at the Municipal Art Society. The positive response to the index and the multiple uses to which it had already been put ensured that it would be taken to the next level of refinement. When it was unveiled in January 1952 as "preliminary, acknowledged incomplete" it came with the disclaimer that it had not yet been "finally screened by our historical experts." It was a work in progress and the recipients were invited to participate by returning it with their comments and any data they could supply."[61] Though much

information had been gathered on the listed sites, with special thanks for this being given to Avery Library, the New-York Historical Society, and Mr. Bolton of the Century Association, in reality the research phase had only begun.[62] The work to refine the list would continue for years. Several times, it would be circulated for review, input, and revision. The sites would be divided into the three categories and again opinions would be solicited to inform that process. Photographs of the sites would be sought and site inspections would be conducted. Efforts would move forward to obtain photographs of the sites.[63]

In the fall of 1953, Steese was able to report the "completion of the Index of Architecturally Historic Buildings in New York City." The list was distributed to members of the Municipal Art Society and the New York Chapter of the Society of Architectural Historians. It was still not public and came with the precautionary note that the "list was not for public distribution at this time." Publicity seems to have been limited to the list of twenty Category 1 sites. In his memo accompanying the list, Municipal Art Society president William Hamilton Russell refers to it as the "final" index, perhaps partially reflecting wishful thinking considering all the energy and resources that had already been devoted to its creation. In reality, neither the index nor the work of the committee was anywhere near to being final. The list would enjoy many further revisions and editions. At this juncture, Steese passed on the leadership of the committee to Mrs. Agnes Gilchrist. Steese would remain involved and later return for another stint as the committee's chair. Gilchrist, a major figure both locally and nationally in the Society of Architectural Historians, would take the project to its next level. The list would continue to be an organic document being reissued at key moments in the years ahead.[64]

The specifics of the 1953 edition of the index offer some insights into the thinking among preservationists at that time in history. The introduction to the list makes it clear that the buildings were selected as worthy of preservation for their "architectural merit and importance, without consideration for any other historical associations." Not surprisingly, architectural and aesthetic concerns continued to dominate the Municipal Art Society's thinking though the list itself does include Castle Clinton, whose architecture we have already seen was only incidental compared to its historical importance.

The list as submitted featured 63 sites, 17 in Category 1 (National Importance), 65 in Category II (Local Importance) and 81 in Category III (worthy of protection). More than half of the sites (93) were in Manhattan, with Brooklyn garnering 30, Richmond (Staten Island) sporting 21, the Bronx having 11, and Queens registering 8. The dominant type of structure nominated was the dwelling house with churches and public buildings next. The earliest building dated from the 1640s and the latest from the 1910s. The nineteenth century dominated the index, capturing 65 percent of the listings.

Three historic neighborhoods appeared on the list. It is clear that they were important to those compiling the list, but it is also clear there was uncertainty on how to incorporate neighborhoods into the structure of the list. After presenting the three categories of individual structures with their 163 buildings, the index presented a list of buildings in Greenwich Village, Gramercy Park, and Brooklyn Heights.

This was followed by yet another list of buildings appearing in the unfortunately named "F" category for "buildings of importance for filing—for future consideration and reference." To dispel any misconception that these were "F" buildings in the grading sense, it is important to note that in the category were such treasures as the Dakota, "Wave Hill," the Pyne-Davidson block front (later the beneficiary of one of the great miracles in the history of preservation), along with a handful of important churches, which if not located in New York City would have been in the top category of most other cities' list of important sites.[65]

Thanks to the index and several other initiatives, preservation had made important strides forward from where it found itself at the dawn of the 1950s. Great effort had been invested in meeting the dual challenges of creating the legal mechanism for a system of protecting landmarks and building a constituency that would demand such protection. As a result, those who cared about preservation now had a much firmer grasp of what was at risk if their efforts failed. The index of buildings proposed for preservation was impressive, both in quality and quantity. There was a heightened awareness among civic organizations as to the need to do something and do it quickly. At this point, preservation was still building a base of support within the civic community. For the most part, preservation still only captured general press attention if there was a major controversy, as with Castle Clinton and the Rhinelander site. Though only baby steps had been taken by the civics to engage the broader public, there was a dawning sense that such efforts could bear fruit.

More sobering was an increased appreciation of the difficulty preservationists faced in devising a system to provide legal protection for the city's worthy buildings. Instead of providing an answer, the search for a legal basis for landmark protection had come up empty-handed. The civics could not find their way over or around the legal hurdles in their path, nor could they see "any possibility of help from the Federal nor City

Governments at this time in securing permanent preservation of these buildings of historical and architectural interest."[66] Despite this, a contemporary preservation movement was coming to life.

The civics had appropriately dismissed the notion that there would be any timely help from the Federal government. There seemed to be no help the executive or legislative branches of government could or would provide to solve the problem. Furthermore, the New York civics had no judicial action of their own pending and that might provide them the solution they needed. In the past, when faced with adversity, New York's preservationists looked to the federal government for salvation and found it. Though not looking there this time, Washington would come to their aid. It would come in the form of a Supreme Court decision. In that decision would be found constitutional ammunition to fortify their cause. Fortunately, this legal development would coincide with a legislative initiative driven by none other than Albert Bard. Fortunately, Bard was smart enough, stubborn enough, and still young enough to appreciate the significance of the court's action and to strategically utilize it to advance his own forward-looking proposal.

ENDNOTES

1. Wood, "Pioneers of Preservation: An Interview with the First Chairman of the Landmarks Preservation Commission, The Late Geoffrey Platt," 7.

2. Municipal Art Society Board Meeting Minutes, October 22, 1951 and March 24, 1952, Municipal Art Society of New York Records, Archives of American Art.

3. From the letterhead of the National Roadside Council, 1941, Albert S. Bard Papers, New York Public Library; Roger William Riis, "The Billboards Must Go—II," *Reader's Digest*, November 1938, 81–84; Bard's draft obituary for Lawton and Lawton's obituary in the *New York Herald-Tribune*, July 8, 1952, Albert S. Bard Papers, New York Public Library.

4. Catherine Gudis, *Buyways: Billboards, Automobiles, and the American Landscape* (New York: Routledge, 2004), 165.

5. Bard to Mrs. W. L. Lawton, August 28, 1951, Albert S. Bard Papers, New York Public Library. Bard's papers include frequent correspondence between the two. Toward the end of their working partnership (Lawton died in 1952), their letters reflect some of the tension between them. On the matter of tactics, she wrote Bard: "You seem quite unable to recognize the fact that your idea of strength and my idea are quite different. To me a statement of fact is much stronger if made in moderation. To you, the strong statement must bristle with innuendo and scathing epithets. . . . We have always differed on these matters and always would, so long as we tried to work together." Lawton to Bard, August 26, 1951, Albert S. Bard Papers, New York Public Library.

6. Riis, "The Billboards Must Go—II," 81.

7. The Albert S. Bard Papers at the New York Public Library include copies of many of his articles and suggest the vast national correspondence he had on this issue.

8. Wm. Boizelle to Mr. E.V.B. von Brandenberg, February 20, 1945, Albert S. Bard Papers, New York Public Library.

9. Bard's notes indicate that he shared at least one of the letters he received from Boizelle with Pierce T. Wetter. Remember that Bard was one of the attorneys representing Wetter, treasurer of the Greenwich Village Historical Society, in the fall of 1941 in Wetter's suit to protect Castle Clinton from Robert Moses. Also receiving copies were E.V.B. von Brandenburg and Owen Grundy of the *Villager*. Boizelle to Bard, February 6, 1946, Albert S. Bard Papers, New York Public Library.

10. Bard's first letter to Boizelle is dated January 16, 1946, almost a year after Boizelle's response to Brandenburg. There is no stated reason for the delay, though it does coincide with the first threat to the Rhinelander property, which was announced in December of 1944. By the fall of 1945, some preliminary demolition had begun on the site before the project was abandoned, only to be resurrected in 1950. Boizelle's responses to Bard are in his capacity as assistant city attorney and come on Law Department letterhead, unlike his response to Brandenburg, which lists him as secretary to the Vieux Carré Commission. Bard to Boizelle, January 16 and February 1, 1946, Boizelle to Bard, January 26 and February 6, 1946, Albert S. Bard Papers, New York Public Library.

11. In 1949, Bard was in correspondence with officials in Paris and received the pamphlet Loi D'Urbanisme du 15 Juin 1943, Albert S. Bard Papers, New York Public Library.

12. Sandra L. Tatman, "Francis Keally, Philadelphia Architects and Buildings," Philadelphia Architects and Buildings Project, www.philadelphiabuildings.org/pab/app/ar_display.cfm (accessed February 28, 2006).

13. "Law Urged to Save Landmarks of City," *New York Times*, March 8, 1950.

14. Ibid.

15. Letter from Hamlin on behalf of the New York Chapter of the Society of Architectural Historians regarding the April 26, 1950 hearing "dealing with the re-zoning of Washington Square and other small park areas," April 26, 1950, Talbot F. Hamlin Collection, Avery Architectural & Fine Arts Library, Columbia University.

16. Jane Taylor and Pamela Peterson to Bard, March 20, 1950, Albert S. Bard Papers, New York Public Library.

17. Owen Grundy to Francis Keally, April 17, 1950, Albert S. Bard Papers, New York Public Library.

18. Bard to National Council for Historic Sites and Buildings, March 15, 1951 and Frederick L. Rath to Bard, March 19, 1951, Albert S. Bard Papers, New York Public Library. Rath suggests Bard be in touch with the person heading up the movement for the Philadelphia ordinance, Leighton P. Stradley, president of the Germantown Historical Society.

19. Municipal Art Society Board Meeting Minutes, March 24, 1952, Municipal Art Society of New York Records, Archives of American Art. In the minutes Coudert is referenced as an assemblyman. At the time a Frederic Coudert, Jr. was serving in the United States House of Representatives; previously he was in the New York State Senate. He is likely the person referenced in the minutes.

20. Memo, January 28, 1952, Albert S. Bard Papers, New York Public Library.

21. Municipal Art Society of New York Board Meeting Minutes, April 28, 1952, Municipal Art Society of New York Records, Archives of American Art.

22. Edward Steese, memo, July 1952, Anthony C. Wood Archive.

23. Municipal Art Society Board Meeting Minutes, May 29, 1952 and October 26, 1953, Municipal Art Society of New York Records, Archives of American Art.

24. Ibid., January 25, 1954.

25. Bard discusses this in his correspondence with Boizelle, explaining the difficulties of obtaining a constitutional amendment in New York State. Albert S. Bard to William Boizelle, January 16 and February 1, 1946, Albert S. Bard Papers, New York Public Library.

26. Two good sources on this period are David Halberstam, *The Fifties* (New York: Ballantine, 1993) and James T. Patterson, *Grand Expectations: The United States, 1945–1974* (Oxford: Oxford University Press, 1996).

27. Halberstam, *The Fifties*, 507–508.

28. Ibid., 126–127.

29. Harmon Goldstone, "The Future of the Past," *Village Views* 4, no. 3 (Summer 1987): 11.

30. Wood, "An Interview with Harmon Goldstone." 17–18. This secretary, who "for some fifty years dedicated herself to the organization—with tact, enthusiasm, and efficiency, helping to steer the Society through the inevitable crises that occur when persons with imagination and zeal work for the public good," was Miss Irene V. Walsh. Nathalie Dana, *1892–1967 The Municipal Art Society: Seventy-five Years of Service to New York* (New York: Municipal Art Society).

31. Program for April 17, 1951 dinner honoring George McAneny and the invitation to February 28, 1949 testimonial dinner for George McAneny, Albert S. Bard Archive, New York Public Library; Gardner Osborn to Ulysses S. Grant III, December 11, 1952, Records of the National Trust for Historic Preservation, National Archives at College Park, Maryland. Bard's papers include the seating list for the City Club dinner. Also receiving an award at that time was Richard S. Childs.

32. "Edward Steese, 78; A Leader in Efforts to Save Landmarks," *New York Times*, August 10, 1981; Goldstone, "Future of the Past," 11; Brendan Gill, interview by Anthony C. Wood, July 2, 1984, 6.

33. Municipal Art Society Board Meeting Minutes, May 21, 1951, Municipal Art Society of New York Records, Archives of American Art.

34. Municipal Art Society Board Meeting Minutes, September 24, 1951, Municipal Art Society of New York Records, Archives of American Art.

35. Ibid.

36. Hamlin to Marie A. Doughney, 112 Grove Street, NYC, November 19, 1951, Talbot F. Hamlin Collection, Avery Architectural & Fine Arts Library, Columbia University.

37. Steese to Hamlin, September 30, 1951, Talbot F. Hamlin Collection, Avery Architectural & Fine Arts Library, Columbia University. By the time the questionnaire was circulated, two other categories of importance, "Ironwork" and "Community Picture," had been added.

38. Annotated by Talbot Hamlin, "Tentative List of Old Buildings of Manhattan Built in 1965 or Earlier, and Worthy of Preservation." November 14, 1942, Talbot F. Hamlin Collection, Avery Architectural & Fine Arts Library, Columbia University; "Questionnaire" circulated with Edgar I. Williams, president, letter "To All Members of the Municipal Art Society," November 1, 1951, Albert S. Bard Papers, New York Public Library.

39. Edgar I. Williams, president, letter "To All Members of the Municipal Art Society," November 1, 1951, Albert S. Bard Papers, New York Public Library.

40. Charles E. Peterson, president, Society of Architectural Historians, to L. Bancel LaFarge, chairman, Brunner Scholarship Committee, November 5, 1951, Talbot F. Hamlin Collection, Avery Architectural & Fine Arts Library, Columbia University.

■ ■ ■ ■ ■ ■ ■

41. Municipal Art Society Board Meeting Minutes, December 17, 1951, Municipal Art Society of New York Records, Archives of American Art.

42. "The Preservation of Historical and Architectural Monuments of Greater New York," introductory statement by Edward Steese, chairman, Committee on Historic Sites, Monuments, and Structures, and Edgar I. Williams, president, The Municipal Art Society, January 25, 1952, Anthony C. Wood Archive.

43. Municipal Art Society Board Meeting Minutes, December 17, 1951, Municipal Art Society of New York Records, Archives of American Art.

44. Among those with such talents was Charles Magruder, managing director of *Progressive Architecture* magazine, previously known as *Pencil Point*. See board meeting minutes of this period, Municipal Art Society of New York Records, Archives of American Art.

45. Their conference included a session "concerned with preservation and restoration of architectural monuments in the New York area as well as a bus tour of Lower Manhattan led by Talbot Hamlin. J. D. Forbes, "S.A.H. News: The 1952 Annual Meeting," *Journal of the Society of Architectural Historians* 11, no. 1 (March 1952): 31–32.

46. Municipal Art Society Board Meeting Minutes, February 25, 1952, Municipal Art Society of New York Records, Archives of American Art. A printed program for the 1952 Society of Architectural Historians Annual Meeting refers to the "Special Exhibition" by this name. James Grote Van Derpool Collection of Papers, Avery Architectural & Fine Arts Library, Columbia University.

47. Municipal Art Society Board Meeting Minutes, January 28, 1952, Municipal Art Society of New York Records, Archives of American Art; A printed program for the 1952 Society of Architectural Historians Annual Meeting refers to the exhibition at the League by the title: "Historically Important New York Buildings," James Grote Van Derpool Papers, Avery Architectural & Fine Arts Library, Columbia University.

48. "Maj. Gen. Grant to Speak," *New York Times*, April 9, 1952.

49. Municipal Art Society Board Meeting Minutes, April 28, 1952, Municipal Art Society of New York Records, Archives of American Art; "20 Buildings in City on Preservation List," *New York Times*, April 17, 1952.

50. "New York Architectural Heritage," *Journal of the AIA* 17 (June 1952): 261–262. This list of twenty would change over time.

51. Municipal Art Society Board Meeting Minutes, April 28, 1952, Municipal Art Society of New York Records, Archives of American Art.

52. Ibid., February 25, 1952.

53. Ibid., December 23, 1952; Bard clipped the November 29, 1952 article, "Listed for Saving by Art Society," *New York World-Telegram and Sun*, November 29, 1952, Albert S. Bard Papers, New York Public Library.

54. The involvement of the Municipal Art Society was such that the book includes the same legal disclaimer language that resulted from the Society's concern that its listing of buildings might negatively impact their value and expose the Society to legal suit. Huson Jackson, *A Guide to New York Architecture 1650–1952* (New York: Reinhold Publishing, 1952), Acknowledgment.

55. The Historic Buildings Committee of the AIA felt that on the entire matter of "Historic Buildings" there should be the "closest possible association" not only with the Municipal Art Society but the "American Scenic and Historic Preservation Society, the Museum of the City of New York and the New-York Historical Society." Minutes of the Historic Buildings Committee, New York Chapter, American Institute of Architects, January 19, 1954.

56. Municipal Art Society Board Meeting Minutes, December 31, 1953, Municipal Art Society of New York Records, Archives of American Art.

57. Ibid., September 22 and December 23, 1952.

58. Ibid., May 25 and October 26, 1953.

59. Ibid., November 26, 1951, January 28, 1952, and May 19, 1952. Though it seemed clear from the legal research that the society had no liability, in true "belt and suspender" fashion, it was decided that the publication of the list would contain the statement: "Neither the publisher nor the Municipal Art Society assumes any legal responsibility for appreciation or depreciation in the value of any of the premises listed herein by reason of their inclusion in this listing." When the list was formally published for the first time in 1957 it would be with such a disclaimer.

60. Ibid., September 22, 1952.

61. "The Preservation of Historical and Architectural Monuments of Greater New York," introductory statement by Edward Steese, chairman, Committee on Historic Sites, Monuments, and Structures, and Edgar I. Williams, president, The Municipal Art Society, January 25, 1952, Anthony C. Wood Archive.

62. Municipal Art Society Board Meeting Minutes, February 25, 1952, Municipal Art Society of New York Records, Archives of American Art.

63. Ibid.; Municipal Art Society Board Meeting Minutes, September 28, 1953, Municipal Art Society of New York Records, Archives of American Art.

64. Ibid.; William Hamilton Russell to Members of the Municipal Art Society and New York Chapter, Society of Architectural Historians, October 1953, Albert S. Bard Papers, New York Public Library.

65. Municipal Art Society, "Index of Architecturally Historic Structures in New York City," August 15, 1953, Albert S. Bard Papers, New York Public Library. Page 6 consists of an "Analysis by Mrs. J. M. Gilchrist Showing Distribution of Buildings."

66. Steese noted in his April 27, 1953 report to the Municipal Art Society's Board that he could not see "any possibility of help from the Federal nor City Governments at this time in securing permanent preservation of these buildings of historical and architectural interest." Municipal Art Society of New York Records, Archives of American Art.

■ ■ ■ ■ ■ ■ ■

SIX

THE BARD ACT

"To the Barricades: This seems to be the season for tearing down buildings. New York—which has been destroying and reconstructing itself at a rate unheard of even for this most changeable of cities—has now achieved a record in architectural inconstancy." With these words, *Harper's* magazine ushered in 1955. Confronting these same sobering realities, the sentiments of architect and Municipal Art Society president, L. Bancel LaFarge, were only slightly more encouraging: "While there appears that no constitutional legislation can be devised to preserve our privately owned architectural masterpieces, there still remains the great force of public opinion." Unrecognized by both *Harper's* and LaFarge was a blessing that had quietly been bestowed on America's municipalities during the 1954 Thanksgiving season by the United States Supreme Court. It would become a beacon of hope in the darkness of the mid-fifties and offer the vision of brighter days ahead for historic preservation.[1]

On November 22, 1954, the Supreme Court issued its decision in the now-landmark case of *Berman v. Parker*. The decision upheld the constitutionality of the District of Columbia's Redevelopment Act and, in so doing, affirmed the government's right to acquire private property—in this case, a department store—as part of its efforts to redevelop a blighted neighborhood. On its face, the decision did not appear to be a boon for historic preservation, but indeed it was. In upholding the District of Columbia's right to redevelop 712 Fourth Street, S.W., Washington, D.C., the court also affirmed the power of municipalities to prevent the redevelopment of thousands of other structures. The language of the court's decision, crafted by Justice William O. Douglas, helps us understand the wider implications of the ruling.

"It is within the power of the legislature to determine that the community should be beautiful as well as healthy, spacious as well as clean, well-balanced as well as carefully patrolled. . . . If those who govern the District of Columbia decide that the Nation's Capital should be beautiful as well as sanitary, there is nothing in the Fifth Amendment that stands in the way."[2] Albert Bard must have broken into a huge grin when he first read this decision. For decades, he had been asserting that aesthetics was an appropriate realm for governmental concern and that cities had the right to be beautiful. Since at least 1913 when he drafted the recommendations of the "Report on the Mayor's Billboard Advertising Commission," Bard had been waiting for the judiciary to catch up to his interpretation of the Constitution. It had taken over forty years, but it had finally happened. Bard now had the words of Justice Douglas to support his contention that under the police powers, government could protect the "patrimony of the people"!

The month after the Supreme Court decision, Bard turned eighty-eight years old. He was "tiny, very frail, and absolutely indomitable."[3] He was very deaf and would come to meetings with a hearing aid the size of a small suitcase. Frequently, it would emit a loud whistle and disrupt the entire proceedings.[4] Bard turned his humor on his own deafness, joking that if he didn't like what you were saying, he could just "tune you out."[5] By the late 1930s, Bard had already lost most of the sight in his right eye due to a cataract.[6] Even the ever-youthful-appearing Bard was showing signs of age. In the spring of 1954, Bard underwent a "serious operation." In personal terms, it would have been a tragedy had he not survived to witness the *Berman v. Parker* decision. For the history of preservation, it would have been a disaster. Fortunately, his operation was a success.[7]

FIGURE 6.1 This portrait of Albert S. Bard by Lewis Salomon for Chi Psi Fraternity was painted in 1953, the year before Bard drafted the act authorizing cities in New York State to adopt local landmark laws. Largely thanks to Bard's efforts, on April 2, 1956 the Act became law. Age 89 at the time, Bard would promote the utilization of the Act by New York City until his death on March 25, 1963.

After recovering from surgery, Bard resumed his decades-old routine, going to his office at 25 Broad Street in lower Manhattan five days a week. His weekend office visits had been reduced to the occasional Saturday. He commuted from East Orange, New Jersey via bus, train, and ferry. "I take a bus from East Orange to the Ampere railway station, take the Delaware Lackawanna & Western to the Hoboken ferry, get off the ferry at Barclay Street, and walk three-quarters of a mile. It takes an hour and a quarter but it's worth it not to have to live in New York."[8] Critical of what was happening to New York City and particularly distressed by modern architecture, he once quipped, "Now I go to the city to curse it."[9] Despite these and his other harsh words to the contrary, Bard's continued dedication to the civic life of New York is evidence that, in fact, he never gave up on New York City.

At eighty-eight, Albert Bard also retained his feisty spirit, commenting some years later on his advocacy strategy: "I have another theory which I have found works. Have a bad temper. Disguise it in some form of humor, but don't forget the bad temper. I have a bad temper."[10] Worn but not weary, disappointed but not disillusioned, vigorous in spirit and undaunted in behavior, Bard was still on his crusade for aesthetic regulation and had not sat idly by waiting for the Supreme Court to catch up with his initiatives. When it did, he recognized the importance of the Court's decision and, despite his age, retained the clarity of thought and chutzpah to take full advantage.

Bard was particularly immersed in the subject of aesthetic regulation in the early 1950s. Since 1953, he had been serving as a very involved volunteer legal counsel to the Joint Committee on Design Control of the New York Chapter of the American Institute of Architects and the New York Regional Chapter of the American Institute of Planners. The Joint Committee had been charged with several tasks. It was to collect and analyze existing laws in the U.S. and abroad dealing with the appearance of buildings and places, both private and public, and report on the mechanisms for "effectuating such regulations." Going beyond study, it was to recommend "new and better regulations and other procedures." Lastly, it was to make the results of its study available as a document that could be distributed to the field.[11] The committee's report appeared in May 1958.

The committee was chaired by Robert C. Weinberg and comprised of distinguished representatives from the two organizations. In Weinberg, the committee had an architect, planner, and preservationist as its leader.[12] Passionately devoted to Greenwich Village, serving on its Community Planning Board for a quarter of a century and an active member of both the

FIGURE 6.2 Largely forgotten today, Robert C. Weinberg was once a familiar name in New York City planning, architectural, and preservation circles. Like Bard, he shared a fascination with the subject of the role government could play in advancing beauty and harmony in community appearance. Over the decades, his work helped spur planning and preservation efforts that to this day continue to contribute to the beauty of the city he loved so deeply.

Washington Square Association and the Greenwich Village Association, Weinberg's dedication to New York City went beyond allegiance to any one neighborhood. Like Bard, he was involved with multiple civic organizations. Over a forty-year period, from the end of his Harvard days in 1931 through his death in 1974, he served on dozens of boards and committees.[13]

Perhaps best remembered through Robert Caro's account of his 1930s-era clash with Robert Moses, Weinberg was an astute observer of the civic scene. In writing, on the radio, in the classroom, and at the meeting table, he addressed planning, design, and preservation issues. He was not a disengaged observer of the urban scene, but rather a full-fledged participant engaged in both local and citywide issues—often working most effectively behind the scenes. Though possessing a keen intellect and sufficient personal resources to allow him time to pursue his extensive civic undertakings, these blessings were frequently undermined by his razor-edge personality. So dominant was this trait that the biographical essay accompanying the guide to his collected papers addresses it head on: "At times

Weinberg seemed unnecessarily abrasive."[14] Like Bard, Weinberg's tongue and pen could slice through others and regularly did. Unlike Bard, Weinberg wore his bad temper on his sleeve, not bothering to "disguise it in some form of humor."

Despite their thirty-six-year age difference, Weinberg and Bard's mutual respect and shared affiliations and interests made them well-suited colleagues.[15] Weinberg, like Bard, had a long history of being interested in "the aesthetic control of public and private buildings," and as early as 1941 was writing the Municipal Art Society president Ely Jacques Kahn suggesting that the society form a committee to "give some attention to the matter."[16]

Bard's reputation as a national expert on the subject of aesthetic regulation made him the logical choice for legal counsel to Weinberg's Joint Committee. As the committee began its work, it had to grapple with the issue of the legality of "planning for community appearance." Bard advised: "Proceed on the assumption that esthetic control of private property in the interest of the community is a legal exercise of the police power."[17] For years prior to *Berman v. Parker*, this had been Bard's firm conviction. It was this conviction, not the Supreme Court decision that initially prompted him to draft legislation to advance aesthetic controls. The *Berman v. Parker* decision proved Bard correct and affirmed the wisdom of Weinberg's committee to follow Bard's prescient advice.

We know that Bard was at work drafting his aesthetic legislation for New York State at the very same time the Supreme Court was considering *Berman v. Parker*. The case was argued before the Supreme Court on October 19, 1954. At the October 26, 1954 Municipal Art Society board meeting, Bard presented a resolution deploring "the absence of adequate consideration of the factor of appearance in the planning and zoning of the city." This generated a discussion on the "necessity for creating new legislation." At the next board meeting, on November 22, the same day that the *Berman v. Parker* decision was actually issued, "Mr. Bard stated that in connection with his report at the last meeting regarding special zoning treatment for special places, he has since drafted an amendment to the general city law to provide that that cities in the state shall have power to provide for special treatment for special cases as there seems to be some doubt as to how far they can go."[18]

All indications are that Bard was unaware of what was transpiring at the Supreme Court as he was drafting his amendment to the general law of New York State.[19] His words were on paper before he had read the inspiring ones written by Justice Douglas. This sequence of events is of

particular interest because of the singular importance of Bard's legislation. It would ultimately be passed in Albany, become known as the Bard Act, serve as a rallying cry for action, and provide the legal underpinning for New York City's own Landmarks Law.

Until now, it has been the accepted wisdom that it was *Berman v. Parker* that prompted the drafting of the Bard Act.[20] The evidence now available clearly indicates that the earliest draft version of Bard's legislation predates the court decision.[21] This means that instead of being inspired to put pen to paper because of the good news from the Supreme Court, Bard was just doing what he had been doing for decades, seeking a way to push the legal envelope by drafting legislation to advance aesthetic regulation. What was different this time was serendipity. Bard's effort coincided with the new language from the Supreme Court that gave his initiative a new legitimacy.

Current events in New York City in 1954 offer compelling clues to why Bard was at work drafting legislation.[22] Bard's draft of his amendment coincides with the breaking preservation story of the day: the threatened demolition of Grand Central Terminal. In September 1954, plans to replace the terminal were announced. We have Bard's own words to suggest the impact of this pending threat. In a letter dated November 24, 1954, his amendment already having been drafted, he writes to Lawson Purdy, a noted expert on municipal taxation: "At the City Club, the Citizen's Union, the Municipal Art Society and elsewhere we are now puzzling our noodles over a method of saving from destruction important buildings that are an asset to the city. The problem arises particularly because of the proposal of the New York Central Railroad to tear down Grand Central Station [sic] and build a skyscraper in its place." Bard closes this letter, which seeks advice on a possible tax solution to the problem of saving the terminal, with typical wry Bard commentary: "An autocratic government could quickly dispose of the whole problem by doing as it pleased. But other methods are necessary here."[23]

The threat to Grand Central Terminal gave a new urgency to Bard's efforts, and his work with the Weinberg Committee offered a particularly yeasty environment to nurture them. At the Joint Committee's meeting of November 18, 1954, some four days before the Supreme Court decision, Bard presented a draft of his proposed legislation. After discussion and with some minor modifications, Weinberg was asked to "pass the proposal on to the proper authorities so as to get it 'into the hopper' for the coming session of the State Legislature."[24] In December, Weinberg reported on "the correspondence between Mr. Bard, himself, and Senator Mitchell regarding introduction in the State Legislature of Mr. Bard's

FIGURE 6.3 Threats to Grand Central Terminal have time and again prodded New Yorkers to take action to advance the cause of historic preservation. A threat to the station in 1954 was one of the factors that motivated Albert S. Bard to draft the Bard Act. Fortunately, unlike Pennsylvania Station, it would survive until it could be afforded the protection of the Landmarks Law.

clause for the General Cities Law providing a basis for consideration of aesthetic aspects, etc. This will be followed up as the legislature meets the early part of the new year."[25] Bard not only drafted his legislation prior to the Supreme Court decision, but it was now on its way to being introduced in Albany.

The Supreme Court's ruling did create a more hospitable climate for advancing the Bard Act. Now it would no longer be just Albert Bard asserting that aesthetics was an appropriate realm for legislative authority. Bard credited Weinberg for initially bringing the *Berman v. Parker* decision to his attention. This further underscores the important link between Bard's efforts and the work of the Joint Committees.[26] When Bard studied

the Court's decision, he quickly realized its importance and immediately began to spread the news of this change in judicial thinking. At the December 1954 Municipal Art Society board meeting, he reported "the encouraging recent decision of the United States Supreme Court," noting that the decision "emphasizes the right of a community to regulate private property upon the basis of community beauty and appearance, regardless of the more usual factors of health, safety, morals and public convenience. The case is likely to become a leading case in the law of planning and on the controversial matter of public control of private property with respect to exterior appearance."[27] Time has proven Bard's assessment correct.

In order for the Supreme Court's decision to help change the political landscape, its existence needed to be known and its importance recognized. Bard set to work to bring the decision, and his interpretation of its significance, to both national and local audiences.[28] In preparation for writing about the decision, Bard sought to learn more about it. In vintage Bard fashion, he was soon in correspondence with the lawyers who argued the case before the Supreme Court.[29]

In promoting the Court's decision, Bard stressed its importance, but was also careful not to oversell it. He noted that "the decision itself does not expressly state that esthetic considerations alone—the making of a pleasanter and more sightly city—will support such legislation, nor that esthetic considerations by themselves will support the regulation of land uses, but the language of the opinion by Mr. Justice Douglas may be claimed to go so far as to support such a case."[30] Bard did see in the language of Justice Douglas a battle cry for aesthetic regulation and it was that language that made this case, in Bard's words, "a leading case on esthetics and the police power." For Bard, the Court's decision had not gone far enough, but it had helped close "the gap" between where the law was and where it should be.[31] Fortunately, the decision and the words of Justice Douglas went far enough to strengthen the case for the pending Bard Act.

The timing of the *Berman v. Parker* decision was indeed fortuitous for Albert Bard's efforts. As discussed at that December 1954 meeting of Weinberg's Joint Committee, Bard's proposed amendment to the General City Laws of the State of New York was to be introduced in January of 1955. On January 18, Bard received a telegram from the Honorable MacNeil Mitchell informing him that he introduced the legislation in the New York State Senate and was now at work seeking a sponsor in the Assembly.[32] The bill, Int. 708, would amend the general city law by inserting the following new section:

■ ■ ■ ■ ■ ■ ■ ■

To provide, for places, buildings, structures, works of art, and other objects having a special character or special historical or aesthetic interest or value, special conditions or regulations for their protection, enhancement, perpetuation or use, including appropriate control of the use or appearance of neighboring private property within public view, or both. In any such instance such measures, if adopted in the exercise of the police power, shall be reasonable and appropriate to the purpose, or if constituting a taking of private property shall provide for due compensation, which may include the limitation or remission of taxes.[33]

This, with a minor change in one phrase, would be the text of the Bard Act as passed and signed into law.[34]

Successful legislation often takes on the name of its legislative sponsors, but in this instance, that would not be the case. The fact that this law has come to be known as the Bard Act is more a testimony to Bard's close association with it than any negative reflection on its lead sponsor, MacNeil Mitchell.[35] With Greenwich Village in his district, Mitchell was certainly well known to a Village activist like Weinberg, so approaching him to introduce Bard's legislation would have been the natural thing to do. Mitchell had already supported earlier efforts to protect the Village. Senator Mitchell was also well known to the civic community. As a reflection of how he was perceived, at the Citizens Union fiftieth anniversary dinner, he was seated at the same table as Albert Bard.[36] As chair of the Senate Committee on Affairs of the City of New York and of the Joint Legislative Committee on Housing and Multiple Dwellings, he was an important player and well positioned to be the champion for Bard's proposed legislation.

Bard is not only the uncontested author of the Bard Act; he is truly its father.[37] Though it was nurtured by his involvement with Weinberg's Joint Committee, it was the product of his life's work. Its roots were in Bard's 1913 proposed amendment to the New York State Constitution. He indicated that he wrote the bill for the Citizens Union and the Fine Arts Federation. In reality, it was at

To Be Honored

Senator MacNeil Mitchell

FIGURE 6.4 Time and again, State Senator MacNeil Mitchell would help advance the cause of preservation in the halls of government in Albany. From 1947 to 1964, he represented State Assembly District 20, which included such landmark-rich territory as Greenwich Village and much of midtown Manhattan and the Upper East Side. Mitchell introduced and succeeded in securing the passage of the Bard Act in 1956 and would later help deliver the legislation needed to save Carnegie Hall.

his own behest that Bard wrote the bill for New York State. If the Citizens Union or the Fine Arts Federation had in some way formally requested him to draft such legislation, such a request would likely have been the result of Bard's own instigation. After all, for years he had been an officer and leader of both organizations.

Bard reached out to others to build support for the legislation. At its February 28, 1955 board meeting, the Municipal Art Society agreed to support the bill and to use its newsletter to ask all its members to do the same. Knowing that it would bolster his request for support, Bard provided the society enough copies of his *American City* article on *Berman v. Parker* so it could be mailed to the members with their issue of the society's newsletter.[38]

Thanks to these and other efforts, the bill passed both the New York State Assembly and Senate.[39] Among those urging the governor to sign the bill was Robert C. Weinberg, writing on behalf of the New York Chapter of the American Institute of Architects Civic Design Committee. He noted that "when this bill becomes law it will be possible for New York City's Planning Commission to introduce zoning regulations directed towards this objective."[40] Unfortunately, the bill did not fare as well with the governor as it had done in the legislature. New York's Governor Averell Harriman vetoed it. He did so citing the bill's "great uncertainty as to (1) the extent to which municipalities can act to effectuate its purposes, (2) the manner in which it is to be carried out, and (3) the geographic scope and bounds which may be embraced in any resultant program."[41]

Bard wrote of this setback, "I have always felt that the Governor (or whoever was advising him) completely misunderstood the bill and its purpose. There was no hearing before the Governor on the bill."[42] As to the substance of the governor's concerns, Bard felt he totally missed the point. The legislation was "purposely general and open in phraseology in order to enable municipalities to pass their own local legislation in whichever way they want it." Bard continued to believe that Harriman had been misadvised.[43] The good news was that despite his veto, the governor felt the purpose of the bill was "laudable" and welcomed its revision and reintroduction in the next session of the Legislature.[44]

What was another year to a man who had already devoted so much of his life to this cause? When that man was eighty-eight, it could have meant everything. By March 8, 1956, the Mitchell Bill, as Bard respectfully called it, had again passed both houses in Albany and was back before the governor.[45] It had not been substantially changed and remained as purposefully general as Bard intended. It came with impressive backing.

■ ■ ■ ■ ■ ■ ■ ■

Along with a Memorandum of Support from the Municipal Art Society, authored "Of counsel" by Bard, were letters of support from Robert F. Wagner, mayor of the City of New York, noting support for the bill from the New York City Art Commission, and from Frederick L. Rath, Jr., of the National Trust for Historic Preservation (who included with his letter Justice Douglas' opinion in *Berman v. Parker*). Also of note was the support of the American Scenic and Historic Preservation Society and, of course, the Citizens Union.

Perhaps of greatest importance were communications from the State of New York Department of Law, under the signature of Jacob K. Javits, attorney general, finding "no legal objection" to the bill and a letter from the state comptroller, Arthur Levitt, "offering no objection to the bill."[46] Levitt's letter also comments favorably on the slight modification to the bill's language since previously vetoed by the governor.[47] The only recorded opposition to the bill came from the Architects Council of New York City: "We have considerable fear that many abuses and inequities could arise, and that under this amendment, great, unwarranted hardships could be foisted on property owners."[48]

On April 2, 1956, with the approval of the governor and with some very impressive support, Mitchell's bill, soon to be referred to as the Bard Act, became law.[49] Bard gave public credit for the passage of Chapter 216 of the Laws of New York, 1956 to "the persistent efforts of Senator MacNeil Mitchell of New York City and the Citizens Union of New York."[50] Bard also went out of his way to make sure the Municipal Art Society credited Mitchell, introducing a motion to that effect after the passage of the law.[51] Despite these efforts, it was well known that Bard deserved the lion's share of credit for the legislation.[52]

The importance of the Bard Act is impossible to overstate. Years later, Harmon Goldstone, president of the Municipal Art Society from 1960 to 1962 and the second chair of the Landmarks Preservation Commission, would marvel at the passage of the Bard Act: "How he did this, I don't know, but it was done skillfully and politically, so deftly that nobody noticed it." As to its significance, Goldstone said, "Now, that little Bard Law was crucial, because when we wanted to do something official and legal in New York, we had an enabling anchor in Albany. Without that it would have been the cart before the horse. So I bless Albert Bard for many things, but I bless him for getting that written into the state enabling act."[53]

From today's vantage point, it seems surprising that a bill of this significance attracted such modest opposition and was passed with such little fanfare. When one thinks of the public controversy over site-specific

■ ■ ■ ■ ■ ■ ■ ■

preservation battles, such as Castle Clinton, it is a surprise that a law that would ultimately protect thousands of buildings was a nonstory. There are several possible explanations for this. The campaign on behalf of the bill was not a very public one. Support for it came from the civic organizations and their supporters. In addition, the bill's language was both intentionally vague and rather understated, leaving much to the reader's imagination.

The Bard Act was not exactly stealth legislation, but few really grasped its full possibilities. Even if they had, the nine-year gap between the Bard Act's passage and the passage of the New York City Landmarks Law proves that having enabling legislation and using it are two very different things. Syracuse would go forward to utilize the Bard Act before New York City did. Perhaps the threat the act posed to real estate interests seemed too distant and theoretical to have stirred up a defensive response at the time it was introduced. Then again, those interests may have been focused elsewhere.

From his years of experience, Bard knew that the only way the new legislation would actually lead to action in New York City was if people knew about it. He went to work publicizing the new bill. In addition to writing about it, he personally brought it to the attention of numerous civic organizations. By the fall of 1956, in response to the passage of Chapter 216, the Municipal Art Society had formed a subcommittee, which included Bard and Weinberg, "to consider ways and means of having such legislation implemented with respect to New York City."[54] In fact, anticipation of the bill had been so keen that even when it had been vetoed the year before, the Civic Design Committee of the American Institute of Architects had gone ahead and appointed a subcommittee to approach the City Planning Commission about drafting a local law that would then be ready when, and if, the bill was reintroduced and passed.[55]

The reason for such eagerness is found in the ever-escalating number of threats to prominent and beloved New York City buildings. In the mid-1950s, Grand Central Terminal was in immediate peril. It was not alone. Storm clouds were gathering over Pennsylvania Station, Carnegie Hall, and the Jefferson Market Courthouse. When William Zeckendorf's plans to replace Grand Central Terminal became public in 1954, the threat not only encouraged Bard to draft his amendment, but also caused a storm in architectural circles. *Architectural Forum* published an open letter to the railroads involved asking them to save the Grand Central Concourse. The letter was endorsed by 220 people in the architectural and planning professions, including Philip Johnson, Ely Jacques Kahn, Harmon Goldstone, Talbot Hamlin, and Vincent Scully.[56]

■ ■ ■ ■ ■ ■ ■

Of Grand Central's concourse, *Architectural Forum* wrote that it is "probably the finest big room in New York. It belongs in fact to the nation." Responding to *Architectural Forum*'s plea, the Municipal Art Society decided to take action to publicize the cause.[57] Not dissuaded by any of this, several different schemes to replace the terminal would be advanced over the next few years with perhaps the most daring being I. M. Pei's Hyperboloid.[58] *Harper's* lamented the general state of affairs: "And now the boys with the sledge hammers and crowbars have a new target; the next proposal is to tear down Grand Central Station, on the grounds that it is uneconomical."[59]

There were other indications that "the boys with the sledge hammers" were going to have a bright future. In 1955, yet another Zeckendorf vision was unveiled. The site of Pennsylvania Station would become home of the Palace of Progress, the "world's largest building" and a "permanent World's Fair and Merchandise Mart." As the media would report, Mr. Zeckendorf, "a fabulous figure in real estate circles because of the magnitude of his deals," added more luster to the deal by enlisting "as his lieutenant to help realize his vision the impresario Billy Rose, who, with Maj. Gen. William J. Donovan, will go on the road in a world tour to enlist interest, exhibitors and tenants."[60] Though the word demolition was not used in the major press accounts of the new project, it was obvious that demolition was required to realize the scheme. The plan would never become a reality, being abandoned in January of 1956 when Zeckendorf announced an even more ambitious project for the site.[61]

If these threats to New York City's two great train stations were not enough, New York also was facing the possible loss of Carnegie Hall. Rumors about its future led to the formation of the Committee to Save Carnegie Hall in the spring of 1955. That summer, Edward Steese, writing "not only as a lover of fine music . . . but also on account of [his] interest in preserving New York's architecture and cultural landmarks," warned that "to tear down Carnegie Hall would be a loss not only to the city and the nation but, on account of its renown, to the world." The rumors were proven true with the announcement of the sale of the hall for replacement by an office tower.[62] As was the case with Grand Central Terminal and Pennsylvania Station, for reasons other than preservation, the initial redevelopment plan would not come to fruition. Carnegie Hall's future, like that of the stations, remained uncertain.

Not commanding enormous press attention nor threatened by such a grandiose new vision was Jefferson Market Courthouse. Warning signs about its future appeared in "The Talk of the Town" in the *New Yorker* of 1956: "This is a city notoriously careless of its possessions. The latest precious

FIGURE 6.5 The grand dreams of real estate mogul William Zeckendorf, president of Webb & Knapp, scared preservationists into action in the mid-1950s. His 1954 proposal to replace Grand Central Terminal helped spur Bard to draft his legislation. Pictured here in a 1955 photograph, Zeckendorf (in the center speaking into the microphone with Billy Rose at left) discusses his vision for replacing Pennsylvania Station with the "Palace of Progress."

landmark to be threatened with demolition is the Jefferson Market Court-house, at Sixth Avenue and West Tenth Street—a dingy, invincibly romantic confection of Philadelphia pressed brick, Ohio stone, and dainty stained glass, leaping skyward in a cluster of gables, chimneys, turrets, and towers."[63] Having outlived its usefulness as a Courthouse, it was underutilized as a local Civil Defense headquarters and its future was at best uncertain. In short order, its preservation would become a Greenwich Village cause célèbre. The uncertain fate of all these beloved buildings would continue to influence events, leading to the passage of the Landmarks Law.

As the focus intensified on the fate of many of the city's architectural treasures, the Municipal Art Society pursued with new vigor and creativity its efforts to build a constituency for historic preservation. These efforts would benefit greatly from changes beginning to take place within the society itself. Of the society at this time, Harmon Goldstone remembered, "I hate to say it was moribund, but it was certainly ossified." The society was "this bunch of idealistic old fogies." Goldstone credits Mrs. Richard Henry Dana with helping bring some new young faces onto the society's board. She helped recruit Goldstone and Bancel LaFarge, both future society presidents, as well as the likes of Geoffrey Platt and William Jayme.[64] In 1952, with the death of George McAneny, the society lost a great friend. In 1954, his daughter, Ruth McAneny Loud, offered the society her assistance, which was eagerly accepted. She would become a prominent figure in the society's rejuvenation. Coming aboard at that time was future society president, the architect Giorgio Cavaglieri.[65] Brendan Gill gives considerable credit to the attorney Whitney North Seymour Sr., for his efforts to revive the society. Seymour particularly appreciated the need to build membership to increase the appearance of the organization having some real power.[66]

The new blood, mixing with the old, advanced the society's efforts to build interest in the cause of preservation. The society was still painfully aware of the pressing need to build a constituency for preservation. Whatever it may not have been in those days, it was certainly "a vehicle to put on a show."[67] Having enjoyed the success of its 1952 exhibits, the society was game for more. In 1953, Edward Steese, a member of the University Club, had encouraged a small exhibit on buildings based on selections from the club's library. That experience had been so positive that the University Club allocated funds to do a much larger exhibit to be "based on the buildings on the Society's index of structures to be preserved." The initial plans for the exhibit called for four groups of buildings from the list. "Buildings of national importance, shown under national colors. Buildings of local importance, under the city colors. Buildings that have been demolished, draped in black. Buildings that are threatened, draped in red." The exhibit would feature models, tracings, photographs, original drawings, and renderings.[68] Curating the exhibit was Henry Hope Reed, a man who would influence the fields of architecture and preservation for years to come.

Titled "Monuments of Manhattan: An Exhibition of Great Buildings in New York City, 1800–1918," the exhibit ran from January 1 to March 15, 1955.[69] Under the joint sponsorship of the University Club and the

Municipal Art Society, it filled three walls of the Club's College Hall. Not satisfied to rely only on materials from museums and historical collections, Henry Hope Reed tracked down original materials that had not been seen in years. He tells the story of finding items belonging to the architect George Brown in sealed storage barrels that had been sitting in Brown's great-grandson's barn in Cold Spring Harbor for decades.[70]

The exhibit included a wide range of treasures, from watercolor drawings of City Hall and the United States Subtreasury building (Federal Hall) by Alexander Jackson Davis to a plaster model of the Morgan Library lent by the firm of McKim, Mead & White. There were pencil drawings of Trinity Church by Richard Upjohn and of the base of the Statue of Liberty by Richard Morris Hunt. Bronzes by Augustus Saint-Gaudens joined sketches, watercolor drawings, and elevations, bringing New York's architectural treasures to life.[71] Visitors were thrilled. The club's location gave luster to the exhibit, though the restrictions of it being a private club severely limited access. Special arrangements were made for at least some outside groups to view it. So successful was the exhibit that the society discussed the possibility of touring it to other locations in Manhattan and Brooklyn that would be open to the general public. The society also explored the possibility of mounting other exhibits. At least one future exhibit would focus on classical architecture in Brooklyn.[72]

"Monuments of Manhattan" had the intended impact. Timing could not have been better to pique interest. As the newspaper headlines reported the futuristic plans for Grand Central Terminal and Pennsylvania Station, in the exhibit New Yorkers could see what architectural treasures were about to be lost. A watercolor of the interior of Pennsylvania Station and the original Whitney Warren sketch of the south face of Grand Central Terminal were on display, ominously keeping company with longitudinal sections of architect George B. Post's demolished mansion built for Cornelius Vanderbilt II. The message was clear, powerful, and poignant.

As Goldstone noted, "people were very interested. They opened their eyes. This was something they hadn't realized—you took these things for granted you see. They were always there, old New York. Only a handful of people were interested. I don't know who invented the term, but it was certainly applicable: this was 'the lunatic fringe.' A few perfectly nice, harmless people, amusing themselves with old New York. And they weren't doing any harm."[73] Preservation would not instantly grow from the concern of this "lunatic fringe" to a popular public cause, but the exhibit did take the preservation message out of the boardrooms of a few civic organizations, effectively bringing it closer to the public.

■ ■ ■ ■ ■ ■ ■

The society was able to maximize the message of the exhibit. At its membership meeting held in the University Club during the run of the show, it presented its certificate of merit to Mr. John A. Kouwenhoven for his *Columbia Historical Portrait of New York*, published in 1953 on the "three-hundredth anniversary of the establishment of the first municipal government in what is now the City of New York."[74] Honoring this publication in the context of the exhibition only helped reinforce the preservation message.

Inspired by and including many of the buildings listed in the society's index of buildings worthy of preservation, "Monuments of Manhattan" was a wonderful vehicle for publicizing the index. Since the exhibition focused on the architecture of Manhattan, the society distributed a version of its index—"Buildings in Manhattan Built Before World War I Designated as Worthy of Protection"—to attendees. Some one thousand copies were distributed.[75] The index came with a foreword by society president L. Bancel LaFarge, partially quoted at the beginning of this chapter. Conveying the urgency of the society's work, he pointed out to exhibit visitors that "of over two hundred and fifty buildings named" in the society's inventory, "over twenty percent were torn down or drastically altered between the inception and the completion of the listing." Considering that the list project began in late 1951 these losses are staggering.[76]

The society knew it had to bring its message to the broader public. In 1955, it turned to the airwaves to do just that. Russell Lynes—managing editor of *Harper's*, "critic, lecturer, pundit," author of the *Tastemakers*, and "inventor of 'Highbrow, Middlebrow, Lowbrow' a now-famous satire on American cultural preferences"—was recruited to the society by Mr. William Jayme for this purpose.[77] The forum was to be a fifteen-minute program with Russell Lynes as moderator and featuring Agnes Gilchrist as historian. Lynes had specifically joined the board of the society because of his interest in promoting the radio broadcasts.[78]

The funding prospectus for the program went for the jugular. "One monument to America's past is demolished every week of the year, and if it often seems to the New Yorker that most of this demolition goes on in his backyard, it is because the five boroughs have been unusually unsuccessful in preserving buildings of public interest." It goes on to recite the losses of the "first marble mansion in New York," the John Taylor Johnston site and the Rhinelander Mansion, it invokes the name of the Collegiate Church of St. Nicholas, and suggests that "even bulk is no guarantee of permanence, as the patrons of the Ritz (and of Grand Central Station) recently came to learn." Declaring its goal for the radio program "to make these historic sites in New York City more widely recognized and appreciated," the society outlined a first season of twenty-six broadcasts with guest panelists ranging from Bennett Cerf, president of Random House, talking about the Henry Villard Houses where its offices were located, to Mrs. Robert Wagner on the subject of Gracie Mansion. Among the other sites to be featured were the Bowne House, Central Synagogue, Sailors' Snug Harbor, Jefferson Market Courthouse, and Grant's Tomb. The society board loved the concept. It was serious in its desire to reach a broader public.[79]

It has been assumed that the radio shows were actually taped and aired. However, it has not been possible to find any documentation to support that belief. It now seems doubtful that the series, at least as it was fully envisioned, ever materialized. Getting Russell Lynes involved did prove to be a wise move; years later, he would serve on the Landmarks Preservation Commission.[80]

In addition to its efforts to bring preservation to the airwaves, the society decided to take it to the streets. There preservation would be warmly greeted and have a profound impact. As captured in the Municipal Art Society minutes of September 26, 1956, the idea emerged innocently enough from a suggestion by Mrs. Gilchrist that the society offer a walking tour from Chelsea to Washington Square "patterned on the tour arranged some time ago by Mr. Hamlin." As was the society's way of doing business, a committee was soon formed. Key among its members was Henry Hope Reed, the acknowledged father of the New York architectural walking tour.[81] The committee itself provided the $15 cost to launch the first tour. Originally, the tours would be offered to members of the Municipal Art Society and the Society of Architectural Historians. Despite the wintry weather, on April 8, 1956, forty of the ninety who registered for the first tour showed up. Joining Reed on that inaugural tour were Whitney North Seymour "in his bowler," Giorgio Cavaglieri, Brendan Gill, and Harmon Goldstone. Interest was so great that the tour was offered again later that month. [82]

The idea caught on. A "Talk of the Town" piece in that fall's *New Yorker* regaled readers with an account of the society's second walking tour, this one from Federal Hall to Battery Park. Over a hundred people came and were divided between four tour guides. The author of the article, Brendan Gill, who had joined the society that June (having been sponsored by Edward Steese), was captivated by Henry Hope Reed, "who, though comparatively young in years and, unlike most members of

FIGURE 6.6 Little did they know it as they braved the wind and snow on April 8, 1956, but this intrepid band of New Yorkers was making history as they went on the Municipal Art Society's first architectural walking tour. An account of this most curious site with this photograph appeared in the next day's *New York Times*. In 2006, this original tour was re-created to celebrate the fiftieth anniversary of the birth of a beloved New York institution: the architectural walking tour.

his profession, beardless, proved a veritable patriarch in his architectural convictions." Reed waxed eloquently on the virtues of the Wall Street District: "Only the Acropolis and the Campidoglio in Rome deserve to

be compared to it." Reed not only helped people see these New York treasures hidden in front of their eyes, but awakened people to the need for their salvation. "In light of the destruction now being carried out in this city in the name of 'modern' one ought to feel something approaching reverence for these examples of the American Renaissance." Gill noted that at the utterance of the word "modern," "Mr. Reed's voice shook with eloquent contempt." Because of their success, the tours soon outgrew the society's capacity to manage them, and they were offered under the auspices of the Museum of the City of New York.[83]

Today, architectural walking tours are an established part of New York life with a seemingly endless variety of places to visit and themes to explore. It is hard to imagine they ever were innovative, but indeed they were when pioneered by the Municipal Art Society. The tours became a powerful advocacy tool to reach the public. The tours brought the message of preservation face-to-face with real New Yorkers. Decades after those first tours, Henry Hope Reed clearly articulated the importance of the medium: "The walking tour is the key device of introducing the general public—you could go on and on about preservation on paper, and it didn't mean a damn thing. But if you walked with New Yorkers and showed them buildings. . ."[84] Seeing was believing.

Tours were also accessible to the general public. One didn't have to belong to a club to participate. In those days, there was no Urban Center, no Neighborhood Preservation Center, and no Center for Architecture. There were few opportunities for the civics to make meaningful contact with the public. The walking tour was a powerful opportunity to persuade and to educate. As Brendan Gill wrote in the *New Yorker*, "For on Wall Street too, we saw as if for the first time buildings we had looked at all our life." Person by person, tour by tour, New Yorkers were learning to see old New York with new eyes and they liked what they saw. They were also exposed to the infectious enthusiasm of the tour guides, veritable pied pipers for historic preservation.[85]

Reflecting on the impact of Henry Hope Reed's walking tours, Harmon Goldstone commented, "Henry's tours had great impact in building up a constituency for preservation. We owe a great deal to him and his colleagues. He encouraged a groundswell of public opinion, by showing people what they had—the city's great architectural heritage—and how fast they were losing it. You know, when you propose something to politicians they want to know: who supports it? Where's the constituency? Well, when the Landmarks Law was proposed in the early 1960s, it passed unanimously in the City Council, because people were aware and enthusiastic about preservation, largely thanks to Henry's activities."[86]

Another way to highlight the city's architectural treasures hidden in plain view was to put a plaque on them. In February 1955, while some New Yorkers were viewing "Monuments of Manhattan" at the University Club, the Municipal Art Society began its discussions of the idea that would ultimately become the "Landmarks of New York" plaque program. Thanks to this program and those that followed, hundreds of such plaques are still seen across the city. The idea seems to have been the brainchild of Whitney North Seymour, at that time the Municipal Art Society's president, and Mr. Ralph Hayes, then the director of the New York Community Trust. Seymour was on the Trust's Distribution Committee, which had approved funding for the idea. The concept was to mark buildings drawn from the society's list of important structures. The society board was excited about the possibilities of the program and, of course, a committee was appointed. The partnership evolved with the society providing data, text, and other support for the program, and the trust covered the cost of the plaques. The trust also gave the society financial support to further develop its index of important structures worthy of preservation so it could serve as a resource for the plaque program. With this grant support, the society promised the Community Trust a more refined version of its index by December 1956.[87]

Thanks in part to the plaque program and the Municipal Art Society's partnership with the New York Community Trust, in January of 1957 the society finally formally printed for public distribution the list of important buildings it had been working on since 1951. Appearing under the name of *New York Landmarks: An Index of Architecturally Notable Structures in New York City*, the index was of such interest that by 1960 it was in its fourth edition. The list was presented as the result of the combined creative efforts of the Municipal Art Society and the Society for Architectural Historians, but it was clear that the index was primarily a Municipal Art Society project. The 1957 list, unlike its earlier incarnation, did not stop at buildings built before World War I, but included those built up to 1930.[88]

Shortly after the publication of the index, the New York Community Trust publicly unveiled its plaque program. In November of 1957, at an inaugural luncheon in the Jade Room of the Waldorf-Astoria Hotel attended by some two hundred people, the first group of twenty plaques were dedicated, with another twenty on the way. The press release for the program noted: "Buildings of architectural distinction as well as those with historical associations are among those being identified." Among

FIGURE 6.7 After years of refinement and research by the Municipal Art Society and the Society of Architectural Historians, the Index of Architecturally Notable Structures in New York City was finally published in 1957 as *New York Landmarks*. Modest in appearance, mimeographed and stapled with its only visual being this cover drawing from *Magical City* by Vernon Howe Bailey, its impact was monumental. It provided the intellectual capital for many landmark public education efforts, helped guide the work of the Landmarks Preservation Commission, and was the basis for Alan Burnham's hardcover and well-illustrated book of the same title appearing in 1963.

the first twenty sites to receive their tablets were Grand Central Terminal, Grace Church, the University Club, the Woolworth Building, St. Paul's Chapel, and Central Synagogue.[89] In unveiling the markers, Seymour noted, "Millions of our fellow Americans say they like to visit New York but wouldn't want to live here. For all of these, the plaques will help to explain why so many of us prefer to visit elsewhere and live here." The unveiling of the plaque program triggered a *New York Times* editorial, which both referenced the recent publication of the "book listing the landmarks of New York City" and Seymour's remarks at the unveiling when he said it is "high time that New Yorkers and visitors have some way to identify our historical and architectural treasures."[90]

In a variety of ways—exhibits, radio shows, walking tours, publications, and plaques—the Municipal Art Society was trying its best to bring the preservation message to a broader audience. These efforts included a letter to the *New York Times*, which cited these various initiatives and, in a very genteel way, suggested that the "program outlined obviously requires far broader financial support that this nonprofit organization has at hand," and invites those "who have an interest in preserving the landmarks that still remain in New York" to contact the Municipal Art Society.[91]

The Municipal Art Society was able to take its scholarly effort, the list of buildings, and use that intellectual capital to shape a variety of opportunities to raise the public's preservation consciousness in a way the list on its own could not have. The society also was able to partner successfully with a range of civic groups, from the Society of Architectural Historians to the University Club to the New York Community Trust, to leverage the energy, resources, and networks of these organizations to reach more and more people. Though still having just scratched the surface and years away from preservation entering the mainstream, the society's efforts to capture the hearts and minds of New Yorkers were beginning to catch on. Preservation had started its journey to reach out beyond the "lunatic fringe."

The society's educational programs were gaining traction at the same time that the Bard Act was slowly and quietly advancing in Albany. The society's educational outreach efforts were not specifically linked to advancing the passage of the Bard Act. At times, reference is made to the existence of proposed legislation in Albany, as in the case of Edward Steese's letter to the *New York Times*. More of the time, the message being sent to the public is that legal means to save landmarks continue to be elusive, and that public sentiment is the recourse most available to save landmarks. These educational programs and the efforts to pass the

FIGURE 6.8 The New York Community Trust's program of placing plaques on important New York City buildings helped increase public appreciation for the city's landmarks. Lüchow's, the famed German restaurant at 110 East 14th Street with its magnificent interiors and rich cultural history, received its plaque in 1965. Even with the Landmarks Law and the subsequent amendment to it permitting the designation of certain interiors, the Landmarks Preservation Commission failed to designate Lüchow's and it was demolished in 1995.

Bard Act in Albany were, at some level, informed by and related to one another, but not in the highly scripted, strategic way contemporary legislative efforts are linked to publicity and educational campaigns.

At the time the Bard Act became law, New York City was experiencing the beginnings of a rediscovery of its history and its architectural heritage and confronting a continuing stream of headlines prophesizing impending doom for some of the city's signature buildings. One would think this hothouse climate would have been a perfect one for the Bard Act to seed, sprout, and grow some form of landmark protection for New York City. With the passage of the Bard Act, the civics had formed their committees, next steps were to be explored, and interest was high.

Bard had also been at work spreading the gospel of aesthetic regulation. The passage of the Bard Act coincided with the publication of Bard's definitive article on aesthetic regulation, "Aesthetics and the Police Power."[92] Appearing in several forms over the next few years, it received favorable notice from sources as diverse as Supreme Court Justice Felix Frankfurter to those on the streets laboring in the vineyard of preservation.[93] Henry Hope Reed wrote to Bard that the article was "one of the most encouraging statements for the future of municipal art that I have seen." Reed went on to indicate that he was having copies sent to friends who are "very much interested in the problem of community beauty in Charleston, Germantown (Pa.), San Francisco and New Orleans."[94] Bard's article helped educate people to "the revolution that has taken place in fifty years with respect to the legal power of the community to deal with the individual landowner in his dealing with his own land, including, what, in response to individual taste, whim ambition, or cupidity, the owner plans to make his property look like to the public."[95] Bard continued his work to foment such a revolution in New York City and beyond.

The passage of the Bard Act made 1956 a banner year in New York City's quest for a landmarks law. A less well-known event would add even further significance to the year. In January of 1956, James Felt was sworn in as chairman of the New York City Planning Commission and "in the light of the enormous changes that have taken place in the last few years, his sights were set on tackling the city's zoning resolution"[96] In July, he announced plans for a major study of the city's zoning, which led to a two-and-a-half-year effort by the architectural firm Voorhees, Walker, Smith, and Smith. The results would be released in February of 1959 and trigger a series of public hearings.[97]

Would this rezoning provide the civic organizations the vehicle they had been looking for to advance the Bard Act from mere potential to reality? Or would it be the speeding train that forced their efforts off the track? The hearings over the new zoning would find the citywide civic organizations requesting the inclusion of "provisions for some controls for the preservation of historic and architectural values in the new Zoning Resolution."[98] Their reasoned and regulated voices would be joined by an informed and passionate chorus from two of New York's most historic and preservation-conscious neighborhoods, Greenwich Village and Brooklyn Heights. Both neighborhoods saw the need to include preservation in the new zoning resolution. Flying under the banner of the Bard Act, residents from Brooklyn Heights and Greenwich Village demanded action.

Unfolding events would bring to James Felt's zoning hearings the Municipal Art Society, its colleague citywide civic organizations, and the denizens of Greenwich Village and Brooklyn Heights. All came to deliver the message that New York City needed a legal mechanism to protect its threatened landmarks. Having followed the long journey that brought the art and preservation societies to this point in their efforts to obtain a landmarks law, our story necessarily turns to the origins of similar sentiments in Greenwich Village and Brooklyn Heights. What led their leaders to appear at Felt's hearings? What was stoking the preservation fires burning in the Village and the Heights?

ENDNOTES

1. "After Hours: To the Barricades," *Harper's*, January 1955, 85; L. Bancel LaFarge, foreword to Municipal Art Society, "Buildings in Manhattan Built Before World War I Designated as Worthy of Protection," 1955.
2. Berman v. Parker, 348 U.S. 26 (U.S. Supreme Court 1954).
3. Wood, "An Interview with Harmon Goldstone," 22.
4. Henry Hope Reed comments at the public program "In Search of Albert S. Bard, a Lecture on Albert S. Bard," May 8, 2002, transcript, New York Preservation Archive Project. On another occasion, Reed reminisced that Walter Lord likened Bard's whistle to those used by the peanut vendors of the time, noting that the Municipal Art Society's board meetings would be punctuated by "Albert Bard's peanut whistle." Henry Hope Reed, interview by Anthony C. Wood, June 11, 1998, New York Preservation Archive Project.
5. "Albert S. Bard Dies At 96," *Purple and Gold* 80, no. 2 (Winter 1963): 59.
6. Bard to Gordon and Marjorie Switz, April 1, 1937, Albert Bard Archive, New York Preservation Archive Project.
7. Secretary to Mr. Bard to Mr. Ross, executive director, Keep America Beautiful, March 16, 1954, noting Bard's March 8 operation, Albert Bard Archive, New York Preservation Archive Project.
8. "Bar's Bard," *The New Yorker,* February 23, 1957, 25; "A. S. Bard, at 90, Sets Brisk Pace," *New York Times,* December 19, 1956; "Outdoor Ad Foe Turns Strong 95," *New York Times,* December 20, 1961. It has been suggested by Gilmartin, *Shaping the City,* 357, that Bard moved to New Jersey because he was so disgusted with the "modern skyscraper city." There is no doubt Bard was upset with the modern city, but based on Bard's personal papers at the New York Preservation Archive Project

and conversations with members of the Switz family, a disillusionment with New York City was not the primary motivation for Bard's move. In 1935, initially on a temporary basis, Bard moved into his own set of rooms in the East Orange home of the Switz family. Bard considered the middle Switz boy, Gordon, his "adopted son" and since the 1920s had taken the entire family under his wing, playing the role of a surrogate father and, later, grandfather. The move was most likely prompted by the combination of changes at 122 East 30th, the house in Manhattan in which Bard had kept rooms since 1916, and pressures, most likely financial, caused by Gordon and Marjorie Switz's December 1933 arrest and subsequent trial for spying in Paris. Totally dedicated to the young couple, Bard devoted his time and financial resources to seeing them through their trouble.

9. "E.O. Man Has Pet Peeve; It's Bad Architecture," *Newark Sunday News*, February 3, 1959.

10. "Civic Group Hails Its Hothead at 95," *New York Times*, December 21, 1961.

11. Meeting Minutes, Joint AIA-AIP Committee on "Design Control," December 7, 1954, Albert S. Bard Papers, New York Public Library.

12. Weinberg believed in preservation, but at times was in conflict with it. Just as he took on Robert Moses, he also broke ranks with fellow Greenwich Villager Jane Jacobs and criticized her wholesale dismal of the planning profession. He believed there was a distinctive role for the professional architect and planner and felt that preservation could be misapplied "in the hands of the well-intentioned laymen." Albert Fein, "Biographical Sketch," in Albert Fein and Elliott S. M. Gatner, eds., *A Guide to the Professional Papers of Robert C. Weinberg* (New York: Department of Urban Studies, Long Island University, 1984), 15–36.

13. Under the auspices of the New York Preservation Archive Project, research on Robert C. Weinberg continues. Currently available are Rudie Hurwitz's "Unsung Urbanist: Robert C. Weinberg, New Yorker Behind the Scenes," paper presented January 20, 2005, New York Preservation Archive Project and Christopher Neville's "'Building and Rebuilding New York:' the Radio Urbanism of Robert C. Weinberg, 1966–71," 2007.

14. Caro, *The Power Broker*, chapter 25. There are other references to Weinberg in the text; see Caro's index. Also of interest is the biographical sketch of Weinberg by Albert Fein in *A Guide to the Professional Papers of Robert C. Weinberg*.

15. One example of the relationship is that it was Weinberg who arranged for Bard to speak on preservation to the Friends of Democracy, Inc. in the Village in 1950. Jane Taylor and Pamela Peterson to Bard, March 20, 1950, Albert S. Bard Papers, New York Public Library. Bard and Weinberg were involved with the Citizens Union and the Municipal Art Society.

16. Weinberg to Ely Jacques Kahn, September 24, 1941, Professional Papers of Robert C. Weinberg, Long Island University.

17. Henry Fagin and Robert C. Weinberg, eds., *Planning and Community Appearance* (New York: Regional Plan Association, 1958), 8.

18. Municipal Art Society Board Meeting Minutes, October 26, 1954 and November 22, 1954, Municipal Art Society of New York Records, Archives of American Art.

19. Further supporting this is correspondence between Bard and lawyers who argued the case before the Supreme Court. Joseph H. Schneider, on the losing side, noted that "neither side presented any argument concerning seizure of property by eminent domain for aesthetic purposes." Joseph H. Schneider to Bard, January 12, 1955, Albert S. Bard Papers, New York Public Library.

20. Gilmartin, *Shaping the City*, 359.

21. The earliest known draft of the Bard Act is dated November 1954 and appended to the meeting minutes, Joint AIA-AIP Committee on Design Control, November 18, 1954. The minutes report that Bard presented a draft to the committee for discussion at the meeting. The minutes indicate that the draft attached to them includes minor modifications discussed at that meeting. The minutes are available in the Professional Papers of Robert C. Weinberg, Long Island University.

22. Was one of these events the plans for the redevelopment of Pennsylvania Station? That threat to the station would have added fuel to the fire, but it is unlikely it was an actual motivator. November 30, 1954 press accounts broke the news of the agreement that William Zeckendorf would buy the station's air rights and build a new building with a "thoroughly modernized below the street level" passenger station. One of those stories indicates that the contract for that deal had been closed in September of 1953, but there is no indication that there was any earlier public knowledge of that deal. By the time of the November 30 stories, Bard already had written a draft of his legislation. Prior to the press stories, there might have been rumors about the station's future, but based on our present knowledge, we can only speculate about what Bard might have known. "Webb & Knapp Now Seeks to Use Air over New York's Penn Station," *Wall Street Journal*, November 30, 1954.

23. Damon Stetson, "World's Loftiest Tower May Rise on Site of Grand Central Terminal," *New York Times*, September 8, 1954; Bard to Hon. Lawson Purdy, November 24, 1954, Albert S. Bard Papers, New York Public Library.

24. Meeting Minutes, Joint AIA-AIP Committee on Design Control, November 18, 1954, Professional Papers of Robert C. Weinberg, Long Island University.

25. Meeting Minutes, Joint AIA-AIP Committee on Design Control, December 7, 1954, Albert S. Bard Papers, New York Public Library.

26. Bard to Weinberg, January 4, 1955, Albert S. Bard Papers, New York Public Library. When did Weinberg learn of the decision? The discussion of the Joint Committee at its December 7, 1954 meeting includes a conversation on the recent Court decision. Bard was absent from that meeting. Though it is only conjecture, perhaps it was in briefing Bard on what he had missed at the meeting that Weinberg brought the decision to Bard's attention.

27. Municipal Art Society Board Meeting Minutes, December 28, 1954, Municipal Art Society of New York Records, Archives of American Art.

28. Bard quickly produced "Esthetics and the Police Power" for *American City*, February 1955. Copies of the article, which included a long extract from the case, were made and distributed. For a more New York audience, in the printed "Report of the Committee on City Development," for the Fine Arts Federation of New York's April 28, 1955 annual meeting, three pages are devoted to "Planning Power: Esthetics and the Police Power," with the subject being the *Berman v. Parker* decision. The committee report appears under the names of Albert Bard and Geoffrey Platt.

29. Bard to Hon. Simon E. Sobeloff, December 27 and 31, 1954, and January 4, 1955, Simon E. Sobeloff, solicitor general, Washington, D.C. to Bard December 28, 1954, Joseph H. Schneider, Lindas and Schneider Attorneys at Law to Bard, January 12, 1955, Bard to Joseph H. Schneider, January 17, 1955, Albert S. Bard Papers, New York Public Library.

30. Bard, "Esthetics and the Police Power," *American City*, February 1955.

31. Ibid.; Albert S. Bard, "Aesthetics and the Police Power," *American Journal of Economics and Sociology* 15, no. 3 (April 1956): 275.

32. Western Union Telegram from MacNeil Mitchell to Bard, January 18, 1955, Bard to Hon. MacNeil Mitchell, January 18, 1955, Albert S. Bard Papers, New York Public Library.

33. State of New York, Int. 708 In Senate, January 18, 1955, Albert S. Bard Papers, New York Public Library.

34. See note 47.

35. Even Bard, always generous in giving out credit, never mentions the sponsor of the Assembly version of the bill, A. Int. 1626, Douglas. Based on Mitchell's telegram to Bard, Douglas must have been the assemblyman Mitchell recruited to this task.

36. In 1945, as an assemblyman he was supportive of the restrictive zoning proposal to prevent the construction of towers on Washington Square North. "Zoning Change Sought," *New York Times*, March 9, 1945. According to the seating list for the event, Bard and Mitchell were assigned to table 20. Albert S. Bard Papers, New York Public Library.

37. There are numerous statements supporting Bard's authorship of the bill, among them "Here is the bill I drew for the Citizens Union and the Fine Arts Federation of New York for the 1955 New York Legislature" from a letter Bard wrote to Allen Fonoroff. City Planning Commission, Cleveland, Ohio, August 11, 1955, Albert S. Bard Papers, New York Public Library. Another is a reference to the bill with the statement "Mr. Bard, who had drafted the bill," in the Board Meeting Minutes, February 28, 1955, Municipal Art Society of New York Records, Archives of American Art.

38. Municipal Art Society Board Meeting Minutes, February 28, 1955, Municipal Art Society of New York Records, Archives of American Art.

39. Edward Steese, now flying the flag of the American Institute of Architects, joined the effort, writing "Perhaps by growing request, some legislative means may be established in Albany or Washington to preserve our artistic and cultural landmarks without hardship to the private owner. Such bills are now under consideration and should be encouraged." Edward Steese, letter to the editor, *New York Times*, April 2, 1955.

40. Robert C. Weinberg, chairman, Civic Design Committee, New York Chapter, American Institute of Architects to the Honorable Averill [sic] Harriman, April 15, 1955. Letter found in April 18, 1955 Veto Jacket #58 of Nos. 709, 1905, Int. 708, In Senate, State of New York, January 18, 1955, New York Public Library, Science, Industry and Business.

41. Averell Harriman, Memorandum, April 18, 1955 filed with Senate bill, Introductory Number 708, Print Number 1905, entitled "An Act to amend the general city law, in relation to providing for places, buildings, structures, works of art and other objects having a special character or special historical or aesthetic interest and for their protection, enhancement, petpetuation [sic] or use," Memorandum found in Veto Jacket #58 of Nos. 709, 1905, Int. 708, In Senate, State of New York, January 18, 1955, New York Public Library, Science, Industry and Business.

42. Bard to Allen Fonoroff, August 11, 1955, Albert S. Bard Papers, New York Public Library.

43. Meeting minutes, New York Chapter of the American Institute of Architects Civic Design Committee, May 12, 1955, Albert S. Bard Papers, New York Public Library.

44. Averell Harriman, Memorandum.

45. Bard to Hon. MacNeil Mitchell, March 8, 1956, Albert S. Bard Papers, New York Public Library.

■ ■ ■ ■ ■ ■ ■

46. Robert F. Wagner, mayor, to Harriman, March 13, 1956; Frederick L. Rath, Jr., director, National Trust for Historic Preservation to Harriman, March 8, 1956; telegram from Alexander Hamilton, president, American Scenic and Historic Preservation Society to Harriman, March 22, 1956; George Hallett, executive secretary, Citizen Union to Hon. Daniel Gutman, Counsel to the governor, March 29, 1956; Jacob K. Javits Memorandum to the governor, March 19, 1956; Arthur Levitt, state comptroller, by Joseph Kelly, deputy comptroller, to Harriman, March 15, 1956. All materials in Bill Jacket, No. 1279, Int. 1218, April 2, 1956, New York State Library.

47. The original version of the bill had a phrase that read "including appropriate control of the use," while in the final version it was replaced by the phrase "which may include appropriate and reasonable control of the use." Levitt's letter notes the change, indicting now "the proposed control of the use or appearance of the property is now expressly limited to not only 'appropriate' control as provided in the 1955 bill, but also to 'reasonable' control as set forth in the present bill." Levitt to Harriman, March 15, 1956, Bill Jacket, No. 1279, Int. 1218, April 2, 1956, New York State Library.

48. Richard Roth, chairman, Committee on Legislation to Averill [sic] Harriman, March 24, 1956, Bill Jacket, No. 1279, Int. 1218, April 2, 1956, New York State Library, New York State Library.

49. Laws of New York, 1956, Chapter 216, 908. By 1959, Mitchell's bill was publicly being called the Bard Act, "Brooklynites Set Action on Heights," *New York Times*, April 21, 1959.

50. Albert S. Bard, "Municipal Regulation of Esthetics Advanced," *American City*, September 1956.

51. Municipal Art Society Board Meeting Minutes, May 15 and September 24, 1956, Municipal Art Society of New York Records, Archives of American Art.

52. Typical of Bard's behind-the-scenes work to advance the legislation is his letter to the state historian, following up on a previous meeting and requesting a letter be sent to the governor in support of the bill. The historian replies he has not only already sent in such a letter, but has urged the National Trust to do the same. Bard to Albert B. Corey, state historian, March 9, 1956, Albert B. Corey to Bard, March 12, 1956, Albert S. Bard Papers, New York Public Library.

53. Interview with Harmon Goldstone by Charles B. Hosmer, Jr., conducted on or about June 23, 1982 under the auspices of the Eastern National Park and Monument Association, the University of Maryland at College Park, 1991, National Trust for Historic Preservation Library Collection and Archives, University of Maryland at College Park Libraries.

54. Minutes of meeting held October 30, 1956, Committee on Government Action, The Municipal Art Society, Albert S. Bard Papers, New York Public Library.

55. Meeting minutes, New York Chapter of the American Institute of Architects Civic Design Committee, May 12, 1955, Albert S. Bard Papers, New York Public Library.

56. "Can the Grand Central Concourse Be Saved?" *Architectural Forum* 101 (November 1954): 134–39.

57. Ibid.; Municipal Art Society Board Meeting Minutes, November 22, 1954, Municipal Art Society of New York Records, Archives of American Art.

58. Stern, *New York 1960*, 1139–1140.

59. "After Hours: To the Barricades," *Harper's*, January 1955, 85.

60. "New Zeckendorf Project to House World's Fair," *Washington Post and Times Herald*, June 7, 1955; John C. Delvin, "Zeckendorf Maps New Penn Station," *New York Times*, November 30, 1954; "Proposed Building in N.Y. Would be World's Biggest," *Chicago Daily Tribune*, June 8, 1955; "Palace of Progress," *New York Times*, June 9, 1955.

61. Hilary Ballon, *New York's Pennsylvania Stations* (New York: W.W. Norton, 2002), 95-98; "'Palace' Plan Out; Bigger One Urged," *New York Times*, January 6, 1956.

62. "Song Not Yet Over for Carnegie Hall," *New York Times*, July 26, 1956; Edward Steese, AIA Chairman, Committee on Historic Architecture, the Municipal Art Society, letter to the editor, "To Preserve Carnegie Hall," *New York Times*, August 3, 1955.

63. "Talk of the Town," *New Yorker*, March 24, 1956. At the society's March 26, 1956 board meeting, Steese credits this article to Brendan Gill.

64. Interview with Harmon Goldstone by Hosmer, 2; Wood, "An Interview with Harmon Goldstone," 17–19; Gilmartin, *Shaping the City*, 353–355.

65. Municipal Art Society Board Meeting Minutes, November 22, 1954, Municipal Art Society of New York Records, Archives of American Art.

66. Brendan Gill, interview by Anthony C. Wood, July 2, 1984, 4–5.

67. Wood, "An Interview with Harmon Goldstone," 17–19.

68. Henry Hope Reed, interview by Anthony C. Wood, 7; Municipal Art Society Board Meeting Minutes, April 26 and October 26, 1954, Municipal Art Society of New York Records, Archives of American Art.

69. A seven-page essay by Henry Hope Reed with illustrations titled "Monuments of Manhattan" accompanied the exhibit. Municipal Art Society of New York Records, Archives of American Art.

70. Henry Hope Reed, interview by Anthony C. Wood, 8.

71. Typed list of contents of the exhibit "Monuments of Manhattan," 13 pages, provided to author by Henry Hope Reed.

72. Special viewings included one for the members of the Municipal Art Society and another for the Society of Architectural Historians who were back in New York City for a three-day meeting. Whether their gathering helped inspire the exhibit, as had been the case in 1952, is not known. Since these two visits to New York coincided with such key events one could only wish that during this period they had met in New York City more frequently. Municipal Art Society Board Meeting Minutes, November 22, December 28, 1954 and January 25, September 26, October 24, 1955, Municipal Art Society of New York Records, Archives of American Art. Henry Hope Reed remembered doing a show with the photographer John B. Bayley in Brooklyn under the Municipal Art Society's auspices. Wood interview with Reed, June 11, 1998.

73. Wood, "An Interview with Harmon Goldstone," 20.

74. Municipal Art Society Board Meeting Minutes, March 1 and December 28, 1954, Municipal Art Society of New York Records, Archives of American Art; John A. Kouwenhoven, *The Columbia Historical Portrait of New York* (New York: Harper and Row, 1972), preface.

75. In addition, 200 copies were distributed at the Society for Architectural Historians New York Conference. Municipal Art Society Board Meeting Minutes, January 25, 1955, Municipal Art Society of New York Records, Archives of American Art.

76. LaFarge, foreword, "Buildings in Manhattan Built Before World War I Designated as Worthy of Protection."

77. "Landmark," a seventeen-page narrative description of the proposed radio series for perspective advertisers, Municipal Art Society of New York Records, Archives of American Art. The document is undated but most likely is from late 1954 or early 1955.

78. Russell Lynes' first-year membership dues were waived because of his interest in promoting the radio show for the society. Municipal Art Society Board Meeting Minutes, October 26 and December 28, 1954, and April 25, 1955, Municipal Art Society of New York Records, Archives of American Art.

79. "Landmark," Municipal Art Society Records. It remains unclear how much of the series was actually developed. Though there was no reference to it in the society minutes of this period, in the late 1930s the society had also turned to radio. "Municipal Art Society Bulletin," December 1937, Municipal Art Society of New York Records, Archives of American Art.

80. Gilmartin, *Shaping the City*; the Municipal Art Society Board Meeting Minutes report on the idea for the radio show but do not report on actual broadcasts. Lynes served on the Commission from 1962 into 1968.

81. Reed recalled his impatience at the slowness with which Gilchrist moved the tour idea forward and finally he and his friend Ed Jones just went ahead and organized it. Wood interview with Reed, June 11, 1998.

82. Municipal Art Society Board Meeting Minutes, September 26 and November 28, 1955, January 23 and April 23, 1956, Municipal Art Society of New York Records, Archives of American Art. Others on the Committee were Mr. Burnham, the painter Ed Powis Jones, and Mr. Roudebush. The guides on the April 29th tour were Henry Hope Reed, John Bayley, and Alan Burnham. Henry Hope Reed, "Remembering Ed Jones, A Founder of MAS Walking Tours," Municipal Art Society Newsletter, January/February 1999.

83. "Talk of the Town," *The New Yorker*, October 13, 1956, 35–36; Municipal Art Society Board Meeting Minutes June 4 and October 22, 1956, Municipal Art Society Records, Archives of American Art. Reed took the tours to the Museum because Ruth McAneny Loud of the Municipal Art Society Board was at the Museum. Wood interview of Reed, June 11, 1998.

84. Wood interview with Reed, June 11, 1998.

85. "Talk of the Town," *The New Yorker*, October 13, 1956.

86. James Sanders, "Henry Hope Reed, Jr.," unedited article, 1984, later appearing as "After Years in the Cold, A Feisty Critic is Back in Style," *Avenue*, February 1985.

87. Municipal Art Society Board Meeting Minutes, February 28, December 19, 1955, March 26, April 23, 1956, Municipal Art Society of New York Records, Archives of American Art. Other Members of the Municipal Art Society engaged in the plaque program were Goldstone, Jayme, Gilchrist, and Steese.

88. Municipal Art Society, *New York Landmarks: An Index of Architecturally Notable Structures in New York City* (New York: The Municipal Art Society, 1957).

89. The program was announced as a memorial to Andrew McKenzie, "a prominent Brooklyn architect who had died in 1926," New York Community Trust, *The Heritage of New York* (New York: Fordham University Press, 1970), 13–21. In addition to support from trust funds established by his widow, Isabel C. McKenzie, additional funding came from the late Lucy Wortham James of New York and Newport. New York Community Trust, "*Landmarks of New York*," Press Release, November 21, 1957, Albert S. Bard Papers, New York Public Library.

■ ■ ■ ■ ■ ■ ■

90. Edith Evans Asbury, "Landmark Signs Dedicated Here," *New York Times*, November 22, 1957; "Landmark Signs," *New York Times*, November 26, 1957.

91. William N. Jayme, Board of Directors, The Municipal Art Society, to the editor, *New York Times*, November 10, 1955.

92. Albert S. Bard, "Aesthetics and the Police Power," *The American Journal of Economics and Sociology* 15, no. 3 (April 1956), 265–275. Bard had been approached to write the article as part of a special issue of the journal honoring Mr. Harold S. Buttenheim on his eightieth birthday. The text of the article was submitted by January of 1956. Appreciating how important the article would be, Bard requested 400 reprints instead of the 100 gratis copies provided. Mabel Walker, executive director, Tax Institute to Bard, 1955 and January 23, 1956, Bard to Walker, January 27, 1956, Albert S. Bard Papers, New York Public Library.

93. It would appear as its own chapter in Weinberg's report, "Planning and Community Appearance," and it would be published in a slightly expanded form in a pamphlet issued by the Citizens Union Research Foundation in November 1957, when Bard was 91, Felix Frankfurter to "Dear Albert," Bard, May 22, 1956, Albert S. Bard Papers, New York Public Library.

94. Henry Hope Reed to Bard, May 28, 1956, Albert S. Bard Papers, New York Public Library.

95. Bard, "Aesthetic and the Police Power," 265.

96. "Plan Chief Urges Rezoning of City," *New York Times*, February 12, 1956.

97. Stanislaw J. Makielski, Jr., *The Politics of Zoning: The New York Experience* (New York: Columbia University Press, 1966), 85–106.

98. "Architects Favor Aesthetic Zoning," *Villager*, June 11, 1959.

SEVEN

THE VILLAGE PEOPLE

THE YEAR WAS 1960. THE MONTH WAS MAY. SEVEN HUNDRED Brooklynites rallied in the ballroom of the St. George Hotel. They heard Richard H. Howland, the president of the National Trust for Historic Preservation, "beat an eloquent drum for Heights preservation." Earlier that March, a "Save the Village" petition to protect Greenwich Village from the "ravages of big buildings" was unveiled at city hall with sixteen thousand signatures.[1]

Hundreds attending meetings demanding preservation? Thousands signing petitions requesting it? These numbers are a far cry from the modest attendance at the award banquets and annual meetings of the citywide civic organizations valiantly striving to save the city's landmarks. Such numbers commanded attention then and command ours now.

The historic neighborhoods of Greenwich Village and Brooklyn Heights had the essential ingredient that the citywide civic organizations lacked: a readymade, sizeable constituency primed to support preservation. Looking back years later, first chair of the Landmarks Preservation Commission, Geoffrey Platt, stressed the importance of that constituency and the signature role played by these neighborhoods: "We had the people in Greenwich Village and Brooklyn Heights who produced a lot of people, a lot of numbers, vociferous numbers. So we had a big and a wide constituency and the legislators felt this tremor."[2]

The Municipal Art Society's *New York Landmarks: An Index of Architecturally Notable Structures in New York City* had pointed out the treasures that needed to be saved. The Bard Act gave cities the ability to save them. Important as this scholarly base and legal foundation were, they would not be enough to produce the Landmarks Law. What was still missing was the political will to save New York's landmark treasures. The "vociferous numbers" from Greenwich Village and Brooklyn Heights would go a long way toward creating that political will. These grassroots preservationists not only filled the halls and hearing rooms, signed the petitions, and took to the streets, at key moments they also led the charge. As a result, theirs is an important chapter in the story of how New York won its Landmarks Law.

What brought Greenwich Village and Brooklyn Heights to the boiling point at such a propitious moment? How did these grassroots efforts evolve? Were they related to one another? Did they have links to the city-wide efforts? A full telling of the history of preservation in these neighborhoods would itself fill a volume. Again, our focus must narrow in on the events that placed these neighborhoods in the forefront of those calling for a system to preserve the city's landmarks.

Greenwich Village has long had a strong sense of identity. Ever since 1822 when it was "discovered" and subsequently overrun by New Yorkers escaping the yellow fever epidemic that threatened their city two miles to the south, the Village has attracted outsiders yet managed to preserve its own identity, even when fully surrounded by the larger city that engulfed it. In some respects, the Village remains "a country village within a city, a tight-knit community that embraces its nonconformists and fiercely opposes outside intervention."[3] Physically more homogenous in mind than in reality, the Village conjures up images of beautiful streets, named not numbered, lined with low-rise brick buildings, punctuated with churches, dotted with institutional buildings, and enriched by the occasional alley or mews.

Then as now, the Village featured a range of architectural styles from all its periods of settlement. It embraced the Federal style row houses from its earliest days and the Greek Revival row houses encouraged by the creation of Washington Square Park. The late-nineteenth century brought European immigrants and, with them, tenements. The early-twentieth century brought immigrants of another type: the artists and bohemians. Each wave of newcomers had their impact. Single-family homes became multiple dwellings and artist studios. Old buildings would take on new lives and the new buildings would be absorbed into the fabric of the Village. It was when the new started to rip holes in the cherished fabric of the old that the preservation instincts of the Village would become aroused.

Complementing the bricks and mortar of the Village streets and their resulting distinctive sense of place is the cultural identity that supports the often-voiced notion that the Village is as much a state of mind as it is a physical place. "The Village has been called 'the most significant mile in

American cultural history,' 'the home of half the talent and half the eccentricity in the country,' 'the place where everything happens first.'" Having served as home, even if for many only temporarily, to "nearly every major American writer and artist," the "Village has held such a mythic place in the American imagination that it has often served as kind of iconographic shorthand."[4]

The Village has always had a keen sense of its own distinctiveness:

> There is probably no safer generalization one can make about Greenwich Village than that this is a community preoccupied, indeed obsessed, with a sense of its own identity. . . . The remarkable fact is that artists and politicians, and for that matter housewives and businessmen, agree on something. As a group of people, we Villagers have what a psychologist might call an edifice complex. We are a community of savers, not lost souls helplessly clinging to a host of remnants, bygones and genealogies as we are often mistakenly caricatured, but concerned citizens wise enough to know that our physical surroundings condition, to some degree, our inner being and that a community which loses contact with its past loses a dimension, and a considerable one, of its existence in the present.[5]

Aware and appreciative of Greenwich Village's rich and distinctive physical and cultural history, villagers were unwilling to see this special place overcome by the winds of change. Preservation DNA ran in their veins. Blessed with a long tradition of social activism, villagers were also well equipped to do something other than just lament the passing of the Village they loved. Their struggles would at times predict as well as mirror larger New York City preservation battles. Because of its prominence, villagers would not be alone in their defense of "the greatest place in the world."[6] Well-known preservationists such as George McAneny and C. C. Burlingham joined residents in their preservation battles. Also drawn to the ranks of those fighting for the Village would be national voices for preservation.

Pre-World War II New York City found Greenwich Village facing the same force of nature that would soon threaten the Battery and Castle Clinton: Robert Moses. The then newly appointed parks commissioner had his eyes set on a redesign of Washington Square Park. Even at this time, the park and the square were perceived as historic.[7]

To this day, proposals to alter Washington Square Park are the subject of major controversy. The reaction to the 1935 Moses plan was no different and for good reasons. Perhaps its most disturbing element was the solution it advanced to a problem that would vex the Village until it was finally solved in the fall of 1963. The problem was how to manage traffic through Washington Square Park. At the time of this proposal, traffic from Fifth Avenue proceeded south through the park, passing under the great Arch. At first glance, the Moses plan seemed an improvement. His idea was to reroute traffic from the park onto a great one-way circular drive around it. It did not take long for the problems created by this solution to become clear. To manage the flow of cars and buses, it seemed likely that the streets around the park would need to be widened. In addition, access to the park would require pedestrians, including children and New York University students, to brave a flowing stream of traffic. This, combined with the proposed more formal landscape treatment and the loss of the park's old trees, was enough to ignite and unite the Village.

As Emily Folpe notes in *It Happened on Washington Square,* "In proposing a redesign for Washington Square before consulting the local population, Moses unwittingly launched a movement of tenacious civic activism."[8] Indeed, over the next decades, Moses would time and again fuel Village activism, inadvertently building a constituency for preservation. With the local population organized and in a frenzy, Moses decided to turn his attention elsewhere. In temporarily retreating from this battleground, he noted of Greenwich Village, "There are all sorts of people around Washington Square, and they are full of ideas. There is no other section in the city where there are so many ideas per person, and where ideas are so tenaciously maintained. Reconciling the points of view . . . is too much for me."[9] It is useful to remember this skirmish with Robert Moses predated the civic community's 1939 battle with him over the Brooklyn-Battery Bridge.

For several years, Moses ignored the park's deteriorating condition. In the summer of 1939, he came back, resubmitting essentially the same plan. This return to the Village did not mean Moses had built up a new capacity for "reconciling" different points of view; instead, he had perfected his ability to ignore them. Fueled with WPA money, he bulldozed the plan forward, threatening the community that if the "controversy" over his plan did not "cease by Nov. 1," the department would put Washington Square Park "at the bottom of the list" of its projects. Fearing that the park would be left to "continue as a dust bowl" the Washington Square Association, with a vote of a nineteen to eighteen, reluctantly approved the plan.[10]

Fortunately, others in and out of the Village were not to be bullied by Moses. A new group, the Volunteer Committee for the Improvement of

Washington Square, chaired by Pierce Trowbridge Wetter, was formed to take up the fight. The Village would not accept the "bathmat" plan, as it had been christened by Henry H. Curran, another of its opponents, without making a splash. New York University students rallied, a petition drive netted two thousand signatures, public meetings were held, and working with Robert C. Weinberg, the committee proposed its own plan for the park.[11]

The Village was blessed with considerable local talent. Leading the fight against the Moses plan was Pierce Trowbridge Wetter, a consulting engineer who lived at 24 Washington Square North. Though a Quaker and pacifist, when it came to confronting Moses, he showed a true fighting spirit. He would battle Moses twice, once over Washington Square and shortly thereafter, as we have seen, he would bring suit to defend Castle Clinton. Wetter's efforts earned his obituary the subhead, "Tilted with Moses to Save Fort Clinton at Battery."[12] Joining Wetter in the struggle were Henry H. Curran, a magistrate and former borough president and deputy mayor, and Robert Weinberg.

The villagers were not alone in their battle. Speaking at the rallies, sending in letters of protest, backing the alternative plan, and providing support in numerous ways were a host of citywide organizations. Among those lining up against the Moses plan were the Municipal Art Society, the Fine Arts Federation, the New York Chapter of the American Institute of Architects, the New York Society of Landscape Architects, the City Club, and the Citizens Union.[13] The brushfire in the Village had spread citywide, reaching the chambers of the Board of Estimate, whose approval was needed. A final showdown was averted when in February 1940, Mayor Fiorello LaGuardia pronounced the likelihood of the project's implementation "remote" and the press reported that the Moses plan has been "postponed indefinitely."[14]

Washington Square Park had again dodged a Robert Moses bullet. Compared to what was to come only a year later when Moses launched his assault on Castle Clinton, the Village had only experienced Robert Moses "light." At the 1939 New York University student rally against Moses' plan for the park, Pierce Trowbridge Wetter announced he "came to praise Moses but also to damn him." Continuing in this Shakespearean vein, he "asserted that the commissioner had all the qualifications of 'a very fine dictator because he doesn't resent criticism but just pays no attention to it.'"[15] Wetter's confrontation with Robert Moses over Castle Clinton would prove his words in error. Robert Moses did pay attention to criticism. He viciously attacked those who voiced it.

■ ■ ■ ■ ■ ■ ■

The Village's early battles with Moses helped prepare it to deal with future assaults. They energized grassroots citizens' resistance, they helped forge links between villagers and the citywide civics, and they gave the civic community an advanced taste of what their future held. The struggle with Moses also produced the following admonition from Alfred Geiffert Jr., president of the Municipal Art Society, which still rings true today: "Vigilance, as a safeguard to the orderly and esthetic development of our city, is a duty we must accept as individuals and as a Society. Large civic programs such as those undertaken by our Park Department demand our attention. We are being served. We should show interest and give assistance by pointing out to the authorities our needs, likes and dislikes for their guidance."[16]

Efforts to protect the neighborhood of Washington Square go back at least as far as the 1920s. Proclaiming it in 1926 "the last great historical locality of New York that remains today virtually unimpaired," the Joint Committee for the Saving of Washington Square (one of many such committees that would be formed over the decades) announced a campaign to seek height limits to preserve the square from "being submerged under a belt of skyscraping structures."[17] In 1936, there was a scare when one of the large village landowners, Sailors' Snug Harbor, announced plans to demolish some of the structures facing the North Side of Washington Square, east of Fifth Avenue.

In addition to troubling residents, the proposal triggered the Municipal Art Society to send a letter to the trustees of Sailors' Snug Harbor "presenting the desire of many citizens to have these structures retained in view of their historic and sentimental character." The controversy simmered. Robert Weinberg, then serving on a Municipal Art Society Committee, urged the society to encourage Sailors' Snug Harbor to consider his alternative plans "to preserve the character of the Houses." The society passed a resolution, stating its interest in "preserving the houses as historical relics" and deploring the "fact that anything should happen to them."[18] Talbot Hamlin, writing as Avery Librarian, underscored the importance of preserving the threatened structures, stressing that they "made the Square itself the oasis it is, and have set the tone of Greenwich Village."[19]

Sailors' Snug Harbor's decision to retain the façades of these threatened buildings is celebrated in a *New York Times* editorial, "The Row," that reads like an architectural love letter:

Is there any bit of New York cherished by more memories and seen with kinder eyes than the little block in North Washington Square,

just east of Fifth Avenue . . . that warm, friendly brick, those little Ionic porticoes, those gracious steps and rails and fences, those
charming doorways, those hospitable windows shining in the sun. . . .
In its more than a hundred years "The Row" has come to be not only
a landmark but a sort of kindly neighbor or crony to anybody with a
little bit of imagination who has the good fortune to see it often or to
visit it in recollection.[20]

Though a far cry from what today's preservationists would find acceptable, at least the character of the "The Row" was preserved in its new
treatment.[21]

The postwar period would find the Village continuing its battle with
Moses, redoubling its efforts to fight out-of-scale apartment buildings and
facing the problem of a burgeoning New York University. The need for
more housing put the Village under enormous pressure. To preserve Village
ambiance, the Washington Square Association launched a planning effort
in 1944 to "preserve the residential character of the Washington Square
and Greenwich Village sections of Manhattan" calling for "protection of
historic and picturesque buildings." Arthur Holden, architect and planner,
produced the plan, which was unveiled in a 101-page booklet published in
1946. Receiving attention in the *New York Times*, it was reported that the
plan recommended that the area "around Washington Square and north
to Fourteenth Street be guarded as a high-class residential section, that
Greenwich Village be redeveloped to retain its essential character but with
a periphery of high apartment buildings. . . . The majority of buildings in
Greenwich Village should not be disturbed."[22] Though a valiant effort,
the plan, having no power of law behind it, had little immediate impact.
Over a decade later, it would be pulled from the dustbin of history to play
a supporting role in reforming zoning in the Village.

As the Washington Square Association was at work planning, so too
were developers. It was in December of 1944 that the Rhinelander property on the northern edge of Washington Square Park west of Fifth Avenue
changed ownership, resulting in the controversy that would ultimately lead
President Keally of the Municipal Art Society to issue his 1950 call for a
landmarks law. The immediate threat to those properties abated at the
end of 1945, though their future remained clouded and the community
concerned.

With the developer's plans for the northern edge of the square temporarily on hold, the next assault was on the square's southern flank. This attack
would come from within. In 1946, New York University stated its intention

to build a law center facing Washington Square. Though its location was still unannounced, by the fall of 1947, the smart money was betting the site would be on the South Side of Washington Square. The Village began to organize. The Save Washington Square Committee was formed under the leadership of Harold D. Fleming. One concern was that such a dramatic increase in the university's presence on the square would "ruin one of New York City's most picturesque and historically important landmarks."[23]

In relatively short order, significant opposition formed. Almost twelve thousand signatures on petitions opposing the project were presented to the university. In a poignant coincidence, just as it celebrated its twenty-fifth anniversary, the Greenwich Village Historical Society joined this chorus urging preservation. The Washington Square Association went on record against the proposal, as did local clergy and such high profile New Yorkers as Eleanor Roosevelt and the Right Rev. William T. Manning, retired bishop of the Protestant Episcopal diocese of New York.[24] Novelist Fannie Hurst chimed in: "For realistic reasons of historic values, Washington Sq. should be treasured. For reasons of sentiment, without which a community lacks soul, it should be preserved."[25]

The situation was at least slightly embarrassing for New York University. The press was happy to remind the public that the university had endorsed the Holden plan, which called both for keeping the square residential and for university expansion elsewhere. In addition the university's vice chancellor was Dr. Leroy Kimball, a former president of the American Scenic and Historic Preservation Society.[26] Though useful in such struggles, embarrassment alone would not be enough to stop the demolition. Ultimately, the Law Center would be built, replacing the last block of artist's housing on Washington Square South.[27]

This battle demonstrates an emerging pro-preservation constituency. It also produced an early cry for a landmarks law. During this campaign, the Save Washington Square Committee announced that it would "ask the Legislature to pass a law to protect 'public monuments, historical and traditional spots, and artistic and picturesque sites.'" The Committee referenced the example of the French Quarter of New Orleans. We have already seen that as early as 1945, villagers were interested in the Vieux Carré model and were in consultation with Albert Bard.[28] In a public meeting subsequent to the Committee's call for such legislation, Pierce Trowbridge Wetter echoes the theme, recommending "special zoning regulations for Washington Square, in view of the fact that it is of historical importance as well as being a recreational area."[29] Villagers were calling

FIGURE 7.1 Appearing in the 1949 book *Greenwich Village Today and Yesterday,* this Berenice Abbott photograph, "The last artist block on Washington Square South," suggests what was at stake and ultimately lost in the failed efforts to protect the southern perimeter of the square. The block, demolished in 1949, was sacrificed for New York University's Law School.

for some version of a landmarks law at least two years before the Municipal Art Society's Keally sounded his clarion call for such legislation.

Also in the battle over the law school is a historical footnote of interest because we have the advantage of knowing the ending to the story of New York's quest for a landmarks law. In the spring of 1948, in Judson Memorial Church at a Save Washington Square protest rally, a telegram from Robert F. Wagner, Jr. is read to the gathering. At this time, Wagner was at the beginning of his short tenure as chair of the City Planning Commission. In the telegram, Wagner offers his "support of the committee's activities . . . and noted that he was 'interested in the preservation of the city's landmarks.'" Seventeen years later, in the spring of 1965, he would demonstrate this interest by signing the Landmarks Law.[30]

Even before the law center controversy was resolved, a second threat to Washington Square South surfaced only blocks from the law center's ultimate site. A builder was seeking to evict tenants to clear the block between Thompson Street and West Broadway (today LaGuardia Place). The block was home to the "Red Row." The *New York Times* felt compelled to explain that this nickname was the result of the color of the buildings, "not the politics" of its former artist and writer inhabitants.[31] The cultural jewel of the row was No. 61 Washington Square South, known as the "House of Genius." It was "considered a landmark by students of the city's artistic and literary history." For years, it had been run as a "rooming-house for the great, the near-great and the might-have-been great of the musical and cultural world." Passing through were such residents as O. Henry, Theodore Dreiser, Steven Crane, Willa Cather, and John Dos Passos.[32]

The Village was having to fight two preservation battles simultaneously. Involved in both was eighty-two-year-old Bishop William T. Manning. With the courts permitting the evictions of the tenants, a plan to save "Genius Row," as the House of Genius and its neighbors were dubbed, by converting them into an art center was put forward by Bishop Manning, the artist John Sloan, Justice Henry H. Curran, and Carl Van Doren.[33] The unfolding saga of Genius Row was followed closely in the press. Demolition began in the spring of 1948. Then a mandated retrial of the eviction proceedings bought more time for Bishop Manning to seek funding for the art center. With the tenant issues resolved by the summer and with the failure of the effort to raise sufficient funds to purchase the site, Genius Row was lost.[34]

In a particularly painful postscript to the story, as the site was being cleared, the builder suddenly abandoned his "well-advanced plans to erect tall apartment houses" and sold the property to New York University. The university had long desired the site. The builder indicated he had received a "strong plea" on the University's behalf from a public official, reported to be Robert Moses wearing his hat as city construction coordinator.[35] The university's acquisition of the site further incensed those in the Village, who were in the midst of the fight over the law center.

The loss of two historic blocks of Washington Square South to the expansion needs of New York University could only have increased the desire of villagers to preserve what was left of their square. One writer

FIGURE 7.2 New Yorkers picked up their *New York Times* on Friday, July 16, 1948 to be greeted by this image of the ongoing demolition of "Genius Row," 61–64 Washington Square South. This image accompanied an article on the surprise selling of the site by the builder Anthony Campagna to New York University. Number 61 was known as the "House of Genius" and was "considered a landmark by students of the city's artistic and literary history."

observed, "The friends of the Square are a militant lot," and indeed the events of the day gave them no other option.[36] As we have already seen, the successful struggle with Sailors' Snug Harbor and New York University over Washington Square North had engaged both villagers and those beyond its borders in preservation efforts. The failed heroic efforts to save the Rhinelander properties in 1950 and 1951 further raised preservation consciousness.

The *Herald-Tribune*'s 1950 assessment of the critical state of preservation in New York City, particularly in the Village, seems depressingly on point:

> New York despite its 300 and more years has no list of historic places marked for preservation against a brash and scornful modernity. Each effort to save something of the past must be made separately; Central Park, Gracie Mansion, and now Castle Clinton are among the very few separate battles won. The long fight for Washington Square, by citizens who feel that New York has a culture and a history worth recollecting in small islands of original and distinctive brick and stone, has been a series of forced retreats.[37]

Despite calls from villagers and others for some sort of legal protection, the neighborhood remained under siege. People like Talbot Hamlin understood the larger challenge facing the Village: "What the citizens of Greenwich Village should do is to work for an over-all scheme of preservation and of city planning—something, perhaps, approximating the Vieux Carré Commission in New Orleans—for the problem in the Village is one much deeper than even the preservation of selected single monuments. It is, rather, the preservation of the character and the beauty of an entire quarter."[38] Hamlin had visited New Orleans in 1939 and had commented positively on the Vieux Carré, deeming it "a much finer thing than even Williamsburg, because it is a living thing." He saw in the Vieux Carré Commission, as did so many villagers, a solution for Greenwich Village. He went even further: "If some such body could be erected in every city to watch over its older portions, would not great strides in this movement be made? How about a Greenwich Village Commission here in New York?"[39]

The special needs of the Village were being recognized. In 1954, the Historic Buildings Committee of the New York City Chapter of the American Institute of Architects lent its support to a call from the Greenwich Village Chamber of Commerce for special "George-town" type zoning to protect the Village. One of the Committee's members, Robert Weinberg, also saw such zoning benefiting other neighborhoods.[40]

The assaults on Washington Square South had attacked the Village's artistic heritage and the inroads into Washington Square North had eroded its patrician origins. New losses would strike at its very persona. Permanently preserved in American literature, the Brevoort Hotel would fare less well in reality. Formed from three existing five-story buildings converted into a hotel in 1854, the Brevoort was a Village landmark. On the east side of Fifth Avenue between Eighth and Ninth Streets, the Brevoort was a favored destination of European visitors and attracted its share of exotic dignitaries. Helping lure them to the Brevoort were an eclectic group of Village artists and writers that frequented its French-themed basement cafe. "It was the club of all the wits—as the Algonquin presumed to be a generation later. Mark Twain was seen there—he lived a bit up the avenue—and John LaFarge."[41]

The Brevoort was the center of international attention on June 16, 1927, when its owner and maitre d', Raymond Orteig, presented his $25,000 prize for the first nonstop flight from New York to Paris, to the adulated Charles Lindbergh. A gathering place for both world travelers and villagers alike, it was dealt a blow during the depression and, despite a modernization in the 1940s, declined to the point where its renowned cafe and restaurant operated downstairs from a closed hotel. In 1952, its fate was sealed with the announcement of its acquisition for an apartment building. The Brevoort, the site of rallies to save threatened landmarks, had itself became one. Late on the morning of January 27, 1954, "Wreckers plunged their crowbars into its walls."[42]

When demolition came to the Brevoort, it would also take with it a row of townhouses, among them a beloved neighbor, the Mark Twain House at 21 Fifth Avenue. Designed by the architect James Renwick, the son-in-law of a Brevoort, this early 1840s townhouse was the home of Mark Twain from 1904–1908. Though brief, his stint as a villager caught the popular imagination as he walked its streets in his signature white serge suit. The impending loss of the Village's physical link to its Twain history spurred the Greenwich Village Chamber of Commerce to action. They sought to raise $70,000 to move the building out of harm's way. The drama unfolded in the *Villager*: "The wrecker's ax hangs over the historic Mark Twain House. . . . Unless a miracle happens, it will fall some time this week." There was to be no miracle and the house, along with the hotel and nine other townhouses, were lost to progress.[43]

On the heels of losing the Twain House and recognizing that Greenwich Village "has a world-wide reputation," with many of its "quaint" buildings having "real architectural and historic significance" but appreciating that "our Village character will soon vanish altogether unless practical steps are taken now to save what remains," the Greenwich Village Association

FIGURE 7.3 Under the headline "Wreckers Attack the Old Brevoort," this foreboding image appeared in the *New York Times* of January 28, 1954. The destruction of this beloved Greenwich Village landmark at Eighth Street and Fifth Avenue further inflamed preservation sentiments. This photograph shows the demolition team starting to work on this one-time world-class hotel that had hosted presidents, foreign dignitaries, and a wild array of other celebrities.

called a town meeting for April 20, 1954. Making a special trip to address the Village on "New Trends in Historic Preservation" would be the executive director of the National Trust for Historic Preservation, Frederick L. Rath, Jr.[44]

FIGURE 7.4 This particularly graphic demolition shot of yet another Greenwich Village landmark being turned into rubble helps explain the vehemence of the calls for preservation emanating from the Village. This photograph depicting the 1954 demolition of the Mark Twain House, Fifth Avenue and Ninth Street, accompanied Whitney North Seymour, Jr.'s *New York Times Magazine* article, "Plea to Curb the Bulldozer," that appeared on October 13, 1963. Only days later on October 28, 1963, demolition commenced on Pennsylvania Station.

The *Villager*'s J. Owen Grundy, one long interested in finding a way to preserve the architecture and character of Greenwich Village, introduced the speaker. Rath acknowledged the Village's recent losses: "I know that many of you feel a sense of urgency as you hear the bells of destruction toll. I know you are concerned about your vanishing landmarks." Tempering his comments, Rath went on, "I think we should fight hard, but that fight should be undertaken only after careful study and then with every weapon at our command."[45]

James Kirk, president of the Greenwich Village Association, billed this "town meeting" the "opening gun in the campaign for adequate laws to safeguard the Village for the future." In fact, it was neither the first, nor would it be the last, "opening gun" fired in the various efforts to obtain "adequate laws" to protect the Village. Unfortunately, it would take the Village another fifteen years to obtain legal protection for its landmarks. This "town meeting" was promising enough to attract the attention of Talbot Hamlin, who reported on it to the American and Scenic Historic Preservation Society.[46]

As villagers battled the new buildings destroying the character of the neighborhood surrounding Washington Square Park, they also continued to defend Washington Square itself. In fact, for the entire decade of the 1950s, Washington Square Park was a civic battleground. The ever-escalating warfare over the Square helped the Village develop its advocacy muscles and hone its organizational skills. This epic struggle would help create an energy and civic momentum that would contribute to the climate of activism essential to advancing the cause of preserving the Village.

By 1940, the Village had fought Robert Moses to a draw in the bout over Washington Square Park. The match, however, was far from over. In the postwar 1940s, there was yet another skirmish over traffic but no physical changes were made. The next encounter was in 1952 and it would set the tone for the rest of the decade. Moses had again focused on the park. In February of that year, villagers became aware of an impending "improvement" to the park. The plan was to create two roads thirty-eight feet wide through the park that would flank the Washington Square arch. South of the arch, between the two roads, would be new playgrounds.[47] The fact that these plans had been approved years earlier by the Board of Estimate in no way discouraged the passionate opposition that erupted as the plan's implementation drew near. The Village went to war.

The *New York Times* headline said it all, "Villagers Defeat New Traffic Plan: Project that Would Put New Roads in Washington Sq. Upset by Women." Indeed, it would be the mothers who brought their children to play in the park that launched this battle against the roads. Led by Shirley Hayes, "wife of an advertising executive and mother of four boys," the Washington Square Park Committee came to life. Hayes worked closely with another park mother, Edith Lyons, who would ultimately devote seven years to efforts to rid the park of traffic once and for all. The Committee quickly gathered four thousand signatures against the project. In May of 1952, the Board of Estimate "quietly shelved" the proposal. The park mothers had thwarted Moses.[48]

FIGURE 7.5 Greenwich Village has been blessed with an incredible array of preservation champions. Shirley Hayes, a mother who brought her sons to Washington Square Park to play, is one of an impressive cohort of Village women who made singular contributions to the cause of preservation. Her battle with Robert Moses over traffic in Washington Square Park transformed that issue from a debate over road width to one successfully questioning the need for any road at all.

Initially unknown to the general public, driving Moses and his quest for a major roadway through the park was the desire to provide a Fifth Avenue address for the buildings to be built in the redevelopment area south of Washington Square. A Fifth Avenue South address would add to the appeal and value of this new area.[49] Jane Jacobs and others opposing the roadway also believed it was being designed to be a "feeder" bringing traffic through the park to Moses' planned Lower Manhattan, Broome Street Expressway project.[50] Because of the larger agendas underlying the road project, the issue would not go away. A series of new plans were offered, including "the Big Ditch," a depressed four-lane highway through the park. The politicians argued over the width of the roads to go through the park. Shirley Hayes and her committee said no to any roads, taking the radical stance that the park should be closed to all but emergency traffic. Over ten thousand postcards supported this request.[51]

With a decision nearing on the roadway, a major new opponent entered the fight. In 1958, the Joint Emergency Committee to Close Washington Square Park to Traffic was formed. Created by Ray Rubinow, a foundation executive who had just played a major role in the saving of Carnegie Hall, the Joint Emergency Committee brought to the ongoing battle with Robert Moses a star-studded roster of New Yorkers.[52] It combined the energy, clout, and brilliance of the likes of Jane Jacobs, Eleanor Roosevelt, Margaret Mead, and Lewis Mumford.[53] The civic equivalent of the marines had landed.

The concern was not just with safety and traffic, but with the heart and soul of the park. As Mrs. Roosevelt proclaimed, "I join with Lewis Mumford and the Joint Emergency Committee in their desire to keep the square a historic place. Too little emphasis is put in this city on points of historic interest, and I cannot bear to see this last bit wiped out without at least entering a protest."[54] Ray Rubinow, the chairman of the Joint Committee, also broadly positioned the battle, stressing that Washington Square was a "symbol of the 'greater general conflict of values over how urban environments are to shape people.'"[55]

What had started in 1952 as a park mother's revolt, with students at St. Joseph's School being asked to contribute dimes to the cause, now had at its disposal some of the most brilliant minds to be found anywhere.[56] Shirley Hayes' original vision of a traffic-free park, which had been "characterized by city experts as everything from 'quixotic' to 'psychotic,'" would become a reality.[57] The advocacy effort of the Joint Emergency Committee deserves an in-depth case study, but for this account only its most brilliant elements will be highlighted.

A member of the Joint Emergency Committee's brain trust was Jane Jacobs, author, critic, and patron saint of civic activism. Described as a "prophet," doing battle in sandaled feet with "straight gray hair flying every which way around a sharp quizzical face," reporter Jane Kramer wrote in 1963: Jacobs "has probably bludgeoned more old songs, rallied more support, fought harder, caused more trouble, and made more enemies than any American woman since Margaret Sanger." Jacobs had moved to the Village, where she raised her family (and plenty of Cain) over what planners were trying to do to the neighborhood. By the early 1960s, her victories included not only the Washington Square campaign, but the defeat of Moses' Broome Street expressway and successfully keeping urban renewal at bay in the West Village.[58]

Jacobs brought incredible savvy to the cause. Norman Redlich, a villager and the pro bono counsel to the Joint Committee, reminisced years later, "Among Jane Jacobs' many brilliant organizing techniques, one of them was always put what you're trying to achieve in the name of the committee, because most people will read no further than that. So it was called the Joint Emergency Committee to Close Washington Square Park to Traffic."

Her direct approach cut to the essence of the problem and offered the solution. Redlich recalled: "We had one objective. And Jane was just brilliant. Our objective was to close Washington Square Park to traffic." Jacobs asked Redlich who could close the park. He started to explore

■ ■ ■ ■ ■ ■ ■

the legal intricacies of changes to the official city map. She said no, "You haven't asked the right question. What I want to know is under the city charter, who has the authority to direct the traffic commissioner to put a sign in the middle of the road saying 'This park is closed'?" That power lay with the Board of Estimate. From this flowed their strategy, one that fully embraced using Politics, with a capital P.[59]

The politics of the Board of Estimate were such that in order to secure victory, villagers needed the support of the Manhattan borough president. At that time, the unwritten rule was that the Board of Estimate did "not override the wishes of a borough president on a matter in his own Borough."[60] As a matter of practice, the borough presidents would vote in a block, so only one additional vote was needed for victory and Village residents knew they had that vote.[61] The key to getting the support of the Manhattan Borough President Hulan Jack was to get the support of the political boss who controlled him. Looking the part of the political "boss" down to the dark glasses was villager Carmine De Sapio, an old-time politico whose reign was beginning to be challenged by changing political realities. The committee's strategy was simple: convince De Sapio that villagers supported the park closing, show him how he could close it, and give him the chance to be the hero.[62]

The strategy worked brilliantly. A campaign to demonstrate popular support for closing the park to traffic unfolded. A petition campaign was launched. Fashion models carrying parasols printed with such slogans as "The Park is not a parkway" and "Parks are for people" strolled through the Park with clipboards, gathering signatures.[63] Petitions with thirty-five thousand signatures were dramatically unveiled on the steps of city hall. Special events kept the issue hot. Busloads of people were organized to attend hearings. The Joint Committee had its own "huge float" in the Village Day parade with a symbolic gold seven-foot papier-mâché "key" to lock the park to traffic. De Sapio presented the key to the mayor as a symbol "of the determination of my community to close Washington Square Park to traffic."[64] As hoped, De Sapio made the issue his own and delivered the road closing. Though the strategy was successful, it had unintended consequences. Some of those working to close the park felt compelled to support De Sapio in the upcoming election because he had come through on this issue. Others eager for political reform in the Village, and actively backing the opposition to De Sapio, were repulsed by their colleagues' support of the old-time political boss. As a result, some of those who had fought side-by-side to close the park to traffic would not speak to one another for decades.[65]

■ ■ ■ ■ ■ ■ ■ ■

Square Saver

Carmine G. DeSapio addressing the crowd in Washington Square last Saturday which turned out to celebrate the trial closing to traffic. Drawing especially for The Villager by Joseph Papin.

FIGURE 7.6 Preservation and politics became bedfellows in Greenwich Village. A key part of the strategy to secure the closing of Washington Square Park to traffic was to convince political boss Carmine De Sapio, depicted here in a drawing by Joseph Papin that appeared in November 1958 in *The Villager,* to make the cause his own. Reflecting the soundness and sophistication of the political instincts of Village activists, the strategy worked.

A key aspect of the strategy to close the park was to avoid getting bogged down by the seemingly unsolvable larger issues such as the need for map changes, new traffic patterns, and bus traffic in the park. Instead,

FIGURE 7.7 Events in Greenwich Village helped demonstrate the popular appeal that preservation could have. Grassroots campaigns in the Village turned out hundreds and generated thousands of signatures on petitions. The successful campaign to close Washington Square Park to traffic, being celebrated on November 1, 1958 by this crowd in front of the Washington Square Arch, helped build neighborhood organizing muscle that would well serve the preservation cause.

the approach used was incremental: Win one point at a time and then leverage that victory to achieve the next. The first victory was the temporary closing of the park. Edith Lyon remembers Jane Jacobs saying, "Let's ask them for a three-month temporary trial, and I bet you when the trial is over, it will have proved our case and it will never be opened again." She was correct.[66]

The temporary closing was celebrated with huge fanfare in November of 1958. A crowd of four hundred watched as the politicians and activists tied a symbolic green ribbon to block traffic. The ceremony was to "tie up the Square with ribbons—not cars." Stanley Tankel, noted planner and chair of the Greenwich Village Study, joined by his family, ceremoniously drove "the last car" through the Washington Square Park. Politicians spoke. Assemblyman Bill Passannate pledged, "I will do my utmost to see that this road is never opened again." The Board of Estimate was honored at a reception following the event.[67] The committee's strategy was working.

The committee lavished praise on all the politicians responsible, particularly Hulan Jack, the borough president and Carmine De Sapio. "We

FIGURE 7.8 Greenwich Village's activists were unmatched in their creativity and theatrics. Here the closing of Washington Square Park to traffic is celebrated with the ceremonial driving of the "Last Car through Washington Square" on November 1, 1958. At the subsequent gala "Community Masquerade Celebration" of the closing, over one thousand villagers gathered and a car was burned in effigy to mark the elimination of the automobile from the park.

praised everybody, and it became impossible after awhile for these people to turn back on what they had been praised for. . . . The temporary closing of course, became indelible." Though there were important battles still to be won, the momentum was in place. Years later in 1963, when the final legal steps to forever clear the park of traffic were actually taken by the Board of Estimate, it was a non-event. "Because it had been accomplished on the ground . . . it was simply no longer an issue. Everybody knew it was going to happen and it happened legally."[68]

The closing of the park to traffic was an empowering victory for Greenwich Village. On June 12, 1959, over one thousand villagers came to the "gala Community Masquerade Celebration of the closing of Washington Square Park to traffic." Awards were presented to those most responsible for the victory and the event ended with the burning of a car in effigy.[69]

Instead of compromising and accepting a narrower roadway through their park (something established Village groups were willing to do), the people had demanded and achieved total victory, something previously unimaginable.[70] After past disappointing compromises and a series of losses, the Village had finally won big. In doing so, it had harnessed the creative powers of its best minds, the star power of its most prominent supporters, and the political power of the people. They had demonstrated that a preservation cause—in this case of their beloved park—could be made a political issue, one on which political campaigns could be won or lost.[71]

Many of those involved would go on to play important roles in Village preservation efforts and beyond. Jane Jacobs and Robert Weinberg are already familiar to us.[72] Others, such as Norman Redlich, would assume important positions and advance the cause of preservation. Redlich, working in the New York City Corporation counsel's office during the early days of the Landmarks Law, would make several contributions to the cause, among them his efforts to ensure a landmark designation for Greenwich Village that would stand up to legal challenge.[73] Another "Square saver," Stanley Tankel would go on to become vice chairman of the Landmarks Preservation Commission from its prelaw formation in 1962 through his tragically early death in 1968. Alan Marcus, who had directed the petition campaign to close the Square to traffic, would go on to launch a similar campaign urging the use of the Bard Act to advance aesthetic zoning for New York City.[74]

The Village emerged from the struggle stronger and wiser. Its leaders were battle tested, their political skills refined, their instincts sharpened. Community organizing, political strategizing, and public relations were becoming second nature to villagers. As the citywide press observed, "One thing about Villagers, though, they're ready to fight City Hall at the drop of a petition. And the Village has more civic organizations than you can shake a guitar at, plus two civic-minded neighborhood newspapers."[75]

All this would serve the Village well as its attention turned to the forces of unrelenting change literally battering down its historic doors and walls. Fortuitously, the escalating crisis in the Village coincided with the debut of the city's new zoning proposal, publicly released in February of 1959. Its importance was not lost on the Village. Stanley Tankel, as a member of the Greenwich Village Association's zoning study committee, urged

■ ■ ■ ■ ■ ■ ■ ■

FIGURE 7.9   Commemorating the fortieth anniversary of the November 1958 ceremonial ribbon-tying marking the closing of Washington Square Park to automobile traffic, the Greenwich Village Society for Historic Preservation gathered a panel of individuals involved in that historic event to share their memories. On this November 1998 program panel were, starting from the left, Shirley Hayes, the park mother who launched the fight, Norman Redlich, who served on the Joint Emergency Committee to Close Washington Square Park to Traffic, Anthony Dapolito, chair of the Village Community Board at the time, and Carol Greitzer, later city council member and then a member of the Village Independent Democrats working to defeat district leader Carmine De Sapio.

villagers to get involved with the proposed zoning, correctly predicting that "zoning is one of the only hopes for Greenwich Village."[76]

That May, at the Borough of Manhattan hearing on James Felt's proposed new zoning, the voice of the Village was heard loud and clear. The Village spoke for historic zoning. The Greenwich Village Association testified in favor of "special zoning safeguards for historical and aesthetic sites." Noting that the concept was "not now before the Commission," it "respectfully" recommended that "the machinery for such designation be established after the present proposed zoning is approved." The borough president's Greenwich Village Planning Board submitted its views, which also included "advocacy of zoning for preservation of historic and architectural values." At the Planning Board's own earlier meeting on the

zoning proposal, Shirley Hayes had urged that the Village be placed "in a special zoning category in order to preserve its historic community character." Naturally, her sentiments were widely shared.[77]

At that same meeting, villagers were reminded they were not alone in their aspirations. A representative of the City Planning Commission told them that hundreds had recently attended a Brooklyn Heights meeting at which the Heights indicated its desire for that same type of protection being sought by the Village. Robert Weinberg, chair of the Village Planning Board's zoning committee, underscored the validity of such a zoning request, stating that "he and the American Institute of Architects had long urged such protection for particular sections of the city." These events, soon to be explored in more detail, suggest the forces coalescing around the cause of preservation.

The Bard Act was very much on the mind of those working for such protection and certainly on the mind of villagers. Owen Grundy of the *Villager*, someone who had been in correspondence with Bard on the general subject of preservation and the Village since at least the early 1950s, wrote to him in June of 1959. His letter frames what would be a key strategic question for those seeking protection for New York's landmarks: "My own feeling is that now is the time to put on a grand push for historic and aesthetic zoning or some similar protection in the City of New York. There are those who feel that we should get behind the proposed Zoning Resolution and get it passed and then discuss historic and aesthetic zoning. But I fear that if we wait, we may never get historic and aesthetic protection in the City of New York." He defers to Bard's expertise, writing "That is a matter of strategy which should be decided upon by you and the wiser heads who have been through these things over the years." However, Grundy was confident that if the decision was to go forward to seek such protection, "we should organize for it on a city-wide basis." In offering to help in such a campaign, he suggests, "We should bring in Brooklyn Heights Assn, Greenwich Village organizations, American Scenic & Historic Preservation Society, Fine Arts Federation, Municipal Art Society, Citizens Union, NYC chapter of the AIA, Staten Island Historical Society and other interested organizations." Though Grundy was uncertain as to the correct timing of such a push for preservation, he was prescient in recognizing the type of coalition ultimately needed to achieve it. Bard responded that because of the 1956 amendment, the city "now has the legal right to do practically anything in the way of planning it wants to do," and suggests that the first step was to produce a draft of "what should go into the new zoning resolution."[78]

■ ■ ■ ■ ■ ■ ■ ■

After decades of self-awareness and an ever-growing appreciation of its historic character, the Village was now facing perhaps its greatest challenge. The new zoning resolution could either open or hold back the floodgates. All the episodic battles the neighborhood had fought were merely preliminaries for this, the big event.

The spring of 1959 found the citywide civics and the villagers entering the battlefield of the new zoning resolution. On that field, they would already find a strong and passionate campaigner for historic zoning. Brooklyn Heights too had recognized the opportunities opened up by the debate over the new zoning resolution. The Heights entered this debate organized, focused, informed, and passionately driven. This was no accident. It was the result of a conscious campaign that would ultimately earn the Heights the right and privilege to become New York City's first legally protected historic district. It is to the story of the emergence of historic preservation in Brooklyn Heights that the winding path ultimately leading to the passage of New York's Landmarks Law now takes us.

ENDNOTES

1. Otis Pratt Pearsall, "Otis Pratt Pearsall's Reminiscences of the Nine Year Effort to Designate Brooklyn Heights as New York City's First Historic District and Its First Limited Height District," *Village Views* 7, no. 2 (1995); "'Saves' Village But Loses Home," *Villager*, March 31, 1960.
2. Wood, "An Interview with the First Chairman of the Landmarks Preservation Commission, The Late Geoffrey Platt," 14.
3. Terry Miller, *Greenwich Village and How It Got that Way* (New York: Crown Publishers, 1990).
4. Ross Wetzsteon, *Republic of Dreams Greenwich Village: The American Bohemia, 1910–1960* (New York: Simon & Schuster, 2002), ix–x.
5. "Our Edifice Complex," editorial, *Villager*, March 31, 1960.
6. Lucille Ball in Wetzsteon, *Republic of Dreams*, 9.
7. "The Municipal Art Society Bulletin of November, 1939," Municipal Art Society of New York Records, Archives of American Art; "Citizen's Union Fights Washington Sq. Plan," *New York Times*, February 8, 1940.
8. Folpe, *It Happened on Washington Square*, 280–283.
9. Ibid.
10. "Park Plan Voted by Washington Sq.," *New York Times*, October 11, 1939; "Work Starts Soon on Washington Sq.," *New York Times*, October 9, 1939; "Fights Moses Plan on Washington Sq.," *New York Times*, January 5, 1940.
11. "Park Permit Allows Rally Against Moses," *New York Times*, November 7, 1939; "Fights Moses Plan on Washington Square," *New York Times*, January 5, 1940; "New Plan Offered on Washington Square," *New York Times*, January 22, 1940; Folpe, *It Happened on Washington Square*, 283–285.
12. "Pierce T. Wetter, Engineer, 68, Dies: Tilted with Moses to Save Fort Clinton at Battery," *New York Times*, May 12, 1963.

13. "Park Plan Voted by Washington Sq.," *New York Times*, October 11, 1939; "'Village' Park Row Will Go to Mayor," *New York Times*, January 24, 1940; "Citizens Union Fights Washington Sq. Plan," *New York Times*, February 8, 1940.

14. "Moses Drops Plan for 'Village' Park—Residents of Washington Sq. Section Conducted Long fight on $600,000 Project," *New York Times*, February 29, 1940.

15. "Park Permit Allows Rally Against Moses," *New York Times*, November 7, 1939.

16. Alfred Geiffert, Jr., foreword, "The Municipal Art Society Bulletin," November 1939, Municipal Art Society of New York Records, Archives of American Art.

17. "Move to Preserve Washington Square," *New York Times*, April 27, 1926.

18. Municipal Art Society Board Meeting Minutes June 17, 1936, Municipal Art Society of New York Records, Archives of American Art; "President's Report of Activities," May 1936–June 1937, Municipal Art Society, June 24, 1937, Anthony C. Wood Archive; Municipal Art Society Board Meeting Minutes, March 15, 1939, Anthony C. Wood Archive.

19. Talbot Hamlin, letter to the editor, Talbot F. Hamlin Collection, Avery Architectural & Fine Arts Library, Columbia University.

20. "The Row," *New York Times*, May 3, 1939.

21. Weinberg wrote of the buildings in question, numbers 7–13: "Demolished in 1939 by the Sailor's Snug Harbor, and replaced with a six-story semi-fireproof multiple dwelling. Following strenuous protests by civic groups portions of the façade were retained and incorporated into the new building with moderate success, as to exterior appearance, although the cornice line is ineptly handled, and the planning and construction of the new building are of such poor quality that they do not indicate an economic life-span of more than another decade or so." Robert C. Weinberg, "Memorandum on the buildings along Washington Square," Talbot F. Hamlin Collection, Avery Architectural & Fine Arts Library, Columbia University. Weinberg credits Hamlin's "intervention" for the preservation of the stoops and the incorporation of some of the original façade in the new building. Weinberg to Edward Steese, April 13, 1955, Professional Papers of Robert C. Weinberg Papers, Long Island University.

22. "Seeks to Improve Lower West Side as a Home Center," *New York Times*, April 23, 1944; "Plan Is Outlined for Village Area," *New York Times*, October 1, 1946; "Washington Square Tomorrow," *New York Times*, October 3, 1946.

23. "Fight N.Y.U. Building on Washington Sq," *New York Times*, September 24, 1947.

24. "Historical Society in Celebration," *Villager*, October 23, 1947; "Oppose 'Use of Square as Campus,'" *Villager*, October 23, 1947; "Mrs. Roosevelt Joins Washington Sq. Drive," *New York Times*, September 6, 1947; "1,800 Fight Change at Washington, Sq.," *New York Times*, September 29, 1947; "Manning Opposes Law Center Plans," *New York Times*, October 6, 1947.

25. "Opposition to Law Center Mounts," *Villager*, November 20, 1947.

26. "Act Sought to Bar Law Center Plans," *New York Times*, October 5, 1947.

27. Berenice Abbott and Henry Wysham Lanier, *Greenwich Village Today & Yesterday* (New York: Harper & Brothers, 1949). By December of 1949, half the site for the Law Center had been cleared of buildings. "Last Tenant Quit Law School Site," *New York Times*, December 23, 1949.

28. "Act Sought to Bar Law Center Plans," *New York Times*, October 5, 1947.

29. "Preservation of Square Is Topic," *Villager*, December 24, 1947.

30. "Manning Presses His Fight on Law Center Proposed by N.Y.U. for Washington Square," *New York Times*, March 17, 1948. In the fall of 1947, Mayor William

O'Dwyer appointed Wagner to become the chair of the City Planning Commission. He served until the end of 1949 having succeeded in his effort to become Manhattan Borough President.

31. "Villagers Strive to Save Landmark," *New York Times*, December 13, 1947.

32. "Evictions Upheld on Washington Square, Clearing of 'House of Genius' and Other Buildings Affirmed to Permit Construction," *New York Times*, January 7, 1948; "Village Evictions Ordered by Court," *New York Times*, January 24, 1948; "Villagers Strive to Save Landmark," *New York Times*, December 13, 1947; "N.Y.U. Purchases in Washington Sq. Stir Controversy," *New York Times*, July 18, 1948.

33. "Art Center Urged to 'Save' Square," *New York Times*, February 1948.

34. "Demolition in Square to Begin Tomorrow but Art Center Group Will Keep Up Fight," *New York Times*, March 16, 1948; "Wreckers Start on 'Genius Row,'"*New York Times*, March 18, 1948; "Retrial Ordered in 'Genius Row' Case," *New York Times*, May 1, 1948; "Art Center Lost, Bishop Announces," *New York Times*, June 28, 1948.

35. Lee E. Cooper, "'Genius Row' Sale to N.Y.U. by Builder Arouses Village," *New York Times*, July 16, 1948; "Moses Faces Sale Query," *New York Times*, July 20, 1948.

36. H. I. Brock, "Embattled Parnassus," *New York Times*, October 26, 1947.

37. "Washington Square North," *New York Herald-Tribune*, April 10, 1950.

38. Talbot Hamlin to Marie A. Doughney, 112 Grove Street, New York City, November 19, 1951, Talbot F. Hamlin Collection, Avery Architectural & Fine Arts Library, Columbia University.

39. Hosmer, Preservation Comes of Age, 303–305; Talbot Hamlin, "Historical Heritage vs. The March of Progress," *Journal of the AIA* 17 (June 1952): 288.

40. With the committee being chaired by Hamlin and among its members Weinberg and Gugler of Greenwich Village, the recommendation comes as no surprise. "Report of the Meeting, Historic Buildings Committee New York Chapter American Institute of Architects," January 19, 1954.

41. Abbott, *Greenwich Village Today & Yesterday*, 107; Jerry E. Patterson, *Fifth Avenue: The Best Address* (New York: Rizzoli, 1998), 31, 39; H. I. Brock, "Embattled Parnassus," *New York Times*, October 26, 1947.

42. Museum of the City of New York, "Brevoort Hotel," www.mcny.org (accessed April 3, 2006); The Raab Collection, "Signed Photograph of Lindbergh Accepting the Orteig Prize," www.raabcollection.com (accessed April 3, 2006); Stanley Turkel, "An Infamous Challenge," www.hotelinteractive.com/index.asp?page_id=5000&article_id=5453 (accessed April 3, 2006); Stern, *New York 1960*, 223; "Wreckers Attack the Old Brevoort," *New York Times*, January 28, 1954.

43. Landmarks Preservation Commission of the City of New York, Greenwich Village Historic District Designation Report (New York: 1969); Patterson, *Fifth Avenue*, 32, 39; "Demolition of Twain House Near; Only Last minute Aid Can Save Old Mansion," *Villager*, March 4, l954; Stern, New York 1960, 223, 1107.

44. "GVA Meeting Called for April 20," *Villager*, April 1, 1954; "Evaluating Historical Landmarks; Expert Says Landmarks Are Cultural Links," *Villager*, April 22, 1954.

45. "Evaluating Historical Landmarks; Expert Says Landmarks are Cultural Links," *Villager*, April 22, 1954.

46. "GVA Meeting Called for April 20," *Villager*, April 1, 1954; 459th Board Meeting, April 21, 1954, American Scenic and Historic Preservation Society Records, New York Public Library.

47. "Villagers Defeat New Traffic Plan," *New York Times*, May 28, 1952.

48. "Villagers Defeat New Traffic Plan," *New York Times*, May 28, 1952; Folpe, *It Happened on Washington Square*, 298; "Washington Sq: No Autos! City to Ban Buses Too," *Village Voice*, April 15, 1959; "Key 'Square Savers' Are Named," *Villager*, May 7, 1959.

49. In 1996, Norman Redlich gave a lecture on his role in preservation in the Village to a class on the history of preservation in the Village taught by Anthony Wood and Vicki Weiner. His remarks were transcribed. He then edited them for accuracy. "Norman Redlich Lecture," NYU School of Continuing Education: Greenwich Village: History and Historic Preservation, November 19, 1996. Redlich explained that "In 1958, however, Robert Moses was running the Slum Clearance Committee. He was running most everything, and he had made a deal with the developers of Washington Square Village, which was a Title One Project, that they would be given a Fifth Avenue address;" Mary Perot Nichols, "NYU is Top Landowner, Buys Washington Square Village," *Village Voice*, December 26, 1963.

50. Roberta Gratz unpublished manuscript, "New York Stories and Conversations with Jane," June 2006; Charles Grutzner, "Strategy Revamped on Washington Sq.," *New York Times*, March 30, 1958.

51. Folpe, It Happened on Washington Square, 303–308; "Hulan Jack For 36 Foot Park Road," *Villager*, November 7, 1957; "'Close Park' Drive Gains impetus," *Villager*, March 27, 1958.

52. Rubinow worked for J. M. Kaplan of the philanthropy bearing the same name. See chapter 10 for the story of Rubinow's and Kaplan's role in saving Carnegie Hall.

53. "New Group Pledges Fight against Washington Sq. Road," *New York Post*, March 28, 1958; "'Close Park' Drive Gains Impetus," *Villager*, March 27, 1958; "Washington Sq: No Autos! City to Ban Buses Too," *Village Voice*, April 15, 1959.

54. "'Close Park' Drive Gains Impetus," *Villager*, March 27, 1958.

55. "'Projects' Assailed as 'Dull Utopoias' at Packed Meeting," *Village Voice*, July 2, 1958.

56. Doris Diether recounted the St. Joseph's episode in the uncut version of her article, "Fight to Keep out Traffic from Washington Sq. Recalled," *Villager,* November 4, 1998, Anthony C. Wood Archive.

57. "Washington Sq: No Autos! City to Ban Buses Too," *Village Voice*, April 15, 1959.

58. Jane Kramer, *Off Washington Square* (New York: Duell, Sloan and Pearce, 1963), 58–64.

59. Redlich, NYU School of Continuing Education: Greenwich Village: History and Historic Preservation, November 19, 1996; Edith Lyon interviewed by Vicki Weiner, February 19, 1997, Greenwich Village Society for Historic Preservation Archive.

60. "Hulan Jack for 36 Foot Park Road," *Villager*, November 7, 1957.

61. That vote was Abe Stark, "he did really care." Redlich, November 19, 1996.

62. De Sapio had a chronic eye disease, which required him to wear dark glasses. Jonathan Kandell, "Carmine De Sapio, Tammany Hall Boss, Dies at 95," *New York Times*, July 28, 2004.

63. Edith Lyon interviewed by Vicki Weiner, February 19, 1997, Greenwich Village Society for Historic Preservation Archive. Edith remembered that Eleanor Roosevelt's niece was a "very top model at the time." Eleanor put Edith in touch with her and the niece got six of her modeling colleagues to gather signatures in the park.

64. Redlich, November 19, 1996; Lyons by Weiner, February 19, 1997.

65. Redlich, November 19, 1996; Jane Jacobs interviewed by Leticia Kent, October 1997, Greenwich Village Society for Historic Preservation Archive. The fortieth

anniversary of the closing of Washington Square Park to traffic was commemorated with a panel discussion in November 1998. On the panel were several of those involved in the fight. Through his involvement in the panel, the author became aware of the decades-long division this clash had caused between Village civic leaders and still felt its presence some forty years later.

66. Lyons by Weiner, February 19, 1997.

67. Mary Nichols, "City Closed Square Saturday," *Village Voice*, November 5, 1958; "Crowd Hails Sq. Ribbon Tying," *Villager*, November 6, 1958; The Greenwich Village Study was a group of "35 city planners, architects, engineers and other professionals" living in Greenwich Village who provided voluntary technical services to help the Village cope with its problems. Joining with Tankel were such Villagers as Jane Jacobs, Harold Edelman, Norman Redlich, and Ray Rubinow." Claire Tankel, letter to the editor, April 22, 1992, Anthony C. Wood Archive.

68. Redlich, November 19, 1996.

69. "Celebration Draws Over 1,000," *Villager*, June 18, 1959.

70. The Washington Square Association and some other eighteen Village groups had indicated their willingness to support the Borough President's proposal for narrower roads than Moses wanted through the park. "New Group Pledges Fight Against Washington Sq. Road," *New York Post*, March 28, 1958. Complete victory, getting the buses completely out of the park and redesigning the park without even emergency roads would take a few more years and a lot more politics.

71. Jacobs interviewed by Leticia Kent, October 1997.

72. In the 1952 effort, a group of advanced students in architecture and city planning from New York University and Cooper Union developed an alternative plan for dealing with the problem. The New York University students worked under Robert Weinberg. "Villagers Defeat New Traffic Plan," *New York Times*, May 28, 1952.

73. Redlich, November 19, 1996.

74. Ed Klein, "Citizens Fight to Keep Village From Being Built Out of Being," *New York Daily News*, December 6, 1959. Alan Marcus also led the petition campaign to "bring free Shakespeare back to Central Park."

75. Raymond Price, Jr., "They're Fighting Back in Greenwich Village," *New York Herald-Tribune*, January 3, 1960.

76. "GVA Zoning Study," *Villager*, May 7, 1959; Makielski, The Politics of Zoning, 90.

77. "Villagers at the Zoning Hearing," *Villager*, May 14, 1959; "Village May Be 'Historic' Zone to Preserve It," *Village Voice*, April 29, 1959.

78. Owen Grundy to Bard, June 8, 1959 and Bard to Grundy, June 9, 1959, Albert S. Bard Papers, New York Public Library.

EIGHT

The View from the Heights

WHEN THOSE REPRESENTING BROOKLYN HEIGHTS APPEARED AT THE spring 1959 public hearings on James Felt's proposed new city zoning resolution, they came not only urging the creation of special historic zoning for neighborhoods like their own, but with actual proposed text for such an amendment. On its own, drafting the ordinance was a remarkable accomplishment. However, making it truly extraordinary was the fact the Heights had only months earlier learned of the existence of the Bard Act and had just determined its own worthiness for possible protection under it.

Unlike Greenwich Village, which had a well-developed sense of its own historical and architectural importance and a track record of seeking to protect those qualities, Brooklyn Heights was much more of a convert to the formal concept of historic preservation. When residents ultimately "discovered" historic preservation, the Heights embraced it with a passion and purpose that even surpassed some long-time preservation devotees.

The epic seven-year campaign to achieve landmark protection for Brooklyn Heights is the best-documented chapter in the story of New York City's preservation movement prior to the passage of the Landmarks Law. For this, we have the lawyer and preservationist Otis Pratt Pearsall to thank. Noted for his "perseverance and a passion for documentation," Pearsall and his wife Nancy were lead players in the Heights drama. Because a conscious effort was made to document the history of the campaign for the Heights, we can follow it from its origins as an idea conceived over cocktails in a Willow Street basement apartment in the late summer of 1958 through its gestation in the undercroft of the Height's

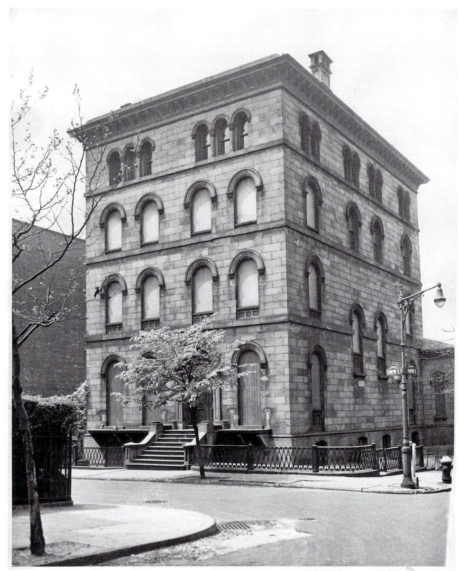

FIGURE 8.1 When it came to historic preservation, Brooklyn Heights' great awakening occurred in the late 1950s. Before that, many treasures, including 1 Pierrepont Place, the Old Pierrepont Mansion, would be lost. Designed by noted architect Richard Upjohn, the mansion was demolished in 1946.

First Unitarian Church to its emergence as a full-fledged movement that would rally hundreds of people, mobilize Brooklyn Heights, and command the attention of the entire city.[1]

The young people who rediscovered the Heights in the mid-1950s fell in love with a neighborhood that owed its distinctiveness to its past. The warmth of its old homes and the intimacy of its historic streets, just minutes away from the daunting towers and teeming life of lower Manhattan,

were inseparable ingredients in the magical formula that created a distinctive charm and powerful sense of place.

New arrivals could envision their dreams unfolding in Brooklyn Heights. When they realized that the past that contributed so much to the quality of their daily lives was threatened, they knew they were too.

Perched on a fifty-foot high ridge offering unparalleled views of lower Manhattan, Brooklyn Heights attracted those able to articulate its worthiness for preservation. Among them was acclaimed architectural historian Clay Lancaster. Lancaster would be recruited to provide the intellectual capital needed to support the landmark designation of the Heights. His prose succinctly captures what was then at risk: "The charm of the real Brooklyn Heights, with its tree-shaded streets and bluestone-paved walks lined by rows of fine old brick and brownstone houses behind decorative iron fences, and distinguished churches in the romantic styles, dating back to an era when this was the most easily accessible, desirable, and aristocratic suburb of New York."[2]

Lancaster carefully surveyed and studied the neighborhood, publishing his definitive *Old Brooklyn Heights: New York's First Suburb* in 1961. Though only at best a modest eight blocks wide by fourteen blocks long, within this compact residential enclave he found hundreds of buildings that even then were over a hundred years old. As a result, in 1965 the official document designating the Heights an historic district could report what was true then and remains so today: "Block after block looks much as it did at the start of the Civil War with many excellent buildings, some of which were designed by outstanding architects."[3] To walk Brooklyn Heights in the twenty-first century is to experience the nineteenth, with its distinctive sense of place intact.

The history of the Heights is tied to that of transportation. Brooklyn's "first and finest" suburb began to take shape shortly after the arrival of steam ferry service in 1814. In a pre-subway New York with its commercial heart still south of City Hall, Brooklyn Heights' desirability could be summed up in three words: location, location, location. As a result, it "became famous for having some of the most substantial residences in Greater New York," and by 1890 it was "one of the wealthiest communities in the nation."[4]

Improvements in transportation would be a double-edged sword for the Heights. They would open up the neighborhood to a wave of newcomers: first white-collar workers and later ethnic immigrants, while at the same time luring its longtime residents away. The influx of the new and the exodus of the old became a leitmotif through the history of the Heights. The early 1900s would see the departure of some of the neighborhood's wealthiest families. Many of those replacing them would be apartment dwellers, whether in converted one-family homes or in the new buildings that would begin to appear in the Heights.[5]

With a growing worry that its glamour days might be behind it and its future uncertain, efforts ensued to stabilize and maintain the standards of Brooklyn Heights. Protecting its residential character became the mantra. Leading this effort from its founding in 1910 to the present day was and is the Brooklyn Heights Association. In 1937, the Association published *Brooklyn Heights Yesterday Today Tomorrow*, by B. Meredith Langstaff, lawyer, Brooklyn civic leader, and a future president of the association. Intended, but not realized as an annual publication, this widely circulated pamphlet was an effort at civic boosterism.[6]

Noting that theirs was "the most convenient and the most delightful residential section of the whole city," Langstaff wrote: "The present condition of the Heights is deplorable in many sections, but that is your fault. If you, present residents, will do the best you can in beautifying your own property and if you will induce friends and acquaintances who would make acceptable neighbors to come and live near you the whole problem of Brooklyn Heights will clear itself." Distancing himself from the "defeatists in our midst, the mourners of the 'lost' golden age," he looked to the future: "We are no longer living in past times. The locality has proud traditions but it is not good sense to live off them. Let us preserve whatever of beauty or interest remains but go forward as fearlessly as did our predecessors."[7] Though extolling the residential quality of the Heights, his comment on beauty is as close as the pamphlet gets to touching on the Heights' architectural richness or aesthetic qualities.

Coping with disinvestment, the arrival of the apartment building, the influx of "new residents," and other challenges to its established residential character, the Heights approached the war years. In the mid-1940s, like Greenwich Village and the citywide civics, the neighborhood would collide with Robert Moses. Almost inevitably, the issue would be a highway, in this case the Brooklyn Queens Expressway. Originally, the Brooklyn Heights Association had been led to believe that the new highway would skirt along the western edge of their neighborhood. That changed in the fall of 1942 with the announcement that the proposed highway would bisect the Heights. Fearing the "ruination of the residential character of the Heights" and the probable loss of the First Unitarian Church, which at that time was preparing to celebrate its centennial, the association launched an effort to have the path of the highway returned to the originally planned westerly route at the edge of the Heights.[8]

Why was Robert Moses pushing a plan that would bisect the Heights? Henrik Krogius, a journalist and longtime resident of the Heights, delving into public hearing records and other original sources, presents an answer that, in light of all we have come to know about Moses, is not surprising. Running the highway through the Heights was the most direct way for the new highway to connect with other thoroughfares. Krogius suggests there was an additional factor in favor of this route. Among those in 1939 who had helped torpedo Moses' cherished dream of a Brooklyn-Battery Bridge were denizens of Brooklyn Heights. In fact, in his book on his life in public service, Moses fingers residents of Brooklyn Heights as being behind Eleanor Roosevelt's involvement in helping stop his beloved Brooklyn-Battery Bridge. Bisecting the Heights with the new highway could provide Moses with the ultimate in revenge. It became his choice for the path of the highway.[9]

The battle over the route of the expressway was not a lengthy one. Because of the higher cost of condemning private property for Moses' preferred route, his own engineers had problems with running the highway through the heart of the Heights. In addition, the Brooklyn Heights Association was able to muster considerable political opposition to the scheme. Brooklyn borough president, John Cashmore, who seems to have had more success than most in his dealings with Moses, is credited with convincing Moses to abandon the route that would have bisected the Heights.[10]

By the March 10, 1943 City Planning Commission hearing on the highway, the proposal under discussion was no longer the one that would have bisected the Heights. The proposal was now a six-lane, seventy-foot wide highway running at its western edge. This too presented serious problems for the Heights. The Brooklyn Heights Association raised concerns about the width of the highway taking up too much of the embankment. It questioned "the height of the proposed highway and its effect upon the future development of the Heights." Key leaders in the struggle with Moses included the association's then president, the physician, lawyer, and civic leader Roy Richardson. He was joined by a businessman and fellow board member Ferdinand W. Nitardy, and Paul Windels, former city corporation counsel.

During the course of the hearing, they discussed how to reduce the impact of the highway on the Heights. It was suggested the highway could be narrowed by having its lanes decked one over the other. If the top deck was covered, a portion of the backyards along the escarpment that would be taken for the highway could be returned to their owners. The entire

structure could be kept below the bluff so as not to deny residents their views. Krogius has found evidence, not public at that time, that prior to the hearing Moses already had developed plans for such a decked, cantilevered highway to be covered with a public promenade, similar to what exists today. A key difference between his vision and the one being advanced by Heights residents was the creation of the public promenade. It was Moses who wanted the deck covering the highway to become a true promenade, not a few isolated viewing areas separated by restored private gardens of the homeowners along the bluff. It would have been in keeping with Moses' general philosophy to seek to create such a magical and grand space for public enjoyment.[11]

Krogius suggests a possible additional motivation behind Moses' desire to create a public promenade. Unable to have his revenge by bisecting the Heights, here was an alternative: creating public access "across the harbor side of its most desirable residences." The public promenade took something that formerly had been primarily reserved for private enjoyment and transformed it into an amenity for the general public. Not only did the promenade diminish the size and quality of the rear yards of the homes along the bluff, it also created an elevated public walk impeding the garden level views of the homes along the bluff. If indeed the creation of the promenade was conceived in part as an act of revenge against the Heights and its leaders, considering how cherished it has become, one has to wonder who ultimately had the last laugh.[12]

Comparatively speaking, the Heights confrontation with Moses over the Brooklyn-Queens Expressway was relatively short-lived and civilized. Thanks in part to their political acumen and connections, Heights residents had dodged what could have been a fatal bullet. The expressway did inflict some damage, primarily the loss of buildings at the northwest corner, but considering what could have befallen the Heights if it had been bisected or if the six-lane highway had been constructed instead of the decked highway, the neighborhood survived nearly unscathed.

Those defending the Heights during this struggle cited surprisingly little about its architectural or historical importance. Perhaps these attributes were implied when its defenders talked of "residential character," but its historical and architecture heritage were certainly not noted as reasons to spare the Heights.

When something it treasured was at risk, the Heights could do battle with the best of them. For decades, residents kept a close eye on anything that might block their breathtaking harbor views.[13] In 1953, again under the leadership of the Brooklyn Heights Association, the community mobilized against an effort to allow taller buildings to be built on the docks below the Heights. Hundreds turned out at a "Town Meeting" called by John Cashmore, the borough president, and some five hundred letters of protest were mailed. Thanks in great part to Cashmore, the situation was turned around and a fifty-foot height limit was placed on new waterfront buildings. The jubilation over this victory was short-lived when the limitation was challenged. The headline reporting the story notes that the court challenge "Renews Biggest Fight on Heights Since 1940 Expressway Bid." The association raised funds so it could join with the city in defense of the height restrictions. The final hero of the drama was the Port Authority. It acquired the dock property, thus ending the legal challenge.[14] In battling for its view, the Brooklyn Heights Association demonstrated its muscle. It could mobilize citizens, deliver politicians, master zoning, and when necessary, go to the courts to defend its turf.

That considerable muscle had yet to be focused on protecting the Heights' architecture as a distinctive component of the neighborhood's special character. In 1946, the Old Pierrepont Mansion at 1 Pierrepont Place, a creation of the noted architect Richard Upjohn, was demolished. Robert Moses is credited with advancing the idea, as early as 1940, that the "then boarded-up" house be razed and that the plot be converted into a children's playground. There is no indication of a public outcry over the loss of the building.[15]

In 1947, Meredith Langstaff, perhaps in some way influenced by the loss of the mansion, upon his ascendancy to the presidency of the Brooklyn Heights Association, unveiled his plans for its future directions. They included a rare mention of preservation. He suggested: "The Association sponsor plans for saving points of interest and for calling public attention to the tradition and historical significance of the neighborhood."[16] The minutes of subsequent meetings reveal no concrete actions resulting from this statement. In 1950, the topic is mentioned again. At the Brooklyn Heights Association's annual meeting, Langstaff submits ten questions for the consideration of the membership. The first question concerned cleaner sidewalks. Question ten was: "Do you wish to take measures to preserve what still remain of historical and cultural monuments on the Heights?" There is no indication in the historical record that any measures were taken as a result of this question.[17]

The lack of traction for Langstaff's suggestions is partially explained by the predominance of lawyers and bankers on the all-male leadership of the Brooklyn Heights Association. In addition to lacking the aesthetic concerns of architects, several of whom would be included in the influx of new arrivals, the Height's old leadership also had a narrow sense of history. They appreciated the early history of the Heights, meaning its role in the revolution, but the significance of the history of its buildings and of the nineteenth century failed to capture their interest.[18]

In 1954, the growing interest in preservation that we saw evolving at the Municipal Art Society earned major coverage on the front page of the *Brooklyn Heights Press*. Under the heading, "Historic Heights Buildings Must Be Preserved Says Municipal Art Society," the Society's list of thirty-three important buildings in the Heights is printed. The article ends noting that with the appearance of the society's report, "the time seems ripe for the formation of a Brooklyn Heights committee to classify buildings in this area as to their age, and as to their historical and architectural importance." The time was indeed ripe for preservation action in the Heights, but there is no indication that any was taken.[19]

In lamenting the late arrival of preservation to Brooklyn Heights, Clay Lancaster calls out a series of lost treasures. Starting with the Pierrepont Mansion, he continues noting the "several blocks of the northwest corner of the Heights," including the Long Island and Atlantic National Bank Building, lost in 1953 as part of the Brooklyn-Queens Expressway project. Next was the 1954 loss of 222 Columbia Heights. Though surely regretted by some on the Heights, these demolitions did not trigger a call to action.[20] Like Greenwich Village, Brooklyn Heights had, and lost, its own "House of Genius." This one had been home to the likes of Carson McCullers, W. H. Auden, and Gypsy Rose Lee. Unlike its namesake in the Village, the 1954 loss of Brooklyn's House of Genius did not become a cause célèbre.[21]

Prior to the Heights' great preservation awakening in 1958, the closest thing to an architectural preservation campaign was the successful effort to save its "Willow Town" section from slum clearance.[22] Even in that struggle, the debate was framed around saving housing, not preserving aesthetics or history. Willow Town, the southwest corner of Brooklyn Heights, features among its treasures, the enchanting block, Willow Place. Though the Municipal Art Society list of important buildings, published in the *Brooklyn Heights Press* only two years earlier, had called out the importance of the four colonnaded row houses on this block, Willow Town's defenders did not call out its architectural quality as a compelling reason to spare it from the bulldozers. Today, one cannot walk this block without being overwhelmed by its architectural richness and powerful historical ambiance.

■ ■ ■ ■ ■ ■ ■

FIGURE 8.2 In the late 1950s, long before the demolition of Pennsylvania Station, Brooklyn Heights became a hotbed of preservation sentiment. In 1959, over four hundred Brooklynites flooded a meeting intended to advance the creation of some legal mechanism to protect their threatened neighborhood. This great awakening of interest in preservation came too late to save 222 Columbia Heights, pictured here on the left, lost in 1954.

Slum clearance, under federal Title One legislation, had come to Brooklyn Heights. One of Robert Moses' many official roles was that of chairman of the city's Slum Clearance committee. Willow Town was the northwest corner of a much larger site that had been identified for clearance. Its defenders were not against slum clearance; they supported it for the area to their south. They argued, however, that Willow Town was not a slum and should not be included. Such fine distinctions as to where slum areas began and ended were lost on Moses in his desire to create a new urban vision unencumbered by the remains of the old.[23]

Willow Town's fate would be decided by the Board of Estimate in the fall of 1956. The community organized a strong defense. Signed by over two hundred residents, petitions stating that "Willow Town is not a slum" were submitted by the Willow Town Association. Meredith Langstaff, still active but no longer president of the Brooklyn Heights Association, stated

FIGURE 8.3   Stunningly beautiful, this colonnade row 43, 45, 47, and 49 Willow Place, Brooklyn would have been lost to "slum clearance" if the community had not risen up to battle Robert Moses in 1956. Moses would go after Willow Town again in 1958. Captured here in a photograph appearing in Clay Lancaster's 1961 *Old Brooklyn Heights: New York's First Suburb,* the row survives today as one of the hidden treasure of Brooklyn Heights.

of the slum clearance of Willow Town: "It's impossible. I can beat that plan with one hand tied behind my back." Moses reacted to the opposition as he had done elsewhere. He wrote in response to a polite question from a Heights resident: "We can leave the Heights alone entirely, so far as Title One is concerned, if the residents and leading citizens can't agree on anything constructive or want to be left alone as you suggest."[24] It would soon be clear that though Moses might be convinced to leave Willow Town alone, he would continue to pursue modernizing the Heights.

The Willow Town Association, with the help of its supporters, prevailed at the Board of Estimate and Willow Town was saved. Reports credited borough president John Cashmore with persuading Moses to drop the plans. Heralding the community's victory as proof that citizens could fight city hall, at least one community activist, though appreciative of Cashmore's role, stated that the fight could have been won without it.[25]

There is another version of the saving of Willow Town that gives much of the credit to Mrs. Darwin R. James III. Heiress to the Underwood typewriter fortune, "the grande dame of Brooklyn Heights" and a major player at the Municipal Art Society, Mrs. James was a personal friend of Robert Moses. Devoted to the preservation of the Heights, at times she used her own fortune to purchase threatened houses in order to save them. She had Robert Moses come to her apartment where "she had a group there, and talked to him very earnestly about how destructive to the Heights that would be, and succeeded in persuading him to give up that particular development plan that would have torn down all of Willowtown." Adding to the plausibility of this is the fact that her husband had been supportive of Moses early in his career and had later supported his political ambitions.[26]

Ultimately more important than who actually saved Willow Town from slum clearance is the fact it was saved. In 1958 Moses would go after Willow Town again but fail to rid New York City of such a "slum."[27] Today, New Yorkers still revel in the beauty of this hidden corner of Brooklyn Heights. The near miss in the saving of Willow Town underscores the tragedy of what New York City lost elsewhere due to the excesses of slum clearance.

Even in the campaign to save architecturally and aesthetically rich Willow Town, the banner of historic preservation had yet to be unfurled. This would soon change as the Heights was "discovered" by a new generation of residents. In November of 1950, *Cue* wrote "Brooklyn Heights sits like a somewhat battered dowager on the cliffs above the harbor, her hat a trifle askew, her Victorian bombazine gown a bit worse for wear, but observably a great lady, nevertheless." By mid-decade, the great lady was beginning to attract a new wave of admirers.

They arrived not a moment too soon. In his slightly over-the-top interpretation of the history of the Heights, one-time resident Truman Capote depicts the neighborhood that awaited the newcomers:

> By 1910, the neighborhood, which comprises sly alleys and tucked-away courts and streets that sometimes run straight but also dwindle and bend, had undergone fiercer vicissitudes. Descendants of the Reverend Beecher's stiff-collared flock had begun removing themselves to other pastures; immigrant tribes, who had first ringed the vicinity, at once infiltrated en masse. Whereupon a majority of what remained of genteel old stock, the sediment in the bottom of the bottle, poured forth from their homes, leaving them to be demolished or converted into eyesore-seedy rooming establishments.

As critical as he was of the indigenous population of the Heights, Capote was complimentary of the newcomers who would indeed be its salvation. Lamenting the loss of the older homes of the Heights, he opines that no one cared about them: "No one did; until soon after the war, the Heights commenced attracting a bright new clientele, brave pioneers bringing brooms and buckets of paint; urban, ambitious young couples, by and large mid-rung in their Doctor-Lawyer-Wall Street-Whatever careers, eager to restore to the Heights, its shattered qualities of circumspect, comfortable charm."[28]

Arriving in the fall of 1956 as part of Capote's "bright new clientele" were Otis and Nancy Pearsall. They came to live in the basement apartment of a Greek Revival house on Willow Street with aspirations of some day becoming homeowners in the Heights. Soon they were meeting "newly-minted lawyers, bankers, architects and the like," singles and couples, who had either moved to or recently returned home to Brooklyn Heights.[29]

Individually, these newcomers were beginning to observe some troubling events that would soon unite them into a powerful new constituency for the old Heights. On the Pearsall's own block, an "ugly apartment building" bore witness to the loss of five "good 1830's houses" that had only recently been demolished to make way for its construction.[30] In late 1957 and spilling into the spring of 1958, the *Brooklyn Heights Press* covered a fierce controversy over a proposal by the Watchtower Society to raze five buildings—three on Willow Street—and construct a ten-story dormitory on Columbia Heights. The Watchtower Society, the Jehovah's Witnesses, had brought their headquarters to the Heights in 1909 and had been thriving there ever since. The main focus of the public controversy was over the fate of the tenants living on the site.

The Brooklyn Heights Association did oppose the dormitory on the grounds it would "destroy the principal charm of the Heights." The association explored with the City Planning Commission the possibility of establishing a height limit, but by the fall of 1958 had concluded that "there was nothing to be done to stop the erection of the ten story dormitory" and the decision was made to take no further action. As to pursuing a height-zoning restriction, the association's Board of Governor's felt they needed "strong community support to persuade the Planning Commission to act with favor thereon and even then it was doubtful if much could be done at the present time." By January of 1959, demolition was well underway.[31]

If the threat of more apartment houses and additional demolitions by the expanding Jehovah's Witnesses was not enough to galvanize the newly arrived young professionals on the Heights, there was another source of motivation: Robert Moses. His "Slum Clearance Committee was preparing to swallow up the entire northeast corner of the Heights through the Cadman Plaza project." Moses and Title One had Brooklyn Heights in their sights. Entire blocks were targeted for removal. Those not upset by the loss of the old were upset by the plans for the new. The proposed Title One housing was not to be "subsidized, middle-income, family-sized apartments" believed to attract a population having a greater interest in the community, but "efficiency apartments, small apartments, small, very expensive apartments."[32]

Seeing the erosion of their neighborhood beginning to accelerate before their eyes, the Pearsalls and others like them began to talk among themselves. They quickly discovered they were not alone in their concerns: "Somehow we did find each other and we gathered together our friends and our friends' friends, all young recent arrivals on Brooklyn Heights, who strongly felt the impending threat to the stability of this delightful corner of New York in which we had settled." As Otis Pearsall remembers, "Something new was in the wind."[33]

Something new was needed. Though they were experiencing the same events troubling the newcomers, the traditional leadership of the Heights was failing to respond. After years of service, perhaps they were just worn out. In 1955, the association's board of governors had discussed the "lack of attendance" at board meetings, and Meredith Langstaff talked of the "desperate looking situation facing the Association. Namely that the Association is running out of money."[34]

■ ■ ■ ■ ■ ■ ■ ■

Perhaps they saw these unfolding events as just part and parcel of what had been going on in the Heights for years. Had they become resigned to the inevitability of such events as the demolition of the two sets of Willow Street houses? Their inaction strongly suggests a feeling that these events were beyond their ability to control. At this point, the association's ability to address larger systemic problems was at its nadir. Whatever the reasons for it, as Pearsall aptly analyzed the situation: the old timers "did not view things through the same prisms" as the newcomers.[35]

Over the years, it has been preservation's experience that the fresh eyes of outsiders or newcomers are often needed to help restore vision to those whose familiarity with a place has blinded them to its beauty. The newcomers to the Heights would play this role. Not only could they see the full beauty of their neighborhood, they could clearly see the threats to it. They also brought the energy and idealism that allowed them to reject the inevitability of the gradual erosion of the Heights. Because they did not know it was impossible to stop the hemorrhaging of Heights' architecture and history, they were able to achieve success. As Pearsall observed of his fellow new young defenders of the Heights, they "possessed a youthful buoyancy and expectation of success that was wholly undiminished by any real idea of the obstacles this City arrays in the path of everything. . . . So lacking the wisdom or cynicism of experience, we were simply too ignorant and naïve to be much dismayed by repeated delay and disappointment." Considering the road ahead of them, this proved to be a very good thing.[36]

As we saw in the battle over traffic in Washington Square Park, sometimes a new organization is required to solve a perplexing problem whose solution has eluded established groups. It is often hard for longstanding civic groups to achieve the laserlike focus the solution to such seemingly intractable issues demands. Existing groups have histories and relationships that can constrain the advocacy options available to them when confronting a single issue. Existing groups also have the distractions and limitations of their own ongoing organizational needs and procedures. The nimbleness, flexibility, focus, and adrenal rush often required to successfully tackle the seemingly impossible at times is best provided by a new organization.

The newcomers to the Heights were freed of any institutional history. In relatively short order, their informal conversations about the threats facing their neighborhood turned into formal meetings. Soon they had coalesced into the Community Conservation and Improvement Council, CCIC (pronounced "kick"). In practice, its full name was almost immediately and completely abandoned in favor of its acronym.[37] CCIC was not formed to oppose the established Brooklyn Heights Association, but

FIGURE 8.4 The new arrivals to Brooklyn Heights in the late 1950s included Nancy and Otis Pratt Pearsall. Both became leaders in the effort to preserve Brooklyn Heights. Shown here in the early 1960s, Nancy Pearsall surveys historic fabric in the neighborhood. For a photograph of Otis Pearsall see Figure 12.7.

reflected the fact that the association was "remote and unknown" to the new activists. With much of the association's leadership in their sixties and the organization fixed in its ways, the Brooklyn Heights Association, in the words of Otis Pearsall, did not "appear to have a structure which could accommodate and harness our energy and enthusiasm." It was also clear the association did not regard the threats to the Heights with the same urgency CCIC did.[38]

CCIC went public at an open meeting in December of 1958. It presented its agenda to the community. At a special meeting of its board of governors, the Brooklyn Heights Association discussed this upstart group

that had appeared on its turf. Referring to it as the "Unitarian Group," because it met in that church's basement, the report to the governors apprised them that the new group was "very interested and would probably become quite aggressive in connection with ideas for future housing on Brooklyn Heights." The plank of the "Unitarian Group's" agenda dealing with historic preservation was not specifically noted in this report. If indeed preservation registered at all with the association, it was condensed into the observation that the new group's plan called "for rehabilitation of our neighborhood."[39] The association's response was to create a new committee to look at the concerns raised by CCIC and to commit to work closely with the new group. Fortuitously, this new association committee was chaired by one of its younger and more active members, the attorney William Fisher. Not only would he be instrumental in helping to bridge the important work of the two organizations, but several years later he would become a member of the Landmarks Preservation Commission.

Both the council and the association went to great pains to avoid any public appearance of being in competition or in conflict. That being said, the appearance of a new group in such a small neighborhood with an established civic group in place had to raise eyebrows. Behind the scenes, they were wary of each other: "It was inevitable that the old timers would view CCIC as an upstart and a threat and that CCIC would view the BHA as crippled by a good case of hardened arteries." Fortunately for the Heights, the leadership of both groups was smart enough to see that it was imperative that they cooperate with one another. CCIC selected three co-chairman to lead its efforts. In addition to two of its founders, Martin Schneider and Otis Pearsall, CCIC demonstrated its good political instincts by appointing the Brooklyn Heights Association's own Bill Fisher as its third co-chair. This was a conscious effort to send a strong signal to both the community and the association that CCIC would work in close partnership with the Heights' traditional community voice. Though publicly discussed, an actual formal merger of the groups was never consummated.[40]

CCIC would have a short life, but a permanent impact on the Brooklyn Heights Association. Thanks to the emergence of CCIC, the association refocused its efforts, received an injection of new blood, and refreshed its thinking. To its great credit, the association quickly recruited to its own board of governors, key CCIC leaders. Soon they would become the leaders of the association. By 1960, "for all practical purposes" CCIC had been "absorbed into" the association. CCIC's leadership, energy, and agenda were now fully embedded in the Brooklyn Heights Association.

Whether a virtual merger, a civic marriage, or an invited takeover, because of CCIC, the Brooklyn Heights Association and the neighborhood would never be the same.[41]

The public unveiling of CCIC in December of 1958 created quite a stir. Its statement of objectives was reprinted in full in the *Brooklyn Heights Press*. News accounts still framed the issues in the language of housing. In fact, the first story on the creation of CCIC was headed "New Group Charts Plan for Housing." Housing was indeed one of CCIC's major concerns, but its greatest legacy would be the second plank of its platform: "Our houses, historic structures and the architectural character of the Heights must be vigilantly preserved and safeguards must be developed to this end."[42] The language of preservation was finally spoken in the Heights. Once uttered, it would spread like wildfire and fundamentally change how Brooklyn Heights thought about itself and how it presented itself to the world.

It is curious why the language and consciousness of preservation as we know it took so long to manifest itself in the Heights. Housing, residential quality, and neighborhood stability were the lenses through which the Heights had traditionally seen itself as it confronted issues. Though for years, its own newspaper, the *Brooklyn Heights Press*, had used the tag line, "Reflecting the Traditions of the Historic Heights," a conscious public articulation of the importance of the Heights as an historically and architecturally significant place only appears with the arrival of CCIC. Had those qualities been consciously discounted before or had they just been taken for granted? Prior to its awakening, the Heights, unlike Greenwich Village, had not invoked the Vieux Carré or Historic Charleston as its civic kin. Was it the Heights' smaller size and more insular nature that made it so different from the Village in this respect? The questions remain for others to explore.[43]

Having gone public with its call for preservation of the "architectural character of the Heights," CCIC, soon in full partnership with the Brooklyn Heights Association, faced the same preservation challenges that had confronted the Municipal Art Society in the early 1950s. The buildings and places that one wanted to preserve had to be identified and documented. An appropriate mechanism to provide for their protection had to be researched and created. And an educated and engaged citizenry was needed. For the Heights, as with the Village, the last of these concerns would be the least of their challenges.

As their Manhattan counterparts had done, the defenders of the Heights took up these challenges simultaneously, each one being inextricably entwined with the other. Fortunately for the Heights, by late 1958, the preservation movement had evolved to the point that there was information and advice to be had. Past preservation initiatives would contribute to success in Brooklyn Heights. Among organizations Heights residents turned to were the National Trust for Historic Preservation and the Municipal Art Society. In addition, there was a small but growing active network of well-informed and passionate individuals who cherished places like the Heights and were happy to come to its defense.

Those leading the preservation charge in the Heights reached out in all directions and at a frenzied pace for information and help. Starting with a vague awareness of Beacon Hill's experience in preserving an intact historic Boston neighborhood, the Heights proceeded to give itself a crash course in historic preservation. Early on in this effort, a packet of material was received from the National Trust. In addition to including a sampling of historic district ordinances from around the country and a virtual "How To" booklet by John Codman, "the guiding spirit of the Beacon Hill success," the trust also provided a copy of New York State's own "Bard Act." We know from Otis Pearsall's reminiscences the excitement residents felt at learning of the Bard Act.[44]

Knowing that through the Bard Act New York State had given the city legal authority to protect "places, buildings, structures, works of art and other objects having a special character, or special historical or aesthetic interest or value," Pearsall and his compatriots were further delighted to discover that Brooklyn Heights had already attracted favorable attention from preservation allies from beyond its borders. Three publications provided valuable information and inspiration to the Heights activists as they moved forward.[45]

The earliest was Huson Jackson's *A Guide to New York Architecture 1660–1952*, prepared for the American Institute of Architects' national meeting in New York City in June 1952. Of Brooklyn Heights, Jackson wrote: "This neighborhood, having remained outside the main stream of great population increases for a relatively long period, has remained intact to a much greater extent than comparable neighborhoods in Manhattan, such as Greenwich Village or Chelsea . . . though there are not many individual buildings of great distinction, the character and residential scale of the neighborhood remain." He continues calling out a handful of those particular houses.[46]

The Heights was also represented in *New York Landmarks: An Index of Architecturally Notable Structures in New York City*, that ever-maturing child of the union of Edward Steese's Municipal Art Society Committee and the Society of Architectural Historians. Finally publicly released in 1957, the index included a special listing of "Buildings on Brooklyn Heights."[47]

■ ■ ■ ■ ■ ■ ■ ■

Most validating of all was Robert Weinberg's great work, *Planning and Community Appearance*. Years in the making, the report had appeared in May 1958 offering much encouragement to the young preservationists of Brooklyn Heights. In addition to the report's reference to the important *Berman v. Parker* decision and its chapter by Albert Bard on legal concepts, it confirmed what CCIC had recently concluded: Brooklyn Heights was exactly the kind of place envisioned for the type of protection authorized by the Bard Act.

The Weinberg report noted: "Areas of historic and esthetic value which are endangered by increasing real estate pressures are exemplified by Greenwich Village and Brooklyn Heights. . . . Their careful protection should be an important part of the municipal design plan and program where they are located. The 1956 New York statute . . . which Mr. Bard drafted, was drawn to enable this kind of protection"[48] For Heights advocates, in the words of Pearsall, this was the "piece de resistance."[49] Coming from a document prepared by committees of both the New York Chapter American Institute of Architects and the New York Regional Chapter American Institute of Planners, the statement had the true ring of authority.

Knowing they were on to something, the Brooklyn team continued reaching out for advice and support. Through networking, they connected with Henry Hope Reed of Municipal Art Society walking tour fame. Having curated with John Barrington Bayley the exhibit "Classical Brooklyn: Its Architecture and Sculpture" at the Long Island Historical Society Library in Brooklyn Heights, now the Brooklyn Historical Society, in January 1957, Reed was familiar with the treasures of the Heights.[50] He suggested the group contact the Municipal Art Society.

Characteristically, the Municipal Art Society responded by creating a committee. In this case, it was a special subcommittee of the Committee on Historic Architecture, the one responsible for developing and maintaining the society's index of buildings. Following in the footsteps of Edward Steese, Agnes A. Gilchrist, and Walter Knight Sturges, the architectural historian Alan Burnham was at this point chairing the committee and would now also chair this special committee to meet with the representatives from the Heights.

Burnham would play a special role in advancing preservation in New York City and beyond. His research is credited with laying the "intellectual foundation for the architectural preservation movement in New York." Brendan Gill said that Burnham was one of the "very first people in the whole country to care about the preservation of the architectural past."[51] Serving on the special Municipal Art Society committee with Burnham

FIGURE 8.5 Preservationist and architectural historian Henry Hope Reed helped connect Brooklyn Heights' nascent preservation efforts with the Municipal Art Society. Reed was well aware of Brooklyn's architectural treasures, having curated the exhibit "Classical Brooklyn: Its Architecture and Sculpture" at the Long Island Historical Society (now the Brooklyn Historical Society) in 1957. He served on the Municipal Art Society's special committee created to meet with the preservationists from the Heights. Reed, on the left, is seen here a decade later shaking hands with architectural historian Clay Lancaster.

were Henry Hope Reed and Albert Bard. Burnham would later serve as the executive director of the Landmarks Preservation Commission.

Hosting the meeting of the special committee and the residents of the Heights was the Municipal Art Society's own Mrs. Darwin R. James III, one of the saviors of Willow Town. Remembered as both a meeting and as a cocktail party, the gathering took place at her home, 2 Pierrepont Place, one of the Brooklyn Heights buildings listed in the Municipal Art Society's index. At it would be representatives of both the Brooklyn Heights Association and CCIC.[52] Mrs. James was a bridge between the old Heights and the new. She had taken Otis and Nancy Pearsall "under her wing, along with other people" and "had parties at her house at which she tried to have all these young people introduced to one another."[53]

For Otis Pearsall, the meeting at Mrs. James' home was "one of the most memorable of our movement's defining moments." Gathered in Mrs. James' top-floor apartment with its commanding views of the Harbor spread out before them, the sages of the Municipal Art Society and the neophytes of Brooklyn Heights discovered they were kindred spirits. "The discussion was excitedly animated and clear-cut that Brooklyn Heights had every entitlement to become the first historic district under the Bard law." Bard not only confirmed that the Heights fit the language of the act bearing his name, but as Pearsall recalls, Bard "did his very best to reinforce the enthusiasm he sensed in us for the importance of our cause." As Pearsall watched Alan Burnham and the "sprightly" ninety-two-year-old Bard admiring the gems of Willow Street as they walked through the Heights, Pearsall was "left with the euphoric sense that we were on to an idea that was truly meant to be." The Municipal Art Society was on board: "Our committee is prepared to stand by you and will be glad to endorse any plans which you might care to outline to us in the future."[54]

The preservation effort was ready for the next step. Pearsall remembers: "Having satisfied ourselves that the legal structure was available and the architectural history case was there to be made, the next step was to make it." Fate would have it that the perfect person to undertake this effort was a resident of Brooklyn Heights. Again, it took outsiders to find a treasure the Heights didn't realize it had. When CCIC asked Henry Hope Reed, Alan Burnham, and others who was the right person to document Brooklyn Heights, the shared response was Clay Lancaster. "Modest and unassuming, but toweringly authoritative," this "greatly respected architectural historian" would become the Heights' "intellectual guru." What began with a note slipped into his mailbox seeking help turned into a meticulous, highly professional architectural survey of Brooklyn

FIGURE 8.6 Brooklyn Heights preservationists knew that in order to successfully make the case that their neighborhood deserved protection, they would need to document its historical and architectural significance. As fate would have it, the ideal person to undertake that effort, the architectural historian Clay Lancaster, lived on Cranberry Street in the Heights. Shown here in April of 1959 taking members of CICC on an architectural tour of the Heights, he would become the preservation pied piper of the Heights.

Heights which morphed into Lancaster's book *"Old Brooklyn Heights: New York's First Suburb.* It provided "the uncontested credibility and solid scholarship" to support the campaign to preserve the Heights and would guide the Landmarks Preservation Commission's work when it was finally in a position to protect the Heights.[55]

Events were moving quickly and the strategy for how to preserve the Heights was becoming clear. The City Planning Commission's spring hearings on the proposed new zoning resolution provided an enticing forum and a sense of urgency. CCIC and the Brooklyn Heights Association decided to combine their considerable talents to seek "Historic Zoning." Not settling to appear at the hearing and merely state their support for the concept of some type of "Historic Zoning" and demand that it be applied to their neighborhood, Heights residents committed to present the text of an actual zoning ordinance at the hearing.[56]

Drafting the ordinance would be a team effort. Leading the team was the Brooklyn Heights Association's Arden Rathkopf, "a delightful firebrand of a lawyer who was the author of a leading treatise on zoning." He would be assisted by Sy Shulman, a zoning consultant brought in by the association, and Arthur Hooker, one of the young CCIC activists and a lawyer at Lord, Day & Lord.[57] In the process of developing the ordinance, Hooker was in correspondence with a very supportive Albert Bard. A concern was whether the word "place" in the language of the Bard Act could be interpreted broadly enough to encompass an entire neighborhood like the Heights? Responding in a series of three short letters all written the same day, Bard replied that it was indeed his intent for "place" to mean "any kind of place, large or small, which had any sort of unity calling for planning of any sort." In a very Bard-like note, he did point out that his "mental intention does not settle the matter." He advised, "Why not try for anything that the neighborhood wants in the way of protection or development? This would appeal to other organizations like those interested in Washington Square, Gramercy Park, the Fifth Avenue Association."[58]

A strategic decision needed to be made. Should the draft ordinance be "potentially applicable throughout the City pursuant to which Brooklyn Heights, not necessarily alone, could be designated an historic district," or should the ordinance be solely directed at preserving Brooklyn Heights? In the belief that the proposal would attract less potential opposition if limited to protecting only the Heights, CCIC argued for the Brooklyn-only ordinance. Rathkopf, the zoning maven among the group, believed it was unrealistic to seek such special treatment for one area. He felt the citywide approach was the way to proceed. Deferring to his greater expertise, the citywide ordinance was the approach adopted. Though this would be the approach ultimately followed by the city, it would be so long in coming that the Heights would soon abandon this strategy and strike off on its own.

With the decision made, the proposed ordinance was drafted. At the April 13, 1959 City Planning Commission public hearing, Rathkopf presented the ordinance on behalf of the Brooklyn Heights Association with Ted Reid representing CCIC. The seven-point ordinance would have created a five-member advisory design board appointed by the mayor. The ordinance would have empowered that board to protect both districts and individual buildings. "Echoes" of this proposed ordinance can be heard in the text of New York's Landmarks Law, whose passage was still years away.[59]

The Heights was beginning to buzz about preservation. The vision it offered was starting to capture people's imagination. Preservation was emerging as the popular cause it would soon become. This was in no small measure thanks to the editor and publisher of the *Brooklyn Heights Press*, Richard Margolis. The press had generously covered the advent of CCIC. It was supportive of the new while tipping its hat to the achievements and importance of the old. Once the concept of historic preservation emerged, the paper embraced it. A published story on the decision of the two civic groups to ask for historic zoning was followed by the editorial, "How to Make History." It applauded the concept and went on to encourage residents to help the "few people on the Heights" doing all the work. Its coverage helped build interest in the growing campaign. In early April, its front-page story announced the launching of Clay Lancaster's architectural survey.[60]

A special supplement to the *Heights Press*, paid for by CCIC, provided even greater visibility for the cause of preservation. Attention was focused on the architecture of the Heights with two articles on that subject, one by Clay Lancaster and one by Alan Burnham. CCIC's agenda was spelled out in detail. Articles ran on historic zoning and even a part of the Bard Act was printed.[61]

This flood of attention helped set the stage for what would be CCIC's "zenith," a town meeting on April 21, 1959. Even more important than the banner headline the event received in the *Brooklyn Heights Press* was the "morning of" story it generated in the *New York Times*. Under the headline, "Brooklynites Set Action on Heights," the first paragraph said it all: "A new generation of Brooklyn Heights residents is trying to get the city to act under a never-invoked state law to preserve the architectural charm and family-life advantages of the community." The effort to use the Bard Act to save the Heights was now citywide news.[62]

If there had been any doubt about public support for preserving the Heights, it was put to rest by the meeting. Over four hundred citizens, "an all-time Heights attendance record for a non-political meeting," packed the house as CCIC's agenda was presented. Moses' Slum Clearance Cadman Plaza Title One Project was a major topic. Also commanding attention was CCIC's preservation plan presented by Pearsall. The keynote speaker at the meeting was state senator MacNeil Mitchell, sponsor of the Bard Act and an author of the state's Urban Renewal Law. Offering urban renewal as the antidote to "Mr Moses' bulldozer approach to slum clearance," Mitchell suggested urban renewal with spot clearance could be the vehicle to preserve "the best of the neighborhood." Of this impressive meeting, Mitchell commented, "When I see this kind of crowd I know that you have the voice and the leadership to raise such a hue and cry that the city's administration will have to listen." Awareness and interest would continue to grow. In May at its annual meeting, the Brooklyn Heights Association featured James Felt speaking on "Zoning for a Better City." It also included a brief presentation on the Bard Law, "Its Possible Value in Preserving the Heights," by Arden H. Rathkopf. Preservation was now on the Heights agenda to stay.[63]

It had taken a wave of newcomers with fresh eyes to rediscover the special beauty of the Brigadoon-like Heights. It took youth and energy to confront the harsh reality that dramatic action would need to be immediately taken if the forces threatening the Heights were to be checked. It took their optimism and naiveté to believe they could indeed battle these forces and triumph over them.

Their arrival led to a new activism on the Heights. The threats the neighborhood was facing, primarily from Robert Moses and the Watchtower Society, spurred the new arrivals to take action. In doing so, they blew off the ashes that had been smothering the still-burning embers of the neighborhood's longtime civic advocate and watchdog, the Brooklyn Heights Association. The traditionally valued qualities of the Heights, its residential quality and charm, found new appeal in the language of preservation. In the words of Pearsall, "The physical aspect of the Heights, in fact, translates itself into a way of living. Our Heights way of life. The house and tree-lined streets impart to us a calm and dignity of an earlier time." The architecture of those houses and the history of those streets would emerge as the public policy rationale for the neighborhood's preservation.[64]

■ ■ ■ ■ ■ ■ ■

Like the Village, the Heights was threatened by Moses, an expanding institution, and the spread of apartment buildings. Both neighborhoods found in the Bard Act the hook on which to hang their future. Both communities enjoyed the support of the local press. Both neighborhoods knew how to command the attention of their elected officials. The promulgation of the new city zoning resolution provided both the opportunity and urgency to organize and focus.

Ironically, it was Brooklyn Heights, the neighborhood newest to the language and formal concepts of historic preservation, that would appear at the zoning hearings with a fully formed, "plug and play," ready-to-be-implemented historic zoning ordinance—only months after the Heights had learned about the Bard Act. Even more recently, the Heights had made its first contact with Albert Bard. Greenwich Village had known of the Bard Act since its passage and leading Villagers had been in touch with Bard since at least the late 1940s. Despite this, it was the Heights that first came forward with a concrete proposal for how to implement the Bard Act in New York City.

Having followed different paths at different speeds, Greenwich Village and Brooklyn Heights arrived in the spring of 1959 at the same place: before the City Planning Commission seeking historic zoning for their neighborhoods. They would find themselves in good company. Neither knew at the time that their quest for legal protection would require additional years of advocacy and angst. Fortunately, the passion and commitment that had brought them this far would help sustain them as they continued to face the pressures that set them in search of landmark protection.

ENDNOTES

1. Clay Lancaster, *Old Brooklyn Heights: New York's First Suburb*, 2nd ed. (New York: Dover, 1979), 9. Otis Pratt Pearsall's recollections of the campaign to preserve Brooklyn Heights have been captured in a variety of forms over the years, including his written account and several oral histories. The most definitive version is a thirty-three-page letter with over a hundred supportive documents from Otis Pearsall to Clay Lancaster as background information for the foreword to the 1979 Dover edition of Lancaster's book. Otis Pearsall to Clay Lancaster, September 7, 1976, Otis Pratt Pearsall Papers, New York Preservation Archive Project. Of additional value is "Otis Pratt Pearsall's Reminiscences of the Nine Year Effort To Designate Brooklyn Heights as New York City's First Historic District and Its First Limited Heights District," *Village Views* 7, no. 2 (1995): 5–22. At least two formal oral histories have been conducted with Otis Pearsall. One is: Anthony C. Wood, "Pioneers of Preservation: Brooklyn Heights and the Landmarks Law: An Interview with Otis Pratt Pearsall," *Village Views* 7, no. 2 (1995): 29–48, and the other: Charles B. Hosmer, Jr., "Interview with Otis Pearsall," June 25, 1982, Eastern National Park

and Monument Association, Charles Bridgham Hosmer, Jr. Papers, National Trust for Historic Preservation Library Collection and Archives, University of Maryland at College Park Libraries. Also of interest is a six-part article, "Battling for Brooklyn Heights," written by Martin L. Schneider that appeared between September 14 and October 19, 1995 in the *Brooklyn Heights Press*. Martin L. Schneider email to author, November 17, 2006.

2. Lancaster, *Old Brooklyn Heights*, 13.

3. Ibid.; Landmarks Preservation Commission of the City of New York, Brooklyn Heights Historic District Designation Report (New York: 1965), 1.

4. Lancaster, *Old Brooklyn Heights*, 20; Charlotte W. Elkind, "The Brooklyn Heights Association" (prepared for an M.A. in history, New York University, 1988), 4.

5. Elkind, "The Brooklyn Heights Association." Dozier Hasty, "Brooklyn Families Use Heights as a Springboard, Many 'Spring Back,'" *Brooklyn Heights Press*, October 3, 1974.

6. Langstaff reported to the board of governors of the association that he had "distributed about 3,000 copies of his booklet." Board of Governors Meeting Minutes, June 8, 1937, Brooklyn Heights Association Archive.

7. B. Meredith Langstaff, *Brooklyn Heights Yesterday Today Tomorrow* (New York: Brooklyn Heights Association, 1937).

8. Board of Governors Meeting Minutes, Minutes December 8, 1942; January 11, 1943, Brooklyn Heights Association Archive.

9. Caro's *The Power Broker* supports the notion that leaders on the Heights did play a role involving Eleanor Roosevelt. He tells the story of Paul Windels, a resident of the Heights, who approached Burlingham, who devised the Roosevelt strategy. Caro, *The Power Broker*, 671; Robert Moses, *Public Works: A Dangerous Trade* (New York: McGraw-Hill, 1970), 202. Henrik Krogius also notes that Moses had an additional though "lesser complaint" against the Heights. The Brooklyn Heights Association had worked against the Moses plan to permanently close the pedestrian walkway across the Brooklyn Bridge. Henrik Krogius, "Pearl Harbor Day: 50 Years Since Promenade's Completion," *Brooklyn Heights Press & Cobble Hill News*, December 6, 2001; Henrik Krogius, "'That Is Not a Promenade...' Or How the Idea Was Born," draft copy of an article, 1993.

10. Henrik Krogius, "Pearl Harbor Day; 50 Years Since Promenade's Completion," *Brooklyn Heights Press & Cobble Hill News*, December 6, 2001; Krogius, "'That is Not a Promenade...'"

11. Henrik Krogius, "Pearl Harbor Day; 50 Years Since Promenade's Completion," *Brooklyn Heights Press & Cobble Hill News*, December 6, 2001; Krogius, "'That is Not a Promenade...'; Board of Governors Meeting Minutes, April 13, 1943, Brooklyn Heights Association Archive; Elkind," The Brooklyn Heights Association." Both Richardson and Nitardy were facing the loss of some of their rear gardens to the highway. Nitardy particularly pushed for the covered highway with the hope that it would allow for the restoration of the lost garden area.

12. Krogius, "'This is Not a Promenade...'", 4; Henrik Krogius, "Pearl Harbor Day; 50 Years Since Promenade's Completion," *Brooklyn Heights Press & Cobble Hill News*, December 6, 2001.

13. In 1938, the Brooklyn Heights Association achieved a zoning change to limit the height of buildings on Brooklyn Heights, only to have it turned back by the courts later that year. Board of Governors Meeting Minutes, October 11, 1938, February 7, 1939, December 12, 1939, Brooklyn Heights Association Archive.

14. "Residents Fight Attempt to Raise 50-Foot Limit," *Brooklyn Heights Press*, April 23, 1953; "Town Meeting Thursday to Discuss H'ts Zoning," *Brooklyn Heights Press*, April 30, 1953; "Estimate to Act Today on Waterfront Zoning," *Brooklyn Heights Press*, May 14, 1953; "Cheers for Mr. Cashmore," *Brooklyn Heights Press*, July 30, 1953; Elkind, "The Brooklyn Heights Association," 23–24.

15. Martin J. Starfield, "Secrets of a Walk on the Heights," *Starfield's Brooklyn Historical Sketches of Brooklyn Heights*, 1984; Lancaster, *Old Brooklyn Heights*, 29. Neither the *Brooklyn Heights Press* nor the minutes of the Brooklyn Heights Association report any concern over the loss of the building. Instead, there was worry that the park project might not move forward and when it did, concern was voiced over its public comfort station. Board of Governors Meeting Minutes, April 13, 1948, Brooklyn Heights Association Archive.

16. Board of Governors Meeting Minutes, May 13, 1947, Brooklyn Heights Association Archive.

17. Minutes of the annual meeting of the Brooklyn Heights Association, May 10, 1950, Brooklyn Heights Association Archive.

18. Anthony Wood conversation with Otis Pratt Pearsall, May 3, 2006.

19. "Historic Heights Buildings Must Be Preserved Says Municipal Art Society," *Brooklyn Heights Press*, February 11, 1954.

20. Lancaster, *Old Brooklyn Heights*, 29.

21. "Brooklyn Chauvininsts, 1940: 'A Queer Aggregate of Artists' Keeping House in a Middagh Street Commune,'" *Phoenix*, March 4, 1976.

22. According to the press, the boundaries of Willow Town were from "Hicks to Columbia Place and from Joralemon to State." "Willow Town Association Opposes Slum Study of Area," *Brooklyn Heights Press*, August 2, 1956.

23. Ibid.; "Langstaff Has Another Plan," *Brooklyn Heights Press*, July 12, 1956.

24. "We Can Leave Heights Alone, Moses Writes," *Brooklyn Heights Press*, August 2, 1956.

25. "Willow Town Drafts Petition for Survival," *Brooklyn Heights Press*, August 23, 1956; "Langstaff Has Another Plan," *Brooklyn Heights Press*, July 12, 1956; "Willowtown Wins; Faces Old Problem," *Brooklyn Heights Press*, October 4, 1956.

26. Wood, "Pioneers of Preservation: Brooklyn Heights and the Landmarks Law: An Interview with Otis Pratt Pearsall," 30–31. For the Darin James–Robert Moses connection, see editor's footnote 1 of the article. In several conversations with the author, Pearsall stressed how personally committed and involved Mrs. James was and how she had personally intervened to save threatened houses in the Heights. Wood conversation with Pearsall, May 3, 2006.

27. "Willowtown: The 2nd Round," *Brooklyn Heights Press*, October 16, 1958.

28. Truman Capote, *A House on the Heights* (New York: The Little Bookroom, 2001), 17, 20–21. This first appeared in the February 1959 issue of *Holiday* under the title, "Brooklyn Heights: A Personal Memoir." Its upcoming publication received the top front-page headline of the *Brooklyn Heights Press*, "Capote Tells Nation Why He Chose Heights," January 15, 1959.

29. "Remarks of Otis Pratt Pearsall at The Brooklyn Heights Association's Annual Meeting Regarding the 25th Anniversary of The Landmarks Law and Brooklyn Heights Historic District Designation," February 27, 1990, Otis Pratt Pearsall Papers, New York Preservation Archive Project.

30. Pearsall to Lancaster, September 7, 1976, 3; Otis Pratt Pearsall Papers, New York Preservation Archive Project; "Remarks of Otis Pratt Pearsall," February 27, 1990, 2.

31. "'Witnesses' Ask to Demolish 5 Buildings—Tenants Fight," *Brooklyn Heights Press*, December 26, 1957; "The Way of the World," *Brooklyn Heights Press*, January 2, 1958; "Witnesses Tell Why They Want a New Dormitory," *Brooklyn Heights Press*, January 2, 1958; "'We Must Operate on Profit Basis'—Jehovah's Witness," *Brooklyn Heights Press*, January 9, 1958; "Heights Association Speaks Against Witness' Dormitory," *Brooklyn Heights Press*, January 23, 1958; "The Opposition," *Brooklyn Heights Press*, January 23, 1958; "'Tenants' Answer Charges Witnesses Own a Larger Dorm Site Near Plant," *Brooklyn Heights Press*, February 6, 1958; "Witnesses Must Build on Heights, Commission Told," *Brooklyn Heights Press*, February 13, 1958; "The Fight's Over—Tenants Are Satisfied," *Brooklyn Heights Press*, March 13, 1958; "Who Won the Fight?" *Brooklyn Heights Press*, March 13, 1958; "Witness Compromise Offer Accepted at Tenant Meeting," *Brooklyn Heights Press*, March 6, 1958; "Love Thy Neighborhood," *Brooklyn Heights Press*, January 15, 1959; Board of Governors Meeting Minutes, January 14, 1958, February 6, 1958, and October 4, 1958, Brooklyn Heights Association Archive.

32. Pearsall to Lancaster, September 7, 1976, 3, Otis Pratt Pearsall Papers, New York Preservation Archive Project; Wood, "Pioneers of Preservation: Brooklyn Heights and the Landmarks Law: An Interview with Otis Pratt Pearsall," 44–45. The controversy over the Cadman Plaza Redevelopment project would swirl in the Heights for years. Though it helped awaken the Heights to the need for some form of landmark protection, the battle over the project and the battle for historic designation would become separate. Those working for landmark protection felt that becoming too involved in battling Cadman Plaza, which was felt to be an "irreversible fait accompli . . . would involve an unacceptable risk to the larger goal of Heights preservation." "Otis Pratt Pearsall's Reminiscences," *Village Views*, 14.

33. Pearsall to Lancaster, September 7, 1976, 3, Otis Pratt Pearsall Papers, New York Preservation Archive Project; Hosmer, "Interview with Pearsall," 3.

34. Board of Governors Meeting Minutes, March 8, 1955, Brooklyn Heights Association Archive.

35. Hosmer, "Interview with Pearsall,"4.

36. "Remarks of Otis Pratt Pearsall," February 27, 1990, 2.

37. Because one can so easily and quickly get lost in the alphabet soup of organizational acronyms (MAS, SAH, AIA, ASHPS, BHA, RPA, etc.), they have not been employed in this account. However, in the case of CCIC, an exception is made because to refer to it by its complete name would be historically inaccurate since its acronym was so frequently used that its real name was almost forgotten by its own members.

38. Pearsall to Lancaster, September 7, 1976, 3, Otis Pratt Pearsall Papers, New York Preservation Archive Project.

39. Board of Governors Meeting Minutes, December 18, 1958, Brooklyn Heights Association Archive.

40. Pearsall to Lancaster, September 7, 1976, 4, Otis Pratt Pearsall Papers, New York Preservation Archive Project; "CCIC and Association Talk Merger," *Brooklyn Heights Press*, January 8, 1959; "It Takes Heap of Housing to Make the Heights a Home," *Brooklyn Heights Press*, April 2, 1959.

41. Pearsall to Lancaster, September 7, 1976, 15, Otis Pratt Pearsall Papers, New York Preservation Archive Project.

42. "New Group Charts Plan for Housing," *Brooklyn Heights Press*, December 24, 1958; "CCIC Lists Housing Goals," *Brooklyn Heights Press*, January 1, 1959.

■ ■ ■ ■ ■ ■ ■

43. In terms of their official historic districts, the Village has over one thousand more buildings in it than the Heights.

44. "Remarks of Otis and Nancy Pearsall," New York Landmarks Conservancy's Lucy G. Moses Awards Radio City Music Hall, April 25, 2000, Otis Pratt Pearsall Papers, New York Preservation Archive Project; "Otis Pratt Pearsall's Reminiscences," *Village Views*, 7; "Comments of Otis Pratt Pearsall at the Albert S. Bard Program," May 8, 2002, New York Preservation Archive Project.

45. Pearsall, "Otis Pratt Pearsall's Reminiscences," 7.

46. Jackson, *A Guide to New York Architecture 1660–1952*, 42–45.

47. *New York Landmarks: An Index of Architecturally Notable Structures in New York City*, 19, also see 15–18.

48. Fagin, 47–48.

49. "Otis Pratt Pearsall's Reminiscences," *Village Views*, 7.

50. Ibid., 8; Maryalicia Crowell, "Building Show Wrecks Moderns," *Brooklyn Heights Press*, January 17, 1957.

51. Gerald Fraser, "Alan Burnham Is Dead at 71; Architect and Preservationist," *New York Times*, March 21, 1984.

52. Alan Burnham wrote a thank-you note to Irving G. Idler of the Brooklyn Heights Association expressing his pleasure at meeting him at "Mrs. James' delightful party." Idler presided as president of the Brooklyn Heights Association at its May 11, 1959, annual meeting. Alan Burnham to Irving Idler, March 4, 1959, and Alan Burnham to Mrs. Darwin R. James III, March 4, 1959, Albert S. Bard Papers, New York Public Library.

53. Wood, "Pioneers of Preservation: Brooklyn Heights and the Landmarks Law: An Interview with Otis Pratt Pearsall," 32.

54. "Comments of Otis Pratt Pearsall at the Albert S. Bard Program," 3; "Otis Pratt Pearsall's Reminiscences," *Village Views*, 8; Alan Burnham to Otis Pratt Pearsall, March 4, 1959, Albert S. Bard Papers, New York Public Library.

55. "Otis Pratt Pearsall's Reminiscences," *Village Views*, 9.

56. "Ask 'Historic Zoning' for the Heights, *Brooklyn Heights Press*, February 26, 1959; Pearsall to Lancaster, September 7, 1976, 6–9, Otis Pratt Pearsall Papers, New York Preservation Archive Project.

57. Pearsall to Lancaster, September 7, 1976, 7, Otis Pratt Pearsall Papers, New York Preservation Archive Project.

58. Arthur B. Hooker to Bard, March 4, 1959, Bard to Hooker, March 6, 1959, initial letter followed by No. 2 and No. 3, Albert S. Bard Papers, New York Public Library.

59. "Arden Rathkopf's Historic Zoning Proposal of 1959," *Village Views* 7, no. 2 (1995), 23–28; "BHA Pleads for 'Historic Zoning,'" *Brooklyn Heights Press*, April 16, 1959; "Otis Pratt Pearsall's Reminiscences," *Village Views*, 10.

60. "Otis Pratt Pearsall's Reminiscences," *Village Views*, 7; "How to Make History," *Brooklyn Heights Press*, March 5, 1959; "Historian to Survey Local Architecture," *Brooklyn Heights Press*, April 9, 1959.

61. Alan Burnham, "An Architect's Ramble," *Brooklyn Heights Press*, April 16, 1959; Clay Lancaster, "Some of Our Fine Houses," *Brooklyn Heights Press*, April 16, 1959; "Historic Zoning for Heights," *Brooklyn Heights Press*, April 16, 1959.

62. Pearsall to Lancaster, September 7, 1976, 15, Otis Pratt Pearsall Papers, New York Preservation Archive Project; Charles Grutzner, "Brooklynites Set Action on Heights," *New York Times*, April 21, 1959.

63. "Record Crowd Hears CCIC's Housing Proposal," *Brooklyn Heights Press,* April 23, 1959; "Mitchell Urges Urban Renewal," *Brooklyn Heights Press,* April 23, 1959; "Program," The Brooklyn Heights Association 50th Annual Meeting, May 11, 1959, New York Preservation Archive Project.

64. Otis Pearsall's Speech to the CCIC Town Meeting Held at the Bossert Hotel April 29 [sic], 1957 [sic], actually held April 21, 1959, error on original, Otis Pratt Pearsall Papers, New York Preservation Archive Project.

NINE

HEARD. DEFERRED. REFERRED.

Mayor Wagner did not appoint James Felt, chairman of the New York City Planning Commission, to advance the cause of historic preservation. And James Felt did not assume the chairmanship to champion a preservation agenda from within the Wagner administration. Nor was Felt's revision of New York City's Zoning Resolution undertaken to provide the focus needed to energize preservation's supporters. Neither was it intended to be a forum to call attention to the unresolved issue of protecting New York's besieged landmarks and eroding historic neighborhoods. All accidental, such were the results of the above actions. Together, these unintended consequences would bring New York City tantalizingly closer to the day when it would have the ability to protect its landmarks.

As a third-generation real estate man specializing in "assembling land for big private developments" and as a governor of the Real Estate Board of New York, James Felt seemed an unlikely candidate for "preservation hero." Yet the critical role he played in advancing the Landmarks Law would lead two people intimately involved in the law's history, Geoffrey Platt and Harmon Goldstone, to see him in this light. The first and second chairs respectively of the Landmarks Preservation Commission used identical words when talking about Felt's singular role in the efforts that led to the creation of the Landmarks Law: "We couldn't have done it without him."[1]

More easily understood than Felt's support of preservation is Wagner's selection of Felt for the role of chair of the City Planning Commission. Felt was "an almost ideal appointment."[2] Having been immensely successful in business, "reputedly a millionaire," when he entered public service he "cut all private business ties." Prior to being sworn in as chair of the Planning

Commission in January 1956 he had held a variety of appointed public positions. He was highly respected within and outside of the real estate community. Known for his personal integrity, as a child Felt had aspired to become a rabbi. His appointment was greeted positively by several good government organizations, including the Municipal Art Society.[3]

In addition to prodigious energy, great knowledge, and a deep love of the city, he brought to the chairmanship just the right personality needed to address the challenges facing his agency. Described as having both "inner toughness and outer mildness," his style was not to "hammer down his opposition;" instead he was "both persistent and ingratiating, achieving goals by indirection."[4] Blessed with "great personal charm and persuasiveness," he would need all these traits to energize the City Planning Commission.[5]

Felt inherited an agency in which public confidence "was so low that its very survival was in question."[6] Years later, the *New York Times* described his appointment as getting "the unenviable job of pulling the City Planning Commission out of the doldrums in which it had languished much of the time since its creation in 1938."[7] The agency had been thwarted in its efforts at zoning reform and, daunted by the task of master planning and mastering the city's capital budget, "it was having difficulty keeping the thin shreds of prestige that remained to it." It was an agency on life support. Felt knew he had to demonstrate that the agency could play a vital role in the affairs of the city.[8]

James Felt had an ally in the mayor. Having himself briefly held the chairmanship of the City Planning Commission, Robert Wagner appreciated the role it could play. Unlike his predecessors, the mayor elevated the importance of the City Planning Commission, bringing Felt into his own "cabinet." The "felicitous" relationship between the mayor and Felt would serve them both well.[9] It would also come to serve well the cause of preservation. Felt succeeded in quickly building up the infrastructure of his agency. Next was proving it was capable of a major policy win. He turned his attention to revising the city's outdated zoning resolution.[10]

In choosing zoning reform as his priority, Felt had not selected an easy target. In fact, the agency had been bloodied twice before in previous efforts to tackle the issue. The most recent attempt at reform was in 1951. Despite the impressive work of planning consultants Harrison, Ballard & Allen, critical acclaim of the proposal, and over a thousand public meetings, the effort had failed. Though the commission had "stood its ground," politics had defeated the initiative. Behind those defeats were also the machinations of Robert Moses. As difficult as it would be, "Felt

■ ■ ■ ■ ■ ■ ■

saw zoning reform as the issue with which he could most effectively rally support for the commission."[11] Though it had been defeated in the past, a new zoning resolution was still needed by the city and desired by its good government groups. In an ironic turn of events, just as Robert Moses' heavy-handed actions had produced the unintended consequence of recruiting individuals and entire neighborhoods to the cause of preservation, his previous efforts to torpedo zoning reform had actually set in motion Felt's reforms, which in turn would create the very forum that had long been sought by those seeking historic and aesthetic zoning.

The process of revising the city's zoning resolution would provide the advocates of preservation numerous opportunities to advance their agenda. In February 1956, early in Felt's tenure, he sent the signal he would tackle rezoning. In July, he announced a new zoning study to be undertaken by Voorhees, Walker, Smith and Smith that would take over two years to complete. In February 1959, their proposal, *Rezoning New York City*, was released to the public. The City Planning Commission held a round of "informal" hearings on the proposal in April and May. It was these hearings that attracted so much interest from residents in Brooklyn Heights and Greenwich Village, and at which those two neighborhoods were so well represented. By December 1959, a revised version of the proposed new zoning resolution was released to the public. In March 1960, it was the subject of a round of formal hearings. The City Planning Commission held its final hearings in mid-September. They would adopt the new zoning ordinance in October 1960. The next and final stop for the ordinance was the Board of Estimate, which held its hearings in November. With their approval in December 1960, New York City would have its new zoning code.

Well before the informal hearings in the spring of 1959, James Felt was aware of the existence and the content of the Bard Act. In January 1957, Bard had sent Felt a copy of his *American City* article "Municipal Regulation of Esthetics Advanced." Bard had written the article to spread the word of the exciting new development in aesthetic regulation that the Mitchell Bill—soon to be popularly known as the Bard Act—represented.[12] In January 1958, while the zoning study was underway, Felt asked the Municipal Art Society for its suggestions on revising zoning. This opportunity was discussed at a society board meeting where it was suggested that the society should respond by raising the subject of Chapter 216 of the Laws of 1956, the Bard Act.[13]

These early attempts to advance the implementation of the Bard Act by injecting aesthetic zoning into the new zoning resolution failed. When the 376-page draft proposal was released in February 1959, the absence of any "provision in the new law regarding the appearance of our city" immediately caught the attention of one of its avid readers, Robert Weinberg. He was not surprised by the omission and surprisingly not discouraged. In correspondence with his colleagues at the Municipal Art Society, Weinberg states: "Ralph Walker, head of the firm that prepared the proposal, told me quite some time ago already that any type of aesthetic controls had not been included in the assignment given them, even though he for one felt that it could very well be added to the new ordinance before it becomes law." Weinberg approached Geoffrey Platt, chair of the appropriate Municipal Art Society committee, about the society testifying at the upcoming zoning hearings in support of including aesthetic regulations in the final version of the new zoning. In Platt, he found a receptive ear.[14]

Platt had served with Weinberg on the joint committee that had produced the still very new report *Planning and Community Appearance*. In this capacity, he was well versed on the Bard Act and what it could do for New York City. Like countless other civic organizations, the society had received its copy of the Voorhees, Walker, Smith and Smith study and was considering a response. At the society's March meeting, Platt reported that "it would be best for this Society to concentrate on the aesthetic considerations of the Zoning Resolution as at present no recommended control of any kind is included, as Mr. Felt thought it should not be in the original docket; and that he believed the Commission will be extremely interested in having some suggestions along these lines." This approach was approved for the society's participation at the April hearings.[15]

For the Municipal Art Society, the hearings on the proposed new zoning resolution were yet another step in its long march toward aesthetic zoning. For Villagers, the hearings were just the latest battlefield in their crusade to save the Village. For the fresh troops from Brooklyn Heights, the hearings were the first official stop in what they envisioned would be a speedy campaign to secure the Heights' future. The rezoning process would offer both hope and frustration for what was now beginning to be recognized as a preservation movement.

By the end of its round of informal hearings, the City Planning Commission had heard a lot about a subject not even on its agenda: historic and aesthetic zoning. The Municipal Art Society, the New York Chapters of the American Institute of Architects, and the American Institute of Planners had all urged its consideration. The call for historic and aesthetic zoning also emanated from the Village in statements from the Washington Square Association, the Greenwich Village Association, and the borough

■ ■ ■ ■ ■ ■ ■ ■

FIGURE 9.1 New York City Planning Commission chairman James Felt was instrumental in helping advance the landmarks agenda within the Wagner administration. Before he could push for a landmarks law, he had to secure the passage of his new zoning resolution. Felt, center of the table, is seen here at an April 13, 1959 public hearing on the zoning with fellow City Planning Commission members Lawrence M. Orton to the left and Francis J. Bloustein to the right.

president's Greenwich Village Community Planning Board. The Brooklyn Heights Association, in conjunction with CCIC, not only expressed their support for the concept, but presented their draft text of what needed to be added to the zoning resolution to make it happen.

The City Planning Commission heard their pleas. The Municipal Art Society's minutes report that "City Planning Commissioner Felt has expressed appreciation for the Society's recommendations that the Proposed Zoning Regulation be broadened to include various aesthetic considerations which would assist preservation of historic or architecturally

significant neighborhoods and buildings." Additionally, Brooklyn Heights advocates felt the commission had been open to their appeal and not dismissive of their proposal.[16] Public confirmation that the commission had actually heard the advocates and was taking the idea seriously took the form of a quote from Felt reported in an August 1959 story in the *Villager*: "We are considering the feasibility of zoning controls, which will afford necessary aesthetic and historic protection. Our technical staff has been instructed to obtain material from the National Trust for Historic Preservation."[17] Finally, a New York City municipal agency was officially exploring what the civic sector had been talking about for years.

The coming together of the citywide civic organizations, Brooklyn Heights, Greenwich Village, and anticipated support from Staten Island, led the *Villager* to recognize that this chorus crying out for historic and aesthetic zoning was actually a "growing city-wide movement." In August, the *Villager* recognized the addition to this chorus of voices from Gramercy Park, Riverdale, and Richmondtown, noting that "civic organizations in all these areas are actively campaigning for such protection."[18]

A nascent preservation movement had emerged. At this point, those in it were unified only in their ultimate goal, some form of landmarks protection. Of the experiences bringing these various players to the zoning hearings, some had been shared, others unique. At times, those in the movement diverged in their tactics and at other times, they had converged. This was a movement of shared values, not coordinated actions or necessarily similar attitudes and temperaments. The dynamics of the events unfolding in the city and in individual neighborhoods would continue to compel individuals and organizations to pursue a range of different strategies. Some efforts would be unilateral, others done in partnership. Some would be more successful than others. All would play a role in advancing the preservation agenda.

The spring and summer of 1959 were a time of high anxiety for Greenwich Village. As the Village was focusing on the proposed new zoning resolution, other issues continued to command attention. Though the great victory of temporarily closing Washington Square Park to traffic had been realized, the permanency of this accomplishment was still in doubt. The issue remained highly charged politically. Issues such as traffic around the square and bus use of the park remained contentious and would continue to be so for years. Buses would not permanently exit the park until the fall of 1963. At this time, and in the months ahead, considerable energy and attention still had to be focused on the battle over Washington Square Park.[19]

Development and redevelopment pressures on the Village continued to rise. Its postwar conundrum—how to have "more adequate housing, but not at the cost of destroying the Village's unique community character"—remained unsolved. In May, the Greenwich Village Association sought to tackle the problem with the creation of a new housing committee under the leadership of Whitney North Seymour, Jr. They launched a building survey and investigated housing conditions. Seymour described their efforts as part of a "'crash program' to preserve the neighborhood character of the Village."[20] Indeed, the old Village was crashing down and villagers were losing their homes. One villager in particular would not give up his home. His struggle would help mobilize public support to save the Village and focus new public attention on the Bard Act.

The Village resident who would not go quietly was the "well-known" sculptor, Arnold Henry Bergier. His "picturesque studio house" was located in the path of a planned apartment house and parking lot. In true Village fashion, in response to this threat, Bergier convened an emergency meeting in his home. Participating in the discussion were some of the best planning, preservation, and political minds in the Village: Robert C. Weinberg, Arthur C. Holden, and Whitney North Seymour, Jr. Those gathered realized that the only hope for the Village was to change the zoning. A week later on September 10, 1959, the *Villager* announced the creation of a new communitywide organization, Save the Village, with the goal of doing just that. With the "eviction-fighting sculptor" Arnold H. Bergier as its temporary chair, Save the Village announced a campaign "designed to implement the recent state Bard Law."[21]

Over the next several years, Save the Village played a critical role in protecting the Village. It would evolve a multipronged strategy—fighting evictions, seeking rent protection, and pursuing zoning and planning tools—to keep the historic Village intact until a landmarks law could take over the job.[22] In the fall of 1959, with the proposed new zoning resolution still under study by the City Planning Commission, the zoning piece of their strategy was the top priority. This effort would concentrate on two initiatives that together would truly protect the Village: obtaining the type of protection authorized by the Bard Act, and obtaining the passage of "The Save the Village Zoning Amendment."[23] On the latter, they would achieve almost immediate success; on the former, they would help demonstrate popular support for an idea whose implementation was still years away.

The proposed new zoning resolution held great promise for the Village. Felt and his staff were exploring the feasibility of the historic and

■ ■ ■ ■ ■ ■ ■

FIGURE 9.2 At the end of the 1950s, demolition pressure on the historic blocks of Greenwich Village was out of control. To respond to this crisis, a new grassroots organization, Save the Village, was born. It would jump into the city rezoning battle and become a strong voice for historic preservation.

aesthetic zoning the Village had requested. Additionally, the proposed new zoning resolution would "limit the height of new buildings on Village residential streets to the present scale."[24] Along with these positive developments, there was a major problem. On June 24, 1959, in an effort to ease "undercurrents of opposition" to a new zoning resolution, James Felt announced that when a new zoning resolution was ultimately approved, it would not take effect until a year after its passage. This would create a "grace period" that would legally "grandfather in" building projects that followed the old zoning that were started during this period. Though this move disappointed the "reform-oriented groups," it has been seen as a "shrewd political tactic."[25] It clearly reflects the depth of Felt's commitment to get a new zoning resolution passed. As Felt stated: "If I may say so, we shall extend every effort. If it is the last thing that I shall do with the City Planning Commission we will have a new Zoning Resolution."[26]

Whether the one-year moratorium on the activation of the new zoning resolution was a necessary concession to obtaining its passage can never be known. We do know the result of pushing off the effective date of the new zoning until December 1961, a year after its final approval. According to William F. R. Ballad, the chair of the City Planning Commission who followed Felt, "In the rush to get in under the wire of the 1961 cut-off date, applications were filed for a colossal 150,659 multiple-dwelling units. That represented about five average years' worth of housing."[27] That number would have been greater if Robert Weinberg had not anticipated the devastation the grace period would have wrought on Greenwich Village and devised a brilliant, preemptive response: "The Save the Village Zoning Amendment."

While the debate was raging over the contents of the new zoning resolution, Weinberg proposed that Greenwich Village go to the City Planning Commission and request that the existing zoning resolution—the one that would still be in effect during the one-year grace period—be amended to restrict the height of new construction in the Village. If successful, this gambit would protect the neighborhood from the race to get projects in the ground under the old rules before newer, more restrictive zoning went into effect. The zoning that Weinberg's amendment would put in place was reported to the community as "essentially the recommendation made several years ago by Arthur C. Holden in his famous 'Washington Square Survey.'" Apparently, several years meant *fifteen*! The forces in the Village—the Greenwich Village Association, the Washington Square Association, the borough president's Village Planning Board—joined with Save the Village to support Weinberg's amendment.[28]

Thinking was also progressing on how the Village could advance the campaign to have New York utilize the powers authorized by the Bard Act. Arthur Holden, architect, planner, and preservation warhorse that he was, took up the challenge. Having been a civic comrade in arms with Bard dating back to at least the 1939 battle with Robert Moses over the Brooklyn-Battery Bridge, nonlawyer Holden set to work on legislation that would bring the Bard Act to life in New York City. To an extent not fully known, Bard provided him assistance.[29] The *Villager*, following the subject closely, would report in the fall of 1959 that "Mr. Bard and city planner Arthur C. Holden are at work on a New York City law putting this into effect, on behalf of Save the Village."[30] As seen earlier, Bard was happy to advise and encourage any and all who showed interest in putting the Bard Act into practice.

With evictions and demolitions spurring it on, Save the Village mounted its offensive. After only three weeks, it had gathered ten thousand signatures on petitions in support of "various city-wide measures to 'protect New York's cherished neighborhoods, rezone and save Greenwich Village

FIGURE 9.3 Blessed with a youthful appearance most of his life, ninety-three-year-old Albert Bard was finally beginning to look his age at the time this photograph was taken in the Lawyer's Club Library in New York City. He may have looked his age, but he certainly did not act it. Almost until his death at the age of ninety-six, Bard continued to attend public hearings, meetings, and rallies.

from mass demolitions and evictions.'"[31] Directing the petition drive was Alan Marcus, the same man who had organized the massive petition campaign to close Washington Square Park to traffic.[32] Indicative of the Village's media savvy, the first person to sign the Save the Village petition at a kick-off meeting in Arnold Bergier's studio, and the headquarters of Save the Village, was the indomitable Albert Bard. His signature was followed by those of the heads of the major Village organizations and such familiar names as Robert Weinberg and Stanley Tankel.[33]

Just shy of his ninety-third birthday, Albert Bard, the "prominent attorney and veteran crusader for conservation of scenic and historic sites," was no mere figurehead for this cause. Addressing a meeting of the Greenwich Village Association, he exhorted New Yorkers to take action: "The door is now wide open. It is up to Greenwich Village, Brooklyn Heights, Morningside Heights (where Columbia University is located), Gramercy Park, and other historic neighborhoods to take advantage of the new legal provisions."[34] What was more amazing—the general public's rallying to Bard's cause or that Bard had lived long enough to witness it? "Emblazoned with a photo of a steam shovel and wrecker's iron ball," the Save

the Village petitions garnered fifteen thousand signatures by January of 1960.[35]

The Village was making progress. Meetings took place with the City Planning Commission. The revised draft of the proposed new zoning resolution included good news for the Village. New residential buildings would be limited to an average of six stories, not nine. Of equal if not greater importance, the City Planning Commission was willing to consider Weinberg's gambit of amending the existing zoning resolution to immediately implement this change. In grand advocacy style, some seventy-five villagers appeared in support of "The Save the Village Zoning Amendment" at the commission's hearing. Never at a loss for publicity-generating gimmicks, villagers traveled down to City Hall on the Salvador Dalí designed sightseeing vehicle, the "Loconik." Soon thereafter in March of 1960, Save the Village was able to declare victory when the Board of Estimate approved Weinberg's emergency zoning amendment sparing the Village from the orgy of destruction that would almost certainly have otherwise followed the approval of the new zoning resolution. Though villagers would ultimately be frustrated by some of the concessions Felt made to developers, they would turn out in force to support the new zoning resolution as they had braved the ravages of Hurricane Donna to support their own amendment.[36]

When it came to the implementation of the Bard Act, Save the Village would not enjoy the same success it achieved with the passage of Weinberg's emergency zoning amendment. The petition campaign was only one of their efforts to promote the use of the Bard Act. In June of 1960, Arnold Bergier raised the issue of New York's utilization of the Bard Act directly with Mayor Wagner. The mayor had come to the Village for the opening of a new mobile municipal information trailer, unofficially known as the "gripemobile." In a sit-down, face-to-face exchange that was captured on film and reported in both Village newspapers, Bergier discussed the Bard Act with Mayor Wagner. The *Villager* reported that the mayor "promised to designate someone in the city administration to investigate the application of the Bard law to current Greenwich Village housing problems."[37]

In August, it was further reported that Bergier was meeting with the mayor's staff in preparation for a fall meeting with Wagner to discuss "the potentialities of the Bard Law." The liaison facilitating the continuing conversation between Bergier and the mayor was Robert Low, an assistant to the mayor. In 1964, as a member of the New York City Council, Low would be one of the three members to the New York City Council who would introduce Wagner's proposed landmarks legislation.[38]

∎ ∎ ∎ ∎ ∎ ∎ ∎

Appealing To Mayor To Help Village

Photo by John Minutoli, Dep't of Commerce and Public Events

Arnold Bergier, Village sculptor and a spearhead of the Save the Village Committee, urges Mayor Wagner (r.) to invoke provisions of the Bard Law enacted to preserve landmarks and other colorful parts of communities.

FIGURE 9.4 Arnold Bergier, the sculptor who would not go quietly when his studio was slated for demolition, became the temporary chair of Save the Village. Bergier personally urged Mayor Wagner, seen here in a June 27, 1960 photo, to use the Bard Act to protect the Village. The media was there to capture Bergier raising this with the mayor at the Village unveiling of a new mobile municipal information trailer.

Despite the efforts of Save the Village and many other organizations, the neighborhood had failed in its effort to have aesthetic and historic zoning included in Felt's new zoning resolution. It had, however, demonstrated the popular appeal of the idea. Furthermore, the Village had brought the issue directly, and very publicly, to Mayor Wagner's attention. One can only wonder if the miracle-working Village advocates would have had more success in their campaign to include historic and aesthetic zoning in the new zoning resolution if they had not been waging a two-front war: one for aesthetic zoning and the other to amend the existing zoning to protect the Village through Felt's grace period.

Pig Pickets to Save Village

(Associated Press foto)

Mrs. Doris Diether leads pig on leash as she heads group of sign-carrying Greenwich Villagers protesting outside Gov. Rockefeller's office at 22 W. 55th St. Using the rented pig as a symbol of greed and avarice, the Save the Village Committee is seeking to halt demolition of older buildings to make way for luxury apartments.

FIGURE 9.5 To dramatize the "avarice" of real estate developers destroying old buildings in the Village and replacing them with luxury apartments, Save the Village enlisted a pig (at a fee of $50 an hour) to join their protest. Doris Diether, Village activist and zoning expert, is seen here holding the leash of the somewhat reluctant picketer. Appearing under the caption, "Pig Pickets to Save Village," this photograph that appeared on May 22, 1960 in the *New York Daily News* represents the type of media coverage such successful stunts received.

The Brooklyn Heights advocates, who unlike the villagers had arrived at the spring 1959 informal hearings on the new zoning resolution with a draft preservation ordinance in hand, also failed in their efforts to inject preservation into the new zoning resolution. During the long gestation period for the new zoning resolution, the Heights would continue to advance the preservation agenda and demonstrate its popular appeal. After the hearings, under the direction of Clay Lancaster, the Heights would plunge into the essential work of documenting the architectural and historical significance of the neighborhood.

The Heights preservation initiative gained added momentum in the spring of 1960 at the Brooklyn Heights Association's fiftieth anniversary meeting. By then, virtually all the leadership of CCIC had become part of the association. Otis Pearsall, who had been temporarily sidelined from preservation due to a challenging new professional position, returned to the cause and was recruited to the association's board by Bill Fisher. Preservation had become the association's agenda. The speaker at the association's Golden Jubilee annual meeting in the ballroom of the St. George Hotel that May was Clay Lancaster's friend, the president of the National Trust for Historic Preservation, Richard H. Howland. In front of a crowd of seven hundred people, he "beat an eloquent drum for Heights preservation."[39]

Not disillusioned by its inability to have preservation incorporated into the new zoning, after this annual meeting the association created a new committee to concentrate on the preservation of the Heights. Its key strategist would be Otis Pearsall. By that fall, a "Battle Plan for the Preservation of Brooklyn Heights" was in place. It anticipated a two- or three-year effort and created a web of working committees to accomplish its task.[40] Informed by the model of Boston's Beacon Hill, the Heights now "single-mindedly pushed for a standalone Brooklyn Heights Historic District."[41] The focused and increasingly formidable preservation movement in Brooklyn Heights had staked out its strategy. Having failed to secure protection for the Heights through a citywide system for landmark protection, the Heights resolved to pursue what it felt would be a more politically viable option: a preservation ordinance focused just on protecting Brooklyn Heights. Advocates reasoned that such a geographically narrow approach would likely arouse less political opposition from the opponents of preservation than a citywide scheme. Heights residents would soon discover that it was the proponents of preservation, not its opponents, who would be aroused by their proposal and counter their efforts.

FIGURE 9.6   Brooklyn Heights had hoped that the new zoning resolution would be the vehicle to provide protection for its historical and architectural treasures; that was not to be. While developing a new strategy to obtain protection, the Heights concentrated its energies on researching and documenting the case for its preservation. Directing that effort was the architectural historian Clay Lancaster, shown here leading a walking tour.

Like the preservation advocates in Greenwich Village and Brooklyn Heights, the citywide civic groups had also been intently following the work of the City Planning Commission on the proposed new zoning resolution. Shortly after the informal zoning hearings in the spring of 1959, L. Bancel LaFarge, president of the American Institute of Architects, New York City chapter, wrote James Felt expressing the hope that historic and aesthetic values might be included in the new zoning. As a past president of the Municipal Art Society and the chair of the special committee it had created after the passage of the Bard Act to "consider ways and means of having such legislation implemented with respect to New York City," LaFarge was well briefed on the subject. However, at the same time he was urging Felt to move forward with aesthetic zoning, he voiced another opinion that would ultimately trump the first: "There is no desire on our part to further complicate the eventual passage of the new Zoning Resolution."[42]

The Municipal Art Society had also been closely following the work of the City Planning Commission. After the round of informal hearings, it consulted with its architectural and planning sister organizations on advancing some form of aesthetic controls. In late September 1959, Geof-frey Platt updated the society's board on where the issue stood. Though the City Planning Commission had voiced interest in aesthetic controls, since such controls had not been "an integral part of what has been pro-posed," the commission thought that "aesthetic control would have a bet-ter chance of enactment if added later to the Zoning Resolution." It was decided that the society should "work out some control of aesthetics for designated areas and would attempt to have it included in the proposed Zoning Resolution at this time. If this could not be done, it would continue to press for its addition at a later date." At the meeting, participants were reminded of the existence of the Bard Act. It was concluded that: "The question seems to be how shall New York City exercise this power."[43]

When it came to advancing his dream of aesthetic regulation, Bard never gave up hope. As the City Planning Commission was crafting its revised zoning resolution (released in December of 1959), Bard was at work pro-moting an October 6 City Club luncheon in honor of James Felt. He sent a personal note to at least twenty people, among them such familiar names as Arthur Holden, Francis Keally, and Owen Grundy, encouraging them to attend. In his note, Bard displayed both his irrepressible advocacy and his never-flagging optimism: "Mr. Felt is putting new life into the Plan-ning Commission and needs encouragement by an evidence of interest on the part of distinguished citizens especially interested in the appearance of the city. He favors new powers for this purpose to go into the Zoning Resolution now under discussion." Perhaps at the time of Bard's note, Felt was still open to that concept—if so, that would soon change.[44]

In late October 1959, Geoffrey Platt again reported to the Municipal Art Society's board. His committee had met with Bard and Arthur Holden to discuss a draft of possible legislation. This is likely related to Holden's efforts to draft legislation as had been reported earlier in the press.[45] By the November board meeting, Platt was able to report that "good progress" had been made on draft legislation and credited this to Arthur Holden. Platt noted that it was unlikely the commission would include this in the new Zoning Resolution "because it might jeopardize the zoning law and the objects the committee wishes to obtain. The Planning Commission feels it will have a much better chance for enactment if it comes up after the Zoning Resolution is passed."[46]

With the release of the City Planning Commission's Revised Zoning Resolution, Platt's report was proven prophetic. Historic or aesthetic zon-ing had not made its way into that document. In January of 1960, the society concluded that "the Resolution is as good as can be hoped for and therefore every means possible should be taken to get it passed."[47] The door to getting aesthetic zoning into Felt's Revised Zoning Resolution had finally been closed.

This battle had been lost, but Felt made it clear that the war could still be won. Platt recalled Felt telling him: "If you will stop talking about aesthetic zoning, I will do something to help you people with your—the question of preservation of older buildings." Felt went on, "We can't get aesthetic zoning into the new zoning law, and if we keep trying, we're going to scuttle the whole thing." Platt's reaction? "So, I didn't say another word."[48]

Exactly when Platt's conversation with Felt took place is not clear. We know the society continued to explore possible amendments and legislation. In February 1960, Holden was still refining his text and had prepared testimony on the amendment for the upcoming hearings on the zoning resolution. In March, Holden made a presentation to the board on his draft amendment and in April, the society was planning to meet with the American Institute of Architects and the Regional Plan Association to discuss it.[49] At some point prior to the spring 1960 hearings on the zoning resolution, the advocates of historic and aesthetic zoning acquiesced to Felt's wishes. At the March hearings, they supported the resolution. No last-gasp campaign was mounted to force the inclusion of aesthetic zoning into the document. Robert Weinberg and Arnold Bergier did, however, use the opportunity to urge the commission to address that issue after the passage of the resolution, Bergier adding, "and may you pass it soon."[50]

Holden, like Bard, was not one to be easily discouraged. He would continue his drafting efforts. His proposal was no longer a "Proposed Amendment to the Zoning Ordinance of the City of New York," but was now christened a "Proposed Local Law for Preservation of Places and Structures of Historical or Aesthetic Value."[51] In the August 1960 *Villager* report on Arnold Bergier's meeting with Wagner's staff to discuss the Bard Act, it is also noted that Arthur Holden was at work drafting "a city-level zoning law to implement the Bard Law." It might well have added he was "still" at work.[52] Holden, though not well suited to the job of drafting zoning amendments or legislation, was particularly well suited to keeping an issue alive and on the agenda of the Municipal Art Society. His doggedness would soon pay off.

Felt's proposed new zoning resolution, without aesthetic zoning and weakened by compromise, was still seen by reformers as a major improvement. Its adoption became a top priority. By the time of the formal hearings on the revised zoning resolution, the Municipal Art Society and the good government community were focusing their energy on getting it approved. Following the completion of the earlier informal hearings, the Citizens Committee for Modern Zoning was formed with the single purpose of supporting Felt's efforts. It was chaired by two prominent New Yorkers: Robert Dowling and Luther Gulick. Dowling "considered Felt a close and affectionate friend." He was "more than willing to contribute his time and influence to advocating a proposal that Felt saw as important." Soon after these efforts, Dowling and Gulick would be asked to join another committee, whose creation was also engineered by Felt.[53] Its focus would be on advancing landmark protection.

Essential to Felt's strategy for getting the new zoning resolution passed by the Board of Estimate was to be able to demonstrate that it enjoyed broad popular support. The Municipal Art Society's public efforts to support the resolution and to engage its own membership in such efforts were well received by Felt. Arthur Holden, Bancel LaFarge, Frederick J. Woodbridge, and others used the letters-to-the-editor columns to urge the adoption of the zoning.[54]

Felt was totally committed to getting the new zoning resolution adopted although opposition was certain and real. The process was highly political and volatile. His personal skills and his political acumen would be called on time and again. He successfully managed Robert Moses who, as feared, emerged at one point to attack the zoning only to then soften his tone. To get a new zoning resolution passed, Felt was willing to compromise, and he did. Some thought he compromised too much. He made the deals he believed were necessary. Aesthetic zoning was only one of a number of reforms that would be left behind on the road to the resolution's approval. Felt kept his eye on the bigger prize. By the time it was over, Felt even won over the New York Real Estate Board. The new zoning resolution was approved unanimously by the Board of Estimate on December 15, 1960. The process James Felt had initiated in 1956 had finally been brought to a successful conclusion.[55]

The revision of the zoning resolution turned out not to be the vehicle to achieve aesthetic and historic zoning. With the announcement that Felt was going to undertake zoning reform coming only three months after the passage of the Bard Act, it had seemed like the most promising venue for advancing the act's goals. If zoning reform had not been on the city's agenda, one can only speculate what alternative path to advancing the Bard Act might have been followed. Though zoning reform turned out not to be a direct route for the implementation of the Bard Act in New York City, neither was it a dead end. Through it the case for preservation

■ ■ ■ ■ ■ ■ ■

had been powerfully advanced. By the end of the zoning resolution drama, preservation had established itself as a real political issue with an emerging constituency that would not be ignored. Though Felt had heard this constituency, he had deferred action on preservation with the promise of taking it up after the passage of the new zoning resolution.

ENDNOTES

1. "The Mild Budgeteer: James Felt," *New York Times*, August 20, 1962; "James Felt, Former Chairman of City Planning Agency, Dies," *New York Times,* March 5, 1971. Though interviewed separately, both Platt and Goldstone used the exact same language. Wood, "An Interview with the First Chairman of the Landmarks Preservation Commission, the Late Geoffrey Platt," 17; Wood, "An Interview with Harmon Goldstone," 28.
2. This assessment and a lot of other good information on the evolution of the City Planning Commission is found in Stanislaw J. Makielski, *Politics of Zoning: The New York Experience* (New York: Columbia University Press, 1966), 83.
3. "The Mild Budgeteer: James Felt," *New York Times,* August 20, 1962; "James Felt, Former Chairman of City Planning Agency, Dies," *New York Times,* March 5, 1971; Municipal Art Society Board Meeting Minutes, December 19, 1955, Municipal Art Society of New York Records, Archives of American Art.
4. "The Mild Budgeteer: James Felt," *New York Times*, August 20, 1962.
5. Makielski, *Politics of Zoning,* 84.
6. Stern, *New York 1960,* 128.
7. "The Mild Budgeteer: James Felt," *New York Times,* August 20, 1962.
8. Makielski, *The Politics of Zoning,* 84–85.
9. Wallace S. Sayre and Herbert Kaufman, *Governing New York City: Politics in the Metropolis* (New York: Russell Sage Foundation, 1960), 375.
10. Makielski, *Politics of Zoning,* 84–85.
11. Stern, *New York 1960,* 128.
12. James Felt to Bard, January 4, 1957, Albert S. Bard Papers, New York Public Library.
13. Municipal Art Society Board Meeting Minutes, January 15, 1958, Municipal Art Society of New York Records, Archives of American Art.
14. Robert C. Weinberg to George H. Fitch, president, Municipal Art Society, March 16, 1959, Professional Papers of Robert C. Weinberg, Long Island University; Charles Grutzner, "New Zoning Plan Offered to Guide Growth of City," *New York Times,* February 16, 1959.
15. Municipal Art Society Board Meeting Minutes, March 23, 1959, Municipal Art Society of New York Records, Archives of American Art.
16. Ibid., April 27, 1959. Author's conversation with Otis Pratt Pearsall, May 3, 2006.
17. "Study Zoning of Other Cities," *Villager,* August 13, 1959.
18. "Architects Favor Aesthetic Zoning," *Villager,* June 11, 1959; "Study Zoning of Other Cities," *Villager,* August 13, 1959.
19. "Washington Sq: No Autos! City to Ban Buses Too," *Village Voice,* April 15, 1959; "Square Closing Not Set, City to Decide in Fall," *Village Voice,* July 1, 1959; "No Christmas in July," *Village Voice,* July 1, 1959; "Rubinow Blasts DeSapio for Bringing Sq. into Politics, Call for his Defeat at Polls," *Village Voice,* September

16, 1959; "Moses Again with Park 'Doormat'," *Villager*, October 1, 1959; "Keep It Safe for Buses!" *Village Voice*, April 6, 1961; "DeSapio Accuses Wagner on Park," *New York Times*, August 16, 1961; Paul Crowell, "Road Ban Sought in Washington Sq.," *New York Times*, February 14, 1962; Mary Perot Nichols, "NYU is Top Landowner, Buys Washington Square Village," *Village Voice*, December 26, l963.

20. "GVA Committee: Seeks Housing That Will Retain Village Character," *Village Voice*, April 8, 1959; Charles Grutzner, "Housing Surveys Begun in 'Village,'" *New York Times*, August 11, 1959.

21. "Emergency Plans to Protect Village," *Villager*, September 3, 1959; "'Save the Village' Vigilante Formed," *Villager*, September 10, 1959.

22. Doris Diether phone conversations with the author, March 13, 1995 and February 3, 2006. Diether was chair of Save the Village's tenant committee, became its vice-president and ultimately its president.

23. "10,000 Here Sign 'Save' Petition," *Villager*, November 19, 1959.

24. Ibid.

25. Makielski, *Politics of Zoning*, 93, 88.

26. "City Zoning Rules Due for Restudy," *New York Times*, July 23, 1956.

27. Richard J. Whalen, "A City Destroying Itself," *Fortune*, September 1964, 122.

28. Owen Grundy, "The Boiling Cauldron-GVA," *Villager*, October 22, 1959.

29. Bard's papers include a copy of a letter from Holden to Moishe H. Goldstein of New Orleans thanking him for "material in regard to the Vieux Carré Commission." Holden to Goldstein, December 3, 1959, Albert S. Bard Papers, New York Public Library.

30. "Accelerate Drive to 'Save Village,'" *Villager*, November 12, 1959.

31. Ibid.

32. Ed Klein, "Citizens Fight to Keep Village From Being Built Out of Being," *New York Daily News*, December 6, 1959.

33. "Accelerate Drive to 'Save Village,'" *Villager*, November 12, 1959.

34. "Boiling Cauldron-GVA," *Villager*, October 22, 1959.

35. Ned Schnurman, "Greenwich Village Group Fights for its Brownstones," *Newark Sunday News*, January 31, 1960.

36. "Zoning Revision May Save Old Houses in Village," *Village Voice*, December 23, 1959; "Greenwich Villagers Give Colorful Backing to Zoning Change Plan," *New York Times*, February 18, 1960; "'Save Village' Trek to City Hall Wins Support," *Village Voice*, February 24, 1960; "Savers Don 'Old Hats' For Hearing," *Villager*, March 10, 1960; "'Save the Village' Wins at City Hall," *Village Voice*, March 30, 1960; "Local Groups Act on Area Zone Changes," *Greenwich Village News*, September 8, 1960; "New Zoning Now Held a Threat," *Villager*, August 25, 1960; "Village Girds for Final Zoning Fight," *Greenwich Village News*, September 2, 1960; "Villagers Brave Hurricane to Press for New Zoning," *Village Voice*, September 15, 1960; "Villager Leaders to Thrash Out Zoning With Felt," *Greenwich Village News*, September 16, 1960.

37. "Mayor Guarantees Zoning Help," *Villager*, June 27, 1960; "Save All! Villagers Tell Mayor," *Village Voice*, June 30, 1960.

38. "'Bottle Up' Village," *Villager*, August 4, 1960.

39. "Otis Pratt Pearsall's Reminiscences," *Village Views*, 11.

40. Memorandum from Pearsall to Brooklyn Heights Association, Committee on Historic Preservation, regarding "Battle Plan for the Preservation of Brooklyn Heights," October 28, 1960; "Brooklyn Heights Association Bulletin," December 1960. Both documents in the Otis Pratt Pearsall Papers, New York Preservation Archive Project.

■ ■ ■ ■ ■ ■ ■

41. "Otis Pratt Pearsall's Reminiscences," *Village Views*, 11.

42. "Architects Favor Aesthetic Zoning," *Villager*, June 11, 1959.

43. Municipal Art Society Board Meeting Minutes, September 28, 1959, Municipal Art Society of New York Records, Archives of American Art.

44. Bard typed note attached to "People Written to by A.S.B. to Attend City Club Luncheon Honoring Commissioner James Felt," October 6, 1959, Hotel Roosevelt, Albert S. Bard Papers, New York Public Library.

45. Municipal Art Society Board Meeting Minutes, October 26, 1959, Municipal Art Society of New York Records, Archives of American Art.

46. Ibid., November 23, 1959.

47. Ibid., January 25, 1960.

48. Wood, "An Interview with the First Chairman of the Landmarks Preservation Commission, the Late Geoffrey Platt," 8.

49. Municipal Art Society Board Meeting Minutes, March 28 and April 25, 1960, Municipal Art Society of New York Records, Archives of American Art.

50. The hearings began on March 14, 1960 and continued on March 15, 18, 21, 22, 23, and 25. Weinberg and Bergier testified on March 22, 1960. "Transcript of Public Hearing before the City Planning Commission March 22, 1960 in the Matter Of..." prepared by Department of City Planning, C.P. 15278, Volume 5.

51. "Memorandum No. 5, Suggestions from Arthur C. Holden, Proposed Amendment to the Zoning Ordinance of the City of New York, Revised to November 5, 1959," and "Memorandum No. 6, Suggestion, from Arthur C. Holden, Proposed Local Law for Preservation of Places and Structures of Historical or Aesthetic Value, April, 1960," Professional Papers of Robert C. Weinberg, Long Island University.

52. "'Bottle Up' Village," *Villager*, August 4, 1960.

53. Makielski, *Politics of Zoning*, 91–92.

54. Ibid., 83–106; Municipal Art Society Board Meeting Minutes, January 26 and March 28, 1960, Municipal Art Society of New York Records, Archives of American Art; Simon Breines, Robert W. Cutler, M. Milton Glass, G. Harmon Gurney, Michael M. Haris, Arthur C. Holden, Robert H. Jacobs, Morris Ketchum, Jr., L. Bancel LaFarge, Frederick J. Woodbridge, letter to the editor, *New York Times*, September 20, 1960.

55. Makielski, *Politics of Zoning*, 83–106.

■ ■ ■ ■ ■ ■ ■

TEN

A Series of
Near Misses

During the years that Felt's zoning revision dominated the land-use policy landscape of New York City, all the pressures driving preservationists to seek some form of protection for landmarks exponentially increased. In these long years, losses in their neighborhoods had sustained, advanced, and inflamed the advocacy efforts that were unfolding in Brooklyn Heights and Greenwich Village. The rest of the city had suffered from the same destructive forces. A series of unfolding preservation crises would help begin to spread the preservation gospel to a larger audience.

More and more New Yorkers were experiencing the loss of buildings they cared about. Change seemed to be spinning out of control. According to Harmon Goldstone, by 1958—even prior to the informal hearings on the new zoning resolution—"ten per cent of the buildings on the Municipal Art Society's highly selective list had already been torn down."[1] Columnist John Crosby would write in the fall of 1960, "No civilized city in the world desecrates its past so constantly and so contemptuously as New York.... What New York most urgently needs is a beaux arts commission which is empowered to designate its great and beautiful buildings, whether they are in private or public hands, as belonging to the ages, and therefore to be preserved for the spiritual nourishment and esthetic enrichment of the whole city."[2] While the creation of such a commission, beaux arts or otherwise, was still years away, the preservation controversies continuing to swirl around some of New York's most cherished buildings would help bring it closer to reality.

Even prior to the saga of the new zoning resolution, such iconic New York buildings as Carnegie Hall, the Jefferson Market Courthouse, Pennsylvania

Station, and Grand Central Terminal had barely missed their dates with the wrecking ball. As the zoning resolution drama unfolded, these sites and others would face new threats. In 1958, Carnegie Hall had narrowly escaped the indignity of being replaced by a red porcelain/enamel-skinned skyscraper. According to its proponent, real estate investor Louis J. Glickman, the proposed forty-four-story office tower on stilts would have been set back from the street in a sunken plaza to "continue West Fifty-Seventh Street as the Rue de la Paix of Manhattan."[3] (Which Rue de la Paix could he have had in mind?) Thanks to an apparent lack of financing, the project died, but the threat to the great concert hall would live on.[4]

Hardly had the confetti ushering in the 1960s fallen to the ground before a new threat to Carnegie Hall emerged. On January 5, 1960, Robert E. Simon, Jr., owner of the controlling interest in Carnegie Hall, announced that demolition of the hall would begin that summer. Simon indicated that one "factor in forcing his hand" was his desire to get a bigger building in the ground before the new zoning resolution took effect."[5] At that time, the revised resolution had only just been released for discussion. Already the hall's ownership was thinking ahead, eager to utilize the window of opportunity created by Felt's grace period to maximize the use of the site before that window closed. The race to save Carnegie Hall from the wrecking ball was on.

It was Carnegie Hall's historical and cultural significance, its acoustics and the magic conjured up by its very name, that motivated those seeking to save it. This battle was not about architecture. Carnegie Hall was included on the Municipal Art Society's list of buildings worthy of preservation, but only after the society had learned of the earlier threat to the building. Edward Steese himself recognized its painful omission from the earlier version of his list.[6] That oversight would be an early demonstration of the inherent limitations in viewing potential landmarks primarily through the lens of architecture and aesthetics. Too often, historic and cultural importance eludes mere visual inspection.

Many New Yorkers would work in multitudinous ways to save Carnegie Hall. Early on, a special committee and fund to save the building were created. Musicians, some whom were tenants in the building, organized for its preservation. Its defenders took to the streets to demonstrate and circulate petitions. In an effort to keep the issue in the press, there was even an attempt to enlist Nikita Khrushchev in the cause. Tchaikovsky was slated to conduct Carnegie Hall's opening concert that year; this was the bait on the hook to attract Khrushchev's interest. At concerts and during broadcasts, prominent musicians would bring the preservation cause directly to their audiences. Though these efforts were not well positioned enough to save the hall, they did succeed in attracting the attention and involvement of those who were.[7]

It is to the great violinist Isaac Stern and to the talented team his passion and dedication to saving Carnegie Hall attracted that New Yorkers owe their thanks for the saving of this landmark. "For me," Stern wrote, "Carnegie Hall was the Holy Grail, the be-all and end-all of musical life in this country for all performing artists. No other place we played in had its unique history. The whole measure of American musical performance was created at Carnegie Hall." Stern was greatly disturbed by the impending demolition and became convinced that "the usual route of protest meetings and save-Carnegie Hall committees was the way *not* to go . . . a practical plan that was a solution—*that* was what we needed."[8]

In December of 1959, Stern turned for help to his friend the noted philanthropist, Jacob M. Kaplan. Not just a check-writing philanthropist, when Kaplan embraced a cause he was willing to roll up his sleeves and jump into the fray. That's what he did for Carnegie Hall. Kaplan brought his mind, money, and muscle to the effort. He provided funding to help cover campaign expenses, bring on an administrator and strategy consultant, and retain legal counsel. He also made available to the cause his esteemed associate, the civic advocate Ray Rubinow.[9] As the successful campaign to close Washington Square to traffic demonstrates, Rubinow was blessed with considerable strategic and political skills. When years later, during his final illness, Rubinow's personal papers were sent to a dumpster, many of the behind-the-scenes details of the campaign to save Carnegie Hall campaign were undoubtedly lost.[10]

With the January 1960 announcement that demolition of Carnegie Hall would begin in the summer, preservation efforts went into light speed. In February, the creation of the Citizen's Committee for Carnegie Hall, "a reputable group of public spirited citizens," was announced. Stern and Kaplan were its co-chairs. Its honorary chair was the longtime friend of threatened city treasures, Eleanor Roosevelt. Also joining the crusade was the patron of the arts, businessman and philanthropist Frederick W. Richmond, as well as the familiar Robert Dowling. In addition to these lead players, the drama also attracted many supporting players. A preservation struggle of this magnitude could not fail to attract the support of Albert Bard, and he logged in with letters to the *New York Times* and to the mayor.[11]

The strategy for saving Carnegie Hall was to create a nonprofit entity to preserve and operate it. The Hall would pay for itself over time. The leap of faith was the belief that New York City could support two major performing venues, Carnegie Hall and the new Lincoln Center. With impending demolition facing Stern and his team, the only hope to implement their strategy was immediate government intervention. Legislation would be needed, as would a lobbying effort to get it passed. The group meeting at Jacob Kaplan's apartment had been strategically expanded with this in mind. It now featured influential Republicans to help deliver the state legislature and powerful Democrats to secure the support of the city's Democratic Mayor, Robert Wagner.[12]

Two pieces of legislation were required. One would enable cities in New York state "to acquire by condemnation any property 'with special historical or esthetic interest or value.'"[13] That bill also allowed for such property to be turned over to a tax-exempt organization created for such a purpose. Again, Senator McNeil Mitchell would show his preservation colors. With his political standing and Carnegie Hall in his district, he was the perfect choice to take the lead. His bill sailed through the state legislature. The other part of the strategy was to obtain the passage of legislation creating the Carnegie Hall Corporation as the nonprofit to own and operate the site. Drafted by the counsel for the Citizens Committee for Carnegie Hall, this legislation also enjoyed success in Albany. In April, both bills were signed by Governor Rockefeller.[14]

Like the Bard Act, the enabling legislation to acquire Carnegie Hall and similar sites only gave the city permission to do so. It did not force it to take action. Unlike the case with the Bard Act, this time the city would move quickly to use its new authority. Only days after Rockefeller's signing of the bill, Mayor Wagner announced that the city would move forward to buy and preserve Carnegie Hall. On June 30, 1960, the City of New York became the owner of Carnegie Hall and leased it to the new nonprofit corporation with the five-million-dollar price tag to be amortized over the life of the lease. The committee's strategy to save Carnegie Hall had gone from dream to reality in a matter of months.

Its success resulted from a variety of factors. Primarily, the fight to save Carnegie Hall enjoyed both popular and press support. Its advocates had the creativity and financial resources to devise an economic solution to the problem. They had a clear strategy and the sophistication and clout to implement it. They were also able to use the crisis to create opportunity.[15]

The Carnegie Hall story is also instructive because it underscores the relationship of preservation to politics. The successful legislative efforts demonstrated the true bipartisan nature of historic preservation. Saving Carnegie Hall proved popular with the general public as well as members of the power elite. The fact that J. M. Kaplan, a financial supporter of the mayor's campaign, was so personally committed to Carnegie Hall's preservation was certainly not lost on the mayor.[16] The *New York Times*, which had followed the issue closely, including running several supportive editorials, called out politicians, among others, for special praise: "A flourish also ought to be sounded for State Senator McNeil Mitchell and Mayor Wagner for the part they have played in seeing this project through."[17] The public hoopla over the reopening of Carnegie Hall in September, with its ribbon-cutting opportunities for the mayor and other elected officials, vividly demonstrated that preservation held great promise for politicians who would embrace it.[18]

FIGURE 10.1   Unlike others, the preservation drama over Carnegie Hall had a happy ending. At the debut of the redecorated and reopened hall, in a "burst of musical enthusiasm," Mayor Wagner took over the baton and directed the Department of Sanitation Band. This photo and story accompanying it in the September 27, 1960 *New York Times* was a rare and welcomed preservation good news story.

Saving Carnegie Hall was like catching lightning in a bottle. Many of the traditional players had assumed it was hopeless. Harmon Goldstone recalled, "It seemed like a totally lost cause at the time, because you had all the steamroller pressure of Lincoln Center coming along; and, obviously, they didn't want a competing concert hall."[19] Lost cause or not, preservation advocates realized just how lucky the city had been and how close New York had come to losing such a signature site. For Goldstone, the experience was instructive. "Carnegie Hall was miraculously saved after a cliff-hanging operation. But these constantly recurring, and only occasionally successful battles convinced us that there ought to be some more orderly and efficient way of saving our architectural heritage than intermittent guerilla warfare."[20] He was right, but that better way continued to elude New Yorkers.

As the legislation to save Carnegie Hall was being advanced in Albany, guerilla warfare would break out in defense of other prominent New York landmarks. One such battle was over a corner of Central Park. It would be hard to find a more beloved and jealously guarded precinct in New York than Central Park. Over the decades, its dedicated defenders, ranging from civic graybeards to mothers pushing prams, have successfully turned back a dizzying array of ill-conceived projects. If implemented, these projects would have incrementally transformed Central Park into anything but what visionaries Frederick Law Olmsted and Calvert Vaux had intended and the city has come to cherish. When New Yorkers awoke the morning of March 14, 1960 to read that the City of New York had accepted the munificent offer from Huntington Hartford to build a cafe pavilion in the southeast corner of Central Park, it should have been no surprise to the powers that be that this proposal would not be greeted with open arms. That, however, was of no concern to the cafe's proponents.

It was not the "gay continental style" of the two-story, one-thousand-seat cafe by the donor's handpicked architect, Edward Durell Stone that created the stir. What incensed its opponents was that the cafe was to be in Central Park, and building it could serve as a precedent for future incursions.[21] The full list of objections to the cafe was long and detailed. The promotional material for the proposed Huntington Hartford Pavilion, which tried to place it in the context of the great cafes of Paris, Venice, and London, entirely missed the point. The *New York Times* did not: "No matter how benevolent the purpose or generous the donation, we think that any and every incursion of new structures in Central Park ought to be stopped." Coincidentally and reflecting the rollercoaster of emotions that those concerned with the city's landmarks must have felt during this, in

FIGURE 10.2 In the early 1960s, some of New York City's most cherished landmarks, including Central Park, were under assault. A one-thousand seat, $500,000, two-story cafe designed by architect Edward Durell Stone and financed by a gift from Huntington Hartford, was planned for the southeast corner of the park across from the Plaza Hotel. The battle over the cafe, seen here in a model (photograph provided by the MTA Bridges and Tunnels Special Archive) again pitted New York's civic community against Robert Moses.

the same newspaper ran the *New York Times* editorial applauding Governor Rockefeller's signing of the legislation making possible the saving of Carnegie Hall.[22]

Robert Moses, still very much the power broker, held a decidedly different point of view. He was the one who had suggested the idea of the cafe to Huntington Hartford, the supermarket heir.[23] Though about to step away from his role as parks commissioner and become the maven of the New York World's Fair, Moses had left Central Park and this pet project securely in the hands of his acolyte and successor, Newbold Morris. For Morris, the project was "an accomplished fact."[24] With the city taking the

position that no public review was required for the cafe project, its opponents had no recourse but to revert to "guerilla" warfare, once again, with the likes of the Municipal Art Society, the American Scenic and Historic Preservation Society, the Citizen's Union, the Fine Arts Federation, and old preservation warhorses such as Albert Bard, Francis Keally, and Edward R. Finch lined up on one side of the issue with Moses on the other side.[25]

The individuals and organizations that had been battling Moses off and on for some twenty years must have felt the déjà vu quality of the situation. For a newer generation of civic leaders and preservationists, this was their baptism by fire. The battle would not only harden them, but inculcate in them the same sense of civic outrage, indignation, and motivation that drove their predecessors. Among these emerging new leaders was Harmon Goldstone. This would be the battle in which he cut his advocacy teeth. Having just assumed the position of president of the Municipal Art Society, Goldstone helped lead the campaign against the Huntington Hartford Cafe. He served as the temporary chairman of a consortium of five civic organizations that had joined together to defeat the project.[26] He took to the editorial pages and the airwaves, and when Huntington Hartford attacked the opposition in the *New York Times* suggesting "if the societies which have objected were put all together, they probably wouldn't number as many people as would use the cafe in one or two days," it was Harmon Goldstone who replied.[27]

Goldstone and the Municipal Art Society were far from alone in their opposition. Numerous editorials appeared. Lawsuits were threatened and one was actually filed by Tiffany & Co. Prominent civic figures demanded a public hearing.[28] Throwing a bone to the growing opposition, and knowing it posed no real danger to the approval of the project, the Board of Estimate agreed to hold a hearing on the acceptance of Huntington Hartford's gift. At the hearing, twenty-two people spoke against the project, five in support.[29] Among those speaking was the future landmarks preservation commissioner from Staten Island, Loring McMillen.

In reporting on the hearing to the American Scenic and Historic Preservation Society, on whose board he served, McMillen wrote: "I came, I saw, I spoke and like the rest of those appearing was conquered. It was obvious that the cafe would be approved by the Board of Estimate since all members as well as the Park Commissioner were in favor of it."[30] The controversy would move into the courts where it would spend years in litigation. The fate of the cafe and the southeast corner of Central Park would only be resolved in 1966 with a new mayor and with a new park commissioner who would ask the city to return to Mr. Hartford his $862,500.[31]

■ ■ ■ ■ ■ ■ ■ ■

FIGURE 10.3 The civic community's battle against the Hartford Pavilion, the proposed cafe, for the southeast corner of Central Park, was a baptism by fire for a new generation of preservationists. The issue was followed closely by the press as evidenced by this photograph of the Board of Estimate Hearing on the cafe, which appeared in the *New York Times* on July 28, 1960. The white-haired gentleman sitting to the left of the sculptural niche is likely Albert Bard.

Each of these preservation episodes had their own lessons to teach. The saving of Carnegie Hall vividly demonstrated the uncertain future of even New York's most famous structures. The battle over the Huntington Hartford Cafe taught a new generation the frustration of being on the wrong side of the exercise of virtually absolute discretionary governmental power. The next preservation struggle, the saving and adaptive reuse of Jefferson Market Courthouse, would provide preservation its "how to" success story. In short order, it would be serving as a much-needed poster child for the pending Landmarks Law. The Courthouse, "the most conspicuous architectural ornament of Greenwich Village," and its uncertain future had just been brought to the city's attention in a lyrical and humorous *New Yorker* piece credited to Brendan Gill. In it, he

wrote of the tour he took of the structure with the architectural historian, Alan Burnham. Gill described the building as "a delightful experiment in something loosely known as Venetian Gothic," a style that he concludes is "exuberant, if somewhat addleheaded." Things had only gotten worse since Gill had sounded the alarm in 1956.[32]

As early as 1952, Alan Burnham had started his efforts to build appreciation for the courthouse in the Village, a creation of the architectural team of Frederick C. Withers and Calvert Vaux. "Old Jeff" appeared in the 1954 Municipal Art Society and Society of Architectural Historians list of important buildings. Over the years, it stirred a wide range of architectural emotions. It had the distinction of appearing on an 1877 list of the ten most beautiful buildings in the country, but by the twentieth century, "Any popularity poll would have made it one of the 10 homeliest buildings in the United States."[33] The Municipal Art Society could see its beauty and in 1956, when it learned that it was threatened, the society's president, Whitney North Seymour Sr. wrote the *New York Times* urging that "every effort should be made to preserve old Jefferson Market Courthouse . . . our reservoir of architectural treasures in New York is running dangerously low." Worry increased as pieces of debris were reported falling from its fanciful clock tower. Seymour was assured by the administration that some municipal purpose would be found for the building and "therefore its preservation seems assured at least for the moment."[34]

The immediate crisis had passed, but Villagers knew the reprieve was only temporary. Efforts were begun to find "some enterprising use for the building." In February 1958, Stanley Tankel, chair of the Greenwich Village Study, and Robert Weinberg reported positively to the Greenwich Village Community Board on the suitability of the building for other uses. The memo ended with the "minor" but extremely important observation that the clock in the tower of the old courthouse had its own separate entrance and that its repair could be pursued as "an entirely separate item." The memo's two points, the suitability of the courthouse for a new use and the ability to separately address the issue of the clock, reflect a two-pronged strategy that would ultimately save the courthouse. Finding a new use would be key, but without a constituency fighting for the site's preservation, the will to advance what was at that time such an unconventional notion would certainly falter.[35]

What better way to engage and excite the public than launching a highly public, grassroots campaign? While not initially aimed at the seemingly Herculean task of preserving this admittedly odd-looking building, it instead set out to accomplish something much more achievable and readily embraceable—bringing the tower's clock back to life. Such was the thinking behind the creation of the Committee of Neighbors to Get the Clock on Jefferson Market Courthouse Started.[36] As seen in Brooklyn Heights, great preservation ideas are often hatched over cocktails, and such was the case in December 1957 when a group of villagers, lamenting the possible loss of the courthouse, decided that getting the clock running was the perfect wedge issue to advance its preservation. They sent a wire to the mayor asking that he rehabilitate the clock as a Christmas present to the Village. The mayor was not yet ready to play Santa, but the campaign had been launched![37]

The preservation phenomenon largely responsible for this effort was Margot Gayle, a well-networked villager, writer, and activist who learned politics and community organizing through almost a decade of involvement in the Democratic Party. A dollar-a-year lease was negotiated with the city and the effort to raise money to fix the clock began in earnest. Raising funds, dollar-by-dollar, the community responded, and on Sunday, October 16, 1960, the Jefferson Market Courthouse clock that had been stuck for years at 3:20 was ticking again. The next manageable project was raising money to electrify and illuminate the clock. The campaign for the clock generated wonderful publicity and good will. Villagers did care for their clock, its tower, and the courthouse. And they were not alone.[38]

Key to saving the courthouse was finding and championing a new use for the building. Whitney North Seymour, Jr., joined with Robert Weinberg and Stanley Tankel on a special Greenwich Village Association committee working toward this end. Reuse of the building was far from a sure thing and certainly far from standard practice in the early 1960s. A proposal to demolish the courthouse and the neighboring House of Detention for a

FIGURE 10.4 It is because of the women of New York City that so many of its most cherished landmarks have been saved. High on that preservation honor role is Margot Gayle. A leader in the effort to save Jefferson Market Courthouse, she successfully used her political organizing and public relations skills to rally New Yorkers to the cause of saving "Old Jeff."

sixteen-story building and a five-hundred-seat theatre had also been floated and was much more in keeping with the predominant thinking of the day.[39] By the end of 1959, the property had found its way into the hands of New York City's bureau of real estate for "ultimate disposition."[40] By early 1960, the idea of converting the building into a branch of the New York Public Library, a notion going back to at least 1954 and credited to the *Villager's* Owen Grundy, started to gain traction. At the request of Weinberg and Tankel, Pratt Institute professors and students developed the concept into a proposal and presented it to the New York Public Library. Originally less than enthusiastic, the library came around to embrace the notion.[41]

By the spring of 1961, efforts to convert the building into a library swung into full gear with the creation of the "Committee for a Library in the Jefferson Courthouse," another of the Village's famous single-issue committees. The idea captivated the imagination and attracted broad support from organizations ranging from the Gotham Kennel Club to the American Institute of Architects. The Municipal Art Society closely monitored the fate of the building and joined in the call for its re-use as a library. The allocation of city capital funds for the conversion of the courthouse to a library was one of the sticking points. To address this, a delegation from the committee met with James Felt because of his role in the capital budget process.[42] The proposal enjoyed enormous popular support. As Stanley Tankel emphasized to Felt, "I have never see seen such unanimity on an issue in Greenwich Village as the idea of a library in the Courthouse has inspired."[43]

The cause of preserving the structure was brought directly to the attention of the mayor. By the end of the summer, he had received petitions with over nine thousand signatures. In addition, some sixty-five civic and community organizations had endorsed the project. In August, Mayor Wagner publicly came out for the project, noting how gratifying it was "to give new life to an architecturally unique building by using it for a vital community service."[44] This announcement would come two months after an even more important landmark announcement, the creation of a mayoral committee to study landmark preservation. Clearly, the preservation of Jefferson Courthouse was an issue very much in front of the mayor and his administration at this key moment. As we have seen, it was only one of several preservation issues of the time. The mayor, civic leaders, and concerned citizens were trying to manage multiple preservation dramas playing out simultaneously.

Yet another preservation crisis would contribute to the growing swirl of uncertainty engulfing the city's landmarks and historic neighborhoods. Its

■ ■ ■ ■ ■ ■ ■

fortuitous timing would provide the civic community the perfect opportunity to yet again advance its preservation agenda with the Wagner administration. As it was with the threat to Grand Central Station in 1954—one of the events prompting Bard to draft his legislation—it would be another threat to Grand Central that would move New York City a step closer to utilizing the Bard Act to save is landmarks.

When Robert Moses looked at the southeast corner of Central Park, he saw a "wasted" piece of real estate, "too steep for walks or playgrounds," but space that could productively house a cafe serving thousands of New Yorkers every day. When his critics looked at it, they saw a cherished piece of parkland.[45] Similarly, when the owners of Grand Central Terminal looked at the empty space above the floor of the station's cavernous waiting room, they saw an unused asset that could generate needed rental income for the flagging terminal. Instead, their critics saw "the most beautiful station waiting room in the United States."[46] This collision of competing values: passive vs. active use, aesthetic value vs. economic worth, private benefit vs. public enjoyment, was as fierce then as it can be, at times, today.

Traditionally during the month of August, when many New Yorkers are on vacation, the city's civic watchdog organizations are less vigilant operating at "summer speed." Hence, late summer is a favored time for unveiling projects that might otherwise trigger negative public reaction. So it was that in August 1960 plans were announced to create the "Grand Central Bowl." The vision was to put to use the fifty-eight feet of empty air space above the floor of the terminal's waiting room to house a three-floor bowling center. Actually, the first eleven feet would still be used for the waiting room. Shoehorned into the 210- by 60-foot space would be a bowling center with 44 lanes, arena seating for competitions, and a restaurant and bar. Noting the "serious annual deficit" of the terminal, its manager pointed out that in addition to the economic benefit of the proposal, other benefits came with it. "The entire area will be brightened and air-conditioned. These innovations will indeed add to the comfort of our passengers while providing them with a recreational outlet. At the same time it will not disfigure the building which has so long been a landmark in New York City."[47]

Among those with a different opinion was Robert Weinberg. Reminding the readers of the *New York Times* that the "misguided" bowling alley proposal would require government approval since such a use was not authorized under the zoning ordinance, he correctly predicted that if the railroad sought such permission, "every civic organization, from the

FAÇADE, DEPEW PLACE, GRAND CENTRAL TERMINAL, NEW YORK.
WARREN & WETMORE AND REED & STEM, ASSOC. ARCHITECTS.

FIGURE 10.5 In the early 1960s, demolition was not the only threat to New York's landmarks. A proposal to insert a three-floor bowling center into the space above Grand Central Terminal's waiting room caused yet another major controversy. This threat underscored the continued vulnerability of the city's architectural treasures and led to renewed calls for a process to legally protect them.

Municipal Art Society to the local taxpayers' groups, will be out in force to argue against it."[48]

Joining Weinberg would be Harmon Goldstone and the Municipal Art Society, the distinguished architect Victor Gruen and the New York Chapter of the American Institute of Architects, the Citizens Union, the Fine Arts Federation, the National Trust for Historic Preservation and other voices decrying the "desecration of a nationally renowned classical building."[49] The controversy also triggered a passionate editorial in the *New York Times*. Characterizing the proposal as "one more step in the disastrous erosion of architectural values that is reducing the heart of this city to a shambles of mediocrity," it marked the editorial debut of the renowned architecture critic, Ada Louise Huxtable.[50] Her presence at the *New York Times* would become a deciding factor in helping shift the balance of power in favor of preservation in the public debate over landmark protection.

By January 1961, the bowlers' dream and preservationists' nightmare was over. The Board of Standards and Appeals, the government agency empowered to grant the required zoning variance, denied the application in a unanimous vote. Though a victory for preservation, it only underscored the continued vulnerability of the terminal and the city's landmarks in general. Grand Central's waiting room was spared only because the proposed use, bowling, required a variance. If the proposal had been for a use permitted by the zoning, it could have gone forward without review. Victor Gruen, a leader in the opposition to the bowling center, realized this had only been a "skirmish, not the main battle." Recognizing this, the American Institute of Architects created a special subcommittee, chaired by Gruen, to keep its eye on the vulnerable terminal.[51]

Gruen realized that a "new legal weapon was needed to protect public, quasi-public and historic buildings against architectural changes that would detract from their distinction." This, of course, was part and parcel of what the American Institute of Architects and its civic partners had unsuccessfully tried to advance during the zoning revision process. One critical thing was now different. Only a month earlier, James Felt's hard-won zoning resolution had been approved by the Board of Estimate. Now it was time to draw his attention to an important piece of unfinished business. In a January 24, 1961 letter to Felt, Gruen reminded him of his request to the Municipal Art Society and the American Institute of Architects to "wait" on advancing their agenda to protect "historic buildings and other buildings of public importance—as well as of public spaces," until after the new zoning resolution was passed. "Now that you have

been so singularly successful in the passage of the new zoning regulations, we feel that the time has come to bring this matter up again."[52]

Felt had not forgotten his promise. Even before Gruen's letter was sent, there were indications that Felt was getting ready to address the deferred issue of some type of historic and aesthetic zoning. At a January 21 preservation committee meeting of the Brooklyn Heights Association, Arden Rathkopf, author of the preservation amendment Brooklyn Heights had proposed for the new zoning resolution, reported that "the New York City Planning Commission is likely to take up the matter of aesthetic zoning in the near future." Rathkopf's active zoning practice gave him regular access to well-placed people in city planning, putting him in a position to get such information.[53] Felt hardly needed reminding on this issue. It had been hammered home during the hearings on the new zoning resolution, and the Village had continued to beat the drum for legislation based on the Bard Act, and the seemingly endless series of preservation issues had very much kept the subject alive. Felt was primed to do something.

Thanks to a wonderful confluence of events put into motion by the Municipal Art Society, action would finally be taken. Having realized that aesthetic and historic zoning would not make it into Felt's new zoning resolution, the society had explored other options. As reported earlier, Arthur Holden, a society board member and Village leader, had long been at work drafting possible amendments to the zoning resolution and new legislation to achieve the society's ends. Passionate on the subject and "very public-spirited," but an architect, not a lawyer, his drafts missed the mark. In the words of his good friend and admirer, society president Harmon Goldstone, Holden's attempt "was the most hopelessly complicated piece of writing I have ever read." Geoffrey Platt, the society's point person on zoning matters, knew this effort was "floundering." He suggested it was time to turn to a professional, James Felt. Goldstone and Platt concluded that the time was right to have a private talk with the chair of the planning commission.[54]

Robert Weinberg had also concluded it was time to approach Felt but for another reason. In a memo to Platt, he commented on the latest versions of Holden's proposals. In doing so, Weinberg framed his comments around his broader interest in seeking the regulation of community appearance through the creation of special design districts that would deal with the appearance of "all buildings and open spaces, whether new or old." He reminded Platt that several times, beginning as far back as at least 1957, versions of such an idea had been presented to Felt. "Chairman Felt put us off at that time with the remark that such an amendment would better go into the new resolution. When the amendment failed to show up in either the first or second version of the new ordinance, Felt said that he feared it might make passage more difficult but that we could re-submit the idea as an amendment after the new one had passed. So now is the time to call his bluff."[55]

Seeking his help and perhaps to call his bluff, Platt and Goldstone requested their private meeting. Years after the lunch, Goldstone would recall that he learned from Felt's secretary that their lunch invitation had arrived at "just the right psychological moment." A lunch for the three of them was scheduled for May 9, 1961.[56] Fortuitously, the day before the lunch, at its sixty-ninth annual meeting, the Municipal Art Society presented an award to James Felt for the new zoning resolution.

In his acceptance remarks, Felt thanked the society for its "recommendations and suggestions," and then went on to address the subject near and dear to the society's heart. Noting an "emerging awareness on the part of the general public," he cited the irony that in World War II, efforts had been made to spare art treasures from destruction, but that "we have no plan to protect our architectural and historic landmarks from becoming casualties of a peacetime real estate market." Stating his belief that New York City was now ready to "seriously consider a program of saving some of the city's most important structures," he announced: "Very soon, I hope to call a meeting with representatives of your Society and related organizations to work out a plan for insuring the preservation of these landmarks."[57]

Perhaps realizing that this audience might mistake his remarks as a manifesto for rampant preservation, he followed them with cautionary language. He stressed the need to distinguish between structures of "nostalgia or special group interest" and those of "true value to society." He pointed out that "New York, unlike Venice, cannot afford to offer antiquity as one of its major products. The genius and strength of New York lies in its dynamic vitality and its continuing self-regeneration. To be sure we must cherish our past but we must not let it lure us to looking backwards instead of looking ahead." Noting that there "will be difficulties—legal and economic problems are intertwined," Felt observed that "other cities have worked out some of these problems, and I feel that we can do the same."[58] These comments coming from such a prominent government official, even with the caveats, were revolutionary.

It appears that Felt had been prepared to make an even stronger statement. According to Robert Weinberg, Felt had told him in a "long conversation" that he had planned to announce something more concrete at the society's event. Felt had planned to reveal that the "Planning Commission was going to introduce an amendment to the Zoning Ordinance 'for the preservation of buildings of historical significance.'" Weinberg then sought to convince Felt to "change that announcement to something closer to what the Joint AIP–AIA Design Committee has always had in mind, namely the establishment of a design district where new as well as old construction would be given consideration."[59]

Perhaps because of Weinberg's comments, Felt realized that the solution to the preservation problem was going to be more complex than he had first imagined, and concluded that it was precipitous to announce a particular solution to it without benefit of more serious study. If on May 8, 1961, Felt had announced a proposed preservation zoning amendment, it is likely the course of preservation in New York City would have taken a decidedly different turn. Instead of a separate agency devoted to preservation, that assignment might have fallen to the City Planning Commission. It is also probable that since the path leading to a zoning amendment was well known, if the issue of preservation had been advanced along it, the policy debate over the protection for the city's landmarks would have been joined much sooner than it was. All this is intriguing, but merely conjecture.

By serendipity, the "very soon" time frame Felt announced in his speech for reaching out to the society turned out to be the next day. Felt's remarks had set the stage for a truly remarkable lunch. Both parties arrived with the same agenda—"there was no need for proselytizing or explanations."[60] In Goldstone's memories of this critical lunch, he sensed that Felt had come looking for help on how to tackle the landmark issue—a subject that had only gotten hotter with the passage of time. Goldstone believed that Felt was looking for a partner he could work with to tackle the issue. He found a willing and able one in the Municipal Art Society. The society was looking for a way to gain traction for their long-held desire to find a way to protect sites of aesthetic and historic value. Frustrated by the homegrown attempt to draft such a proposal and thwarted in their efforts to advance such regulation from outside the government, they were eager to find a champion to advance the idea from within.[61] Platt's key memory of the lunch was Felt's statement: "If you're willing to give the Mayor the credit for this activity, we can do something." Willing they were. Felt went into action.

At lunch, Felt coached Goldstone and Platt on what was needed to be done. The society should write a letter formally requesting the appointment of a mayoral committee to study the matter. Felt would make sure that the mayor responded positively.[62] The letter, largely drafted by Felt, was then sent to the mayor. Felt "walked the letter through channels. . . .

■ ■ ■ ■ ■ ■ ■

Felt was the catalyst; we couldn't have done it without him."[63] From this lunch forward, Goldstone and Platt would look directly to Felt for guidance. As a child, Felt had wanted to be a rabbi, and in the political sense, he had just become one for preservation.

By recommending that the issue of landmarks protection be explored by a mayoral policy advisory committee, Felt was proposing a change in venue for the issue. Since the process of revising the zoning resolution had begun, the City Planning Commission had been seen as the agency for advancing this issue. Even when it was clear that aesthetics and history were not going to be included in the new zoning resolution, attention continued to be focused on subsequent amendments to the resolution. Though not taking the City Planning Commission entirely out of the picture, Felt now saw it playing only a "technical liaison role" to the new mayoral committee that would study the problem. Felt's suggestion of a committee created a new, broader forum for the exploration of the issue. It also dramatically opened up the range of possible solutions to the landmark protection problem.[64] At least partially due to Weinberg, Platt, and Goldstone, Felt's initial thinking on the matter had changed.

Felt had promised to deliver the mayor, and he did. How difficult a task was that? Felt truly enjoyed the mayor's confidence. This helped his efforts. But there are also indications that it was not that hard a sell. Leaders of the Jefferson Market Courthouse and the Carnegie Hall efforts have noted the genuine receptiveness and helpfulness of the Wagner administration in both instances.[65] As we have seen, the question of preserving landmarks was one that had been brought directly to the mayor's attention. Not only had he heard the call to implement the Bard Act, he was personally well aware of the efforts to save Jefferson Market and had been successfully enlisted in the campaign to save Carnegie Hall. He had also been publicly asked to use his influence at the Board of Standards and Appeals to defeat the bowling center in Grand Central Terminal.[66] This string of preservation crises, one after another, could only have made it clear to the mayor that the issue of preserving New York's heritage was not going to go away, and that his administration was being looked to for a solution.

By early summer 1961, the mayor's attention was appropriately focused on his reelection. Though thousands of signatures had been gathered for various preservation causes, usually in Greenwich Village, and editorial pages, letter-to-the-editor columns, and public hearing rooms were regularly populated by passionate voices urging the preservation of one threatened site or another, when it came to the larger public, preservation was still a nonissue. Even so, Wagner would have been well aware of the role the closing of Washington Square Park to traffic had played only a few years earlier in Village elections. For many, it was seen as a preservation issue. Wagner also knew the issue of historic and aesthetic regulation was a high priority on the policy agenda of many civic groups.

Not to overemphasize the political importance of preservation at that time, it is important to note there was at least a degree of political calculation in the Wagner administration's decision to move the preservation agenda forward when it did. In reporting to Whitney North Seymour on his and Geoffrey Platt's "off-the-record lunch" with James Felt, and asking Seymour to consider chairing the new mayoral study committee, Goldstone wrote: "For the first time, after years of talk, the climate seems favorable for effectively implementing the Bard Act if a sensible, workable proposal can be presented to the Mayor at least a month before election day."[67] It seems likely that this reference to election day was triggered by a comment made by Felt.

Shortly after the appointment of the committee, the mayor went public with his support for preserving the Jefferson Market Courthouse by converting it into a public library. That press release, issued August 23, 1961, also recounts some of the mayor's other preservation achievements, reminding its readers of the mayor's "concern for city beautification and preservation of buildings of architectural and historic interest." It concludes, mentioning "his recent appointment of a committee of prominent architects and other citizens to frame a systematic approach to ensuring that the city retain its treasures from the past."[68] Someone in the mayor's press office saw the value of highlighting the mayor's preservation record.

Whatever his motivations, the mayor appointed the Committee for the Preservation of Structures of Historic and Esthetic Importance on June 19, 1961. The committee was charged to work with the Municipal Art Society and the Fine Arts Federation. Announcing that "we cannot and should not ignore the past history of our city, nor permit its beauties to vanish if they can be preserved," Mayor Wagner named Geoffrey Platt, chair of the committee of thirteen. Among those serving with Platt would be such civic figures as Harmon H. Goldstone, Robert W. Dowling, Luther H. Gulick, Arthur C. Holden, Clarence G. Michalis, Whitney North Seymour, Sr., and Frederick J. Woodbridge.[69] Candidates for the committee had been suggested by Goldstone, Platt, and Felt. The diversity of professions represented by the committee—architect, lawyer, planner, realtor, banker—was no accident. Some twenty years later, Goldstone would stress: "And from the start (and this is very significant) we recognized that

Principals At Courthouse Library Rally

Photo by Dan Miller

Paying close attention and waiting their turn to speak at the rally Tuesday night to convert the Jefferson Market Courthouse into a branch library are (l.-r.): Margot Gayle, deputy chairman of the courthouse committee; Alan Burnham, architectural historian; author-attorney Philip Wittenberg, library group chairman; John Crosby, Herald-Tribune columnist; and Stanley Tankel, a member of the coordinating committee of the courthouse committee. The event was held at Greenwich House during a regular GVA meeting.

FIGURE 10.6 Securing the adaptive reuse of the Jefferson Market Courthouse as a branch of the New York Public Library was the winning strategy Villagers devised to secure its preservation. Seen here at a rally supporting this plan are, from left to right, preservationist Margot Gayle, architectural historian Alan Burnham, author–attorney Philip Wittenberg, John Crosby, *New York Herald-Tribune* columnist, and Stanley Tankel, planner.

the whole problem of preservation was much broader than just architectural historians, that you needed a very broad spectrum, and we wanted the initial committee to have it."[70]

Goldstone also suggested a panel of consultants to be "invited to present their views or special interests to the Committee but not to serve as regular members." Albert Bard, now ninety-four and a half, was on that list.[71] Between its members and its consultants, the committee pulled together the individuals and groups that had for years been advancing the cause of landmark protection. Those who had been outside advocates had now been brought inside the tent.[72] What for years had been unconventional thinking was on the verge of becoming conventional. Reality had almost caught up with the vision of the prescient Albert Bard.

From its passage in 1956, there had been great hope that the Bard Act would pave the way for some form of landmark protection for New York City. The timing of its passage, coinciding with James Felt's arrival and his campaign to revise the zoning resolution, was both fortuitous and problematic. The zoning revision process provided proponents of preservation the forum they had long been seeking to advance their cause, but it also was the source of painful delay. Though preservation advocates had been heard, Felt deferred action on their request—keeping his eye on the larger prize of the zoning resolution. Heard but deferred until after the passage of the new zoning, the issue was then referred to the mayor's new Committee for the Preservation of Structures of Historic and Esthetic Importance.

To some, referring the issue of preserving New York's landmarks to a committee for study might appear to be a delaying tactic. In light of the long and tortured road the issue traveled up to that point, the creation of a mayoral committee to study the idea was truly a significant step forward. Finally, the question of landmark protection was going to be addressed in an official way. The civics were now in partnership with the Wagner administration. As Harmon Goldstone would later say, "We were moving away from guerilla warfare, which was lots of fun, into the responsibilities of government."[73]

Without such a partnership there was no hope that preservation would ever become public policy. With it came great dangers. For decades, the civics had been playing the outsider game, but to advance their goal, they had to become adept at winning as insiders. What trade-offs might this require? What concessions might they be called on to make? How would the grassroots preservation advocates in the neighborhoods react? Bard's dream had come a long way. Whether it would become a reality was still to be decided.

ENDNOTES

1. Harmon Goldstone, "The Future of the Past," 12.

2. John Crosby, "Crosby Column: Vision and Money," *New York Herald-Tribune*, November 21, 1960.

3. John P. Callahan, "Red Tower Is Set for Carnegie Site," *New York Times*, August 8, 1957.

4. Harold C. Schonberg, "Longer Life Won by Carnegie Hall," *New York Times*, July 4, 1958.

5. Ross Parmenter, "Concert Season Shifts to Hunter," *New York Times*, January 6, 1960.

6. Steese, letter to the editor, *New York Times*, August 3, 1955.

7. "Song Not Yet Over for Carnegie Hall," *New York Times*, July 26, 1956; Lisa Greenwald, unpublished monograph, "History of the J. M. Kaplan Fund," May 2004, 53–57; Richard and Theodora Schulze, "Isaac Stern Savior of Carnegie Hall," www.carnegiehallfund.org (accessed March 7, 2006); Michael Zuekal, a tenant of the hall and president of the World Brotherhood Foundation, was behind both the demonstration and the effort to recruit Khrushchev. In January of 1960, he wrote Khrushchev and in March he was one of a dozen who demonstrated at city hall on behalf of Carnegie Hall. "Maybe Mr. Khrushchev Can Save Carnegie Hall," *New York Times*, January 27, 1960; "Carnegie Hall Protest Held," *New York Times*, March

30, 1960; "Telemann Concert Is Preceded by Plea to Save Carnegie Hall," *New York Times*, January 4, 1960; Bard, letter to the editor, *New York Times*, April 2, 1960.

8. Stern, *My First 79 Years*, 143.

9. Stern, *New York 1960*, 1113; Greenwald, "History of the J. M. Kaplan Fund," 53–57; Stern, *My First 79 Years*, 143–153.

10. Suzanne Davis, who had worked at the J. M. Kaplan Fund with Ray Rubinow, email message to author, May 20, 2006.

11. Stern, *New York 1960*, 1113; Greenwald, "History of the J. M. Kaplan Fund," 53–57; Stern, *My First 79 Years*, 143–153; Bard to Robert F. Wagner, Mayor, April 20, 1960, Albert S. Bard Papers, New York Public Library.

12. Stern, *My First 79 Years*, 143–153; Greenwald, "History of the J. M. Kaplan Fund," 55.

13. "Saving Carnegie Hall," *New York Times*, March 21, 1960.

14. "Saving of Carnegie Hall Enabled in Bills Signed by Rockefeller," *New York Times*, April 17, 1960.

15. "City Move Nears on Carnegie Hall," *New York Times*, April 21, 1960; "Carnegie Hall Is Bought by City; Philharmonic Will Stay There," *New York Times*, July 1, 1960.

16. Greenwald, "History of the J. M. Kaplan Fund," 56.

17. "Saving Carnegie Hall," *New York Times*, March 21, 1960; "Carnegie's Lights Look Brighter," *New York Times*, April 19, 1960; "Lights Up at Carnegie Hall," *New York Times*, May 2, 1960.

18. "Reborn Carnegie Makes Its Debut; Wagner Cuts Tape to Open Redecorated Auditorium—Conducts Band on Street," *New York Times*, September 27, 1960 with large photo caption, "Carnegie Reopens to Mayor's Scissors and Baton."

19. Wood, "An Interview with Harmon Goldstone," 24.

20. Goldstone, "The Future of the Past," 12.

21. M. Jay Racusin, "Hearing to Be Demanded on Central Park Cafe Plan," *New York Herald-Tribune*, May 12, 1960.

22. "Every Foot of the Park," *New York Times*, April 19, 1960; "Carnegie's Lights Look Brighter," *New York Times*, April 19, 1960.

23. Robert Moses, *Public Works: A Dangerous Trade*, 17.

24. M. Jay Racusin, "Hearing to Be Demanded on Central Park Cafe Plan," *New York Herald-Tribune*, May 12, 1960.

25. Bard, letter to the editor, *New York Times*, June 2, 1960; Edward R. Finch, Jr. coauthored the Brief of Amicus Curiae for the Municipal Art Society in 795 Fifth Avenue Corporation, Walter Hoving, Fifth Avenue and 59th Street Corporation and Andrew Y. Rogers against the City of New York, Robert F. Wagner as Mayor of the City of New York, Newbold Morris as Commissioner of Parks of the City of New York for the Borough of Manhattan, April 7, 1961; Francis Keally, letter to the editor, *New York Times*, May 30, 1961.

26. Peter Kihss, "Out-of-Park Site Is Urged for Cafe," *New York Times*, July 20, 1960.

27. Harmon H. Goldstone, letter to the editor, *Manhattan East*, March 30, 1961; Goldstone appeared on Bill Leonard's "Eye on New York," Saturday, July 16, 1960, "Municipal Art Society News," July 1960; Peter Kihss, "Out-of-Park Site Is Urged for Cafe," *New York Times*, July 20, 1960.

28. Harmon Goldstone, "The Proposed Huntington Hartford Pavilion at the Southeast Corner of Central Park," Municipal Art Society, July 3, 1960, Anthony C. Wood Archive.

29. Paul Crowell, "City Accepts Gift for Cafe in Park," *New York Times*, July 28, 1960.

30. Loring McMillen to Gardner Osborn, August 8, 1960, American Scenic and Historic Preservation Society Records, New York Public Library.

31. Moses, *Public Works: A Dangerous Trade*, 18.

32. "Landmark," *The New Yorker*, March 24, 1956, attributed to Brendan Gill by Edward Steese, Municipal Art Society Board Meeting Minutes, March 26, 1956, Municipal Art Society of New York Records, Archives of American Art.

33. Ada Louise Huxtable, "The Salvage of Old Jeff," *New York Times*, September 23, 1964; Ada Louise Huxtable, "'Old Jeff's' Conversion," *New York Times*, November 28, 1967.

34. Whitney North Seymour, letter to the editor, *New York Times*, June 21, 1956; "Building Peril Ended," *New York Times*, July 7, 1956; Municipal Art Society Board Meeting Minutes, September 24, 1956, Municipal Art Society of New York Records, Archives of American Art.

35. Whitney North Seymour, letter to the editor, *New York Times*, June 21, 1956; memo to chairman, borough president's Local Planning Board #2, regarding Old Jefferson Market Courthouse, from Robert C. Weinberg, February 18, 1958.

36. It was also called the Village Neighborhood Committee for the Clock on Jefferson Market Courthouse since its work continued beyond just getting the clock started. "Clock in the 'Village' Running Again," *New York Times*, October 17, 1970.

37. A photo caption accompanying a picture of Old Jeff's Clock, in the *Village Voice* of July 2, 1958, reports on the achievements of Margot Gayle and Harold Birns' The Committee of Neighbors to Get the Jefferson Market Courthouse Clock Started. This, along with the article mentioned in the preface of this book, suggest that Margot's oft-repeated memory that the effort got started in December of 1959 is mistaken. Whether launched in December of 1957 or 1959, the accomplishment was incredible. Wood unpublished interview with Margot Gayle, April 26, 1984, Anthony C. Wood Archive; Christopher Gray, "A Stopped Clock Sired the Preservation Movement," *New York Times*, April 3, 1994; "The Return of Old Jeff," *Progressive Architecture*, October 1967, 175–178; "Old Jeff's Clock," Village Voice, July 2, 1958.

38. Wood interview with Gayle, April 26, 1984; "Jefferson Market Clock Ticks Again," *Greenwich Village News*, October 21, 1960; "Courthouse Clock Bows to Progress. It Is Now Electric," *New York Times*, September 1, 1962; "Wrecker, Stop that Ball," *Newsweek*, January 25, 1965, 54–55.

39. *Villager,* November 25, 1959; "'Old Jeff,' 82, Still Has a Life Left, Official Indicates," *Village Voice*, December 4, 1959.

40. "'Old Jeff,' 82, Still Has a Life Left, Official Indicates," *Village Voice*, December 4, 1959.

41. H. Robert Mandell, treasurer, Committee for a Library in the Jefferson Courthouse to James Felt, March 10, 1961, Archives at Jefferson Market Courthouse Library; Wood interview with Gayle, April 26, 1984; Ada Louise Huxtable, "Old Jeff's Conversion," *New York Times*, November 28, 1967.

42. Edith Evans Asbury, "'Villagers' Fight to Save Building," *New York Times*, February 19, 1961; Ada Louise Huxtable, "The Salvage of Old Jeff," *New York Times*, September 23, 1964; Municipal Art Society Board Meeting Minutes, November 24, 1958 and November 23, 1959, Municipal Art Society of New York Records, Archives of American Art; Margot Gayle notes of the meeting, Archives at Jefferson Market Courthouse Library.

43. Stanley B. Tankel to James Felt, June 23, 1961.

44. "Committee Jubilant as Mayor Urges Library in Courthouse," *Chelsea Clinton News*, August 31, 1961; office of the mayor, press releases, "Mayor Wagner Backs Jefferson Market Courthouse for a Library," August 23, 1961; Melanie Gregurina, "The Jefferson Market Courthouse Conversion and Its Influence," paper for course at Pratt Institute, Landmarks Preservation Practices, July 14, 1985.

45. Harmon H. Goldstone, president, Municipal Art Society, letter to the editor, *New York Times*, August 19, 1960.

46. Victor Gruen, quoted in Edmond J. Bartnett, "Bowling Plan Hit in Grand Central," *New York Times*, December 4, 1960.

47. Gordon S. White, Jr., "Terminal to Get Bowling Alleys; Three-Floor Center Will Be Built into Waiting Room of Grand Central," *New York Times*, August 4, 1960; S. T. Keiley, manager, Grand Central Terminal, letter to the editor, *New York Times*, August 24, 1960.

48. Robert C. Weinberg, letter to the editor, *New York Times*, August 16, 1960.

49. Goldstone, letter to the editor, August 19, 1960; Charles Grutzner, "Bowling Barred at Grand Central," *New York Times*, January 11, 1961.

50. Anthony C. Wood interview with Ada Louise Huxtable, March 13, 2006; "Bowling over Grand Central," *New York Times*, January 10, 1961.

51. "Architects to Keep Their Guardian Eye on Grand Central," *New York Times*, January 24, 1961.

52. Ibid.; Victor Gruen, Chairman, AIA Grand Central Subcommittee to James Felt, January 24, 1961.

53. January 21, 1961 Meeting Minutes of the Preservation Committee of the Brooklyn Heights Association, Otis Pratt Pearsall Papers, New York Preservation Archive Project; Wood interview with Otis Pratt Pearsall, May 3, 2006.

54. Hosmer interview of Goldstone, June 23, 1982; "How the Landmarks Law Happened," Harmon Goldstone's handwritten notes for his talk "How the Landmarks Law Happened," before the Century Association, February 3, 1972, Anthony C. Wood Archive.

55. Holden had been working on the document for years. Robert Weinberg's papers produced two versions of the document, a "Memorandum No. 5, Suggestions from Arthur C. Holden, Proposed Amendment to the Zoning Ordinance of the City of New York, Revised to November 5, 1959," and "Memorandum No. 6, Suggestion, from Arthur C. Holden, Proposed Local Law for Preservation of Places and Structures of Historical or Aesthetic Value, April, 1960." Memorandum from Robert C. Weinberg to Geoffrey Platt, February 7, 1961. All materials from the Professional Papers of Robert C. Weinberg, Long Island University.

56. Wood, "An Interview with Harmon Goldstone," *Village Views*, 26.

57. "An Address by James Felt, Chairman, City Planning Commission Before the 69th Annual Meeting of the Municipal Art Society," May 8, 1961."

58. Ibid.

59. Robert C. Weinberg to Harmon Goldstone, May 10, 1961, Professional Papers of Robert C. Weinberg, Long Island University.

60. Goldstone, notes for his Century Association talk, "How the Landmarks Law Happened," February 3, 1972, Anthony C. Wood Archive.

61. Wood, "An Interview with the First Chairman of the Landmarks Preservation Commission, the Late Geoffrey Platt," *Village Views*, 8.

62. In his interview with Hosmer, Goldstone states that after lunch, Felt "called up Mayor Wagner and said, 'I recommend that you appoint a committee to study this thing.'" Hosmer, "Interview with Harmon Goldstone," 11.

63. Wood, "An Interview with Harmon Goldstone," *Village Views*, 28.

64. Goldstone to Felt, May 9, 1961, Goldstone to Whitney N. Seymour, May 10, 1961, Anthony C. Wood Archive.

65. Wood interview of Margot Gayle; *Stern, My First 79 Years*, 147.

66. "Group Hits Bowling at Grand Central," *New York Times*, January 5, 1961.

67. Goldstone to Whitney North Seymour, May 10, 1961, Anthony C. Wood Archive.

68. "Mayor Wagner Backs Jefferson Market Courthouse for a Library," Press Release, City of New York Office of the Mayor, August 23, 1961, NYC Municipal Archives.

69. Other members of the Committee for the Preservation of Structures of Historic and Esthetic Importance were Robert S. Curtiss, Stanley H. Lowell, McKim Norton, Morgan Dix Wheelock, and Bethuel M. Webster; "Mayor Appoints 13 to Help Preserve Historic Buildings," *New York Times*, July 12, 1961.

70. Hosmer, "Interview with Goldstone," 12.

71. Goldstone to Felt, June 1, 1961, Anthony C. Wood Archive.

72. Reporting on "the furious pace at which New York tears down the old and raises up the new," a columnist writing in the *Chicago Daily Tribune* describes the work of the Municipal Art Society on saving landmarks, noting that the mayor's new committee "has society personnel for its chairman, secretary, and seven of its 13 members." Linda Crawford, "Report from New York," *Chicago Daily Tribune*, March 25, 1962.

73. Recording of Harmon Goldstone, "How the Landmarks Law Happened," The Century Association, February 3, 1972, Century Association Archives Foundation.

ELEVEN

The Commission and the Station

ONLY WEEKS AFTER MAYOR WAGNER'S APPOINTMENT OF THE COMMITTEE for the Preservation of Structures of Historic and Esthetic Importance, and only days after its creation was reported in the *New York Times*, the news broke that Pennsylvania Station was again destined for demolition. From that moment on, the painfully slow process of drafting and ultimately securing passage of the Landmarks Law would always be a step or two behind the forces working to demolish the station. It would be under the increasingly darkening shadow of Pennsylvania Station, both before and during its long-drawn-out and highly public demolition, that the mayor's new committee and its successor, the first Landmarks Preservation Commission, would undertake the politically charged task of trying to create a public policy to curtail New York's seemingly insatiable appetite for consuming its past. Pennsylvania Station's uncertain fate would make that task even more difficult while also complicating relationships between organizations, preservationists, and even brothers.

The July 25, 1961 front-page story announcing the demolition of Pennsylvania Station did no such thing. The headline read "New Madison Sq. Garden To Rise Atop Penn Station." The story never mentions the actual demolition of the station.[1] As was the case with earlier schemes to replace the station, the press coverage treated the station as though it consisted only of the below-grade railroad tracks and platforms and ignored the presence of the Charles Follen McKim classical giant that housed it all. Perhaps this was because, as *Architectural Forum* had observed years earlier, "every function of the station, except the glory, occurs below street level."[2] For those who had not read between the lines of the first news

FIGURE 11.1 The sheer size of Pennsylvania Station, captured here in a 1909 photograph taken from the roof of R. H. Macy's & Co., underscores the enormity of its loss. The threat to the station was always several steps ahead of the efforts to create a law that could have preserved it.

accounts, the subhead of the *Times* follow-up story made it clear: "Penn Station to Be Razed to Street Level in Project."[3]

The news of the planned demolition of the station did not trigger an immediate public outcry. Perhaps this was because earlier grandiose schemes to replace Grand Central Terminal and Pennsylvania Station had never materialized, so this latest threat was not taken seriously. Perhaps it was exactly the opposite. The steady decline and cheapening of Pennsylvania Station, through tasteless additions and deferred maintenance, led people to conclude that its demise was inevitable. Others would chalk up the initial silence to the public's general indifference and apathy toward

the city's landmarks. The now-famous picketing of the station that would capture headlines and unleash editorials was still a year away.

That hot summer of 1961 found Mayor Wagner's new Committee for the Preservation of Structures of Historic and Esthetic Importance hard at work. Despite the "dreadful name" which the "mayor inflicted" on it, the committee was "grateful to be appointed" and held the first of its five meetings on July 25 at the Seaman's Bank for Savings at 45th Street and Fifth Avenue.[4] Under Platt's leadership, it examined "relevant legislation in other cities, particularly those of New Orleans, Boston, Providence and Philadelphia."[5] It worked "in consultation with the City Planning Commission."[6] Thanks to Platt's "passion for brevity," on November 27, 1961, the committee reported its findings to the mayor in a one-page memo.[7]

The committee "recommended that a permanent commission be established to be known as the Landmarks Preservation Commission of the City of New York," thus sparing future preservationists the burden of the cumbersome name under which it had labored.[8] The commission would designate for protection "a. Buildings, structures, monuments, statues and works of historic and/or esthetic importance; b. The surroundings of any of the foregoing insofar as needed to protect their character; c. Groups of buildings or districts whose general character is important historically or which are uniquely valuable in design or location." The new commission would also answer preservation questions from public bodies and recommend "appropriate action." Within a year, the commission was to present to the mayor a "detailed legislative program for the effective protection of those portions of designated landmarks that fall within public view." The report then suggested the composition of the commission and the action steps for bringing it to life.[9]

Six days later, on December 3, uncharacteristically quick for the Wagner administration, the mayor issued a press release thanking the committee for its work, accepting its recommendations, and announcing his intent to "take steps immediately which will lead to their implementation."[10] While the mayor's response was remarkably fast, the proposed landmarks law was still over three years away. Events that had transpired since the committee had begun its work, including the breaking of the Pennsylvania Station demolition story literally on the heels of the committee's appointment, likely had something to do with the mayor's speedy actions.

While preservation issues in New York City were reaching the crisis stage, Robert Wagner had been elected to a third term. Having broken with Democratic political boss Carmine De Sapio, Wagner had gone on to impressively win the Democratic primary and then to triumph over his Republican challenger, Louis Lefkowitz, in the general election. To this day, historic preservation has yet to emerge as a decisive issue in any mayoral campaign, but the fact that preservation was an important issue to some in Wagner's camp was not lost on such a savvy mayor. From personal experience, Wagner knew the political importance of preservation in Greenwich Village. The civic community's interest in the issue was also well established. The press release announcing the mayor's support for preserving Jefferson Market Courthouse and converting it into a library (a position taken just prior to the hotly contested Democratic primary) also referenced other examples of the mayor's concern for "city beautification and preservation of buildings of architectural and historic interest."[11] The fact that key Wagner supporters such as Eleanor Roosevelt were also vocal and active supporters of various efforts to save New York landmarks should not be overlooked. His decisive action on the committee's recommendations certainly pleased some of his supporters.

Pressing preservation issues also called for quick action on the committee's report. Platt's letter conveying the report to the mayor captured the growing sense of urgency: "Since its formation, the Committee has received numerous communications requesting support for the preservation of various individual buildings as well as districts and has been increasingly impressed with the necessity for the early establishment of the suggested agency."[12] Not only were there continuing calls for preservation coming from the besieged neighborhoods of Brooklyn Heights and Greenwich Village, the citywide civics also continued to sound the preservation alarm.

In what must have been a delicate political balancing act, on the same day Platt's letter to the mayor conveying the committee's report is dated, the Municipal Art Society, under the name of its president, Harmon Goldstone (also a member of Platt's committee), sent a telegram to the mayor urging delay on a plan for a new building that would have replaced the historic Tweed Courthouse in City Hall Park. The postponement would allow the City Planning Commission time to complete its study of the area. Though not framed explicitly as a call to preserve the building, the request for the delay, which was reported in the *New York Times*, suggests both the growing number of threatened high-profile historic structures as well as the Municipal Art Society's dual challenge of advancing its preservation policy agenda within government while continuing its much needed role as public watchdog.[13]

FIGURE 11.2 Mayor Wagner was proud of his support of the preservation of Jefferson Market Courthouse and its reuse as a branch of the New York Public Library. The campaign to save the courthouse demonstrated the popular appeal preservation could enjoy. The successful saving of the courthouse, seen here in a photograph by Berenice Abbott, would make it a "poster child" for the cause of preservation.

FIGURE 11.3 On September 21, 1961, the question of whether New York City's landmarks should be saved was brought into New York living rooms with the airing of the first prime time television preservation documentary. Producer/writer Gordon Hyatt's crew is shown here filming Pennsylvania Station for the WCBS-TV thirty-minute program, *Our Vanishing Legacy*. Reporter Ned Calmer served as narrator.

While Platt's committee was at work, a new voice for preservation joined the traditional pro-preservation choir. On September 21, 1961, what appears to be the first New York prime time broadcast highlighting the case for historic preservation, aired on New York Channel 2, WCBS-TV.[14] Described by one reviewer as "a persuasive plea for preservation of buildings that are part of the city's architectural heritage," the thirty-minute documentary, *Our Vanishing Legacy*, was written and produced by Gordon Hyatt. Alan Burnham and Henry Hope Reed received special thanks for their help with the program.[15] The broadcast brought the preservation message into the living rooms of more New Yorkers than Henry Hope Reed could have reached in a lifetime of leading walking tours.

Taking on the questions, "Are we just tearing down buildings? Or are we also destroying some of the most precious things in our cultural heritage?", the program showcased preservation causes from saving Carnegie Hall to the threatened Pennsylvania Station. Whether highlighting Jefferson Market Courthouse, the Old Merchant's House, or the interior of Grand Central Terminal, the film captured the beauty of the buildings and reported on their possible fates. The tone was far from neutral.

After singing the praises of Pennsylvania Station, the reporter Ned Calmer observed: "For unless we take a new kind of interest in this building, Pennsylvania Station will be lost." Noting that New York is "far behind" such cities as Charleston and Boston in "recognizing our architectural legacy," the show ended with a view of the New York skyline and the statement, "Should there be a law to protect our unique buildings—to preserve the best of our architectural tradition—to save our vanishing legacy? Maybe there should."[16]

Described as a "provocative documentary" dealing with "our shocking craze for demolishing buildings which have not only historic importance but are gems of architectural beauty," the program did not instantly transform hordes of apathetic New Yorkers into preservation activists, but it did help bring the cause of preservation to the general public.[17] It also brought new hope to the preservation community. Henry Hope Reed wrote Gordon Hyatt: "Tired spirits who have battled for our vanishing legacy were refreshed, weakened they have found new strength."[18] Geoffrey Platt's committee had decided it was too early in their work to offer a statement to be included in the program, but in a letter after its debut, Harmon Goldstone suggests to Hyatt that perhaps a subsequent program might offer a chance to advance the committee's recommendations.[19]

Another voice would emerge to champion the committee's proposals and to dramatically bring the cause for historic preservation to the general public. Though the age of television was dawning, it was the newspaper that remained preservation's best friend. Preservation battles in Brooklyn Heights and Greenwich Village already demonstrated the power that the local press could bring to the preservation battlefield. The role the *New York Herald-Tribune* played in the successful effort to save Castle Clinton earned its chief editorial writer Geoffrey Parsons the prestigious McAneny Award from the American Scenic and Historic Preservation Society in 1949.[20] But, the important role the press had played in the past would pale in comparison to the role the *New York Times* would play in advancing and securing the passage of New York's Landmarks Law.

The release of the Platt committee report and the mayor's positive response to it triggered a *Times* editorial. Noting that in the case of preservation, "New York's action is long overdue," it continues: "For the sake of its future, New York needs a radically increased awareness of its historic and esthetic assets. If we put half of the energy, ingenuity and activity into retaining these assets that we do into ripping them out we can be assured of impressive results. The establishment of a Landmarks Preservation Commission would be a hopeful indication that New York

City is at last moving in this direction."[21] The *New York Times* would radically increase New York's preservation consciousness by running well over twenty pro-preservation editorials between December 1961 and the passage of the Landmarks Law in the spring of 1965. This would be in addition to its impressive news coverage of the ceaseless stream of preservation stories marking that turbulent time.

In this period, preservation was blessed to have at the *New York Times* not only an editor of the editorial page who appreciated the importance of preservation, but a brilliant writer who also embraced its values. That editor was John Oakes, and the writer was Ada Louise Huxtable. After more than a decade of writing "distinguished editorials," Oakes assumed control of the editorial page on April 25, 1961. He immediately injected "new life into what had become a 'dull, heavy, mournful' pastiche of opinion." For the next fifteen years, he would operate with "near autonomy."[22] Under his leadership, the page "dropped its cautious drift and became a stern liberal bellows on most social and economic questions."[23] The environment was a subject of particular interest to Oakes. His opinions were in such close alignment with the advocates of that cause that in 1962 he was invited to join the board of the American Scenic and Historic Preservation Society.[24] This change of editorial leadership and style at the *New York Times* could not have come at a better time for preservation.

Even before Ada Louise Huxtable made history in 1963 as the first full-time *New York Times* architecture critic, focusing "public opinion on the city's built environment as never before," she was writing in its defense.[25] As early as 1961, John Oakes had enlisted her to write editorials for the paper. In this capacity, she authored, without public attribution, a series of forceful editorials that would keep the cause of preservation front and center until and well beyond the passage of the Landmarks Law.[26] With an art degree from Hunter College and advanced courses in architecture from the Institute of Fine Arts of New York University, she had gone to work in the Architecture and Design Department of the Museum of Modern Art during Philip Johnson's tenure. She spent over a decade as a freelance writer focusing on art and architecture. In 1959, she authored for the Municipal Art Society, in partnership with the Museum of Modern Art, a series of walking tours devoted to modern architecture (as a counterpoint to Henry Hope Reed's tours focusing on traditional architecture).[27]

In recounting her work with John Oakes, Huxtable noted that Oakes made the final decisions on all the issues addressed in editorials. Initially, he approached her to write editorials. Soon, she was able to propose her own topics to him. Oakes was a light-handed editor, primarily concerned

FIGURE 11.4 Ada Louise Huxtable made history in 1963 when she became the first full-time architecture critic for the *New York Times,* yet as early as 1961, she was saving history, writing the paper's powerful editorials calling for action to preserve New York City's architecture and heritage. Her brilliant and fiery prose, combined with *Times* editor John Oakes' editorial strategy, helped focus the city's attention on the escalating landmark crisis.

with the solidity of facts. Not welcoming heavy-handed editing from anyone, Huxtable wrote her editorials carefully to size to reduce the chance of being edited. When asked whether there was a concerted strategy behind the *Times'* dogged editorial coverage of key preservation efforts,

she responded that it was the news stories themselves that determined the editorial coverage. If there was a news hook, there could be an editorial. The many twists and turns of such preservation dramas as the fates of Pennsylvania Station and the Brokaw mansions, and the continued efforts toward the Landmarks Law itself, provided an unending series of news pegs for editorials.[28]

Though there was no master plan driving the *New York Times* editorial coverage of preservation issues, the relentless focus on an issue did reflect the strategic approach John Oakes brought to the editorial page. One editorial board member described it as follows: "John firmly believed that the page had to hit at its arguments day after day after day. Once we took a position on a subject, the power came in constant hammering at it. John was very insistent on this. There was always novel ways of making the same argument."[29] When it came to preservation, there were so many hard news stories providing opportunities for editorial comment that novel arguments were not needed. Huxtable gives Oakes great credit for letting her ride with the issue. Preservationists need to give them both enormous credit for helping transform preservation from an obscure subject discussed in civic board rooms, to a vibrant public issue followed at New York breakfast tables.

The mayor had accepted his committee's report with record speed, but the formal wheels of government turned more slowly. In its March 10, 1962 editorial, "Farewell to Landmarks," the *New York Times* commented on this. "By action of the Board of Estimate, New York City now has a Landmarks Preservation Commission and a budget of $50,000 to help it carry out its function. The Fine Arts Federation is busy making up a list of potential commission members to be submitted to the Mayor for appointment. While this due process plods on, the bulldozers have been busy." The editorial looked at the ponderous work confronting the new commission, the drafting of a law and compilation of lists of buildings and areas to be protected, and lamented: "If we are slow enough—and we have set an ignoble precedent on this score—most of New York's architectural heritage and almost all of the city's remaining early nineteenth-century structures of historical interest will be gone. We can then point to our documents, plans, reports and excellent intentions, and say that no one was really to blame."[30]

If the *New York Times* felt the wheels of government were turning at a painfully slow rate, one can only imagine the sentiments of Francis Keally. It was in 1950 that Keally, as president of the Municipal Art Society, had issued his early call for a landmarks law. Now twelve years later,

■ ■ ■ ■ ■ ■ ■

in "partial implementation of the Bard Act," this new commission was being appointed to advance that agenda. Now, serving as the chairman of the Fine Arts Federation's nominating committee recommending the membership of this new commission to the mayor was Francis Keally.[31] If one has the staying power and is blessed with good genes, one can live long enough to witness such advances.

On April 21, 1962, Mayor Wagner appointed the first Landmarks Preservation Commission.[32] Its membership was to include at all times "an architect, a realtor, an historian qualified in the field, a practitioner of the fine arts, a landscape architect or city planner, and a representative of the public at large—one of whom shall be a member of the Art Commission."[33] Of historical interest on this twelve-member body chaired by Geoffrey Platt were individuals linked to the very civic organizations and the historic neighborhoods that for years had been working toward this moment.

On the commission were members of the Municipal Art Society (Geoffrey Platt), the Society of Architectural Historians (Russell Lynes), the American Institute of Architects (Frederick F. Woodbridge, its president at the time), and the American Scenic and Historic Preservation Society (Loring McMillen). Some members had involvements with multiple civic organizations. Two of its members, Platt and Woodbridge, had served on Weinberg's instrumental Joint Committee on Design Control. Also included on the commission were articulate voices from two geographic hotbeds of preservation: Greenwich Village's Stanley Tankel, and Brooklyn Heights' William Fisher (who replaced Robert S. Curtiss, who resigned that fall).

Notably missing from the new commission, and for good reason, was Harmon Goldstone. While Platt's mayoral study committee was still at work, a vacancy had opened up on the City Planning Commission. There was public clamor that the new appointee should be an architect: "Surprisingly, although it deals with many architectural matters, the commission has long lacked an architect member. . . . An architect is the obvious and proper choice for the commission's vacancy."[34] By this time, because of their conversations about landmarks, James Felt had developed a close and trusting relationship with Geoffrey Platt and Harmon Goldstone, both architects. Felt approached them regarding their possible interests in filling the vacancy. Goldstone was appointed.[35]

Goldstone's new position was a boon to the cause of preservation. Though he had to resign as president of the Municipal Art Society and was not available to serve on the first Landmarks Preservation Commission, as a planning commissioner he was able to facilitate a smooth working

FIGURE 11.5   Harmon Goldstone, seen here being sworn into office by Mayor Lindsay in 1971, was not among those appointed to the first Landmarks Preservation Commission on April 21, 1962. He had already been handpicked by chair James Felt to serve on the New York City Planning Commission, where he played an invaluable role advancing the cause of preservation.

relationship between the agencies, both prior to the passage of the law and in the critical early years of its implementation. He was also able to "run interference" for preservation with other city agencies. Meeting "almost every day" with Platt, he was an indispensable, though unofficial, member of the landmarks team. Some years later, Goldstone's preservation work would continue in a new role when he would succeed Platt becoming the second chair of the Landmarks Preservation Commission.[36]

Those who had long sought legal landmark protection were now ensconced in the new official agency tasked with designing that formal system. In addition, in Felt and Goldstone, preservation had allies on the all-important City Planning Commission. Not only was the pro-preservation civic community well represented among the commissioners of the new agency, its professional staff was also enriched with those from its ranks. Among the commission's early staffers were Henry Hope Reed, of walking-tour fame, and Agnes Gilchrist, former president of the Society of Architectural Historians and a major force in developing the Municipal Art Society's *New York Landmarks: An Index of Architecturally Notable Structures in New York City*. Its fourth edition had appeared in January 1960.[37]

Singularly important would be that person who would lead the nascent agency in its day-to-day work, the commission's executive director. At Harmon Goldstone's suggestion, Platt went to Columbia University to seek the counsel of Goldstone's friend, James Van Derpool. Long a professor of architectural history, the Avery Librarian after Talbot Hamlin, and having served as acting and then associate dean of Columbia's School of Architecture, no one was better networked to help Platt find his executive director than Van Derpool. When informed of the job, Van Derpool delighted Platt and "dumbfounded" Goldstone, by offering to fill the position himself: "This is my dream all my life."[38] With a former president of both the local chapter and the national Society of Architectural Historians, a trustee of the American Scenic and Historic Preservation Society, and a nationally recognized expert in the field at its head, the commission's staff would be led by a high profile, respected professional.[39]

The Landmarks Preservation Commission had been appointed and its team assembled in its offices at 2 Lafayette Street. Its charge was clear: identify and designate landmarks, draft a law, and receive and answer preservation questions from other city agencies. Along with this official charge came some unofficial advice from Platt's political rabbi, James Felt. He urged Platt to proceed cautiously: "Take this time that you've got." In Platt's mind, that time was a three-year window. Felt also advised, "Don't surprise anybody in government." Most prophetically, he advised Platt to keep his eye on the prize. "You're going to lose some buildings during this period and don't let it bother you. You just—you're going to lose 'em." Though Platt did not suggest this advice had being given to him in the context of Pennsylvania Station, as the story of the commission and the station unfolds, it is hard not to see it in that context.[40]

FIGURE 11.6 The new Landmarks Preservation Commission received an unexpected boost when high-profile architectural historian James Grote Van Derpool left Columbia University's School of Architecture to become the agency's first executive director. Van Derpool, at left, is shown here on February 5, 1965 receiving the George McAneny Historic Preservation Medal from the American Scenic and Historic Preservation Society.

The Landmarks Preservation Commission immediately confronted daunting political challenges. In addition to the problems any new agency would face as it tried to navigate unfamiliar and often treacherous governmental and public terrain, the commission had to finesse two

political problems unique to its situation. Both were highly politically charged and very public, though one was more so than the other. Either could have wounded, perhaps mortally, the commission. Both problems predated the commission's creation. One involves the unfinished story of Brooklyn Heights' campaign for preservation protection, the other, the growing realization that this time, New York City might really lose Pennsylvania Station.

Having failed in their efforts to achieve some form of historic or aesthetic zoning for New York City's special neighborhoods through the new zoning resolution, residents of Brooklyn Heights set out to achieve protection for themselves. The goal was to achieve so-called stand-alone protection for the Heights by securing passage of a Heights-specific preservation ordinance based on the Bard Act. While citywide events had been unfolding, the Brooklyn Heights Association had been hard at work "identifying every Heights building by date and style, converting Clay Lancaster's detailed report into book form, developing battle plans, organizing committees, delivering speeches, coffee clatches in every corner of the Heights to explain the program, public relations and reaching out to local politicians."[41]

On May 15, 1961, as Platt, Goldstone, and Felt were working behind the scenes to have Mayor Wagner appoint the study committee, the Brooklyn Heights Association held its fifty-first annual meeting in the Grand Ballroom of the Hotel St. George. Its theme was preservation. Five hundred people had come to hear the story of the preservation of Boston's Beacon Hill, the neighborhood that had become the model for the Heights' own vision.[42] "John Codman, the Beacon Hill realtor who had lead the charge for that community's historic zoning, drove home by vivid example the Heights' destiny to achieve no less." Brooklyn Heights was "ready and willing" to embrace legal landmarks protection and did not want to "stand by and suffer possibly years of destruction while the rest of the City caught up."[43]

With the forces of change feasting on the historic architecture of Brooklyn Heights, the calls for neighborhood preservation became louder and more urgent. The "crash program to assure the long-term survival of Brooklyn Heights" presented at the Brooklyn Heights Association's annual meeting was seen as being as "vital" to the future "as was the successful Esplanade-Highway proposal fifteen years ago."[44] Among the many Heights residences recruited to work on the multitude of volunteer committees advancing various pieces of the Heights preservation campaign was a man whose advocacy roots went back to the Esplanade-Highway

struggle, his name was Roy Richardson.[45] The old and new Heights were now shoulder-to-shoulder, fighting for preservation.

The Heights did not regard the announcement of the creation of the Mayor's Committee for the Preservation of Structures of Historic and Esthetic Importance as a positive development. "In fact," as Otis Pearsall has written, "we viewed the Mayor's Committee as a competitor or rival which could well head us off at the pass, require us to fold our project in with theirs, and force Brooklyn Heights to do without preservation indefinitely pending development of a citywide preservation plan." Instead, the Heights sought to be the entity doing the heading off at the pass.[46]

The Heights aggressively advanced its campaign. In December 1961, Clay Lancaster's book, *Old Brooklyn Heights*, was published by Charles E. Tuttle and attracted great attention. It helped generate a major story in the *New York Times*, "'Old Brooklyn Heights' Groups Fighting to Preserve Buildings."[47] As Lancaster's book further established the architectural bona fides of the Heights, the solution for its preservation was being unveiled. The Brooklyn Heights Association, with Otis Pearsall at the reins, had drafted a proposed amendment to the zoning resolution, establishing an "Old Brooklyn Heights" district and creating in the Buildings Department an "Old Brooklyn Heights Architectural Commission" to regulate proposed changes within the District.[48]

Seeking a zoning amendment as their solution, the Brooklyn Heights Association focused their efforts on winning over planning chair James Felt. If Felt was supportive, the path forward would be clear. If not, the alternative governmental route, having Heights preservation become a subject for Platt's new committee, would likely lead to a "city-wide vortex" where Heights preservation could be "delayed for many years."[49] The Heights went after Felt with some success. He "applauded the general aim to preserve the character of Brooklyn Heights."[50] Unfortunately, he was "noncommittal on the issue of immediate historic zoning expressly for Brooklyn Heights." Worse, thought residents, he urged them to work with Platt's committee.[51]

Mrs. Darwin James assisted in making the Brooklyn Heights Association's first contact with the Platt committee. She arranged an intimate lunch in her apartment with Harmon Goldstone, her fellow Municipal Art Society board member and "the member of the Mayor's Committee closest to its Chairman, Geoffrey Platt." The lunch was a success. Pearsall recalled that "Harmon was very excited about Brooklyn Heights and all that we had done. He was very positive in his encouragement and urged us to get together as soon as possible with Platt."[52] Goldstone followed up by sending the Heights' proposed zoning amendment on to Platt with a letter comparing it to the current thinking of Platt's committee. He ended noting that the Brooklyn Heights group is "very conscious of the urgency for getting effective preservation on the Heights enacted as soon as possible. I fully agree."[53] Goldstone ultimately concluded that any landmarks lost while New York worked to achieve a "workable law" for the entire city was a price worth paying to avoid the "chaos" that he believed would result if New York followed the Boston model of stand-alone-districts, each with its own law. He too joined in the effort to "put the brakes on Brooklyn Heights."[54]

Heights residents were soon in direct contact with Platt and their earlier fears were confirmed. It quickly became clear that Platt would not be supportive of their isolationist efforts. Platt was committed to developing a citywide system for landmarks protection. A stand-alone solution for Brooklyn Heights would have taken New York down the path followed by Boston and other cities that had neighborhood-specific preservation ordinances. If Brooklyn had been successful in its efforts, both the history and structure of New York's Landmarks Law would be very different. Years later, Geoffrey Platt would recall the struggle with Brooklyn Heights, saying "they had some rather difficult characters over there."[55]

Not a community to take "no" for an answer, in the spring of 1962, just days after the appointment of the mayoral Landmarks Preservation Commission, the Brooklyn Heights Association formally submitted to the mayor, the commission, "and every other City and Federal official we could think of," its proposal to amend the Zoning Resolution to create an Old Brooklyn Heights Architectural Commission.[56] Presented along with the amendment were "detailed study maps and a comprehensive tabulation describing the buildings in the 50-block area to be preserved as the historic district of 'Old Brooklyn Heights.'"[57] This effort generated some press coverage and elicited a statement by Platt that Brooklyn Heights should have "first priority in any effort to preserve what is left of old New York."[58] Their request also caught the attention of Save the Village and led it to write the Landmarks Preservation Commission requesting the same "aesthetic historic zoning" that Brooklyn Heights was seeking.[59] The Heights had earned a place at the head of the line, but its goal had been to avoid being in any line at all.

Despite its multipronged, multiyear, highly strategic, aggressively public and decidedly well-organized effort to advance its bid for a "separate and immediate statute," the Brooklyn Heights Association had failed to achieve that goal.[60] Their efforts established the Heights' primacy for historic district designation, but it would be years before that chit could be cashed in. The association's intensive organizing and public education efforts did result in a highly preservation-sensitive population that began to enforce, as much as it was possible without the force of law, a preservation ethic in the Heights.[61] The Heights' preservation campaign had received the support of Brooklyn's congressman (and later New York State governor) Hugh Carey. Through his intervention, the Heights' own Bill Fisher would soon join the new Landmarks Preservation Commission, giving the Heights a direct channel into that body.[62] The fact that Clay Lancaster and James Van Derpool were also good friends had to give Heights advocates an additional degree of comfort in the new Landmarks Commission.[63]

On August 12, 1962, James Felt was the guest on the television program *New York Forum* aired on WCBS-TV. Panelists were members of the Association of the Bar of the City of New York. Among them was Otis Pearsall. He took the occasion to again directly raise the issue of the preservation of Brooklyn Heights. In no uncertain terms, Felt made it clear that the issue was now fully in the hands of the new Landmarks Preservation Commission. An end run around the new commission to the City Planning Commission would not be allowed. Even the indefatigable Pearsall finally got the message; the Heights was going to have to wait. Brooklyn Heights' fate was now inextricably tied to that of a citywide landmarks ordinance.[64]

With that answer, Felt removed any threat the Brooklyn Heights single-district campaign still posed for the Landmarks Preservation Commission. The first of the two extraordinary political challenges inherited by the commission upon its birth had been deftly handled. On the *New York Forum* television program, Felt was asked a question about the other high-profile issue facing both Wagner's administration and the new Landmarks Preservation Commission.

> Well, Mr. Felt, last week a group of architects made headlines picketing Penn Station to protest demolition of a landmark they consider to contribute beauty and distinction to the city. Shouldn't the appearance of our city—how it looks—just as bulk and density and height are matters for regulation—shouldn't we immediately enact architectural controls to preserve the heritage of New York, its architecturally and historically important buildings to preserve them for our present enjoyment and the enjoyment of future generations?[65]

The threat to Pennsylvania Station had hit the news again and the infant Landmarks Preservation Commission would soon be in the hot seat.

The *New York Times* announced the appointment of the mayor's Landmarks Preservation Commission in a front-page story on Sunday April 22, 1962. Even in its public birth announcement, the commission was touched by the specter of Pennsylvania Station. The headline "City Acts to Save Historical Sites" was followed by the prominent subhead, "Wagner Names 12 to New Agency—Architects Decry Razing of Pennsylvania Station." Since the story of the station's imminent demise had broken the previous summer, opponents of the demolition had surfaced. The April 22, *New York Times* headline was referencing the opposition of the New York Chapter of the American Institute of Architects, announced in its publication, *Oculus* [66] Also having expressed doubts about the demolition project were the Municipal Art Society and the National Trust for Historic Preservation. [67]

Objecting to the demolition of the station was one thing. Aggressively trying to prevent it was something else. What actually could be done? This was not just another threatened building. Pennsylvania Station occupied nine acres of exceptionally valuable real estate in New York City. The building of Pennsylvania Station had involved the removal of some five hundred buildings. [68] The new construction that would replace the station represented an investment of over $90 million and promised to provide the financially strapped Pennsylvania Railroad $3.5 million a year. In addition, between the new project and the redevelopment of the old site of Madison Square Garden, an estimated $5,000,000 in new tax revenues would be generated for the city. Those were huge numbers for any possible preservation scheme to overcome. [69]

At that time, even though specific details of the new Madison Square Garden project were not available to the general public, some alternative schemes were floated. [70] In February 1962, assuming the building was already a lost cause, parks commissioner Newbold Morris advanced the notion of saving and relocating eighty-four of the station's columns to create a "classical landscape in Flushing Meadow Park." [71] This idea was greeted with the following response from the *New York Times*: "Among the saddest words of tongue or pen—at least from a civic point of view—was Park Commissioner Newbold Morris' recent epitaph for the doomed Pennsylvania Station . . . 'Pennsylvania Station is one of the city's great buildings. I'm working on a plan to save the columns.'" [72]

Slightly better was a proposal by Robert Weinberg that the station's "granite façade with its colonnades and entablature, on Seventh Avenue and along part of the side streets" be incorporated into the design of the new project.[73] The young architect Norval White felt Weinberg had totally missed the point, arguing that the "architecture of Pennsylvania Station is not the superficial architecture of merely a handsome façade attached to an unimportant building. Pennsylvania Station is total architecture, giving commodity, firmness, and delight." White offered a different solution. Noting that all the "basic systems of symbolic arrival" to the city, from the George Washington Bridge to the "splendor of New York harbor," are "controlled and owned by the Port of New York Authority," so, too, should be the city's "great railroad terminals," both Grand Central and Pennsylvania Station.[74] Though intriguing, White's proposal would not carry the day. Norval White, described in the *Village Voice* as "a larger-than-life young architect so passionately involved in the cause of his craft that he brings a sane man's Howard Roark to mind," would shortly emerge as a major public figure in the campaign to save the station.[75]

New York's civic establishment had gone on record opposing the demolition of Pennsylvania Station. It also seemed clear it was largely resigned to accepting the inevitable. The civics had lost buildings before and seemed braced to lose another. Brendan Gill remembered his feelings at the time: "I just felt a kind of despair over it. . . . There was no way to win. It had—it was a project that was underway."[76] The established civic groups knew how hard and unlikely it was to save a building without the force of law (let alone a building of this scale whose demolition was attached to a project of such economic magnitude). At this point, the civics were also heavily invested in working with the Wagner administration in a process that held the greater promise of finally delivering a landmarks preservation law. They wanted to save Pennsylvania Station, but at the same time could not risk excessively rocking the boat. They had worked long and hard to get inside government, securing a place at the decision-shaping table. Having just gotten their foot in the door, was this the time to strain their positive working relationship with the Wagner administration?

The seemingly half-hearted attempts by the traditional organizations to address the Pennsylvania Station situation did not sit well with a new generation of concerned New Yorkers.[77] A cadre of young architects and their friends, many in their twenties, were particularly dismayed by the American Institute of Architects response to the Pennsylvania Station situation. These "young turk" architects banded together to create AGBANY—Action Group for Better Architecture in New York.[78] The officers of the group were: Diana Kirsch, its secretary, Costas Machlouzarides, the treasurer, and Norval White, selected to be its chair because he was "slightly older . . . and more politically astute."[79] Also on the list of its first directors were Jeffrey Aronin, Peter Samton, James Burne, Elliot Willensky, Jay Fleishman, and Joan and Jordan Gruzen.[80]

For these young architects, the threat to Pennsylvania Station was "the first straw," not the last.[81] Years later, one of the key instigators of AGBANY, Diana Goldstein (Kirsch) would recall, "we knew that we would lose, but we wanted to protest, which was why we had the pickets; and we wanted to change the climate."[82] "We felt a moral obligation to protest the tearing down of a great building."[83] These young architects would provide the energy and moral outrage to ensure that Pennsylvania Station would not go quietly into the night.

AGBANY was not totally without the input of some established voices for preservation. Ray Rubinow of Greenwich Village and Carnegie Hall fame joined their board of directors, bringing along his organizational and political experience and recruiting others to the cause.[84] He also opened the door for "moral, and to some extent financial, support from the Kaplan Fund."[85] Lending their names to AGBANY's advisory committee were other longtime preservation supporters Eleanor Roosevelt and Fannie Hurst. Among its financial supporters was Robert C. Weinberg.[86] First and foremost, however, AGBANY was fueled by youth and energy. It would be the efforts of young architects that brought the fight for Pennsylvania Station onto the streets and into the media.

AGBANY succeeded in capturing the public eye with their picketing of Pennsylvania Station from 5 to 7 p.m. on Thursday August 2, 1962. Promoted in advance to the media, launched with a press conference across the street in the Boston Room of the Statler-Hilton Hotel, trumpeted in a same-day advertisement they had purchased in the *New York Times* asking New Yorkers to join them in a "peaceful demonstration of affection for this great and threatened building," AGBANY staged what has gone down in history as "the best-dressed picket line in New York City."[87] Carrying artful placards with slogans ranging from the simple "Shame" to "Progress Is Quality Not Novelty," hundreds picketed the station. Estimates of the number who picketed ranged from 150 to 500.[88] The swirl of the rush-hour commuters around the "two long ellipses" of protesters could only have helped enhance the drama of the event.[89] It was an impressive showing for a demonstration conceived and organized by a young upstart organization with virtually no resources and no political capital.[90]

There may be uncertainty regarding the quantity of protesters, but there is no doubt about their quality. The young architects had been able to attract the blessings and the participation of some established professionals.

Philip Johnson, who would emerge in future years as a preservation rock star passionately involved in efforts to save Grand Central Terminal and St. Bartholomew's Church, walked the picket line. He joined "Mrs. Eero Saarinen, one of the most gifted writers on modern architecture and widow of one of its greatest practitioners;" Mrs. Arthur Drexler of the Museum of Modern Art; Charles Evans Hughes, Jr., of Skidmore, Owings & Merill; Thomas H. Creighton, editor of *Progressive Architecture*; and Paul Rudolph of the Yale University Department of Architecture.[91] Wearing sandals, Jane Jacobs marched with Ray Rubinow. From Robert C. Weinberg to the one-year-old Victoria Lindgren, whose parents carried a sign expressing her wishes: "Don't Let Them Destroy My Heritage," the marchers succeeded in dramatically raising the profile of the campaign to save Pennsylvania Station.[92]

Until AGBANY's efforts, the Wagner administration and the new Landmarks Preservation Commission had been able to sidestep the issue of Pennsylvania Station. In the press story announcing the creation of the new landmarks commission, Geoffrey Platt staked out the commission's initial position: "He personally regretted that his commission had come into being too late to try to save the terminal."[93]

At the end of July 1962 with press interest growing in AGBANY's activities, Platt told the press that he "personally 'deplored' the doom of the station," but asserted "that the commission has no legal powers available now to prevent demolition. It must await instructions from Mayor Wagner even to take a public interest in the issue."[94] Mayor Wagner had been in Europe on vacation and returned the evening of AGBANY's protest at the station. Perhaps it was Platt's comment that led defenders of the station to greet

the scene that one enthusiastic gentleman carrying an orange "SHAME" finally leaned over to a red "STOP GREED" and said: "You know, next we ought to picket the picket lines—and really show 'em how it's done."

The architects, together with an assortment of critics and cultural conservationists, are angry because the Pennsylvania Railroad has sold the air rights over its tracks to the new Madison Square Garden Corporation for the construction of two giant auditoriums and a couple of 33-story office buildings. In the process the railway terminal, designed in 1910 by McKim, Mead, and White after the tepidorium of Caracalla, is scheduled to come down.

Rainbow Display

"You're angry?" The question was put to a mild man in blue summer serge and white straw whose sign—"ANGER" in dripping white on a black field—looked like some old poster from the Grand Guignol.

"I certainly am, I certainly am," he said, whereupon he smiled to greet an old friend who had just waved a blue "RENOVATE, DON'T DESECRATE" in his direction.

ANGER, SHAME, STOP GREED, RENOVATE, and 200 or so other opinions on the intended demolition of Pennsyl-

Voice: Gin Briggs

PICKETERS ALL. Guiding genius of the picket line was NORVAL WHITE (top); other sponsors of the project included JANE JACOBS and RAYMOND S. RUBINOW.

where in the chateau country-

FIGURE 11.7 Though AGBANY (Action Group for Better Architecture in New York) was largely driven by young architects, it was able to attract established activists to its cause. Here Ray Rubinow, veteran of successful efforts to remove traffic from Washington Square and to save Carnegie Hall (who served on AGBANY's board), marches with the urban activist and writer Jane Jacobs at the August 2, 1962 picketing of Pennsylvania Station.

the mayor as he landed at the airport returning from his one-month family vacation. He was welcomed home with a letter "asking him to enlist in the crusade. The letter urged him to call for a report from the Landmarks Preservation Commission that he appointed last April on the architectural and historical importance of Pennsylvania Station, and asked him for a meeting with a delegation next week to discuss the matter."[95]

Pressure was growing. The *New York Times* joined in. "Something should be done, and it can be done, in certain areas. The newly appointed Landmarks Preservation Commission must take clear and immediate positions on threatened buildings of historic or artistic value."[96] City Council member Edward Sadowsky, at AGBANY's request, put forward a resolution in the New York City Council "urging the mayor of the city of New York to request the landmarks preservation commission for an opinion on the desirability of preserving Pennsylvania Station."[97]

One of AGBANY's strategies as proclaimed in its *New York Times* ad was to make "the preservation of our heritage an issue in the forthcoming campaign."[98] Alice Sachs, Democratic-Liberal candidate for the East Side State Senate district, "called on the city . . . to consider setting up a museum of science, technology and industry in Pennsylvania Station."[99] Ironically, Sachs was running against a proven friend of preservation, the man who had introduced the Bard Act in Albany, MacNeil Mitchell.

Attracting greater attention was congressman John V. Lindsay, Republican of Manhattan, who represented the Seventeenth Congressional District. His announcement that he would make the preservation of Pennsylvania Station an issue in his reelection campaign helped fuel such breathless reporting as "other developments in the rising controversy over the fate of the station included."[100] Lindsay formally and very publicly called on James Felt to state the City Planning Commission's views on the future of Pennsylvania Station.[101] Felt made it clear that "the city could not block demolition," but that the new Madison Square Garden would require a permit, which would require City Planning Commission approval.[102]

With its efforts gaining attention and support, AGBANY continued to press for a meeting with the mayor and got it that September. The delegation of twelve meeting with Mayor Wagner was a rich mix of new voices from AGBANY and more familiar ones. Among those joining Norval White were Ray Rubinow, L. Bancel La Farge, and Morris Ketchum, Jr., president of the Municipal Art Society, and Frederick J. Woodbridge, president of the New York Chapter of the American Institute of Architects. Woodbridge had been playing an interesting balancing act as the head of the American Institute of Architects, calling for the preservation of the station while also serving on the mayor's Landmarks Preservation Commission. After their thirty minutes with the mayor, the delegation announced that Wagner had promised to "discuss their objections with James Felt, chairman of the City Planning Commission; corporation counsel Leo A. Larkin, and the city's Landmarks Preservation Commission."[103] This was as close as the issue ever got to the mayor himself. He managed to remain publicly noncommittal on the station as he dragged his feet on asking his Landmarks Preservation Commission to comment on the subject.[104]

Seemingly, the only person in the Wagner administration eager to get involved with Pennsylvania Station was Parks Commissioner Newbold Morris. The day of the delegation's meeting with Wagner, the papers reported Morris' approval of a scheme proposed by Pratt Institute students to use eighteen of the columns from the station to create a colonnade in Battery Park. Woodbridge and Ketchum used the press opportunity of their meeting with Wagner to clarify that though both of their organizations supported this new plan, they were still opposed to the razing of the station and favored the Pratt proposal only if the station was doomed. This new version of Morris' plan to recycle the station's columns did not sit any better with the *New York Times* than did the first. "Parks Commissioner Newbold Morris has proposed that two disembodied rows of eighteen of the eighty-four columns be saved and set up on the Battery mall, colossal crumbs to remind us that New York once had a great building by a fine architect."[105]

On December 12, 1962, the supporters of the station got more bad news. The Municipal Art Society minutes describe a meeting held that day in Deputy Cavanaugh's office at which the Municipal Art Society and AGBANY met with Platt and Van Derpool to discuss Penn Station. "AGBANY had suggested requesting a delay of the demolition plans, in order to conduct a study of the situation. Mr. Platt reported that this was impossible because of financial commitments."[106] The same day, the City Planning Commission officially announced that it would hold a public hearing on January 3, 1963 to consider Madison Square Garden's application for the special permit needed "to construct an arena, auditorium and trade exposition on the site of Pennsylvania Station."[107] The proposal was moving forward.

Any hope the new and powerless Landmarks Preservation Commission might somehow ride to the station's rescue was dashed. Looking back at the situation over twenty years later, Platt would recall: "At one point we thought we should say something about Pennsylvania Station, and we did. It didn't do any good, and it surprised people in other agencies."[108] It is not clear what Platt was specifically referencing, but what is clear is that without the force of law, whatever the commission would have said would have carried little weight. It certainly would have put some wind in the sails of those working to save the station, but when compared against the raging storm that was attacking the landmark, it is unlikely it would have led to a different outcome.

Felt had already made it clear that the City Planning Commission could not deal with the proposed demolition of the station. Its sole focus would be on the permit required for the construction of the new complex. With these ground rules, the outcome of their hearing was predetermined. Despite a robust showing by the station's defenders and a serious effort on their part to fight the permit on planning grounds, they could not win. As was aptly reported in *Architectural Forum*, "To the surprise of few people (but the disappointment of many) the New York City Planning Commission . . . issued the permit."[109]

Looking at a list of those supporting the new Madison Square Garden, one better understands the odds against the preservation of Pennsylvania Station. Joining Madison Square Garden Center, Inc. at the hearing in promoting the benefits to the new project for New York City were the unions and business associations. Local 32B added its voice, and the clout of its forty-two thousand members, to "the many farseeing groups who put the interests of the city ahead of any artificial self-aggrandizement." Further attacking the defenders of the station, the union's president continued: "It should be noted that Pennsylvania Station has no city, state or federal historical significance. . . . It is designed as a copy of an original building in Europe and its removal would in no way affect the historical significance of the original."[110] The Real Estate Board of New York, the New York Board of Trade, Inc., and even the station's famously competitive neighboring department stores, Macy's and Gimbel's, were united in their support of the new project. The statements articulated the prevailing attitude of the time: the "responsible position" for those with "the interests of the city at heart" was to support the new Madison Square Garden.[111]

With the granting of the permit, the station's fate was sealed. On October 28, 1963, with great fanfare and extensive press attention, demolition of Pennsylvania Station began. The station's signature eagles were lowered, and the walls on which they stood would soon follow. The demolition continued daily, up close and personal, in the face of thousands of New Yorkers until it was completed three long years later. As Ada Louise Huxtable would write for the *New York Times* editorial page: "It's not easy to knock down nine acres of travertine and granite, 84 Doric

FIGURE 11.8 On Monday, October 28, 1963, demolition began on Pennsylvania Station. The lowering of the station's 5,700-pound stone eagles from their perch of over fifty years signaled that the battle to save the station had truly been lost. Photographer Norman McGrath captured their descent as part of his extensive documentation of the station's demolition.

columns, a vaulted concourse of extravagant, weighty, grandeur, classical splendor modeled after royal Roman baths, rich detail in solid stone, architectural quality in precious materials that set the stamp of excellence on a city. But it can be done."[112] And it was.

The campaign to save Pennsylvania Station had failed, but not for a lack of energy and sophistication. As witnessed earlier in Brooklyn Heights and Greenwich Village, it took a new group to stand up and lead the preservation charge. Existing organizations, knowing from experience that it was a hopeless cause, never fully engaged. Without AGBANY's outrage and indignation, the defense of Pennsylvania Station would have been limited to a few strongly worded letters of protest. But once AGBANY's efforts began to gain traction, the established civic community came off the bench, although not in full force.

FIGURE 11.9 Photographer Peter Moore was one of many New Yorkers who witnessed the slow destruction of Pennsylvania Station. Unlike most observers, he documented the process on film, visiting the site numerous times from 1963 to 1966. Photo by Peter Moore, © Est. of Peter Moore/VAGA, NYC, from *The Destruction of Penn Station* (D.A.P., 2000).

Driven by the fresh anger of a new generation and enriched by the experiences of a few battle-hardened veterans, the campaign for Pennsylvania Station combined many of the techniques and strategies seen in earlier preservation struggles. From preservation's grassroots tradition it employed petitions, public protests, and placards.[113] It was media savvy and blessed with the editorial support of the *New York Times*. It combined such previously successful strategies as urging public-minded ownership for a threatened site—the Carnegie Hall solution—and suggesting an adaptive reuse, which had worked so well in securing the future of the Jefferson Market Courthouse. The campaign sought to inject the issue into the political arena, turning to both the City Council and to aspiring candidates for public office.

Combining proven tactics with new energy, the proponents of the station waged an impressive campaign. Considering that the group was not a well-established organization, the accomplishment is even more astounding. Unfortunately, neither youthful protestors, campaigning politicians, civic celebrities, council resolutions, press conferences, nor paid advertisements could ride to the rescue of Pennsylvania Station. As Huxtable wrote as demolition began, "Penn Station is a tragic example. Nothing short of legal protection could have stopped its destruction, in spite of the fact that every qualified critic confirms its architectural merit and the beauty and solidity of its materials."[114]

One of the charges to the new Landmarks Preservation Commission was to "prepare for submission to the Mayor, within one year of its formation, a detailed legislative program for the effective protection of those portions of designated landmarks that fall within public view."[115] Receiving this assignment in April 1962 and having only brought on board an executive director in July, when the Pennsylvania Station controversy erupted in August, the commission had had precious little opportunity to focus on drafting a law. As the controversy grew, advocates for the station's preservation reminded the Wagner administration that under the existing Bard Act, the city could directly intervene to save the station.[116] The Wagner administration, however, was not eager to do so. It had no clear incentive to take on the forces pushing for the demolition of the station. Nor was the Wagner administration inclined to deviate from the course it had set, the development of a comprehensive system for landmark protection, in order to save a single building, even if that building was Pennsylvania Station.

With the din of the debate over Pennsylvania Station ringing in their ears, the Landmarks Preservation Commission began to meet with the Corporation Counsel's office in August to start working on a landmarks

FIGURE 11.10 Pennsylvania Station's haunting beauty is captured in this Peter Moore photograph of demolition work in the station's interior. The vastness of the building, the majesty of its spaces, and the tragedy of its loss have all helped elevate Pennsylvania Station to its mythic status among preservationists. Photo by Peter Moore, © Est. of Peter Moore/VAGA, NYC, from *The Destruction of Penn Station* (D.A.P., 2000).

law. "All available legislation in other cities and states was studied, together with other necessary legal background material."[117] However, the preservation challenges facing New York could not be met by just borrowing from other cities. The scope and nature of New York's preservation problems were unique.[118] In November, Geoffrey Platt was able to report to the commission that a "preliminary draft" of the legislation "was nearing completion by the corporation counsel."[119] Many eyes, including those of the Brooklyn Heights preservationists, were closely following the drafting of the law. Otis Pearsall reports that by January of 1963, "the proposed citywide statute had already gone through two or three drafts and by April 1, 1963 the Commission had developed a virtually final draft." It was expected to go to the City Planning Commission for hearings late that spring.[120] By May, an internal final draft existed and reportedly went to the mayor.[121] In July, the press reported that the commission's proposal was expected in the next month.[122]

Goldstone remembered the wisdom behind the drafting process as well as its seemingly endless nature. First, the proposed legislation went through "draft after draft, and everybody reviewed it." Then the Corporation Counsel "sent it round, very wisely, when it was in a semi-final form, to every city department" that might be affected by it. "And it dragged on and dragged on and I thought we'd never be done."[123] Goldstone was not the only one feeling this way. As demolition began on Pennsylvania Station, attention naturally turned to the promised legislation. As demolition crews began their work, Ada Louise Huxtable lamented the status of the law.

> The City Planning Commission meeting to consider protective legislation recommended by the Landmarks Commission, held as a kind of prelude to the Penn Station demolition, ended in another postponement. In the lumbering slow-motion process that seems to be a Parkinsonian accompaniment to any critically needed action, it went back to the Corporation Counsel for further study. New York has the Bard Act, which makes it possible for the city to enact such legislation, but it has studiously avoided using it thus far.[124]

Reporting that the "crucial process of drafting the legislation . . . is bogged down in a morass of legal technicalities and inter-departmental consultations," the *New York World-Telegram* turned to Platt for an explanation. "Platt explained that the whole question of how much authority the city can use to save a landmark is entirely new territory and that drafting legislation with no legal loopholes is a time-consuming

"Where do you want Penn Station?"

FIGURE 11.11   One sign of the growing prominence of preservation as a pressing issue for New York City was the subject's coverage in *New Yorker* cartoons. The loss of Pennsylvania Station rated the following cartoon, "Where do you want Penn Station?" appearing in the *New Yorker* of November 9, 1963.

process." He added, "But we're moving just as fast as we can."[125] They were never able to move fast enough to save Pennsylvania Station.

The race between the demolition of Pennsylvania Station and the passage of the Landmarks Law was over. Demolition had outpaced the drafting of legislation. It had never been a fair competition. The forces pushing for demolition had always been at least a step ahead and had always held the cards. The Madison Square Garden proposal had much going for it. It promised to be an economic engine for the city, enjoyed the support of powerful forces, and certainly fit the prevailing notion of progress at the time.[126] One unanswerable question remains: Did the project also have a highly placed friend in city government?

James Felt, the chair of the City Planning Commission, was the brother of one of the two "prime movers" of the Madison Square Garden project.

Irwin Mitchell Felt was president of the company that controlled Madison Square Garden, and he was the namesake of the Felt Forum.[127] In December 1962, prior to the City Planning Commission's hearing on the permit for Madison Square Garden, James Felt announced his intention to resign as chairman of the City Planning Commission, making it clear he would not attend or participate in the Madison Square Garden hearing. Having been part of the Wagner administration for ten years, he was now resigning to become the unpaid advisor to "the institutions on Morningside Heights which are involved in a General Neighborhood Renewal Plan covering this area."[128] The suddenness of the Felt's announcement came as a surprise. There was some "speculation around City Hall" that its timing was due to the impending hearing of his brother's project and the "possible embarrassment" it might cause.[129]

Actually, it is not Felt's position as chair of the City Planning Commission that raises eyebrows as much as his leadership role on Wagner's team. For all practical purposes, he was the master strategist behind the Wagner administration's embrace of preservation. He had kept aesthetic and historic zoning out of the revised Zoning Resolution. As confidant to the mayor, he had arranged for the creation of the Mayor's Committee for the Preservation of Structures of Historic and Esthetic Importance and handpicked its membership. He had become the political mentor of Geoffrey Platt and Harmon Goldstone. He met with them regularly as the committee did its work, coaching them on the intricacies of government, and he followed the drafting process of the law.[130] His old real estate ties and deep roots in that community certainly would have made him privy to inside information on a major project like Madison Square Garden before it became public. He certainly had the knowledge, ability, and insider access to help influence the timing of events. Could he have manipulated circumstances to help ensure that New York's Landmarks Law would not exist in time to block the demolition of Pennsylvania Station and impede his brother's project?

Both Platt and Goldstone had only the highest opinion of James Felt. Not only had he helped advance their preservation agenda, it would have been hard for these gentleman to imagine anything less than honorable behavior on Felt's part. For them, it was inconceivable that Felt could have played any sort of duplicitous role. They appreciated that his brother's project put Felt in an awkward spot, but felt that he had very different values and interests than his brother.[131] Even the more fiery Otis Pearsall had only praise for Felt's support of preservation: "I don't think the thing would ever have gotten across the goal line had it not been for

Felt's support and efforts. He was the one person in city government that took what appeared to be a genuine interest."[132] James Felt had already made his fortune prior to entering government service. His reputation for personal honesty and public service were unquestioned. It seems highly unlikely that Felt would have consciously schemed to enrich his brother.

That being said, Felt's handling of the new zoning resolution and his willingness to compromise show that in addition to being a political realist, he was not unsympathetic to larger real estate concerns. Real estate, after all, was the world that had shaped him. It is not unlikely that at times his view of what was best for the city would coincide with what was best for the real estate industry. That his "real estate worldview" could have influenced the timing of the law so that its advancement would not impede the redevelopment of Pennsylvania Station is not to be dismissed out of hand.[133] That he also genuinely might have felt this was in the best interests of preservation is not necessarily contradictory.

If indeed Felt was the true friend of preservation that Goldstone and Platt believed him to be, that only provides further reason to think that the dance between the emerging Landmarks Preservation Commission and the great Pennsylvania Station was choreographed and not totally free form. At the time of the Pennsylvania Station controversy, the notion of advancing preservation through public policy was far from accepted. In addition, the Landmarks Preservation Commission had not had sufficient time to put down roots in the soil of city government. This new and unproven agency was no match for the economic, political, and cultural forces driving the Madison Square Garden project. Trying to do battle against those supporting the project would have been suicidal for a neophyte mayoral agency that functioned without statutory power. Working to block the demolition of Pennsylvania Station would have demonstrated that such an agency could be a major threat to real estate interests and would have unleashed the full might and wrath of that industry on the commission and its efforts to secure legal power to protect landmarks. To sequence events so that the new commission would avoid a head-on clash with the Madison Square Garden juggernaut was the type of strategic thinking that came naturally to James Felt.

It was not James and Irving Felt's shared DNA that doomed Pennsylvania Station. It would have taken incredible political will for any administration to stand up to the forces lined up in favor of demolishing the station. As was noted at the time, "Only extraordinary political action could save Penn Station now; and only extraordinary evidence of extraordinary public interest could spur such action."[134] If it had so desired, the

Wagner administration could have used the existing Bard Act to justify some form of intervention on behalf of the station, even without a local landmarks law. But where was the "extraordinary public interest" to compel them to do so? It just did not exist. As pickets marched in August and press coverage of the controversy grew, the *New York Times* predicted, "If AGBANY springs to the barricades the public will not be far behind."[135] Unfortunately, this time Ada Louise Huxtable was wrong.

The on-again, off-again love affair between the people of New York and Pennsylvania Station has been well chronicled.[136] From its formal opening day, November 27, 1910, when a hundred thousand New Yorkers (in addition to those actually riding the trains) flooded the station (as it was proclaimed as the eighth wonder of the world) to the day demolition began, when six architects wearing black armbands picketed the station, New Yorkers' feelings for the station have waxed hot and cold.[137] Through martyrdom, its popularity has soared to a degree that makes it hard to imagine how invisible and unappreciated the station was at the time of its demise. In death, it has become so iconic that its spiritual resurrection is being advanced in the effort to physically transform its sister building, the James A. Farley Post Office, McKim, Mead & White's old general post office, into the latest incarnation of Pennsylvania Station.

Public apathy ultimately doomed the station. Forty years after the picketing, one of the protesters recalled: "What I remember about that day is the indifference of people on the street to the message that we were trying to communicate."[138] Robert Weinberg would write, "Except for that memorable picketing event some of us participated in . . . there was not a scream of protest, nor any real struggle."[139] Years after the effort to save the station, Giorgio Cavaglieri would tell Charles Hosmer, "It was not a mass movement. The architects paraded back and forth. And the fact that some of them (like Philip Johnson) were very well known, made the parade a curiosity for the public. . . . It was not the subject-matter that was their concern."[140] Even applying the most creative math, the number of people who did anything to try and save the station—picketed, testified, wrote a letter, signed a petition—was tiny and inadequate to the task.

Even compared to earlier preservation efforts in Brooklyn and Greenwich Village, support for Pennsylvania Station was disappointing. Pennsylvania Station was in nobody's backyard. It didn't have a resident constituency to rise to its defense. Could New York City have saved Pennsylvania Station without a landmarks law? If there had been an extraordinary outpouring of public support, there would have been a political incentive for the city

FIGURE 11.12 In 2003, forty years to the day of the commencement of the demolition of Pennsylvania Station, surviving preservation veterans who had taken action to save the station were honored as preservation heroes by the New York Preservation Archive Project. This commemorative event is indicative of the growing interest in the history of New York's preservation movement.

to try. AGBANY sought to arouse that support and create that political will. Despite AGBANY's best efforts, and those who rallied to its cause, the station was lost. Instead of preservation's cause being buried in the rubble of the station, the loss of the battle for Pennsylvania Station ultimately helped secure passage of a landmarks law. The fate of the station and the landmarks law are forever linked and, with the passage of time, have become inseparable.

There was one New Yorker who indeed felt all of New York was in his backyard, even though he had been living in East Orange, New Jersey since 1935. In the fall of 1962, Albert S. Bard was approaching his ninety-sixth birthday. It is unclear how involved he was able to be in the battle over Pennsylvania Station. Robert Weinberg copied him on letters dealing with the issue and we know Bard was still active in several civic organizations concerned with the station's preservation. In September 1962, the Fine Arts

Federation sent a telegram to Allen J. Greenough, president of Pennsylvania Railroad, asking for a delay in the station's demolition, and of course the Municipal Art Society had gone on record in the station's defense.[141]

Despite his advanced age, Bard was still very much alive. At the fall 1961 and spring 1962 meetings of the Fine Arts Federation, he would remind the representatives of the civic groups that constituted its membership that the Bard Act existed and could be put to use to advance their interests.[142] At his penultimate Fine Arts Federation meeting, he would be as eloquent as ever in arguing on behalf of aesthetics: "This spring and Easter season, with its emphasis upon the ideas of renewal and a possible Resurrection, suggests the question: When, oh when, will the Sense of Beauty rise again in the wide ranks of the architectural profession, and give the City of New York the beauty which would be appropriate to its size, importance, and power?" After these remarks, being the federation's first meeting since Bard's ninety-fifth birthday, it presented him a special citation.[143]

Bard had lived long enough to see the Landmarks Preservation Commission come into being. In the media coverage of the Pennsylvania Station controversy, the Bard Act would be referenced—and referred to by that name. Though he would not live long enough to see his legislation put to use in New York City, in the spring of 1962, the City of Schenectady became the first municipality in New York State to use the law.[144] Bard died March 25, 1963 as the drafting of the Landmarks Law continued and before trucks would start hauling the debris that once was Pennsylvania Station to Secaucus.

As an adult, Albert Bard had three lifelong passions: Chi Psi, the fraternity he had joined at Amherst College, his commitment to advancing aesthetic regulations, and his devotion to the Switz family. The struggle over Pennsylvania Station may well have interjected some tension between the first two of these passions. As Pennsylvania Station certainly must have complicated the relationship between the Felt brothers, it had the potential for doing the same between Bard and one of his fraternity brothers. In August 1962, during the heat of the Pennsylvania Station battle, A. J. Greenough, president of the Pennsylvania Railroad Company, wrote to the *New York Times:* "Does it make any sense to attempt to preserve a building merely as a 'monument' when it no longer serves the utilitarian needs for which it was erected?"[145] Earlier that year, the *Purple and Gold,* Chi Psi's national magazine, had reprinted the *New York Times* story on Albert Bard's ninety-fifth birthday. On the opposite page, it noted a *Times* magazine mention of Allen Greenough, Π' 27. *Purple and Gold* would

also report on the election of Greenough to the Chi Psi Executive Committee, a body on which Bard had served for many years.[146]

As the battle for Pennsylvania Station was being waged, the brothers of Chi Psi gathered in Ann Arbor, Michigan from August 29 to September 1, 1962 for the 121st Annual Convention. Prominently in attendance were both Brothers Bard and Greenough. Bard, the beloved grand old man of the fraternity, was being honored with the establishment of an award in his name. Greenough was the speaker at the conference banquet. Fate had conspired to bring together at the same time, in the same place, and on the same dais, the man whose living legacy would be the act empowering New York municipalities to protect their landmarks and the man instrumental in the demolition of New York's most famous lost landmark. At the time of their meeting, the futures of the station and that of a New York City Landmarks Law were both uncertain. Did Brother Bard approach Brother Greenough about the planned demolition of Pennsylvania Station? Did he mention the telegram that would soon be sent to Greenough by the Fine Arts Federation? Perhaps in the future, archival material will come forward to shed light on whether the landmark legend and the landmark despoiler ever exchanged words on Pennsylvania Station.[147]

Still going to his Broad Street office until the month before he died, Albert Bard was aware that finally, the slow wheels of government were moving toward implementing the Bard Act in New York City.[148] At the spring Fine Arts Federation meeting, he had heard Harmon Goldstone report on the creation of the new Landmarks Preservation Commission. Earlier in the same meeting, before Goldstone's report, Bard had commented on the six years that had elapsed since the passage of the Bard Act and the fact its powers had yet to be used. Never one to be discouraged, he said of his legislation, "the new power will come in handy some day when the need for

FIGURE 11.13 As fate would have it, during the height of the battle over Pennsylvania Station, Chi Psi fraternity brothers, Albert Bard, Amherst 1888 (standing) and Allen Greenough, Union 1927 (thought to be the second person to Bard's left) appeared on the same dais at the fraternity's 121st annual convention held at the end of August 1962 in Ann Arbor, Michigan. Allen Greenough was the president of the Pennsylvania Railroad Company, then aggressively seeking the demolition of Pennsylvania Station. Albert Bard, who had devoted much of his life to advancing the cause of preserving beauty, was aligned with those seeking to save it.

prompt special action covering some special situation crops up."[149] Bard died knowing that New York was closer than ever to winning the right to protect its landmarks.

With the great Pennsylvania Station now lost and a landmarks law drafted, what more would it take for New York City to finally take action?

ENDNOTES

1. "New Madison Sq. Garden to Rise Atop Penn Station," *New York Times,* July 25, 1961.
2. "Old Setting, New Gleam," *Architectural Forum*, August 1957, 108.
3. Foster Hailey, "'62 Start Is Set for New Garden; Penn Station to Be Razed to Street Level in Project," *New York Times,* July 27, 1961.
4. Goldstone detested the name the mayor had given the committee. Hosmer, "Interview with Goldstone," 12; Wood, "An Interview with the First Chairman of the Landmarks Preservation Commission, the Late Geoffrey Platt," 9.
5. Geoffrey Platt, chair, Committee for the Preservation of Structures of Historic and Esthetic Importance, to Mayor Robert F. Wagner, November 27, 1961, Mayor Wagner Papers, NYC Municipal Archives.
6. Goldstone, president, Municipal Art Society to Gordon Hyatt, Producer, WCBS-TV, September 27, 1961.
7. Hosmer, "Interview with Goldstone," 12.
8. Platt credits Luther Gulick with coming up with the name the Landmarks Preservation Commission.
9. "Outline of Recommendations" to the mayor from the Committee for the Preservation of Structures of Historic and Esthetic Importance," November 27, 1961, Mayor Wagner Papers, NYC Municipal Archives.
10. "Statement by Mayor Robert F. Wagner," for release December 3, 1961, City of New York Office of the Mayor, Mayor Wagner Papers, NYC Municipal Archives.
11. "Mayor Wagner Backs Jefferson Market Courthouse for A Library," Press Release, City of New York Office of the Mayor, August 23, 1961, NYC Municipal Archives.
12. Platt to Wagner, November 27, 1961, Mayor Wagner Papers, NYC Municipal Archives.
13. "Arts Unit Scores City Office Plan," *New York Times*, November 28, 1961.
14. At a May 18, 2005 New York Preservation Archive Project public screening of *Our Vanishing Legacy*, Gordon Hyatt reminisced that the opportunity to do such a public interest documentary was in part the result of the TV quiz show scandal of the late 1950s. To make amends, stations were producing public service programming. In a twist of irony, the focus of the quiz show scandal was Charles Van Doren, the contestant who had been the big winner on the quiz show *Twenty-One*. Ironically, he was the nephew of Carl Van Doren, the writer and historian who had campaigned in the 1940s to save Castle Clinton and "The Row" on the north side of Washington Square. This time, inadvertently, another Van Doren had given preservation a helpful boost.
15. Jack Gould, "TV: Focus on New York," *New York Times*, September 22, 1961; *Our Vanishing Legacy*, Program Transcript, September 21, 1961, WCBS-TV Public Affairs Department.

■ ■ ■ ■ ■ ■ ■ ■

16. *Our Vanishing Legacy.*

17. Ben Gross, "TV Considers Our Town; Kovacs as Zany as Ever," *New York Daily News,* Friday, September 22, 1961.

18. Henry Hope Reed, Jr., to Gordon Hyatt, September 29, 1961.

19. Goldstone wrote Hyatt after the broadcast to express his pleasure with the program. He noted that the only "adverse word" that he'd heard was a comment that the ending statement about the law, "Maybe there should," was "too defeatist and that it did not recognize the serious study that is being given to the matter right now." Goldstone, president, Municipal Art Society, to Hyatt, September 27, 1961.

20. Charles Messer Stow, "Medals Given Two for Service to Fort Clinton," *New York Sun,* June 10, 1949.

21. "Preserving New York's Heritage," *New York Times,* December 9, 1961.

22. Susan Tift and Alex S. Jones, *The Trust* (New York: Little, Brown, 1999), 311, 324, 523.

23. Robert D. McFadden, "John B. Oakes, Impassioned Editorial Page Voice of the Times, Dies at 87," *New York Times,* April 6, 2001.

24. Because of the "daily pressures of his work at the *New York Times,*" Oakes declined the invitation to become a trustee of the American Scenic and Historic Preservation Society. John Oakes to the American Scenic and Historic Preservation Society, April 18, 1962, American Scenic and Historic Preservation Society Records, New York Public Library.

25. Stern, *New York 1960,* 1211.

26. In an interview with the author, Huxtable confirmed her authorship of numerous *New York Times* editorials between 1961 and 1965. She also shared her memories of working with Oakes on editorials. Anthony C. Wood interview with Ada Louise Huxtable, March 13, 2006.

27. Stephen Grover, "Heeded Words: Ada Louise Huxtable Has Formidable Power as Architecture Critic," *Wall Street Journal,* November 7, 1972; Stern, *New York 1960,* 1210; Ada Louise Huxtable, *Four Walking Tours of Modern Architecture in New York City* (New York: Doubleday & Company, 1961).

28. Wood interview with Huxtable, March 13, 2006.

29. Peter Gross, a *New York Times* correspondent and editorial board member from 1972 to 1976, quoted in McFadden, "John B. Oakes, Impassioned Editorial Page Voice of The Times, Dies at 87," *New York Times,* April 6, 2001.

30. "Farewell to Landmarks," *New York Times,* March 10, 1962.

31. Whitney North Seymour, president, Fine Arts Federation to Weinberg, January 31, 1962, professional papers of Robert C. Weinberg, Long Island University; Francis Keally, chairman to Robert F. Wagner, March 13, 1962, Mayor Wagner Papers, NYC Municipal Archives.

32. Named to the Landmarks Preservation Commission were: Geoffrey Platt, architect; William Zinsser, Wm. Zinsser & Co.; Bayrd Still, professor of history; Stanley B. Tankel, planning director, Regional Plan Association; Robert Curtiss, president, Horace S. Ely & Co.; Miss Juliet Bartlett, Women's City Club; Russell Lynes, managing editor, *Harper's*; Leopold Rothschild, lawyer; Frederick Woodbridge, architect; James N. Fosburgh, artist; Loring McMillen, engineer; and Allen Evarts Foster, lawyer, Lord, Day and Lord. Press release, City of New York Office of the Mayor, April 22, 1962, Mayor Wagner Papers, NYC Municipal Archives.

33. Ibid.

34. "An Architect Is Needed," *New York Times,* October 24, 1961.

35. Wood, "An Interview with the First Chairman of the Landmarks Preservation Commission the Late Geoffrey Platt," 16–17; Hosmer, "Interview with Harmon Goldstone," 12–14; Wood, "An Interview with Harmon Goldstone," 33–34.

36. Hosmer, "Interview with Harmon Goldstone," 12–14.

37. "Landmarks Commission Seeks to Preserve Splendor of City's Past," *New York Times*, July 21, 1963.

38. Hosmer, "Interview with Harmon Goldstone," 14–15.

39. City of New York Office of the Mayor, press release, July 1, 1962, Mayor Wagner Papers, NYC Municipal Archives.

40. The commission had not been appointed with a "sunset" date, so it is likely the three years reflected both the length of Platt's term on the commission and the reality that the commission was a mayoral agency and that there were three years until the next mayoral election. Wood, "An Interview with the First Chairman of the Landmarks Preservation Commission the Late Geoffrey Platt," 12, 24.

41. Platt, "Otis Pratt Pearsall's Reminiscences," 11.

42. "Brooklyn Heights Association Bulletin," June 1961, Otis Pratt Pearsall Papers, New York Preservation Archive Project.

43. Platt, "Otis Pratt Pearsall's Reminiscences," 11.

44. "Brooklyn Heights Association Bulletin," June 1961, Otis Pratt Pearsall Papers, New York Preservation Archive Project.

45. Wood interview of Pearsall, May 3, 2006.

46. Pearsall to Lancaster, September 7, 1976, 21, Otis Pratt Pearsall Papers, New York Preservation Archive Project.

47. Martin Arnold, "'Old Brooklyn Heights' Groups Fighting to Preserve Buildings," *New York Times*, December 9, 1961.

48. "Draft Proposed by the Brooklyn Heights Association," Otis Pratt Pearsall Papers, New York Preservation Archive Project.

49. Wood, "An Interview with Otis Pratt Pearsall," 39.

50. "'Old Brooklyn Heights' Groups Fighting to Preserve Buildings," *New York Times*, December 9, 1961

51. Pearsall to Lancaster, September 7, 1976, 20, Otis Pratt Pearsall Papers, New York Preservation Archive Project.

52. Ibid., 22.

53. Goldstone to Platt, October 20, 1961, Otis Pratt Pearsall Papers, New York Preservation Archive Project.

54. In an interview, Goldstone recounted that a trip to Boston and conversations there led him to conclude that Boston's approach of multiple laws was "difficult" and "chaos to have." He recounted a conversation with Otis Pearsall. Pearsall said, "'Well, while you're dragging your feet, we're losing ten houses every week'; and I said, 'Well, we're losing twenty every week—but, you know, let's have a workable law.'" Wood interview with Harmon Goldstone, May 12, 1987.

55. Wood, "An Interview with the First Chairman of the Landmarks Preservation Commission the Late Geoffrey Platt," 23.

56. Pearsall to Lancaster, September 7, 1976, 23, Otis Pratt Pearsall Papers, New York Preservation Archive Project.

57. Brooklyn Heights Association Press Release, April 30, 1962, Otis Pratt Pearsall Papers, New York Preservation Archive Project.

58. John Molleson, "Brooklyn Heights Fights for Life," *New York Herald-Tribune*, April 31, 1962.

59. *Villager,* September 20, 1962.

60. Pearsall to Lancaster, September 7, 1976, 25, Otis Pratt Pearsall Papers, New York Preservation Archive Project.

61. While awaiting the Landmarks Law, the Brooklyn Heights Association continued to advance preservation. It created the Design Advisory Council "to provide free advice, short of actual plans for appropriate work on façades. The Council immediately set to work showering every Heights property owner with educational materials on the types and original characteristics of our architecture, the owner's responsibilities to himself, his neighbors and the community, appropriate practices in renovation and restoration, and how to access the Council's services." Pearsall, "Otis Pratt Pearsall's Reminiscences of the Nine-Year Effort to Designate Brooklyn Heights as New York City's First Historic District and Its First Limited Height District," 16.

62. Pearsall to Lancaster, September 7, 1976, 25, Otis Pratt Pearsall Papers, New York Preservation Archive Project.

63. Lancaster dedicated the second edition of his book to Van Derpool.

64. Program transcript of *New York Forum,* WCBS-TV Public Affairs Department, August 12, 1962.

65. Ibid. It is likely Pearsall also asked the Penn Station question of Felt. The transcript of the program does not indicate who asked the question. Over forty years later, when queried as to whether he had asked that question of Felt, Pearsall stated that he was the only person on the panel who was likely to have done so. Wood conversation with Pearsall, May 3, 2006.

66. Charles G. Bennett, "City Acts to Save Historical Sites," *New York Times,* April 22, 1962.

67. "Penn Station to Give Way to Madison Square Garden," *Progressive Architecture,* September 1961. The same edition of *Progressive Architecture* includes a letter from Robert R. Garvey Jr., executive director of the National Trust, expressing the "serious concern" of the trust over the plans to demolish the station. However, at an October 1962 meeting, the board of the National Trust for Historic Preservation made a decision to "take no action" on a resolution supporting the preservation of Pennsylvania Station. David Doheny, *David Finley: Quiet Force for America's Arts* (Washington, D.C.: National Trust for Historic Preservation, 2006), 282.

68. "Huge New York Station Opens," *Boston Daily Globe,* November 27, 1910.

69. "Plan for Sports Center at Penn Station Filed," *New York Times,* July 27, 1962; Jerome Zukosky, "Salvation on Seventh Ave.?" *New York Herald-Tribune,* July 29, 1962; Foster Hailey, "Battle over Future of Penn Station Continues," *New York Times,* September 23, 1962.

70. In a March 9, 1962 letter, Robert Weinberg refers to the "few sketchy, presumably tentative, plans and sections on which published perspectives of the new group of buildings were based." It seems likely it was not until the *New York Times* reported in late July on the filing of the plans that the full details of the proposal would have been publicly available. Weinberg to Morris Ketchum, president, Municipal Art Society, March 9, 1962, professional papers of Robert C. Weinberg, Long Island University; "Plan for Sports Center at Penn Station Filed," *New York Times,* July 27, 1962.

71. "84 Penn Station Doric Columns May Be Moved to Flushing Park," *New York Times,* February 20, 1962.

72. "Kill Him but Save the Scalp," *New York Times,* March 21, 1962.

73. Robert C. Weinberg, letter to the editor, *New York Times*, May 7, 1962.

74. Norval White, letter to the editor, *New York Times*, May 17, 1962.

75. Roark being the idealistic young architect in Ayn Rand's classic *The Fountainhead*. Jane Kramer, "Picket Penn Station in Fight for Style," *Village Voice*, August 9, 1962.

76. Wood interview with Brendan Gill, July 2, 1984.

77. Weinberg pressed the Historic Buildings Committee of the New York Chapter of the American Institute of Architects to do more regarding the preservation of Pennsylvania Station. In particular, he was "anxious" that the committee press for the preservation of the station's colonnade as he had proposed in his letter to the *New York Times*. Since letters about saving the building had already been sent, the other committee members decided to do nothing more at the time. Minutes of the Historic Buildings Committee, American Institute of Architects, May 4, 1962, Professional Papers of Robert C. Weinberg, Long Island University.

78. Jeffrey Ellis Aronin to Norval White, August 9, 1962, Anthony C. Wood Archive.

79. Christopher Gray, "A 1960's Protest that Tried to Save a Piece of the Past," *New York Times,* May 20, 2001.

80. Resolutions for Unincorporated Club, Society or Association, Irving Trust Company, Action Group for Better Architecture, July 23, 1962, Anthony C. Wood Archive.

81. Unpublished, "An Interview with Commissioner Elliot Willensky," *Village Views.*

82. Anthony C. Wood interview with Diana Goldstein (Kirsch), October 25, 2003.

83. Diana Goldstein (Kirsch), email to Christopher Gray, May 15, 2001.

84. Walter Thabit to Tony Woods [sic] October 29, 2003; "Program for Meeting with Mayor Wagner," for meeting of September 10, 1962 indicating that Ray Rubinow was part of the delegation and designated to speak on "Civic Aspect: Compare to Washington Square and Carnegie Hall," Anthony C. Wood Archive.

85. Self-administered interview, Norval White, April 20, 2006, New York Preservation Archive Project.

86. Costas Machlouzarides, treasurer, "Action Group for Better Architecture in New York Contributions List," August 23, 1963, Anthony C. Wood Archive.

87. AGBANY press release August 2, 1962, Anthony C. Wood Archive; "Save Our City," *New York Times*, August 2, 1962; "The March of the Architects," *New York Daily News,* August 3, 1962.

88. AGBANY's newsletter reported 500 participated, the *Daily News* estimated 250, the *New York Times* reported the size at between 150 to 200. "AGBANY Newsletter," August 24, 1962; *New York Daily News,* August 3, 1962; Foster Hailey, "Architects Fight Penn Station Plan," *New York Times,* August 3, 1962.

89. "Architects Want Penn Station Saved, Their Picket Lines Have Proved It: What Does Public Interest Require?" *Architectural Record,* September 1962.

90. An August 1963 financial report prepared by Costas Machlouzarides, AGBANY's treasurer, reports a total income of $1,314.95. AGBANY's largest recorded expense was $403 to the *New York Times*. Philip Johnson helped in the fundraising efforts. A script for those calling individuals to raise contributions read, "I am calling on behalf of Philip Johnson who is working in conjunction with a recently formed group of young architects to sponsor an advertisement in the *New York Times*." The callers were seeking minimum donations of $10. Anthony C. Wood Archive.

91. "Architects Want Penn Station Saved," *Architectural Record*, September 1962.

92. "Architects Fight Penn Station Plan," *New York Times*, August 3, 1962; Jane Kramer, "Picket Penn Station in Fight for Style," *Village Voice*, August 9, 1962.

93. Charles G. Bennett, "City Acts to Save Historical Sites," *New York Times*, April 22, 1962.

94. Jerome Zukosky, "Salvation on Seventh Ave.?" *New York Herald-Tribune*, July 29, 1962.

95. Foster Hailey, "Architects Fight Penn Station Plan," *New York Times*, August 3, 1962; Charles G. Bennett, "City Asks to Save Landmarks; Names Scholar to New Agency," *New York Times*, July 1, 1962.

96. "Saving Fine Architecture," *New York Times*, August 11, 1962.

97. "AGBANY Newsletter," August 24, 1962; Resolution 300, The Committee on City Affairs, August 21, 1962, Mayor Robert F. Wagner Papers, NYC Municipal Archives.

98. "Save Our City," *New York Times*, August 2, 1962.

99. "Asks Museum in Penn Station," *World-Telegram*, August 2, 1962.

100. "Felt Gives View on Penn Station/Says City Can Affect Zoning But Not Demolition," *New York Times*, August 26, 1962.

101. John V. Lindsay, representative, "News Release," August 15, 1962, Anthony C. Wood Archive.

102. "Felt Gives View on Penn Station," *New York Times*, August 26, 1962.

103. "Wagner Confers on Penn Station," *New York Times*, September 11, 1962.

104. "Battle over Future of Penn Station Continues," *New York Times*, September 23, 1962.

105. "Penn Station Perils," *New York Times*, September 29, 1962.

106. Platt must have been referencing the financial commitments already made by the applicant, not any related to his agency. Municipal Art Society Board Meeting Minutes, December 17, 1962, Municipal Art Society of New York Records, Archives of American Art.

107. City Planning Commission, City of New York, "Press Release," December 12, 1962.

108. Wood, "An Interview with the Late Geoffrey Platt," 12.

109. *Architectural Forum*, February, 1963.

110. "Remarks by Thomas F. Shortman, president, Local 32B, Building Service Employees International Union, AFL-CIO, at a public hearing at the Board of Estimate, City Hall," January 3, 1963, New York Preservation Archive Project.

111. "Statement of the Real Estate Board of New York, Inc. Presented by Edgar I Levy, Chairman," January 3, 1963, Henry L. Lambert, president, New York Board of Trade to City Planning Commission, January 3, 1963, Jack I. Straus, chairman of the board, R. H. Macy & Co., Inc., to Mayor Wagner, "Dear Bob," September 7, 1962, "Statement of Bernard F. Gimbel, chairman of the board, Gimbel Brothers, Inc.," January 3, 1963, James W. Danahy, executive vice-president, West Side Association of Commerce in the City of New York, to City Planning Commission, January 3, 1962, New York Preservation Archive Project.

112. "Farewell to Penn Station," *New York Times*, October 30, 1963.

113. AGBANY's petition, with the statement: "We, the undersigned, deplore the proposed demolition of Pennsylvania Station. We request that immediate action be taken to assure its preservation by the federal, state and city governments," was signed by an unknown number of New Yorkers. AGBANY's August 24, 1962 newsletter reported, "Filled-in petitions have been trickling in steadily since the protest meeting (at which AGBANY received fourteen hundred signatures in little over an hour!)."

114. Ada Louise Huxtable, "Architecture: That Was the Week that Was," *New York Times*, November 3, 1963.

■ ■ ■ ■ ■ ■ ■

115. City of New York, office of the mayor, "Press Release," April 22, 1962, Mayor Robert Wagner Papers, NYC Municipal Archives.

116. "AGBANY Takes Penn Station Issue to P.S.C.," *Oculus*, November, 1962.

117. Statement by Geoffery Platt, chairman, Landmarks Preservation Commission at the Hearing on Bill No. 799, Int. No. 653, Before the Codification Committee of the City Council of the City of New York, Dec. 3, 1964. In addition to the laws, we know that resources such as Preservation of Historic Districts by Architectural Control, by John Codman of the Beacon Hill Civic Association printed by the American Society of Planning Officials in 1956, "reproduced especially for National Trust for Historic Preservation," and Blair Associates' materials on their groundbreaking preservation/planning work on College Hill in Providence, were in Van Derpool's collection of resource materials. James Grote Van Derpool Papers, Avery Architectural & Fine Arts Library, Columbia University.

118. Geoffrey Platt, "What New York City Is Doing to Protect Its Landmarks," *Pace*, September 1962.

119. Minutes of the Tenth Meeting of the Landmarks Preservation Commission, November 8, 1962.

120. Otis Pearsall to Clay Lancaster, Minutes of the Board of Governors of the Brooklyn Heights Association Meeting, January 9, 1963, Otis Pratt Pearsall Archives, New York Preservation Archive Project.

121. Statement by Geoffery Platt, chairman, Landmarks Preservation Commission at the Hearing on Bill No. 799, Int. No. 653; Thomas W. Ennis, "Landmarks Bill Goes to Council," *New York Times*, March 24, 1965.

122. Thomas W. Ennis, "Landmarks Commission Seeks to Preserve Splendor of City's Past/Bid Made to Save 300 Old Buildings," *New York Times*, July 21, 1963.

123. Hosmer, "Interview with Goldstone," 16.

124. Ada Louise Huxtable, "Architecture: That Was the Week That Was," *New York Times*, November 3, 1963.

125. Nina McCain, "This Landmark Is Doomed," *New York World-Telegram*, November 12, 1963.

126. Peter Blake, *God's Own Junkyard: The Planned Deterioration of America's Landscape* (New York: Holt, Rinehart and Winston, 1964), 9; Richard J. Whalen, "A City Destroying Itself," *Fortune*, September 1964, 234.

127. "New Madison Square Garden to Rise Atop Penn Station," *New York Times*, July 25, 1961.

128. James Felt to Hon. Robert F. Wagner, December 16, 1964, NYC Municipal Archives.

129. "Felt, Top Planner, to Quit Post He Held Since 1956," *Village Voice*, December 20, 1962; Stern, *New York 1960*, 131.

130. Wood, "An Interview with Harmon Goldstone," 34.

131. Ibid., 28–29; Wood, "An Interview with the Late Geoffrey Platt," 16–18.

132. Wood, "An Interview with Otis Pratt Pearsall," 43.

133. In discussing this notion with Huxtable, she felt that that the author was "on to the truth." Wood interview with Ada Louise Huxtable, March 13, 2006.

134. "Architects Want Penn Station Saved, Their Picket Lines Have Proven It; What Does Public Interest Require?" *Architectural Record*, September, 1962.

135. "Saving Fine Architecture," *New York Times*, August 11, 1962.

136. There are several must-reads on the station: Lorraine B. Diehl, *The Late, Great Pennsylvania Station* (New York: Stephen Greene Press, 1987); Hilary Ballon, *New York's Pennsylvania Stations* (New York: W.W. Norton & Co., 2002); Eric

J. Plosky, "The Fall and Rise of Pennsylvania Station: Changing Attitudes Toward Historic Preservation in New York City" (Master's Thesis, Massachusetts Institute of Technology, 1999); and for a powerful photo essay, Peter Moore, *The Destruction of Penn Station* (New York: Distributed Art Publishers, 2000).

137. "100,000 Visitors See New Penna. Station," *New York Times*, November 28, 1910; "Huge New York Station Opens," *Boston Daily Globe*, November 27, 1910; Martin Tolchin, "Demolition Starts at Penn Station; Architects Picket," *New York Times*, October 29, 1963.

138. Interview with Laurel Lovrak, who was a student at Cooper Union at the time of protest, conducted at "Remembering Pennsylvania Station," the New York Preservation Archive Project's Commemoration of the 40th Anniversary of the Start of the Demolition of Pennsylvania Station, October 28, 2003, New York Preservation Archive Project.

139. Robert Weinberg, letter to the editor, *Oculus*, June 17, 1964.

140. Charles B. Hosmer, Jr., "Interview with Giorgio Cavaglieri," June 23, 1982, Eastern National Park and Monument Association, Charles Bridgham Hosmer, Jr. Papers, National Trust for Historic Preservation Library Collection and Archives, University of Maryland at College Park Libraries.

141. Weinberg copied Albert Bard on his letter to the editor of the *New York Times*, published May 7, 1962, on preserving the façade of Penn Station, Professional Papers of Robert C. Weinberg, Long Island University. In September the Fine Arts Federation sent a telegram to Allen J. Greenough, president of Pennsylvania Railroad, asking for a delay in demolition. "Fine Arts Unit Asks Delay in Penn Station Demolition," *New York Times*, September 18, 1962.

142. Minutes of the Semi-Annual Meeting of the Fine Arts Federation of New York, held at the Architectural League, November 14, 1961, Minutes of the Annual Meeting of The Fine Arts Federation of New York at the Museum of the City of New York, April 26, 1962 at 4:30 p.m., Fine Arts Federation of New York Records, Archives of American Art.

143. Minutes of the Annual Meeting of The Fine Arts Federation of New York at the Museum of the City of New York, April 26, 1962, Fine Arts Federation of New York Records, Archives of American Art.

144. On May 14, 1962, the City of Schenectady used the Bard Act to protect its "Old Stockade Area." It received little press coverage, but the Society for the Preservation of Long Island Antiquities reported on this "landmark event" in the article "First Historic District in New York State," appearing in their October 1962 newsletter.

145. A. J. Greenough, letter to the editor, *New York Times*, August 23, 1962.

146. *Purple and Gold*, Winter 1961, 90–91; *Purple and Gold*, Autumn 1962, 17.

147. "Albert S. Bard Dies at 96," *Purple and Gold*, Winter 1963, 59; "Remarks Given at 121st Convention Banquet," *Purple and Gold*, Autumn 1962; 20–22, 27–28.

148. "Albert S. Bard Dies at 96," *Purple and Gold*.

149. Minutes of the Annual Meeting of The Fine Arts Federation of New York at the Museum of the City of New York, April 26, 1962, Fine Arts Federation of New York Records, Archives of American Art.

TWELVE

CRISIS AND SACRIFICE

TOO OFTEN, THE DEMOLITION OF A LANDMARK BUILDING RECEIVES attention on the eve of destruction and once again when the wrecking ball strikes the first blow. After that, lost landmarks quickly fade from public consciousness. Pennsylvania Station would be different.

> The city regards the past with contempt and hastens to obliterate its heritage. Symbolic of New York's self-destructive frenzy is the destruction of Pennsylvania Station, now being razed to make way for a 120-million complex including a new Madison Square Garden arena, an exhibition hall, bowling alleys, and a thirty-three-story office tower. This will be the fourth Madison Square Garden in eighty-five years. There will never be another Penn Station.[1]

This bitter observation was penned in *Fortune* almost a year after the station's demolition began. It would only be one of a chorus of cries reminding New Yorkers of a loss, the pain of which would only grow with the passage of time.

Because of the enormity of the project, made even more daunting by the need to continue train service during the demolition, the destruction of Pennsylvania Station was spread out over three years. Instead of receiving one burst of publicity, the long, agonizing dissection of the monument took place publicly for years. It was seared into the collective consciousness of the city. There were endless opportunities to revisit the issue and countless chances for more and more New Yorkers to confront the loss. Reports such as "the commission's race against extinction is dramatized by the current demolition work at Pennsylvania Station" would keep the civic wound open and inextricably link the demolition of the station to the landmark cause.[2]

Each new threat to an historic building would magnify the horror the demolition of Pennsylvania Station had become. "The city's Landmarks Preservation Commission feels that two more landmarks here face the same fate as Pennsylvania Station, which went under the wrecker's hammer on Monday."[3] Now, threatened buildings, in this case the old headquarters of the Brooklyn Savings Bank and the city's oldest house, the 1641 Pieter Claesen Wyckoff home with its rich Dutch heritage, would be directly, or indirectly, coupled with the martyrdom of Pennsylvania Station. The station was becoming preservation's poster child.

Due to the demolition of Pennsylvania Station, threatened buildings throughout New York City gained even greater visibility in the media. No longer were they viewed as individual structures and their threatened demolition an isolated case; they were now kindred spirits with Pennsylvania Station. Their plight was illustrative of the growing landmark crisis. "Even as jackhammers chip at the great pillars of Pennsylvania Station, the Romanesque arches of the Brooklyn Savings Bank and the staid façade of the Black, Star & Frost (nee Gorham) building, the slower, steadier process of decay is destroying the city's lesser known significant buildings."[4]

Speaking for a growing number of New Yorkers, the press logged in: "But a lot of us feel a sense of urgency. It is now or never, and there's not much of a stockpile to play with. It could all be wiped out in our lifetime."[5] Again, with reference to the loss of the Brooklyn Savings Bank and the threat to Wyckoff homestead, the *Brooklyn World-Telegram* reported "there are scores of other landmarks, other pieces of the borough's heritage that need not crumble, if only the Landmarks Commission would work a little faster."[6]

The Landmarks Preservation Commission recognized that the loss of Pennsylvania Station had created a "teachable moment"—or in this case, a series of such moments. The commission had been sidelined in the battle over the station. Goldstone later referred to this inaction as "the heartbreaking inability to intervene in the efforts to save Pennsylvania Station." However, the commission could and would make the most of the loss of the station in its efforts to advance the larger cause.[7] The commission did not downplay the loss nor let the issue die down. The papers would report "James Van Derpool, executive director of the city's Landmarks Preservation Commission, hasn't recovered yet. He considers Penn Station the 'most monumental on the face of the earth' and its destruction a 'tragic loss.' Van Derpool says he has no doubt that 'in the years to come we will

BROOKLYN EAGLE POST CARD, SERIES 4, NO. 22.

BROOKLYN SAVINGS BANK BUILDING, CLINTON AND PIERREPONT STREETS.

FIGURE 12.1   As the Wagner administration internally reviewed drafts of the proposed Landmarks Law, the wrecking ball continued to swing. Its victims were not limited to Manhattan. Seen here in a 1910 image is Frank Freeman's Beaux Arts gem, the Brooklyn Savings Bank building, that once graced the northeast corner of Clinton and Pierrepont Streets in Brooklyn Heights.

be consumed with regret for allowing this supreme example of the architecture of the period to be destroyed.'"[8]

The commission knew all too well that a loss was often needed to prod the public, and ultimately, politicians, into action. Goldstone and his fellow preservation strategists within the government recognized that crisis and, tragically, the sacrifice of a building, were dire yet often essential ingredients for moving the cause forward. Preservation successes up to this point had largely been the result of crisis and sacrifice. The period between the first blow of the demolition hammer on the smooth marble

∎ ∎ ∎ ∎ ∎ ∎ ∎

skin of Pennsylvania Station and the physical signing of the Landmarks Law by Mayor Wagner would be filled with plenty of both.

The hopes of the city's preservationists now rested squarely on the shoulders of the Landmarks Preservation Commission. Often out of the limelight since its creation, the commission had been hard at work. As the demolition of Pennsylvania Station had starkly demonstrated, without legal power, the commission was in no position to forcefully intervene to save threatened buildings. At this point, its task was to lay the groundwork for such a future time, systematically identifying the buildings and places worthy of preservation and working to shape a law that would protect them. In the process of doing both, the commission would help build a constituency that would proactively protect landmarks and ultimately support the new law.

The commission moved forward with alacrity in its efforts to identify the city's architectural and historical treasures. Thanks to the Index of Architecturally Notable Structures in New York City lovingly developed over the years under the auspices of the Municipal Art Society, the commission had a road map to guide its work.[9] In 1963, as the landmarks cause itself continued to evolve from an ad hoc effort to the work of a formal city agency, the index was transformed from a mimeographed document to a "dazzling" hardcover, generously illustrated and professionally published book, *New York Landmarks*, appropriately dedicated to Edward Steese, the man who had been so involved in developing the index.[10]

Described by Brendan Gill as a "veritable Kama Sutra" for devotees of New York, the book had been a multi-year effort conducted on behalf of the Society by Alan Burnham. He had almost single-handedly guided this extreme make-over.[11] The book was yet another vehicle to bring the landmark cause to a broader public audience. Years later, Brendan Gill, who wrote the foreword to the book, stressed its impact: "That book made a mark in the world. It had its consequences ever since."[12]

The release of Burnham's book provided the press yet another opportunity to keep alive the Pennsylvania Station story.

Thus the classic grandeur of ancient Rome began to crumble again Monday as demolition began on the space to be occupied by the arena. There was irony in the timing. Even as the eagles were being unperched, a party was in progress at the Museum of the City of New York launching Alan Burnham's new book entitled, "New York Landmarks." The Pennsylvania Station "certainly should be saved," Mr. Burnham says emphatically. "Its removal is an absolute scandal and a crying shame."[13]

■ ■ ■ ■ ■ ■ ■

FIGURE 12.2 In 1963, the Index of Architecturally Notable Structures in New York City, established by the Municipal Art Society in 1951, took its final form in Alan Burnham's "dazzling" hardcover, *New York Landmarks*. In his foreword, Brendan Gill describes the work as a "veritable Kama Sutra for devotees of New York."

Identifying sites worthy of preservation came naturally to the new Landmarks Preservation Commission. After all, many of its members and staff had been involved in such list-making efforts for years. Only months after its creation, the commission started to officially designate lists of buildings as landmarks.[14] As will become painfully apparent, such designation provided no legal protection for these landmarks, but did constitute an official recognition by the city of New York of the importance of the buildings and places on the list. If threatened, this status could at least be used to help focus additional public and press attention on the sites. In September 1962, as the controversy over Pennsylvania Station raged around it, the commission acted on a "Proposed List of Obvious Buildings and Monuments for Designation." It acted affirmatively on over one hundred buildings. The list included sites in all the boroughs ranging from the Bowne House in Flushing, to the Pieter Claesen Wyckoff House in Brooklyn, to the Bartow-Pell Mansion in the Bronx, to Old Richmond Town on Staten Island. The largest contingent of buildings on the roster was in Manhattan. That list included everything from Castle Clinton, City Hall, and St. Mark's-in-the-Bowery to the Old Merchant's House and the Brokaw mansion.[15]

There was one very important difference between the commission's approach to identifying landmarks and the earlier efforts conducted under the auspices of the Municipal Art Society. The society's index placed buildings worthy of preservation in different categories reflecting their different levels of significance. "That was later dropped," Goldstone would explain, "because we felt, as we were getting closer to a real official list, that it would be dangerous, because then someone might say, 'Oh, this is only a second-string landmark; let that one go.' And we didn't want that; it was a landmark, or it was not."[16]

In the spring of 1963, the commission's designation work received major press attention with a well-illustrated story in the *New York Times*. In announcing the designation of three hundred sites, the story reported that "the commission is making its designations in the first phase of a survey of the five boroughs."[17] By June 1963, the commission tabulated its work as follows: "a) Individual Landmarks 706; b) Upper East Side Historic District—A 341; c) Upper East Side Historic District—B 14; d) Greenwich Village Historic District 2067; e) Brooklyn Heights Historic District, 1192; f) Cast Iron Historic District 50." Total: 4,370.[18] The rigor and selectivity of the commission's work would be remembered by Goldstone: "They rejected as much as they retained; from the start, a policy of critical selectivity was maintained. Everything old could not, and should not be preserved. In a city such as this it was merely realistic to hope to save only the best, only the most significant."[19]

The commission would continue reviewing lists and designating sites in this manner until the passage of the Landmarks Law. These early designations came with no legal protection. Once the law was passed, the commission would start designating anew using the procedures in the law. The new designations would come with the protective powers of the law.

The commission's work identifying and designating sites not only helped generate useful publicity, it also provided a way to engage the constituency in favor of landmarks protection. "Van Derpool with an extraordinary devoted staff and with an equally hard-working corps of volunteers was scouring every corner of the 5 boroughs to discover the most representative surviving examples of the various phases of New York's architectural and political history."[20] As early as the fall of 1962, Van Derpool was on the preservation circuit recruiting help. He and Stanley Tankel spoke at the Greenwich Village Association asking for the "community's help in preparing a diagram of sites—and even whole blocks—in Greenwich Village that are worth saving." A Village Committee was appointed. It was chaired by Ruth Wittenberg. Among its members were such familiar villagers as Doris Diether, Verna Small, Margot Gayle, and Carol Greitzer—all pillars of preservation in the Village.[21]

The success the commission was enjoying in identifying landmarks was in depressing contrast to the progress it was making on completing its other assignment, the shaping of the actual Landmarks Law. This did not go unnoticed by the press. Just prior to the commencement of the demolition of Pennsylvania Station, Ada Louise Huxtable editorialized in the *New York Times*:

In the fifteen months since the staff of the Landmarks Preservation Commission was appointed, it has done a quietly competent job of assessing the city's past. Period by period, it has compiled lists of New York buildings for a comprehensive architectural history

Micki Wolter

Judges evaluating entries in the VID Landmarks Contest are, seated, from the left: James Grote Van Derpool, executive director of the Landmarks Preservation Commission; Mrs. Philip Willenberg, chairman of the Village volunteers working with the Commission; Giorgio Cavaglieri, president of the Municipal Art Society and architect of the Jefferson Market Courthouse remodeling. Standing: Henry Hope Reed Jr., architectural historian and writer for the New York Herald Tribune; and Mrs. Carol Greitzer, Democratic District Leader, who sponsored the contest.

FIGURE 12.3 A landmark contest for Greenwich Village school children was only one of many ways used to publicize the work of the new Landmarks Preservation Commission. In this 1963 photograph, judges are seen evaluating entries in the competition. Sitting from the left: James Van Derpool, executive director of the commission, Ruth Willenberg, Village preservationist, Giorgio Cavaglieri, Municipal Art Society president. Standing are architectural historian Henry Hope Reed and Village political leader, Carol Greitzer.

of the city. But lists and history are only half of the commission's job. The other half—without which scholarly exercises are meaningless—is to recommend landmarks legislation to protect New York's architectural heritage. The commission's recommendations have been ready since last summer. It is time action was taken.[22]

Why was the drafting of the law taking so long? It was not just that the process of circulating drafts to all relevant city agencies was cumbersome; there were also substantive issues to be ironed out. "Problems of administration and enforcement not only had to be workable in themselves but they had to be consistent with and acceptable to every other city department with which the proposed new Agency might overlap or collide." Where was the best place to house this new governmental function? "For a while it was proposed to extend the jurisdiction of the Art Commission. Then it was thought to extend the scope of the zoning resolution. At one dreadful moment it was even proposed that the designating power be delegated to a group consisting entirely of architects!" Goldstone would recall: "Platt, William Fisher and their sub-committee on legislation were in almost continuous session with Morris Handel, Bernard Friedlander and other expert drafters of legislation in the Corporation Counsel's office. The statutes of some 49 other cities were minutely analyzed."[23] Fisher reached out to Otis Pratt Pearsall for help in this effort. Pearsall systematically gathered the statutes from across the country. In addition to contacting, yet again, such obvious places as New Orleans and Charleston, statutes were gathered from locations as diverse as Mobile, Alabama, Frankfort Kentucky, San Antonio, Texas, and Richmond, Virginia.[24]

The arduous drafting process tested the extraordinary patience of Platt and Goldstone but they, more than those outside the process, recognized the qualitative improvements the extensive internal review process made to the emerging legislation. The feedback from other agencies, particularly the City Planning Commission, contributed to this delay, yet ultimately strengthened the legislation. Considering the role the City Planning Commission had played in advancing the cause of landmark preservation, Goldstone, who by then was serving on that commission, expected the draft legislation to sail through the commission "like a breeze." Instead, Goldstone was "decimated" when Frank Blaustein, the vice chairman of the commission, "ripped it apart, absolutely tore it to shreds." Blaustein, with his years of experience, had "put his fingers into legal weaknesses." Both Platt and Goldstone would credit Blaustein with strengthening the law and clarifying the all-important relationship between the two agencies.

Originally thinking Blaustein was trying to sabotage the law, Goldstone quickly realized differently. "I have blessed Frank a thousand times for what he did."[25] Substantive critiques like Blaustein's necessitated the legislation going back to the Corporation Counsel for redrafting. During this review process the original bill went through "several subsequent revisions."[26]

"Finally, or, at the time, it seemed final," Goldstone would remember, on May 7, 1964 the proposed Landmarks Law "was laid on the Mayor's desk. The reaction was astounding. Nothing happened."[27] The long-lamented legislation to preserve the city's landmarks was now sitting collecting dust on the mayor's desk. Why was this the case? In March, the mayor's wife of over two decades had died. It is hard to imagine that this loss did not have an impact on the affairs of state. Or, perhaps less kindly, as the outspoken Greenwich Village activist and journalist Mary Nichols had written a year earlier, "The Mayor is a cultural boob, but he is also a man who has a fervent desire not only to get votes but to be socially respectable in the bargain. One of the charges least likely to bug him at this moment is that he doesn't set a high enough cultural and architectural tone for the city."[28]

Then again, in the eyes of many, inaction on a controversial issue was business as usual for the mayor. "New York, a city of perpetual motion, had a mayor who was a master of deliberate caution. Wagner liked to touch base with every center of power and carefully build a consensus before implementing new ideas. One of his favorite sayings, often quoted by his critics in ridicule, was: 'When in doubt, don't.'"[29] Whether his personal loss, real doubts, or just inertia were keeping the legislation from moving forward, it would spend the summer of 1964 languishing on the mayor's desk. Goldstone recalled the painful wait: "Now all that summer, Geoff and I were just on tender horses; its going to die at this point."[30] The legislation was not dead but something was needed to resuscitate it. Goldstone "suspected that another crisis would probably be needed to launch the law."[31]

Ironically, the real estate industry in New York deserves the lion's share of credit for the existence of the city's Landmarks Law. Real estate developers, as well as institutions cashing in their real estate holdings, provided the necessary impetus to move the Landmarks Law forward. Almost on cue, time and again, real estate interests provided landmark crisis after landmark crisis. Providently timed and accelerating in frequency, they vividly advanced the case for landmarks protection. Without this escalating assault on the city's landmarks and the cries each crisis provoked, the proposed Landmarks Law might have ended up like so many other good ideas lost on a shelf in a governmental office.

The crisis needed to dislodge the draft law from the mayor's desk and propel it into the city council arrived in September 1964. Unintentionally, the mayor himself provided the very context that elevated what might have been just another story about yet another threatened building into a media feeding frenzy that resulted in a clarion call for immediate action. The random events appeared so well orchestrated they looked like a baited trap. Years later, when Goldstone recounted the incident, he felt compelled to stress its truly accidental nature. "But no one dreamed, and honestly, no one planned, the delightful coincidence that actually occurred . . . The irony of the situation was too wonderful to be wasted."[32]

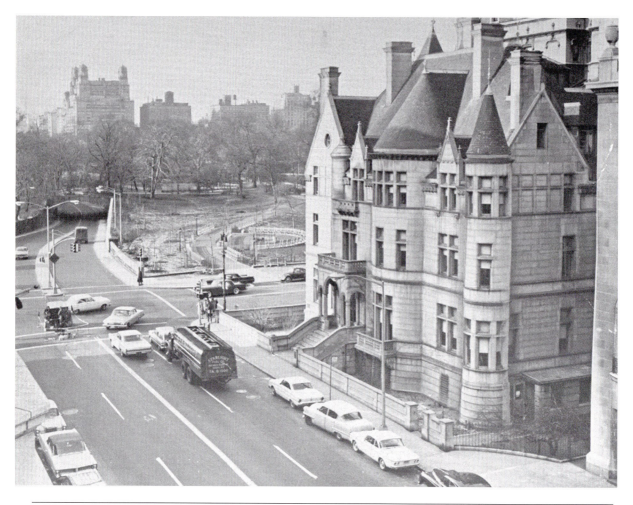

FIGURE 12.4 With the caption, "Going...going...?" this photograph of the Brokaw mansion appeared in the *New York Daily News* on December 10, 1964. Solidly holding down the northeast corner of East 79th Street and Fifth Avenue, it looked secure, though its future was anything but. Only days earlier, the city council had held its public hearing on the law that could have saved this landmark.

On September 17, the press broke the story that the Brokaw mansion at East 79th and Fifth Avenue, along with two adjoining mansions, were to be demolished.[33] Two years earlier on September 23, 1962, the Landmarks Preservation Commission had officially recognized the landmark quality of the building, then in use as the home of the Institute of Radio Engineers. The fact that the city had officially acknowledged the building's importance as a landmark yet was still powerless to save it was hammered home in the press. "Ironically, the Brokaw mansion had been designated by the Landmarks Preservation Commission as one of some 750 buildings worth preserving for historic or esthetic reasons. But the commission, established by Mayor Wagner in 1962, has no real say in these matters. It can recommend, plead, protest and deplore—and that's about all."[34] That alone, however, did not provide this particular crisis with the powerful punch that it packed.

Only a day before the Brokaw crisis broke, the mayor had proclaimed September 28 through October 4 "American Landmarks Preservation Week in New York City." The city was participating in "an international program to advance technical and legal measures for the protection, preservation, and restoration of landmarks throughout the world." Under normal circumstances, such an innocuous announcement would have merited minimal press attention at best. Internationally sponsored by UNESCO (the idea came out of its eleventh annual session in Paris in 1960), the program was sponsored in the United States by the National Trust for Historic Preservation. New York's celebration of Landmarks Week was to consist of the issuing of the mayoral proclamation and a ragtag assortment of activities spread across the five boroughs. Not exactly heart-stopping, headline-grabbing stuff.[35]

Timing is everything. The breaking news about the Brokaw mansion combined with the mayor's otherwise innocent announcement of the upcoming Landmarks Preservation Week, created the perfect media storm needed to advance the Landmarks Law. Sensing a lucky break, representatives of the Municipal Art Society, the American Institute of Architects, the Architectural League, and the Fine Arts Federation dashed off a telegram to the mayor applauding his proclamation and expressing their hope that "this will be the opportunity to make final arrangements for making effective the legislation which was previously presented for your approval," and noting that "such legislation may prevent the impending demolition of the mansions at Fifth Avenue and 79th street whose character has been gracing our city for two generations."[36]

■ ■ ■ ■ ■ ■ ■

FIGURE 12.5 Mayor Wagner's proclamation of September 28–October 4, 1964 as "American Landmarks Preservation Week in New York City" received extraordinary press attention because its announcement coincided with the breaking news that the Brokaw mansion would be demolished. Mayor Wagner, on the left, is seen here holding the proclamation with lawyer Whitney North Seymour, Sr. in the middle and landmark chair, Geoffrey Platt, at the right.

Immediately, the press went after Wagner. "The Landmarks Preservation Commission should either be given meaningful official status and authority or be discarded as an embarrassment—like the small voice of a reproachful conscience."[37] These words of the *New York World-Telegram*

resonated with those coming from the ever-vigilant editorial page of the *New York Times*: "While Mayor Wagner sits on this proposal, and old buildings go down like dominoes, he announces that he will issue a proclamation next Wednesday of Landmarks Preservation Week. The irony of this coincidence would be laughable if the facts weren't so somber. It would be a handsomely appropriate day for the Mayor to make public this long awaited bill, and turn it over to the City Council."[38]

The pressure was growing. Some movement from city hall was detectable. The day the story broke, the mayor's legal aide told the press he had "no idea" when the legislation would move forward; it was still under study by city agencies.[39] Five days later, a "summary of the final draft of the legislation" was made public.[40] On that Wednesday, at the signing of the mayoral proclamation for American Landmarks Week, Wagner did not go so far as to officially unveil the landmarks legislation, nor turn it over to the city council, but he did state: "It is now undergoing final review by my staff, to ensure that it is effective and equitable, and I hope we will be able to point to 1964 as New York's landmark year."[41]

If anything, the mayor's comments only caused the press to turn up the heat: "In a curiously poignant ceremony at City Hall yesterday, Mayor Wagner signed a proclamation establishing 'American Landmarks Preservation Week in New York City' as part of a national and international program to protect landmarks that neither he nor the city has any power to protect. . . . We need more than good intentions. Actions speak louder than proclamations and the only action so far is the steady swing of the wrecker's ball."[42]

Momentum continued to build. On September 26, 1964, citizens took to the streets, rallying in front of the Brokaw mansion demanding legislation that would save it and other landmarks. They were joined by civic leaders and their elected representatives of all political stripes, Democrat, Republican, and liberal.[43] By the formal Manhattan event celebrating Landmarks Week—a September 29 symposium on "Greenwich Village Living Landmarks"—borough president Edward R. Dudley was able to announce, "I left Mayor Wagner 20 minutes ago and he said the bill would be introduced on Thursday of this week." Though off by a few days, his report was essentially accurate.

On October 6, 1964, New Yorkers would wake up to read that "a bill to preserve the city's architectural heritage was introduced into the city council amid a chorus of approval from architects and historians and expressions of misgiving by some of those who would be required to carry out its terms."[44] Though some in the civic community had actually hoped

that the Landmarks Law would be enacted during Landmarks Preservation Week, it is both remarkable and instructive that a benign and innocently designed artificial celebration could actually play such a significant role in advancing New York's Landmarks Law.[45]

Years later, Harmon Goldstone would stress the importance of the threat to the Brokaw mansion, placing it right up there with the loss of Pennsylvania Station: "The Brokaw House, the loss of Penn Station, were the sacrifices that made it possible." He observed, people "will not act until there is a crisis and a sacrifice, and these were the two that impelled it into the council."[46] Though the Brokaw crisis was clearly the event that freed the draft legislation from the mayor's office, the more receptive climate of the early 1960s was also the result of other preservation stories.

In August 1964, it had become public that McKim, Mead & White's 1928 Savoy-Plaza Hotel had been added to that list of architectural dominoes soon to be knocked down. It was to be replaced by a forty-eight-story corporate headquarters for General Motors. This threat generated another unsanctioned activity for Landmarks Preservation Week, a demonstration at the hotel by some one hundred students and faculty from "major architectural schools." Led by AGBANY activist Elliot Willensky, their "funeral march" featured placards, one of which pointedly proclaimed, "Landmarks Preservation Weak." Two other protests scheduled for the same day were rained out: one had been targeted for the Brokaw mansions and the other in front of what would soon become the site of a preservation miracle, the block of mansions between 68th and 69th Streets on the west side of Park Avenue.[47]

The Savoy-Plaza, which one reporter cattily observed was "mourned in death more strenuously than it had been praised in life," would soon attract the support of a constituency much more unexpected than the AGBANY crowd.[48] Calling itself "Save Our Landmarks! Save the Plaza Square," a new committee driven by socially prominent wealthy New York women began plans for a nationwide boycott of General Motors products, both cars and home appliances, to protest the impending demolition. Its honorary chair was Fannie Hurst, the novelist who years earlier had joined in preservation efforts in the Village, and its committee members included many whose names graced the social register. Its chair and spokesperson was Mrs. Helen M. Clark, a lawyer, civic leader, and former president of the New York City Federation of Women's Clubs.[49]

As the demolition derby reached Midtown and the Upper East Side, the landmarks crisis began to attract the interest of growing numbers of

■ ■ ■ ■ ■ ■ ■ ■

FIGURE 12.6   The prominence of the Savoy-Plaza in both the life and look of New York City made the August 1964 announcement of its planned demolition another shock to New Yorkers. In this 1932 stunning photograph by renowned architectural photographer Samuel H. Gottscho, the Savoy is the structure in the middle with the two chimneys on its roof. The photo also depicts the beauty of the southeast corner of Central Park—the site of the hotly contested, proposed two-story, one-thousand-seat Huntington Pavilion.

the area's socially prominent, wealthy, and well-connected residents. Their involvement did not go unnoticed. It was getting harder and harder to continue ignoring the growing preservation crisis. Daily, it was also becoming clear that preservation was no longer solely the province of civic gray-beards, Greenwich Village mothers, sandal-wearing activists, young architects, and young urban professionals. When wealthy, socially prominent women were willing to boycott General Motors to save a landmark, preservation was clearly on the way to achieving a societal tipping point.[50]

The climate surrounding the introduction of the landmark preservation legislation was one largely informed by impending landmark disasters, but not exclusively so. There was also some good news in the midst of crisis. By the fall of 1964, the campaign to save Jefferson Market Courthouse, which had started in December 1957 with the modest goal of getting its massive tower clock running and illuminated again, had evolved to the point where the renovation work converting it to a branch of the New York Public Library was about to commence. Side-by-side on the same page of the September 23, 1964 *New York Times* ran an article on the first public release of the outline for the proposed Landmarks Law and Ada Louise Huxtable's story, "The Salvage of Old Jeff." Under a picture of the courthouse with the headline "Victorian Landmark in Greenwich Village to Be Library Branch," Huxtable's piece told the improbable and empowering tale of how devoted villagers had saved a "notable, but particularly awkward monument, in a city that saves nothing."[51]

The successful effort to save and adaptively reuse Jefferson Market Courthouse would often be cited in the context of the proposed Landmarks Law. The courthouse demonstrated how a landmark could be saved if given a chance. The message was clear: the proposed Landmarks Law was all about creating an orderly process to give the city and its citizens a formal chance to save their landmarks. The intended message was if New York City had such a law, there would be more Jefferson Market Courthouses and fewer Brokaw mansions.[52]

Propelled by the Brokaw crisis, the proposed legislation was scheduled for a December 3, 1964 public hearing at the city council. Introduced by councilmen Seymour Boyers, Robert A. Low, and Richard S. Aldrich, the bipartisan bill arrived at the council with some momentum behind it. Prior to the hearing, the *New York Times* ran two editorials in support of the legislation. "New York's landmarks legislation is no wild-eyed dream of doddering sentimentalists; it is a practical, necessary and equitable means of preserving important civic values. It is expertly tailored

■ ■ ■ ■ ■ ■ ■ ■

for New York's needs and has the backing of the Mayor. It should be made effective promptly, without debilitating compromise."[53] WCBS-TV endorsed the legislation, underscoring the same message: "The legislation is moderate, it's sensible. It would not set up any arbitrary power. It would not block progress in our city."[54] The message was clear: the legislation was sound and should be passed intact and without delay.

The time devoted to crafting and vetting the bill had been well spent. Not only had years of review and study produced a solid piece of legislation, all that hard work had paved the way for the legislation. In addition to the press advancing the concept to the general public, Geoffrey Platt and the commission had been meeting all across the city with organizations of all types, likely proponents and opponents.[55] Despite these efforts, preservationists were worried about two things: possible amendments to the legislation and the prospect of defeat by endless delay. In urging the members of the Fine Arts Federation to work on behalf of the legislation, Whitney North Seymour, Sr., issued a word of caution: "There might be changes proposed and delays which would drag it on." At the same meeting Margot Gayle "emphasized the importance of a quick passage of the Bill."[56]

There was indeed real cause for worry. When the proposed legislation was announced, the press reported the following reaction from a source identified as being "close to the City Council." "I have a feeling that this will create an uproar. Everybody likes the idea of preserving historic landmarks, but the question is how to do it. The procedures in here are pretty rough. If the Council irons all this out, you won't recognize the bill." Reinforcing the fear, "David Ross of the Bronx, the council's majority leader, declared that 'any bill of this magnitude will require a multiple of changes.'"[57]

In planning its public advocacy for the legislation, the Municipal Art Society largely took its cues from the Landmarks Preservation Commission. At a Municipal Art Society board meeting, Geoffrey Platt (both the chair of the Landmarks Preservation Commission and a member of the Municipal Art Society board) reported that "he hoped to call a Citizens Committee to act as a pressure group to work toward the passing of the Landmarks legislation bill which is now before the city council; that the next step was to marshal widespread citizen support for the bill; and that the logical organization to spearhead this is the MAS." Interestingly enough, in a postscript to the minutes of that meeting, Municipal Art Society president Giorgio Cavaglieri reported: "The idea of a prominent Citizens Committee to give luster to the legislation support was abandoned

by the Landmarks Preservation Commission." Cavaglieri then created a task force to mobilize support for the bill and part of this effort involved reaching out to forty-three civic groups.[58]

Among the groups endorsing the legislation was the American Scenic and Historic Preservation Society. James Van Derpool, long a board member of American Scenic, had requested and easily received its endorsement of the commission's legislation.[59] The American Scenic and Historic Preservation Society and the Municipal Art Society had stayed the course. Decades earlier, they had provided assistance to Albert Bard and the mayor's Billboard Advertising Commission of the City of New York. Now, half a century later, that commission's conclusion—that New York City needed the ability to regulate private property on aesthetic grounds—was getting its public hearing. The Billboard Advertising Commission's recommendation had taken a different form and was being advanced by a different commission, but it was moving forward. Bard, despite his remarkable dedication and longevity, did not live to witness this and add his support. Fortunately, these two societies did.

Geoffrey Platt's reasoning for not creating a committee of luminaries in support of the legislation remains a mystery. However, the lack of such a body certainly made it easier for Ada Louise Huxtable to drive home her point in the *New York Times* editorial appearing on the morning of the all-important hearing: "The political pressure groups and the real estate and business lobbies that show up at these hearings regularly with powerful statements of minority interest must be measured against the unorganized but strong public sentiment in favor of this bill. It should be adopted without debilitating compromise."[60]

Advocacy efforts on behalf of the legislation included generating a groundswell of citizen support. Whitney North Seymour, Sr., wearing his hat as chairman of the Committee on Legislation of the Fine Arts Federation, sounded a call for action in his letter to the *New York Times*: "I would urge that all organizations and citizens concerned with the quality and texture of life in our city support this legislation. . . . This may be the last clear chance to get landmarks legislation on the books while we still have some to preserve."[61] Supporters of the bill ranged from the expected, including Stewart Udall, secretary of the Department of the Interior, to the unexpected. The Rabbi of Central Synagogue urged the passage of the law "so that we may save for our untold generations the symbols of the past which may well become the landmarks in their lives."[62] The council received hundreds of letters in support of the legislation.[63]

FIGURE 12.7   Among those eagerly following the progress of the proposed Landmarks Law was Otis Pratt Pearsall of Brooklyn Heights. On December 3, 1964, Pearsall was one of the eighty-four people who testified before the city council's Committee on Codification in support of proposed landmarks preservation law, bill no. 779. Almost a year later, on November 17, 1965, Pearsall would be able to testify in front of the Landmarks Preservation Commission in support of the designation of New York's first historic district, Brooklyn Heights.

The 11 a.m. city council hearing on Thursday, December 3, 1964 was in itself a landmark event. In dramatic fashion, the Municipal Art Society reported on this hearing to its membership: "The session was a stormy one that lasted seven hours, but when the smoke settled, the Landmarks Commission, the Municipal Art Society, and their allies, had carried the day. Eighty-four people had spoken in favor of the bill, and only five against."[64] It was indeed, as the press stated, a "confrontation of civic leaders and real estate interests."[65] Platt would remember one legislator telling him, "We haven't had as much interest in any subject since the Sales Tax."[66] Brooklyn preservation leader Otis Pearsall, who testified at the hearing, remembers sensing that something truly special was happening.[67]

Geoffrey Platt, William Fisher, and James Van Derpool made the presentation for the Landmarks Preservation Commission. The reasonableness of the proposed legislation was stressed. Van Derpool pointed out that the approximately 750 individual buildings that they had identified as landmarks constituted "less than 1/10th of 1% of the total real estate parcels in the city." He concluded: "The time is late; we believe the Bill to be temperate and wise. We certainly need the protection it offers."[68] In his testimony, Harmon Goldstone echoed the call for timely action: "I urge its prompt enactment. If you delay, you may achieve the most perfect document ever designed for the preservation of landmarks, but there may be no landmarks left to preserve."[69]

The opposition was overwhelmed in numbers but was so vociferous that the media reported the controversial nature of the bill.[70] Considering the power of New York's real estate community, their public opposition to the bill, though loud, was surprisingly constrained. The limited scope of at least their public opposition would be credited in part to James Felt. Geoffrey Platt believed Felt used his considerable influence to mute the Real Estate Board of New York's opposition to the bill.[71] Also helping temper opposition to the bill was a series of prehearing meetings held by council member Seymour Boyers with representatives of the building industry and the unions. Boyers had recruited fellow council member Paul O'Dwyer, who had strong ties with these groups, to help him make the case that their interests would not be adversely impacted by the legislation.[72]

Despite these efforts, there was still some opposition. A variety of objections were raised. Among them, government was "too big already;" the bill did not clearly "define what constitutes a landmark;" and that property rights would be curtailed without "compensation to the owners."[73] The Commerce and Industry Association summed it up: "The rub is that the bill now before the City Council is unconstitutional and inadequate. It fails to provide appropriate compensation to the owner of the building. A new bill should be drawn."[74]

The report on the hearing given to the board of the American Scenic and Historic Preservation Society concluded that the city council committee was "favorably impressed with the support expressed by the representation of the many organizations speaking on behalf of the Bill, although slight changes and additions may be required to meet the questions raised."[75] How "slight" could the forces for preservation keep those changes? Though small in numbers at the public hearing, those opposing the bill were anything but powerless. It would have been a huge mistake to underestimate the strength of their opposition or their ability to effectively advance their desired changes behind closed doors. Those aligned against the legislation tended to do their best work behind the scenes, away from the glare of the public. Delaying tactics could easily keep the legislation bottled up in the city council for months, even sentencing it to a lingering death. Alternatively, a few well-worded amendments could easily render it ineffective.

■ ■ ■ ■ ■ ■ ■ ■

Delay and debilitating amendments were what the bill's proponents feared the most. The *New York Times* would editorialize after the December hearing: "Without the landmarks law there will be no color, character or history. Some want to strengthen the bill. Others want to weaken it. The main thing is to get on with it. Protective legislation too late to protect anything would be an ironic outcome."[76] The hearing had demonstrated the public support of the legislation leading David Ross, to state that the legislation would be passed. But uncertainty remained. When would it be passed and in what form? Seymour Boyers, chair of the Council's Committee on Codification, which had held the hearing, confirmed the bill would need to be redrafted. How long would it take? All answers were in months, not weeks.[77] As the *Times* wished, the council would "get on with it" but not without further crisis and additional painful sacrifice.

The city council was suggesting additional months of review. Unfortunately, some of the city's landmarks did not have that much time left. Only two weeks after the public hearing, as New Yorkers were getting ready for the Christmas holidays, another landmark crisis loomed. The grinch poised to steal that Christmas was a developer planning to demolish what was described as "one of the finest groups of domestic architecture in the country" and replace it with a thirty-one-story apartment building. As the *New York Times* ominously noted, "The scaffolding is going up for the demolition of the 68th Street end of the Pyne-Davidson block on Park Avenue." Since demolition had commenced on Pennsylvania Station, the Landmarks Commission had been "keeping an anxious eye" on this architecturally magnificent block.[78]

The westerly block of Park Avenue between 68th and 69th Streets features a bouquet of stately mansions, any one of which most cities would proudly embrace and cherish as a landmark. The result is what architectural historian Andrew Dolkart calls an "extraordinary block which is entirely lined with red brick dwellings inspired by 18th-century architecture." Among the four mansions, 680 and 684 Park were the work of McKim, Mead & White. Occupying the southwest corner of the block is 680 Park, built as the home of the financier Percy Pyne. Next to it, 684 Park was built for his daughter. Mid-block is 686 Park Avenue, a Delano & Aldrich mansion that rubs shoulders to the north with 690 Park Avenue, a building designed by Walker & Gilette.[79] It would be hard to find a more quintessential landmark block in all of New York City.

What to some looked like a landmark block to others resembled the perfect development site. The key corner building, 680 Park and the

FIGURE 12.8   Just how close New York City came to losing this block of architecturally distinguished brick mansions on the west side of Park Avenue between East 68th and 69th Streets is apparent in this photograph from the *New York Times* of January 6, 1965. With demolition scaffolding surrounding the exterior of 680 Park Avenue and interior demolition already underway, the last-second preservation of these buildings more than earned the *New York Times* editorial headline, "Miracle on 68th Street."

building adjoining it on 68th Street, had been owned by the Soviet government. Even though the property sported the balcony from which Nikita S. Khrushchev had made "his famous harangues to the press," the Soviets, no longer needing the buildings, sold them to Sommer Brothers Realty. What was lacking to create an irresistibly sized and highly profitable development site was the adjoining building to the north, 684 Park Avenue.[80]

James Van Derpool understood the pivotal role 684 Park played in the architectural ensemble that made this such an architecturally stunning block and the equally key role it played in blocking the apartment house scheme that would otherwise consume its McKim, Mead & White neighbor to the south. Knowing that it was going on the market, Van Derpool met with its institutional owner and convinced them of its importance

to the city. They agreed to take a lower price for the property, selling it to a client who would save the building—at least for a one-year period.[81] During that time, Van Derpool and the commission aggressively explored various reuse scenarios for the threatened buildings. None worked out. By September the *New York Times* announced that, like the Brokaw houses, the fate of "the Percy Pyne block on Park Avenue appears to be sealed; they will be replaced by apartment houses."[82] New Yorkers were facing a bleak Christmas. In addition to these impending losses, the papers announced that the Astor Library on Lafayette Street, today the Public Theatre, and the Friends Meeting House on Gramercy Park were both for sale and "rumor points the finger at more of the city's fine old mansions."[83]

There is much truth to the old preservation mantra that as long as a landmark remains standing, no matter how dim its prospects may appear, there is still hope that it can be saved. While others were drafting their architectural obituaries, James Van Derpool continued his behind-the-scenes efforts. The mayor held up the wrecking permits as long as possible. Scaffolding started to go up.[84] Van Derpool turned for help to Peter Grimm. For years a leader in New York's real estate community and long immersed in civic affairs, Grimm's interest in historic sites went back to at least 1947 when, as president of the Chamber of Commerce of the State of New York, he attended and spoke about the historical significance of Fort Clinton at the lunch that George McAneny had arranged at Fraunces Tavern to convince the mayor of New York of the importance of saving Castle Clinton.[85]

Grimm was personally committed to saving the block front on Park Avenue. He had arranged the earlier sale of 684 Park at a reduced price to a buyer willing to hold the site while a preservation solution was being sought.[86] Now seeking a sympathetic buyer to step forward and purchase an option on the site, which would give the commission another six months to find that still-elusive preservation solution, Grimm found an "angel" who agreed to acquire and save all three of the threatened buildings, sparing them from the wrecker's ball.[87]

James Van Derpool would recount a final snag in these last-minute efforts, what he called a "tragic impass." Grimm had found a buyer to save the buildings, but could not find the site's developer to make the deal. Sommers had left town for two weeks for an "undisclosed destination for a complete rest." Fate again intervened. Grimm was lunching at the University Club, and "at one moment in the larger dining room all conversation ceased—except at [the] next table." In that sudden moment of unnatural silence, Grimm heard coming from another table one diner commenting to the next: "I drove Mr. Sommers to the airport this morning, he is going to Arizona for a rest." Grimm was able to reach Sommers that afternoon. The sale was negotiated the Saturday before Christmas. Proclaimed by the *New York Times* as the "Miracle on 68th Street" and by others as a "Christmas Carol for New York," the "miraculous last-minute rescue" was a huge win for preservation.[88]

The rescue was so last-minute that the demolition crew had already been at work for ten days wreaking "havoc" on the interior. Sleuthlike, the architects, who would later convert the building for its new nonprofit use, tracked down to Third Avenue antique dealers some of the removed decorative elements and reacquired them for reinstallation. Lost, however, was the decorative flooring and "at least one magnificent chimney piece."[89] Instead of being called a last-minute rescue, the saving of this block is perhaps more accurately called a last-second rescue.

The drama and romance of the story made it a headline grabber for the media. It received national attention. *Newsweek* captured its magic:

> The scene could have been lifted from one of those turn-of-the-century cliff-hanging melodramas. Three New York City mansions—among the finest examples of Federal Eclectic architecture left in the U.S.—were about to be razed for one of the new "luxury" apartment houses that Manhattan needs like another Triangle fire. Demolition workers had set up the scaffolding on Park Avenue, carting off a dozen antique marble mantelpieces, and were tearing up the parquet flooring. Suddenly the president of the wrecking firm, like Dick Dalton himself, rushed in and ordered them to stop.[90]

Versions of this storybook rescue appeared in the editorial columns. Depicted as "freeing Poor Nell from the railroad tracks just as the whistle blows," or as "Belinda the Beautiful Boilermaker was never in greater peril, nor saved more spectacularly from Relentless Rudolph by Hairbreadth Harry," it was a story made for the press.[91] The story received an additional bounce when the identity of the anonymous purchaser was revealed as the granddaughter of John D. Rockefeller, Sr., the Marquesa de Cuevas, first cousin of Governor Rockefeller, "the former Margaret Rockefeller Strong, who inherited $25 million from her grandfather at his death in 1937."[92] The story had much in it to capture the public's attention.

There were several lessons to be learned from this crisis and they were not lost on the press or the civics. In honoring the Marquesa, the American Institute of Architects "pointed out, last-minute cliff-hangers such as this

FIGURE 12.9 Lacking a law to prevent the demolition of these threatened landmarks on Park Avenue, the Landmarks Preservation Commission used its powers of persuasion and its incredible networks to save them. Appropriately, commission chair Geoffrey Platt, left, and particularly its executive director, James Van Derpool, right, received kudos for, in the words of the *New York Herald-Tribune,* "freeing Poor Nell from the railroad tracks just as the whistle blows."

are thrilling, but if the City Council would pass the Landmarks Preservation Bill, which it has been contemplating for over two months, the city could act in the interest of its citizens, instead of the reverse, as is presently the case."[93] The *Herald-Tribune* pointed out that the case demonstrated that "given time, such landmarks can be preserved after all," going on to stress that this is "one of the chief purposes of the landmarks preservation bill now before the city council."[94]

In the euphoria of the moment, others had reached a wishful and wrong conclusion: "Yet the Park Avenue cliff-hanger demonstrates that when the citizenry is aroused, the wreckers can be rolled back." Sadly, this hopeful observation by *Newsweek* was more wish than reality. In the past, New York's citizenry had been "aroused" only to see a landmark turn into dust, and those days were not yet over.[95] Ada Louise Huxtable, on the other hand, nailed it in her *New York Times* editorial, "Miracle on 68th Street." "Miracles and magnanimity are fine, but they are not the legislative answer to preservation. That lies in the hands of the City Council—now."[96]

Sadly, the positive resolution to this preservation crisis was not enough to dramatically speed up the legislative process. After all, Nell had been rescued from the railroad tracks, not splattered all over them. At a meeting on January 20, 1965, over forty people representing sixty-seven civic organizations concerned with landmarks preservation listened as it was reported that councilmember Seymour Boyers was still looking for ways to respond to the objections that had been raised to the bill.[97] Despite the cries from the press and public for speedy action to avoid another landmark crisis, the wheels of government continued to roll slowly. It now would take more than just a crisis and a last-minute rescue to effect much-needed change. It would take a huge sacrifice to force action. The victim would be a very familiar one to the New York residents: the Brokaw mansion.

In early February in "weekend stealth," Associated Wreckers went to work on the landmark. They were under pressure from the new owner, the Campagna Construction Corporation, to move swiftly. Though Campagna's contract had called for the seller of the property to vacate by April 1, Campagna had persuaded them to leave before the end of January. Eighty-year-old Anthony Campagna, senior member and founder of the company, explained the accelerated schedule: "It was common sense. Self-defense. With all the adverse publicity, every day counts." Giving the forces for preservation more credit than they deserved, Campagna feared some last-minute interference. "We got in there a little early. A friend tipped us

off."[98] As Ada Louise Huxtable would write in her editorial addressing that Saturday demolition, "It was a dandy way to do enough massive damage at a time when no normal channels are functioning, to assure the building's doom."[99]

Ever since the fate of the mansion had been announced in the fall of 1964, efforts had been made to try and find a way to save it.[100] With the demolition scaffolding erected on Friday, February 5, 1965 and demolition beginning the very next day, "No Marquesa de Cuevas had a chance to step forward with $2 million to save it. . . . Even if another equally public-spirited good fairy existed in New York, by Monday it was too late."[101] Even though the odds of a second last-minute miracle intervention were miniscule, the brazen weekend assault on the landmark made

FIGURE 12.10 Demolition scaffolding went up around the Brokaw mansion on Friday February 5, 1965 and demolition began the next day. The demolition schedule had been moved up to avoid any last-minute efforts to stop the wreckers. Following on the heels of the miraculous rescue of the Park Avenue mansions, the destruction of the Brokaw mansion infuriated New Yorkers and set off another round of editorials demanding a landmarks law.

FIGURE 12.11   In 1957, the program of placing plaques on landmark-quality buildings was inaugurated by the New York Community Trust. An important public education initiative, the obvious preservation shortcoming of the program was made painfully clear in 1965 when one of the plaqued buildings, the Brokaw mansion, then also known as the Institute of Radio Engineers, was brazenly demolished. Plaques and lists were no substitute for the much-needed Landmarks Law.

its demolition even more offensive precisely because the action was legal.

Contrasted with the fairy tale reprieve of the Park Avenue mansions, the tragic ending of the Brokaw story was another publicity windfall for the forces of preservation. Not only did the audacious demolition offer the press a dramatic and compelling story, it provided a news hook for another round of pro-preservation editorials. Pressure increased on the city council. WCBS-TV would editorialize to its viewers, "Tonight we'd like to talk about inaction; inaction by the City Council, and the high price we're paying for it. The particular issue is the preservation of city landmarks, an issue we've discussed several times in our editorials. While the City Council dallies, landmarks are coming down and more of the city's history is lost, forever."[102]

The loss of the Brokaw mansions also made more credible and urgent the pending threats hanging over other city landmarks. In Flushing, Queens, it was the Kingsland mansion whose fate hung in the balance. If funds could not be raised to move it, this 1774 Georgian Colonial, recognized by the Landmarks Preservation Commission, was to be demolished for a shopping center.[103] Threats in Manhattan ranged from a proposed garage under Madison Square Park to the Huntington Pavilion, the massive cafe planned for the southeast corner of Central Park, still in limbo as the state's highest court considered the litigation against it.[104] The list of blue chip landmarks in danger included everything from the Custom House at Bowling Green, to the Singer Building, the Stock Exchange, the Seventh Regiment Armory, the Metropolitan Opera House, and the Sun Building.[105]

Now joining this list, which included the Astor Library and the Friends Meeting House, was the beloved Old Merchants House at 29 East Fourth Street. Though maintained as a museum since 1936, dire financial conditions propelled the prospect of its demolition into the headlines.[106] This threat and the council's inaction on the pending landmarks legislation led state senator Frederic S. Berman to introduce a resolution in Albany calling on the council to pass the landmarks bill.[107]

In demolishing the Brokaw mansion in such a brazen fashion, Anthony Campagna unknowingly gave preservation a huge boost. The Brokaw mansions actually had "two lives" to give to the cause of landmark preservation. The announcement of the mansion's doom had dislodged the proposed Landmarks Law from its long residence on the mayor's desk, resulting in its introduction into the city council. The actual demolition of the mansion made it virtually impossible for the council to study the legislation any longer, forcing it to take action.

This was not the first time Anthony Campagna unwittingly provided the preservation community with the powerful ammunition of moral outrage at a critical juncture. His first accidental assist to the preservation cause came in 1948. Campagna was an immigrant from Castelmezzano, Italy, who had arrived in America in 1908 "with $60 and a law degree from an Italian university in his pocket." By 1911 he had put up his first building.[108] He was the same builder who, to great public outcry, demolished the House of Genius on the south side of Washington Square Park in 1948. Adding insult to that injury, at the apparent prodding of Robert Moses, Campagna then sold the cleared site to New York University, further infuriating villagers.[109] That controversy in the late 1940s helped lead to the early call for the Landmarks Law as the loss of the Brokaw would crank up the volume of the continuing cries for the law's passage.

As to whether the Brokaw mansion was a landmark, Campagna said: "Who was Brokaw? A man who made ready-made clothes who thought he would get into society. He was ridiculed."[110] Ironically, the Landmarks Law that Campagna twice unintentionally helped advance would be used in 1993 to preserve his own house, the Anthony Campagna Estate in Riverdale. It was designated as "a prime example of the integration of house and setting, virtually unparalleled for its period in New York City."[111] What would Campagna have responded to this landmark designation? "Who was Campagna? A man who destroyed two landmarks?"

The demolition of the Brokaw mansion put huge pressure on the city council and put Seymour Boyers, the chair of the committee studying the bill, on the defensive. A March 15, 1965 *New York Times* editorial reviewed the current status of the bill, noting that Boyers' committee thought it might get "a revised bill to the floor by March 31." Caustically, it continued: "This bill is on the way to becoming an antique itself, and it had better be good when it finally does emerge from City Council." As with the earlier CBS-TV editorial, Boyers felt the need to respond in person. He stressed the complexity of the twenty-eight-page bill, pointing out it was "path-finding legislation." He noted the "series of meetings" his committee had held and the "careful study" it had given to numerous proposed amendments to the bill.[112] Perhaps his most telling response to the charge that the bill had been bottled-up in committee was that a final version of the bill went to the full council on March 23, 1965, ahead of the schedule previously reported in the *Times* editorial.[113]

Geoffrey Platt and Harmon Goldstone had feared the bill might die in committee.[114] The landmark dramas that had played out since the council's December 3, 1964 hearing had helped make sure that would not be the case. As these events had unfolded in a highly public way, Boyers' committee had been doing its work off center stage. It had met seven times and reviewed numerous proposed amendments to the original bill.[115] The bill had survived the committee process, but at what cost? What issues had emerged and how had they been resolved?

The legislation came out of committee recognizable as the bill that had gone in. It still would create the Landmarks Preservation Commission as an independent expert body of eleven members empowered to designate and regulate landmarks and historic districts. It would remain an independent agency and not become part of the City Planning Commission as some had argued it should.[116] The council had added the requirement that each borough be represented on the commission. Despite calls for more precise definitions that would spell out in detail what would constitute a landmark or an historic district, the committee maintained the approach of providing broad conceptual definitions letting the commission make

■ ■ ■ ■ ■ ■ ■

those determinations through its work. By not predetermining landmarks by particular style or building type, the legislation maintained the flexibility that has come to serve the law so well. The council did add one concrete requirement to landmark eligibility, that buildings needed to be "30 years or older."[117]

The bill retained the proposed procedures and processes for the workings of the commission. In particular, it kept intact the hardship provision that created a process through which landmark owners could seek to prove that their landmark was causing them a financial hardship. If successful in making this claim, special tools and a public process would then be activated and citizens and the city would have a specified period of time in which to try and redress the hardship and save the building. If that final opportunity could not produce a solution, then the law permitted the loss of that landmark. The weekend demolition of the Brokaw mansion had underscored the need for such a period of time to respond to crisis situations. In this way, the legislation sought to make sure that no landmark was unnecessarily lost.

Some landmark proponents felt the hardship provision weakened the legislation by allowing the demolition of designated buildings. However, it was landmark opponents who objected the most to how it had been drafted, finding fault with the proposed definition of what should constitute a reasonable rate of return and hence determine when a landmark owner faced a financial hardship. The council's committee held firm on this provision. Goldstone called the hardship provision the law's "safety valve" and the passage of time has demonstrated the wisdom of its inclusion in the law. Ultimately, it has been seen as a key provision strengthening the defensibility of the legislation in the courts.[118]

The proposed Landmarks Law did not come out of committee entirely unscathed. The real estate interests opposing the bill had been able to extract two important concessions. The first dealt with what was reported by both the press and those inside the process to be the main objection to the bill, the so-called "400-foot provision."[119] Under this part of the proposed legislation, the commission would have had jurisdiction over all property within four hundred feet of a landmark in all directions, potentially covering up to eight blocks. As Municipal Art Society president Giorgio Cavaglieri explained the provision, "It simply wishes to have the construction around Landmarks under the supervision of the Landmarks Preservation Commission. That is, it intends to preserve the character and the proportions of the environment of the Landmark."[120]

■ ■ ■ ■ ■ ■ ■ ■

Aesthetically important as such authority could have been, preservationists did not view the elimination of this provision as a great loss—actually quite the contrary. Reminiscing about the horse-trading that went on over the legislation, Platt remembered this provision as a useful bargaining chip. "We had a wonderful bone to throw the 'dogs,' which was that in one of the original drafts it said that an area four hundred feet from each landmark should be under the jurisdiction of the Landmarks Preservation Commission. Nobody thought this was a good idea. They reacted very strongly against this. And so we were able to say, 'Well, we'll give that up' . . . it was put in sort of seriously at first, then, we realized it would never work."[121] The provision had also attracted the attention and concern of the Bar Association of the City of New York.[122]

The second compromise was a true concession and one with possible serious repercussions. Instead of a proposed deletion from the legislation, it was the other threat preservationists had feared: a potentially debilitating addition to the law. The city council, responding to pressure from the real estate interests, inserted a moratorium clause into the bill.[123] After an initial eighteen-month period for designations, there would be a thirty-six-month "hiatus" during which the commission would not be able to designate properties. "Successive 6-month-designating and 36-month non-designating periods would follow."[124]

For Harmon Goldstone, accepting the provision was "a tactical move in winning Council approval of the bill."[125] It was seen differently by the *New York Times*, whose editorial column deplored this provision of the law:

> But its weakness, which has been consistently soft-pedaled, lies in an extraordinary joker in the final revision, called a "moratorium" clause. . . . But this extremely questionable solution is no more than an ironic guarantee of speculative destruction as usual—under protection of the preservation law itself. . . . The effect of this provision is that the law can be used for its basic purpose—selection of buildings or districts for protection—only once every three years. . . . The rest of the time this power stays under glass, like a pressed flower or a lacy valentine.[126]

Platt saw the moratorium differently: "It was criticized quite strongly, and was finally given up some time later, but that's all right; it was really very helpful to the Statutory Commission, because it was absorbing an awful lot of material, so to speak. Hearing all kinds of buildings, wondering what to do about them. People were making threatening noises of one kind or another. That gave the Commission a chance to pull itself together."[127] Those who would have to implement the law saw this silver lining in the moratorium cloud. When the law was amended in 1973 the moratorium provision was eliminated.

Goldstone, in his thoughts on the moratorium, offers an insight into the motivation of those who had proposed it: "Quite frankly, the Real Estate Board and some of our dearest friends thought, 'This idiotic piece of legislation is obviously unconstitutional; give us a year to have it in the courts, and we'll be rid of it; and all the preservationist hullabaloo will die down.'"[128] In his interview with preservation historian Charles Hosmer, Goldstone sheds further light on what he believed to be the real estate community's reasoning behind the clause: "After the first year, the law will be killed; it will be unconstitutional. We'll never have to worry about the next period.' I think that was the cynical backing of it."[129]

This also helps explain why the real estate community seemed willing to focus their energy on amending the proposed legislation rather than trying to kill it outright. Realizing that for the moment they had lost the landmarks battle in the court of public opinion and hence with the politicians, their strategy was to go to the real courts and win the war there, once and for all.

Clearly attributed to the real estate community, it is not clear who specifically originated the suggestion of the moratorium. Though James Felt had stepped down as chair of the City Planning Commission in 1963, he remained on the commission until the end of January 1965. He continued to be a man of great influence. Years earlier, when his proposed new zoning resolution was facing strong opposition, as a strategy to mute the opposition he brought forth the idea of a one-year grandfather period, or moratorium, on the implementation of the new resolution. Knowing Felt's personal involvement in helping launch the pre-law Landmarks Preservation Commission, aware that preservation insiders credit him with helping tone down the real estate community's opposition to the bill, and seeing the similarity of these two tactical responses to opposition, it is hard not to speculate that Felt might have had a hand in developing this moratorium concept. No hard evidence has yet been found to link Felt to the moratorium concept, but his possible involvement in shaping it has been deemed a credible theory by Seymour Boyers, one of the key players in the drama.[130]

The city council was under pressure not only to weaken the law, but to strengthen it. Among others, the *New York Times* called for "the inclusion of provisions for natural and landscaped areas that would safeguard the city's park heritage, presently excluded from the bill."[131] Considering the number of preservation battles fought over parks issues, the request was a natural. At that very moment, the battle over the proposal to build an underground garage at Madison Square Park was raging and, further disheartening the civic community, the New York Court of Appeals had just ruled in favor of the construction of the Huntington Pavilion at the southeast corner of Central Park.[132]

There were also calls to expand the scope of the proposed legislation to include interiors. The original make-up of the commission called for a "practitioner of fine arts," which the council committee dropped, noting that the bill only applied to exteriors, so this was "unnecessary."[133] Indeed, according to Goldstone, both the inclusion of interiors and landscape features had been thought of during the drafting of the law, "but all of us felt, 'Look we're biting off a lot. Let's chew this and then wait for a while.'"[134]

There was concern among supporters of the legislation that attempts to strengthen it might prove true the old proverb, "The best is the enemy of the good." A report to the Municipal Art Society Board on a discussion at the West Side Democratic Club on the proposed legislation observed that "the greatest danger to the legislation are the friends of it. For example, several people at the meeting thought the preservation of the interiors of landmarks should be included in the Bill. This is unwarranted and unnecessary . . . as it might not let the Bill pass in its present form."[135] As Goldstone would comment on those who sought to get more into the legislation, "That was where the zealots don't know how to bend, or when to bend. We were being a little more realistic and we got what we wanted."[136]

The Landmarks Preservation Commission was very much involved in the process of revising the draft law. Its leadership sought to shepherd the legislation through the committee as intact as possible. They were intimately involved in the process of negotiation and compromise. They knew it was absolutely critical to get the bill reported out of committee and for that to happen, a balance had to be struck. Because of the political dynamics of the city council, in all likelihood, the bill reported out of the committee would be passed by the larger body.[137] The Landmarks Commission helped deflect the efforts to expand the scope of the law while accepting the amendments that would curtail its own power.

The game would be won or lost in the council committee and the commission was careful to put a very positive spin on its workings with it. James Van Derpool commented to the press, "This is a good committee, interested, informed, and thoughtful. We have an immense good will working for us now and I am very hopeful that we will see a good bill passed."[138] Goldstone succinctly stated the commission's goal: "We tried to get the essentials of the law, and let people get used to it, and let them live with it, and discover we were not ogres and monsters."[139] Platt and Goldstone and their allies in the process played their cards astutely and achieved that goal.

Speaking from the floor of the council on the day his committee voted on the bill, Boyers was interviewed for the Municipal Art Society's newsletter. He announced that the bill would be voted out of the committee and go to the full council. He accurately predicted, "The bill should be law within a month. I don't anticipate any trouble; the groundwork has been well laid. The bill has been altered a little, but I wouldn't say it has been watered down; if anything, it has been strengthened in spots."[140] Though some would be disappointed that the bill did not go further, those closest to the action were pleased with the results. The American Institute of Architects would call Boyers an "adroit champion" of the bill.[141] Underscoring the magnitude of getting the Landmarks Law through the council, Platt would comment, "In 1960, nobody dreamt that such a bill could be passed."[142]

Though the legislation had successfully emerged from committee and the politically astute were convinced of its passage, preservation forces were too wary to start celebrating. As the Municipal Art Society's newsletter cautioned, "In Spite of Councilman Boyers' optimism, there may be days of reckoning to come. Proverbially, anything can happen in a legislature, so it may be too early to pull the corks and bring on the dancing girls."[143] In fact, events emerged to suggest that the wrecking ball might put in another appearance before that of the "dancing girls."

The threat to the Old Merchant's House was fanning the flames that had ignited into a full conflagration at the demolition of the Brokaw mansions. The *Villager* passionately reported: "Its great dignity and beauty, shabby and threadbare, threatened by the swinging demolitionist's ball to make way for another garage, the plight of the Old Merchant's House at 29 E. Fourth St. may be the *cause celebre* needed to get the Landmarks Bill passed by the City Council."[144] Even the likes of *Cue* joined the fray. Its story "S.O.S. For New Yorkers: Save Our Landmarks," decried:

This appalling lack of civic pride and awareness of our architectural heritage is evident to any visitor of our city. One of the true measurers of a city's maturity is its attitudes toward its architectural heritage, its past. Using this yardstick, New York rates an absolute zero among the world's great cities. . . . New York appears to be a city savagely intent on destroying itself, on transforming itself into a jungle with civilized amenities a vague memory, on finally driving to the suburbs all foolhardy citizens fighting to make the city habitable.[145]

Fortunately, this was not yet the case. There were still many citizen activists willing to fight for New York City and a new generation of them was taking to the streets.

In early March 1965, as Boyers' committee was still hammering away at the legislation, school children in New York City marched to protest the possible demolition of the Old Merchant's House. The *Times* captured the sensation, as some one hundred "placard-carrying, guitar-playing youngsters" marching through the Lower East Side. Winding their way down Second Avenue to the strains of "Where have all the landmarks gone. Gone to ruins, most everyone," the marchers ended up on the steps of the Old Merchant's House.[146] Greeted there by state senator Frederic S. Berman and James Van Derpool, they gathered signatures on petitions destined for city hall. The organizers of this March 6 protest invited other schools and Boy and Girl Scout troops to join with them in a second march planned to bring the petitions to city hall.[147]

Here was another press bonanza for the cause of preservation. The *Villager*, as poetic orator, caught the excitement of the moment: "Blasted from their smouldering state of passive resistance to the loss of their historic landmarks by the plight of the Old Merchant's House, and the recent demise of the Brokaw mansion, the repressed objections of the people of the city of New York have surfaced, resulting in the aroused public opinion that may well have turned the tide destroying their heritage."[148]

Events began to unfold quickly. Boyers' committee reported the bill out on March 23. On the twenty-eighth City Council president Paul R. Screvane publicly announced he was confident the bill would pass the full council. Underscoring the urgency for final council action was yet another breaking story of a doomed landmark. The Friends Meeting House, at 144 East 20th Street, was sold to a developer to be replaced by an apartment house. Seizing the moment, Geoffrey Platt made the most of this development, commenting to the press, "The loss of this handsome, unique building is an example of the necessity for the landmark legislation now pending."[149] The vote on the bill was scheduled for the city council's next meeting.

Sitting in the center gallery of the council chamber on March 30, 1965 to watch the vote were thirty "young leaders of the children's crusade for the Landmarks Preservation Bill to save the Old Merchant's House and other historic landmarks" who had arrived that afternoon at city hall with

Downtown Community students on the march: from the left, Isobel Abzub, Lisa La Preile, Celeste Derr, (partly hidden), carrying sign, and Nina Cohen. Taken for The Villager by Jeff Kamen.

FIGURE 12.12   While the proposed Landmarks Law was still under review by the City Council in the spring of 1965, yet another preservation crisis loomed. The Old Merchant's House at 19 East Fourth Street was threatened to be replaced by a parking garage. Adopted as a cause by a local school, students strumming their guitars singing "Where have all the landmarks gone" marched to protest the threat to the landmark.

more than two thousand signatures on their petitions. As the press would report, these young citizens would get "their first disappointing taste of frustrating delay in government," as it was announced that because the "message of necessity" from the mayor allowing the bill to come to a vote that day had not been received, a required procedural technicality, action would be delayed another week.[150] After this truly final delay, on April 6, 1965, by a vote of thirty-three in favor and with two members absent, the city council passed New York City's Landmarks Law.

The legislation now needed only one signature to become a reality, the mayor's. Was there any doubt he would sign? The legislation had been introduced at his request. Traditionally, the city council followed his lead.[151] His Landmarks Commission had concurred with every change

FIGURE 12.13   Framed by the doorway of the threatened 1832 Old Merchants House, students marching to save the building are greeted by, from the left, Norman Studer, director of the Downtown Community School, State Senator Frederic S. Berman, who had introduced in Albany a resolution calling on the New York City Council to pass the landmarks bill, and James Grote Van Derpool, the executive director of the Landmarks Preservation Commission. The threat to the house kept attention focused on the pending Landmarks Law.

in the legislation. Could there be any doubt of his support? Though conventional wisdom suggested he would sign the bill, even with the amendments limiting its scope and curtailing its application, it was still deemed

controversial. Real estate opposition remained loud and public. As would be reported back to the Fine Arts Federation, at the mayor's public hearing on the legislation held immediately prior to his signing of the bill, "there had been a few anxious moments, when the old enemies of the bill had again brought up the arguments they had presented against its passage."[152]

The real estate interests urged the mayor to send the bill back to the council or to outright veto it. A representative of the Real Estate Board argued that the law would "seriously impede the modern expansion and progress of the city." He went on to recommend, one has to assume with a straight face, that "commemorative plaques" or other such means, be used to "preserve historic landmarks." The plaqued and demolished Brokaw mansion offered a silent, yet compelling rebuttal to his testimony.[153]

Despite this opposition, on April 19, 1965, Mayor Robert F. Wagner signed the Landmarks Law. At the signing of the law, the mayor referenced the controversy over the bill and sought to reassure its opponents. He stressed that if indeed it was found to be "too restrictive on property rights or did not meet the problems of landmark owners," he had assurances from Seymour Boyers that the city council would amend it. This was not exactly a ringing endorsement or a comforting notion to the forces for preservation.

Why did this mayor, habitually opposed to taking strong actions in the face of opposition, sign a bill still opposed by the Real Estate Board of New York, the Avenue of the Americas Association, the Commerce and Industry Association of New York, and the Downtown-Lower Manhattan Association?[154] Years later, speaking of Mayor Wagner, Brendan Gill would observe that Wagner was "the last person on earth you would have thought would have had legislation of this kind pass his desk in his time." Wagner was "a creature of the many powers more stronger than he."[155] So why did Wagner take real action and not just punt on this important issue?

Did Robert Wagner personally support preservation? Opinions are mixed. Not surprisingly, Goldstone's assessment of Mayor Wagner is much kinder and gentler than Gill's. Goldstone felt Wagner was "sincere. He was very cautious, and he was very wise. And I think he felt that landmark protection was awfully good for the city; he was always very supportive."[156] Remembering back to 1949 and early preservation battles in the Village, Wagner, in his brief stint as City Planning Commission Chair, had expressed his "interest in the preservation of the city's landmarks."[157] Years after the passage of the law, looking back over his

FIGURE 12.14 For decades, New York preservationists had been dreaming of this moment, the signing of a law to protect the city's landmarks. Finally, on April 19, 1965, it happened. Mayor Wagner's signing of the legislation, with Seymour Boyers looking on at the left, and chair Geoffrey Platt from the right, was documented by Margot Gayle of Jefferson Market Courthouse fame.

mayoralty, Wagner reflected that "creating the Landmarks Commission was probably the best thing that I ever did while I was the Mayor." Continuing in that vein, he observed, "It was the most lasting contribution from my administration."[158]

It is actually beside the point whether Wagner was personally supportive of preservation or neutral to it. Other variables likely determined his signing the legislation. The city council's committee report accompanying the bill suggests the political reality of the situation: "Testimony discloses that the City has been and is undergoing the loss and destruction of its architectural heritage at an alarming rate, especially so in the last 8–10 years. . . . The public, through individuals, groups, press, organizations and others, has strongly protested such loss and destruction and has widely argued that measures be taken immediately to prevent further loss and destruction."[159]

Not only was the public demanding landmark protection. Powerful people were working on its behalf. Brendan Gill credits Whitney North Seymour, Sr., with playing a key role. Seymour had been appointed by the Municipal Art Society in August of 1964 to serve as "the coordinator of efforts in behalf of the permanent establishment of the city's Landmarks Preservation Commission."[160] Of Seymour's role in getting the law passed, Gill said, "he was absolutely indispensable, because he was the most admired lawyer in New York. . . . I think it was because of Whitney Seymour, who had everyone's ear, and was demonstratively a big show Wall Street lawyer, who earned hundreds of thousands of dollars and had clout. When he said it was something that couldn't be ignored. . . . it couldn't be ignored."[161]

Clearly having the strong, involved support of prominent civic leaders like Seymour greatly assisted the cause, as did the increasing involvement of the rich and powerful. There were, however, equally if not richer and more powerful forces opposing the law, so it is likely its individual backers or detractors were not the determining factor in Wagner's decision. The nonpartisan embracing of the landmarks cause and its growing appeal among potential voters was less easy for a politician to ignore. Perhaps hardest to avoid was the unrelenting and increasingly hard-hitting media focus on the issue. Not only was it supportive of preservation, but, perhaps more importantly, it was increasingly derisive of the administration's inability to respond to what had become generally recognized as an enormous crisis.

Action had to be taken because the situation surrounding New York's landmarks had gotten spectacularly out of control in a highly public manner. Because of the escalating series of crises and landmarks sacrificed, an emergency situation existed both in reality and in the public consciousness. As Ada Louise Huxtable would write, landmarks were being "knocked down like ten-pins." Platt noted, "each time an important building was torn down, the shouts got louder."[162] Finally, as building after building was turned into dust, these shouts got so loud and the attacks on the administration so caustic that Mayor Wagner, even in the face of opposition from powerful special interests, had no alternative but to sign the bill to quiet the pro-landmarks preservation roar. The furor demanded action now, and as he indeed pointed out, the law could always be amended later. The mayor had to do something—and he did.

With the passage of the 1965 Landmarks Law, the story of how New Yorkers won the right to protect the city's landmarks ends. But another story begins. The individuals and institutions that had been working for decades to achieve this momentous accomplishment knew that real victory would be determined by their ability to put the law to work and to defend it from its detractors. They were well aware they had their work cut out for them. There was little time to pause and celebrate their accomplishment. Appropriate awards were given and thanks offered, but immediate action was required to put the law to work to stop the falling of more "architectural ten-pins."

As the *New York Times* editorialized at the law's passage: "It will take imagination, dedication, concern, citizen action, private financing and public cooperation to effect preservation under the new law. The past is yet to be secured for the future. Celebration is premature until we can point to a safe and substantial legacy. New York is still the city that marks its history with gaping holes in the ground."[163]

From the moment the law was passed to the present day, passionate New Yorkers have been hard at work using the law to secure the city's rich past for the future. The knowledge, experience, and expertise gained in the decades of advocacy for a landmarks law became a source of strength and inspiration for New York's preservationists as they sought to put the new law into action. It remains so today.

The story of how New York won the right to protect its landmarks is the shared history of all who continue to passionately campaign to preserve the landmarks of New York. It continues to color and influence preservation. Successes and failures alike, the history of the law provides an indispensable lens through which to better understand preservation's present and to inform its future.

The Landmarks Law, and indeed the history of the law, is a living legacy. What a priceless legacy it is!

ENDNOTES

1. Richard J. Whalen, "A City Destroying Itself," *Fortune*, September, 1964, 234.
2. Henry Lee, "The Fight to Save Old New York," March 1, 1964, Talbot F. Hamlin Collection, Avery Architectural & Fine Arts Library, Columbia University.
3. Thomas W. Ennis, "2 City Landmarks Feared in Danger," *New York Times*, November 1, 1963.
4. Michael T. Kaufman, "Time and Neglect Erode Landmarks," *New York Times*, March 1, 1964.
5. Henry Lee, "The Fight to Save Old New York," March 1, 1964, Talbot F. Hamlin Collection, Avery Architectural & Fine Arts Library, Columbia, University.
6. "Keeping Up with Progress," *Brooklyn World-Telegram*, November 13, 1963.
7. Goldstone notes for his Century Association talk "How the Landmarks Law Happened," February 3, 1972, Anthony C. Wood Archive.

8. Douglas Sefton, "Old Penn Station Reaches the End of the Line, *New York Daily News*, May 8, 1964.

9. Hosmer interview of Goldstone, 27; Geoffrey Platt, "What New York City Is Doing to Protect Its Landmarks," Pace, September, 1962; Alan Burnham, *New York Landmarks* (Connecticut: Wesleyan University Press,1963), 3; an annotated copy of the index is in the Van Derpool papers at Avery Library.

10. Emory Lewis, "S.O.S. for New Yorkers: Save Our Landmarks," *Cue*, March 13, 1965.

11. Gill's foreword to *New York Landmarks*, 14. Gill recalled that Burnham did the book "practically single-handed." Wood interview with Brendan Gill. Harmon Goldstone, who was president of the Municipal Art Society at the time of the book project, remembered that "Alan is a scholar and meticulously conscientious and terribly slow." Goldstone goes on to tell the story of how he embarrassed Burnham into speeding up his work by reporting at the Society's annual meeting (likely in 1961 or 1962), "'If Alan Burnham can maintain his present pace, the book will be published on December 14, 1998, projecting his rate of progress over the last years.' Of course, everybody roared with laughter, and that got the book out within a year!" Hosmer interview with Goldstone, 26–27.

12. Wood interview with Gill.

13. Emilie Tavel, "Architectural Battle Flares," *Christian Science Monitor*, October 30, 1963.

14. The nomenclature used to categorize this aspect of the commission's work is not consistent. In places the sites are referred to as "nominated for designation," in others as designated landmarks, and in still others as preliminary designations. Publicly, it was clear that sites on the commission's list had been officially recognized as landmarks.

15. "Proposed List of Obvious Buildings and Monuments for Designation," and other such lists in the Van Derpool Papers, Avery Library.

16. Wood, "Taking the Long View; An Interview with Harmon Goldstone," *Village Views*, 19.

17. Thomas W. Ennis, "Landmark Commission Seeks to Preserve Splendor of City's Past; Bid Made to Save 300 Old Buildings," *New York Times*, July 21, 1963.

18. Geoffrey Platt to Mayor Wagner, October 28, 1964, reporting on the Landmarks Preservation Commission's "activities for the budget year 1963–1964," Mayor Robert Wagner Papers, NYC Municipal Archives.

19. Goldstone notes for his Century Association talk, "How the Landmarks Law Happened," February 3, 1972, Anthony C. Wood Archive.

20. Ibid.

21. "Pearl E. Michelin Is GVA President," *Villager*, September 27, 1962; Perot Nichols, "Greenwich Village Association: Local Old Guard Sweeps All in Test of Voting Strength," *Village Voice*, October 18, 1962; "Drive Is Started to Save Landmarks," *Villager*, March 14, 1963.

22. "Landmarks Legislation," *New York Times*, October 22, 1963.

23. Goldstone notes for his Century Association talk, "How the Landmarks Law Happened," February 3, 1972, Anthony C. Wood Archive.

24. Pearsall's efforts began just days after the city council hearing on the draft landmark legislation. Clearly, those drafting the law were already well aware of at least some of these statutes prior to this formal survey of the field. The timing also suggests the ongoing nature of the drafting process. William R. Fisher to Bernard Friedlander, Corporation Counsel's Office, December 9, 1964; "Table of Statutes,"

■ ■ ■ ■ ■ ■ ■

prepared by Otis Pratt Pearsall, Otis Pratt Pearsall Papers, New York Preservation Archive Project.

25. Hosmer interview with Goldstone, 16–17; Wood, "An Interview with the First Chairman of the Landmarks Preservation Commission, The Late Geoffrey Platt," 30.

26. Platt to Wagner, October 28, 1964, Mayor Robert Wagner Papers, NYC Municipal Archives.

27. Ibid.; Goldstone notes for his Century Association talk, "How the Landmarks Law Happened," February 3, 1972, Anthony C. Wood Archive.

28. Mary Perot Nichols, "Face of a City: New York Is An Architectural Disaster," *Village Voice*, June 6, 1963.

29. Chris McNickle, *To Be Mayor of New York* (New York: Columbia University Press, 1993), 148.

30. Hosmer interview with Goldstone, 21.

31. Goldstone notes for his Century Association talk, "How the Landmarks Law Happened," February 3, 1972, Anthony C. Wood Archive.

32. Ibid. In her interview with Charles Hosmer, Margot Gayle shared her role in this episode. At the time, she was working in the city's Department of Public Events writing proclamations. She drafted one for preservation week and was told by the mayor's press secretary that "it was not appropriate." She misunderstood him, thinking he said it was appropriate. She sent it out and "everybody landed on poor Mayor Wagner" and, Margot recalled, she was "pulverized." Charles B. Hosmer, Jr., interview with Margot Gayle, June 23, 1982, 33, University of Maryland at College Park, National Trust for Historic Preservation Library Collection & Archives, University of Maryland at College Park Libraries.

33. See chapter 1.

34. "Vanishing Landmarks," *New York World-Telegram*, September 18, 1964.

35. Landmarks Preservation Commission press release, "Landmarks Preservation Week Proclaimed by Mayor Wagner," September 16, 1964; Notes for JGV Talk at Greenwich Village Symposium, auditorium, Loeb Center, New York University, September 29, 1964 in conjunction with American Landmarks Celebration Week in New York City, James Grote Van Derpool Papers, Avery Architectural & Fine Arts Library.

36. Copy of text of telegram on Municipal Art Society letterhead, September 17, 1964.

37. "Vanishing Landmarks," *New York World-Telegram*, September 18, 1964.

38. "The Disappearing Landmarks," *New York Times*, September 18, 1964.

39. Thomas W. Ennis, "City Considering Landmarks Code," *New York Times*, September 18, 1964.

40. Thomas W. Ennis, "Bill Would Save City Landmarks," *New York Times*, September 23, 1964.

41. City of New York Office of the mayor, "Press Release," September 23, 1964, Mayor Robert Wagner Papers, NYC Municipal Archives.

42. "Anything Left to Preserve," *New York Times*, September 24, 1964.

43. Edith Asbury, "City Move to Save Mansions Is Urged: Brokaw Demolition Scored by Speakers at Rally," *New York Times*, September 27, 1964.

44. Lawrence O'Kane, "City Council Gets Landmarks Bill," *New York Times*, October 7, 1964.

45. Minutes of the Meeting of the Officers and Directors of the Fine Arts Federation of New York, October 15, 1964, Fine Arts Federation of New York Records, Archives of American Art.

46. Hosmer interview with Goldstone, 22.

47. Thomas W. Ennis, "Coming Demise of Savoy Plaza Mourned by Student Marchers," *New York Times*, October 3, 1964. The *New York Times* addressed the issue in an editorial, "Down with the Savoy Plaza," which focused less on the importance of the existing building and more on the importance of its site: "On this critical, central New York site anything but the best will spell catastrophe. . . . If the results of this gigantic undertaking are of less than landmark quality it will be an urban disaster," August 24, 1964; Glenn Fowler, "48-Story Tower to Rise on Savoy Plaza Site," *New York Times*, December 16, 1964.

48. Glenn Fowler, "Furor Over Savoy Plaza and 1-Way Traffic Fades," *New York Times*, August 5, 1965.

49. Thomas W. Ennis, "Women Score G.M. On Building Plan," *New York Times*, January 20, 1965.

50. Stern, *New York 1960*, 1123.

51. Thomas W. Ennis, "Bill Would Save City Landmarks," *New York Times*, September 23, 1964; Ada Louise Huxtable, "The Salvage of Old Jeff," *New York Times*, September 23, 1964.

52. Whitney North Seymour, chairman, Committee on Legislation, the Fine Arts Federation of New York, letter to the editor, *New York Times*, November 17, 1964; "Anything Left to Preserve?" *New York Times*, September 24, 1964.

53. "Action to Save Landmarks," *New York Times*, October 19, 1964; "Landmark Legislation," *New York Times*, December 3, 1964.

54. Editorial WCBS-TV, "City Landmarks," November 18, 1964.

55. Wood, "An Interview with the First Chairman of the Landmarks Preservation Commission, the late Geoffrey Platt," 14.

56. Minutes of the Semi-Annual Meeting of the Fine Arts Federation, November 24, 1964, Fine Arts Federation of New York Records, Archives of American Art.

57. Lawrence O'Kane, "City Council Gets Landmarks Bill," *New York Times*, October 7, 1964.

58. Municipal Art Society Board Meeting Minutes, October 26, 1964, Municipal Art Society of New York Records, Archives of American Art.

59. Minutes of the 531 Meeting of the Board, 68th year, December 9, 1964, American Scenic and Historic Preservation Society Records, New York Public Library.

60. "Landmark Legislation," *New York Times*, December 3, 1964. This editorial and the one of October 19 ended with the same phrase: "without debilitating compromise."

61. Whitney North Seymour, letter to the editor, *New York Times*, November 20, 1964.

62. Wire from Secretary Udall to Boyers, Landmarks Preservation Commission scrapbook, Anthony C. Wood Archive; "Rabbi Urges Curb on Razing of City's Historic Landmarks," *New York World Telegram*, October 5, 1964.

63. George Douris and Howard Reiser, "Landmarks Bill Faces Revisions," *Long Island Star Journal*, December 4, 1964.

64. Henry S. F. Cooper, Jr., ed., "News of the Municipal Art Society," March 1965.

65. Roslyn Burton and Joe Barbato, "Queens Councilman Presides at Landmarks Bill Hearing," *Long Island Post*, December 10–13, 1964.

66. Wood, "An Interview with the First Chairman of the Landmarks Preservation Commission, the Late Geoffrey Platt," 15.

67. Wood interview with Platt, May 3, 2006.

68. Statement by James G. Van Derpool, executive director, Landmarks Preservation Commission at the Hearing on Bill No. 799, Int. No. 653 before the Codification Committee of the City Council of the City of New York, December 3, 1964, James Grote Van Derpool Papers, Avery Architectural & Fine Arts Library, Columbia University.

69. Testimony of Harmon Goldstone before the Codification Committee of the city council, December 3, 1964, Harmon Hendricks Goldstone Papers, The New York Historical Society.

70. "City Holds Landmarks Bill Hearing," *New York Times*, December 1964; "Landmark Hearing Fails to End Clash," *World Telegram*, December 4, 1964.

71. Wood, "An Interview with the First Chairman of the Landmarks Preservation Commission, the Late Geoffrey Platt," 24.

72. Anthony Wood with Dorothy Miner and Liz McEnaney interview with Judge Seymour Boyers, October 17, 2006, New York Preservation Archive Project.

73. Roslyn Burton and Joe Barbato, "Queens Councilman Presides at Landmarks Bill Hearings," *Long Island Post*, December 10–13, 1964.

74. Ralph C. Gross, Commerce and Industry Association, letter to the editor, *New York Daily News*, December 16, 1964.

75. Minutes of the 531 Meeting of the Board 68th Year, December 9, 1964, American Scenic and Historic Preservation Society Records, New York Public Library.

76. "The Crumbling Landmarks," *New York Times*, December 22, 1964.

77. "Landmarks Bill Faces Revisions," *Long Island Star Journal*; Roslyn Burton and Joe Barbato, "Queens Councilman Presides at Landmarks Bill Hearings, *Long Island Post*, December 10–13, 1964.

78. Thomas W. Ennis, "2 City Landmarks Feared in Danger," *New York Times*, November 1, 1963; "The Crumbling Landmarks," *New York Times*, December 22, 1964.

79. Andrew Dolkart, *Touring the Upper East Side* (New York: New York Landmarks Conservancy, 1995), 45–46.

80. Anthony Lukas, "Ex-Soviet Mission on Park Ave. Will Reopen as a Latin Center," *New York Times*, September 9, 1967.

81. Thomas W. Ennis, "2 Park Ave. Landmarks Saved from Razing," *New York Times*, January 6, 1965.

82. "Anything Left to Preserve," *New York Times*, September 24, 1964.

83. "The Crumbling Landmarks," *New York Times*, December 22, 1964.

84. "Miracle on 68th Street," *New York Times*, January 8, 1965.

85. Board Meeting Minutes of the Fine Arts Federation of New York, April 3, 1947, report on Fort Clinton luncheon by Albert Bard, Fine Arts Federation of New York records, Archives of American Art.

86. Thomas W. Ennis, "2 Park Ave. Landmarks Saved From Razing," *New York Times*, January 6, 1965; Peter Kihss, "Peter Grimm Dead; Real Estate Expert," *New York Times*, February 17, 1980.

87. Van Derpool's handwritten notes for a talk on the Percy Pyne Project, James Grote Van Derpool Papers, Avery Architectural 7 Fine Arts Library, Columbia University.

88. Ibid.; "Miracle on 68th Street," *New York Times*, January 8, 1965.

89. J. Anthony Lukas, "Ex-Soviet Mission on Park Ave. Will Reopen as a Latin Center," *New York Times*, September 9, 1967.

90. "Wrecker, Stop That Ball," *Newsweek*, January 25, 1965.

91. "Victory Over the Wreckers," *New York Herald-Tribune*, January 9, 1965; "One Who Cares," *New York Journal America*, January 9, 1965.

92. Thomas W. Ennis, "Marquesa Saved 2 Landmarks," *New York Times*, January 14, 1965.

93. "The Case of the Munificent Marquesa," *Progressive Architecture*, February 1965, 54.

94. "Victory Over the Wreckers" *New York Herald-Tribune*, January 9, 1965.

95. "Wrecker, Stop that Ball," *Newsweek*, January 25, 1965, 54.

96. "Miracle on 68th Street," *New York Times*, January 8, 1965.

97. Minutes of the Landmarks Meeting, January 20, 1965 at the Architectural League, chaired by Giorgio Cavaglieri, president of the Municipal Art Society, Municipal Art Society of New York; "A Statement of the Purpose of an Exhibition for Utilization of Landmark Buildings in New York City," April 8, 1965, Anthony C. Wood Archive.

98. "Rape of the Brokaw Mansion," *New York Times*, February 8, 1965; Daniel Selznick, "The Wreck of the Brokaw Mansions," *New York Herald-Tribune*, April 11, 1965.

99. Ada Louise Huxtable, "New York's Architectural Follies," *New York Times*, February 14, 1965.

100. See chapter 1.

101. Ada Louise Huxtable, "New York's Architectural Follies," *New York Times*, February 14, 1965

102. Michael F. Keating, "Landmarks 3," WCBS-TV Editorial, February 24, 1965.

103. Thomas W. Ennis, "Funds Sought to Save Landmark," *New York Times*, February 9, 1965.

104. Municipal Art Society Board Meeting Minutes, February 24, 1965, Municipal Art Society of New York records, Archives of American Art.

105. Included with the August 1964 "News of the Municipal Art Society," was a special Section II consisting of a list of buildings "currently being threatened or destroyed" compiled by Henry Hope Reed, Anthony C. Wood archive.

106. Ada Louise Huxtable, "1832 'Village' Landmark Faces Demolition," *New York Times*, February 18, 1965.

107. "A Landmark May Have Reprieve," *Villager*, February 25, 1965.

108. Daniel Selznick, "The Wreck of the Brokaw Mansions," *New York Herald-Tribune*, April 11, 1965.

109. See chapter 7.

110. Daniel Selznick, "The Wreck of the Brokaw Mansions," *New York Herald-Tribune*, April 11, 1965.

111. Built by Campagna in 1929–1930, the estate, in the style of a Tuscan village and overlooking the Hudson River and the Palisades, was designed by the architect Dwight James Baum. Among his other works are John Ringling's mansion in Sarasota, Florida, and the West Side YMCA on Manhattan's West 63rd Street. Located across the street from Wave Hill, its award winning landscape design was by Vitale & Geiffert. Mervyn Rothstein, "Debating Limits on Landmark No. 1,003," *New York Times*, January 16, 1994.

112. "As the Wrecker's Ball Swings," *New York Times*, March 15, 1965; Seymour Boyers, "Landmarks 4," WCBS-TV Editorial, March 8, 1965; Seymour Boyers, letter to the editor, *New York Times*, March 27, 1965.

113. Thomas W. Ennis, "Landmarks Bill Goes to Council," *New York Times*, March 24, 1965.

114. Hosmer interview with Goldstone, 22.

115. The committee's report provides a detailed account of the changes that the committee made to the legislation. "Report of the Committee on Codification in Favor of Adopting a Local Law to Amend the Administrative Code of the City of New York in Relation to the Establishment and Regulation of Landmarks, Landmark Sites and Historic Districts," Proceedings of the Council of the City of New York from January 6 to June 29, 1965, vol. 1, 499.

■ ■ ■ ■ ■ ■ ■

116. James Whitford, "Everyone Wants to Save Landmarks—but How to Do It," *Staten Island Advance*, January 16, 1965.

117. "Report of the Committee on Codification in Favor of Adopting," Proceedings of the Council of the City of New York from January 6 to June 29, 1965, vol. 1, 500.

118. Ibid.; Hosmer interview with Goldstone, 19.

119. Frederick Woodbridge reported to the Municipal Art Society that the four-hundred-foot provision was the "main objection to the Bill," Municipal Art Society Board Meeting Minutes, February 24, 1965, Municipal Art Society; Thomas W. Ennis, "Landmarks Get City Protection," *New York Times*, April 11, 1965.

120. Giorgio Cavaglieri to E. H. Fullilove, chair, Board of Gov. Building Trades Employers Association, February 9, 1965.

121. Wood, "An Interview with the First Chairman of the Landmarks Preservation Commission, the Late Geoffrey Platt," 14.

122. "News of the Municipal Art Society," March 1965, 2.

123. Ibid., 15; Thomas W. Ennis, "Landmarks Get City Protection," *New York Times*, April 11, 1965.

124. "Report of the Committee on Codification in Favor of Adopting," Proceedings of the Council of the City of New York from January 6 to June 29, 1965, vol. 1, 500.

125. Wood, "An Interview with Harmon Goldstone," 40.

126. "A Landmark Law," *New York Times*, April 27, 1965.

127. Wood, "An Interview with the First Chairman of the Landmarks Preservation Commission, the Late Geoffrey Platt," 15.

128. Wood, "An Interview with Harmon Goldstone," 40.

129. Hosmer interview with Goldstone, 22.

130. Wood interview with Boyers, October 17, 2006.

131. Gilmartin notes that Councilman Paul O'Dwyer "argued eloquently" that historic parks should fall under the jurisdiction of the commission, Gilmartin, *Shaping the City*, 373; "The Crumbling Landmarks," *New York Times*, December 22, 1964.

132. "News of the Municipal Art Society," March 1965, 3–4.

133. "Report of the Committee on Codification in Favor of Adopting," Proceedings of the Council of the City of New York from January 6 to June 29, 1965, vol. 1, 500.

134. Hosmer interview with Goldstone, 24.

135. Board meeting minutes, February 24, 1965, Municipal Art Society Board Meeting Minutes, Municipal Art Society.

136. Wood, "An Interview with Harmon Goldstone," 41.

137. Wood, phone interview with Henry Stern, September 6, 2006.

138. "Immense Good Will for Landmarks Bill," *Villager*, March 11, 1965.

139. Wood, "An Interview with Harmon Goldstone," 41.

140. "News of the Municipal Art Society of New York," March 1965, Anthony C. Wood Archive.

141. "N.Y.C. Landmark Preservation Law Signed," *Oculus*, May, 1965.

142. "News of the Municipal Art Society," June 1965. Anthony C. Wood Archive.

143. "News of the Municipal Art Society," March 1965, 2, Anthony C. Wood Archive.

144. "A Landmark May Have Reprieve," *Villager*, February 25, 1965

145. "S.O.S. for New Yorkers: Save Our Landmarks," *Cue*, March 13, 1965.

146. Bernard Weinraub, "Children Picket for a Landmark, 100 Protest Threat to Tear Down Merchant's House," *New York Times*, March 7, 1965.

147. Photo caption, *Villager*, March 11, 1965; "Passive Resistance Stirs At Last," *Villager*, March 18, 1965.

■ ■ ■ ■ ■ ■ ■

148. "Passive Resistance Stirs at Last," *Villager*, March 18, 1965.

149. "Quaker Building to Be Razed Here," *New York Times*, March 29, 1965.

150. "The Wheels in the City Turn Slowly," *Villager*, April 1, 1965.

151. Dorothy Miner and Anthony C. Wood interview with Robert Low, July 16, 2002, New York Preservation Archive Project.

152. Minutes of the annual meeting of the Fine Arts Federation, April 29, 1965, Fine Arts Federation of New York Records, Archives of American Art.

153. Thomas W. Ennis, "Landmarks Bill Signed by Mayor," *New York Times*, April 20, 1965.

154. Ibid.

155. Wood interview with Brendan Gill, July 2, 1984.

156. Wood, "An Interview with Harmon Goldstone," 39.

157. "Manning Presses His fight on Law Center Proposed by N.Y.U. for Washington Square," *New York Times*, March 17, 1948.

158. Wagner made these comments to the architect and former Landmarks Preservation commissioner Charles A. Platt, who with Diane Coffey, interviewed Wagner on May 27, 1982 to get his thoughts on possible alterations to Gracie Mansion. Charles A. Platt, email message to author, April 27, 2005.

159. "Report of the Committee on Codification in Favor of Adopting," Proceedings of the Council of the City of New York from January 6 to June 29, 1965, vol. 1, 502.

160. "News of the Municipal Art Society," August 1964, Anthony C. Wood Archive.

161. Wood interview with Gill. A fuller appreciation of Whitney North Seymour, Sr.'s role awaits us. His considerable papers are at the New York Public Library. Unfortunately, at the time of this writing, because of the terms of the gift of the papers to the library, they were not yet open to the public.

162. "A Landmarks Law," *New York Times*, April 27, 1965; "News of the Municipal Art Society of New York," June 1965, Anthony C. Wood Archive.

163. "A Landmark Law," *New York Times*, April 27, 1965.

EPILOGUE

WHAT A DIFFERENCE A LAW MAKES!

Without one, there was no salvation for the Brokaw mansions or Pennsylvania Station. With one, New York City has protected over eleven hundred individually significant buildings since 1965. Among them are the Old Merchant's House, the Friends Meeting House, and the Astor Library, all of which faced uncertain futures while the law was being debated.

The vast majority of the over twenty-four thousand structures protected by the Landmarks Preservation Commission are found within the boundaries of New York City's more than eighty-five historic districts. Included in these districts are significant portions of Brooklyn Heights and Greenwich Village, their long-sought protection finally achieved through historic district designation. To describe fully the current inventory of what the law protects, one must add over one hundred historic interiors and a handful of scenic landmarks whose designation was made possible by the 1973 amendment to the law.[1]

It is hard to overstate the full impact the Landmarks Law has had on New York City. When we look at the list of what has been saved since 1965, we see the absolute heart and soul of New York City. However, despite its over forty years in existence, the law has been used to protect less than 3 percent of the city's tax lots.[2] Despite its incredible success, New York City has continued to lose buildings that many believed the law should have saved. In 1967, Ernest Flagg's 1908 Singer Building was demolished. The *AIA Guide to New York City* called this the "city's greatest loss since Penn Station."[3] In 2005, the city suffered the destruction of the façades of Edward Durell Stone's 1964 Gallery of Modern Art

FIGURE 13.1   As Pulitzer-Prize-winning author Arthur M. Schlesinger Jr. has observed: "It is useful to remember that history is to the nation as memory is to the individual." Such is also the case for the preservation movement. Its history, including the near loss of Castle Clinton—seen here in an infrared photograph from 1950—continues to provide inspiration and insight.

(popularly known as 2 Columbus Circle). Of 2 Columbus, architect and historian Robert A. M. Stern said "by any and every standard of what a landmark is, this is a landmark."[4]

Clearly having a landmarks law isn't enough. Preservation ultimately depends on how it is used.

Some contemporary laments are eerily similar to those heard in the Pre-Landmarks Law days. Commenting on the 2006 loss of an unprotected building, Fred Bernstein wrote in *Oculus*, "Has any other society dismantled so many of its monuments so willingly?"[5] Concern has even reached the general press; *amNew York*, a citywide free daily paper, in a high profile, well-illustrated story headlined: "Urban gems under threat," reported "preservationists are astonished by the breadth of the losses, and troubled by the fate of other worthy buildings."[6] Many preservation activists perceive that New York City is again facing a true landmark crisis.[7] When treasures ranging from the historic Officers Row at the Brooklyn Navy Yard to the glorious St. Thomas the Apostle Roman Catholic Church in Harlem are being sentenced to the landfill, there is cause for concern.

The future, however, may well be even more troubling than the present. It is now predicted that by 2030, New York City will be the home of another one million people.[8] The pressure on New York's landmarks, those officially recognized and those yet to be, will increase as New York City begins to address its future housing and

Singer Building, 41 Stories, Highest Building in the World
Broadway and Liberty Street

FIGURE 13.2 Even since the passage of the Landmarks Law, New York City has lost some incredible architectural treasures. High on that list would be Ernest Flagg's stunning forty-seven-story tower, the Singer Building. Built in 1908, it was demolished in 1967.

infrastructure needs. There is talk of the need for new Moses-scale projects. The effort to "rehabilitate Robert Moses" and whet our appetite for new master builders is well under way. Where are the plans and resources needed for securing a future for our threatened past?

There are multiple reasons why the Landmarks Law has, in some opinions, underachieved. High on that long list are soaring real estate values, development pressures, economic realities, political dynamics, and limited New York City resources. Indeed it is remarkable how much has been saved in the face of these powerful forces. In addition to these external forces at work to undercut the law, there are internal ones that have their origins in the law and its history. I would like to posit that the history of the Landmarks Law suggests some interesting additional answers to the question, "Why does New York City continue to lose buildings New Yorkers would rather be saving?" The answers are worthy of some critical investigation.

It is not only the Landmarks Law that is the living legacy. The attitudes and behaviors that were forged by the same sequence of events that hammered out the shape of the law are themselves another legacy that continues to influence preservation today.

As William Faulkner has written, "The past is never dead. It's not even past."[9]

What a difference historical perspective can make! The following possible answers to why we continue to lose important buildings are not offered as proven conclusions. It will be up to historians of the post April 19, 1965 period to ultimately make such judgments. Instead these answers are presented to provoke preservationists into some much-needed thinking about what we do and how we do it, well or not.

The history of the Landmarks Law suggests many buildings are still being demolished because of the historic reticence of the Landmarks Preservation Commission.

The law reads: "It is hereby declared a matter of public policy that the protection, enhancement, perpetuation and use of improvements and landscape features of special character or special historical or aesthetic interest or value is a public necessity and is required in the interest of the health, prosperity, safety and welfare of the people."[10]

"Public necessity" is not public nicety. Providing New York City with a "public necessity" is a compelling mandate. It requires strong and decisive action. From the law's passage in 1965, that has not been the modus operandi of the Landmarks Preservation Commission. Rather, timidity and conservatism have more often characterized the agency's behavior. It is understandable that the commission began its work cautiously. Remember, ringing in the commission's ears was the message Mayor Wagner sent when he signed the law: if it causes problems, it will be swiftly amended.[11]

With a law finally in place, the new commission ventured into unmapped territory. Neither the law nor the Bard Act had been proven in the courts. As Geoffrey Platt would recall years later: "My objective during those— all the years that I was chairman, was to—that the most important thing was to preserve the Landmarks Preservation Commission."[12] Caution was the rule and, as a result, architectural treasures were lost. Conservatism and caution became the commission's mantra. There was, however, a line in the sand it would not cross.

In the early 1970s, the commission confronted a tower proposed for Grand Central Terminal. As Goldstone tells it, "But when it came to Grand Central, I said, we may well be torpedoed, but let's go down with all the flags flying."[13] The Landmarks Preservation Commission chose to risk the law to save the terminal. If the law was unable to save Grand Central, what good was it? By the time the law was affirmed in a 1978 Supreme Court victory, there was another reason for new confidence at the Landmarks Preservation Commission. It now had an established track record of accomplishment, performance, professionalism, and acceptance. Despite these critical changes, conservatism continues to characterize the agency's behavior.

The historical circumstances that shaped the commission's cautious behavior are long gone. After forty years, one would hope the commission has become secure and strong enough to advance preservation as the "public necessity" the law mandates it to be. Yet the old behavior remains, as does its acceptance by most New Yorkers. Have new factors constraining the commission's full application of the law just replaced the historic ones? Or, after all these years, has the commission's timid behavior become an ingrained natural default position? Knowing this answer will help determine what needs to be done to secure for New York City the full benefit of the law that its citizens worked so hard to put in place.

Despite its landmarks law, New York City continues to particularly experience the destruction of sites of cultural and historical significance. Whether it is the 2001 demolition of Catholic Worker cofounder Dorothy Day's cottage at the 1929 Spanish Camp, a Staten Island seaside summer retreat founded by Spanish-American immigrants, or the 2006 assault on St. Brigid's Roman Catholic Church in Manhattan's East Village built by Irish immigrants escaping the potato famine, losses of culturally significant buildings continue to mount.[14]

FIGURE 13.3 When it came to Grand Central Terminal, the Landmarks Preservation Commission was willing to put the Landmarks Law to the ultimate legal test. The Supreme Court case that resulted captured the interest of the nation. Here, Jacqueline Kennedy Onassis, New York City commissioner of cultural affairs, Henry Geldzahler, and the children of two preservationists, at the left Nancy Menapace, daughter of Municipal Art Society President Ralph Menapace and Ariel Hyatt, daughter of Gordon Hyatt, are seen in April of 1978 riding the Municipal Art Society's special "Landmarks Express" train to Washington, D.C. to focus media attention on the case.

Add to these the demolition of the Revere Sugar Refinery in Red Hook, Brooklyn, the doomed Duffield Street Houses in downtown Brooklyn, with their connections to the history of the abolitionist movement, and the still unprotected status of the Beachside Bungalows in Far Rockaway, Queens, and the unmet challenge is apparent.[15] As development pressures now threaten entire communities of historic and cultural importance, the problem only grows.[16] The national phenomenon of teardowns, out-of-scale structures replacing older homes in existing historic neighborhoods

■ ■ ■ ■ ■ ■ ■ ■

FIGURE 13.4 Despite their equal legal footing, sites of cultural and historical significance have not fared as well under the Landmarks Law as those of architectural importance. Seen here is the modest bungalow at Spanish Camp on Staten Island where Dorothy Day, instrumental in the Catholic Worker movement, lived. The bungalow was demolished; the Vatican is considering Day for sainthood.

and eroding their character, is evident in the Bronx, Brooklyn, Queens, and Staten Island.[17]

Again, history suggests at least a possible partial answer to these continuing losses: a deeply ingrained bias against the designation of sites of cultural and historical importance. Despite their equal footing in the Landmarks Law, the designation of architecturally important sites, representing the aesthetic roots of preservation, has long dominated over the designation of sites of historic and cultural value. It was, after all, the art societies, not the patriotic and historical societies, that developed the index of buildings that would initially guide the commission's work, and that list was titled An Index of Architecturally Notable Structures in New York City. The intellectual origins of the law, the architectural focus of the original lists, and the predominance of architects on the commission and architectural historians on its staff all help explain why sites of architectural value have received top priority.[18]

In the 1990s, the highly public and painful loss of several sites of cultural and historical value led the Municipal Art Society to create a Committee

FIGURE 13.5 In April 2001, on the verge of its designation by the Landmarks Preservation Commission, a bulldozer turned Dorothy Day's beachside bungalow at Spanish Camp on Raritan Bay on Staten Island into a pile of rubble. Here, veteran preservationist, Christabel Gough from the Society for the Architecture of the City, inspects the wreckage.

on Historical and Cultural Landmarks.[19] The committee issued a report that concluded: "The Landmarks Commission has never entirely neglected its broader historical and cultural mandate. . . . But despite these worthy efforts and the law's clear intent with respect to historically important structures and sites, the Commission has tended to favor architectural criteria in its decision-making."[20]

Despite the interest generated by the committee, a 1997 conference, and the creation of Place Matters by the Municipal Art Society and City Lore "to foster the conservation of New York's historically and culturally significant places," the preservation of these sites remains one of the most interesting and vexing problems facing preservation today.[21] Recognizing and understanding the bias against buildings of historical and cultural significance is the first step in addressing questions of how to preserve them.

It is not only sites of cultural and historic value that are still in harm's way; architecturally significant buildings from the mid-twentieth century are also filling dump trucks. This problem is not limited to New York

FIGURE 13.6 This June 2006 courthouse rally protesting the planned demolition of St. Brigid's Roman Catholic Church demonstrates the growing concern over threats to New York City's unprotected cultural and historical treasures. A church built by Irish immigrants in the 1840s, its preservation has been championed by parishioners, preservationists, and such prominent Irish organizations as the Ancient Order of Hibernians and the Grand Council of United Emerald Societies.

City.[22] Postwar sites have begun to appear on preservation-endangered building lists, such as the World Monuments Watch List of 100 Most Endangered Sites, the National Trust for Historic Preservation's America's 11 Most Endangered Historic Places list, and the Preservation League of New York State's Seven to Save. Among New York City's losses are Morris Lapidus' 1949 Paterson Silk Building on 14th Street and the historic façades of 2 Columbus Circle.[23] One possible answer to why such losses continue emerges from the attitudes shaped by the years of struggle to create the Landmarks Law. Generations of New Yorkers and preservationists have always been hostile to modern architecture.

The framers of the law wisely did not codify particular architectural styles or building types as determining criteria for landmark eligibility. The Landmark Preservation Commission was given considerable leeway

FIGURE 13.7 Among New York City's unprotected cultural and historic treasures are Far Rockaway's surviving Beachside Bungalows. Dating from the 1920s, these surviving remnants of this once-thriving working class summer resort have been the focus of an almost twenty-year preservation effort. Its leader, Richard George, exemplifies the tradition of civic activism that has helped save so many of New York's truly special places.

in what it could choose to designate as a landmark. The law was well drafted to allow for the protection of buildings from all architectural periods, whether classical or modern. Despite this, New York City has been slow to embrace saving buildings from the recent past.

Helping motivate preservationists in the 1950s was an unrelenting assault on New York City's historic fabric. Often, the design of many new buildings was foreign in appearance to architectural traditionalists. Modern buildings clashed with the sensibilities of many trying to protect what new buildings were replacing. In a spring 1965 call to support the Landmarks Law, Emory Lewis wrote in *Cue*, "Act now. Or the city will be all glass sky-scrapers—shiny and without a past."[24] For many, glass and steel and skyscrapers were the enemy. Preservation leaders such as Albert Bard, Edward Steese, and Henry Hope Reed regularly railed against such architecture. Attitudes about the preservation of the recent past often reflect generational divides among the general public and even within preservation's own ranks.

With great struggle, the Landmarks Law has been successfully utilized to protect some icons of modern architecture such as Lever House and the Seagram's Building. Significant but less well-known postwar buildings have not fared as well.[25] Efforts to build a constituency for saving these buildings emerged in the last half of the 1990s with the promulgation of lists of such sites, the hosting of exhibitions, and some media attention.[26] Current clashes over attempts to preserve twentieth-century buildings demonstrate how far we still have to go to preserve this chapter in New York City's architectural history.

Within the history of the Landmarks Law, one can find a host of plausible explanations for why New York City continues to lose what Albert Bard called "the patrimony of the people." Perhaps the most ironic of these is the possibility that the creation of the Landmarks Law itself inadvertently has contributed to the problem.

Since its passage, the Landmarks Law has been the almost singular preoccupation of New York's established preservation community. It was never intended to be the vehicle that could save everything everyone wanted to save. Yet, since 1965, the law has largely defined preservation efforts in New York City. Other avenues for advancing the preservation agenda, such as direct intervention in the real estate market, the creation of incentives for preservation property owners, the passage of additional laws, or the development of preservation-supportive zoning policies have not been robustly embraced in New York City, though they have been utilized elsewhere.[27]

The limits of the Landmarks Law have largely defined preservation expectations. Understanding how much was invested to pass the law and the passionate hopes those seeking the law had for what it could do for New York City, it is easy to see how the Landmarks Law and its various application have come to dominate New York's preservation scene. So long was a law seen as the missing implement in the preservation toolbox that once it existed, preservationists have put it to constant use.

Has the almost singular focus on the use of the law, at least partially borne out of its history, led preservationists to rely too heavily on it at the cost of developing alternative preservation tools? If all you have is a hammer, does everything look like a nail—have we let the tool shape some of the tasks at hand? Is it time for preservationists to take a more expansive view? Should preservation be more aggressively partnering with those advancing affordable housing and community development? Has the extreme focus on the law limited horizons, frozen creativity, and arrested creative development? Should preservation grow beyond the limits of the

Landmarks Law? A new cadre of preservation thinkers is beginning to ask and explore these questions.[28] The realization that New York preservationists have been living in a cage of their own creation is the first step toward venturing beyond its confines.

Is the law as strong as it needs to be? Are we losing some buildings because it contains inherent weaknesses? It has long been taboo in preservation circles to suggest strengthening the Landmarks Law through positive amendment. Though reasons abound to regard amendments to the law with healthy skepticism, the long reach of preservation's past helps account for the zero tolerance policy that comes in play when alterations to the Landmarks Law are discussed. Having witnessed the decades of struggle that it took to get the landmarks legislation introduced into the city council and having experienced the difficult and delicate maneuvering required to get that legislation through the legislative process, preservation's postlaw leaders were appropriately reluctant to open up the law. Even the successful 1973 effort to strengthen the Landmarks Law through amendments was less than warmly greeted by preservation's elders.[29]

With the exception of those amendments, when it has come to the law, the accepted behavior for preservationists has been to defend it from sporadic misguided efforts to weaken it. The other task has been to watchdog any changes required in the law to bring it into conformity with changing governmental realities, such as the elimination of the Board of Estimate. Preservationists have only played defense. Is it time to consider going on the offensive?

To stem the continued destruction of cherished New York buildings and sites, preservationists need to see their work in an historic context. As Winston Churchill instructed, "The farther backward you can look, the farther forward you are likely to see." Conditions, facts, situations have changed dramatically since 1965. How can preservationists respond to these changes? As the Landmarks Law approaches its second half-century of existence, knowledge of preservation's history should result in better choices and help avoid unnecessary losses.

When I started my search for the history of the Landmarks Law, I was motivated by a desire to know more about the New York City preservation movement that I wanted to join. Over the last almost thirty years, while in search of the origins of the law, I have become a part of that movement. I've had the privilege of working at such major preservation institutions as the Landmarks Preservation Commission, the Municipal Art Society, and the J. M. Kaplan Fund, and of serving on the boards of a wonderful assortment of preservation organizations.

■ ■ ■ ■ ■ ■ ■

For me, gaining an understanding of preservation's pre-Landmarks Law history has given me a more nuanced appreciation of preservation's recent past: the events, behaviors, and attitudes I've witnessed during my time on the front lines of the preservation movement. Looking through the lens of preservation's history, certain things become clearer while others cry out for further questioning. As Deborah Laycock of Kenyon College has aptly observed, "Our understanding of the past changes how we read the present moment."[30] Understanding preservation's history is no antiquarian exercise; it provides essential perspective and context too often absent from preservation today.

Preservation's past reveals at least one positive tradition that offers hope that New York City can meet future challenges. That tradition is citizen advocacy. If the law's history teaches us anything, it is the essential role the citizen advocate played in securing New York's right to protect its landmarks. Landmarks preservation depends on political will, and that begins with citizen advocacy.

The history behind the Landmarks Law is one replete with examples of inspired, dedicated, and passionate citizen activism. New York won its Landmarks Law because the people of New York—as individuals, united within various organizations, represented by their elected officials, having their concerns echoed in the media—demanded a law and, after successes and failures, they finally got one.

Ironically, though advocacy is one of the great legacies of the law, it was hoped, at least by some of the law's proponents, that with its passage, an orderly and rational governmental preservation process would preclude the need for the type of advocacy that had so long characterized preservation efforts.

In 1987, Harmon Goldstone reflected on prelaw preservation efforts and his hopes for how the law would effect change.

One pulled together an ad hoc committee of wonderful volunteers, organized torchlight processions and marches, issued pamphlets and so forth. Loads of fun. But it was a very wasteful procedure, because the minute one battle was over, the next one came up, and you had to go though the whole thing all over again. Of course once in a while it's very valuable to go through these things, because they're good for morale and public education. But both Geoff [Platt] and I—and I think I'm free to talk for him—felt that landmark protection should be an orderly, calm, legal procedure that would take care of itself automatically. . . . To a certain extent, yes: the publicity, the public

relations, and the whoopdeedo—you have to have a constituency; I will grant this. I don't like it, I don't like public actions. . . . And there are still many of these self-appointed committees, and self-appointed organizations, dozens of them who don't realize we have a law, we have a procedure, we have a method.[31]

Despite Goldstone's reservations, preservation advocacy has continued to serve preservation well. Though the law established an orderly process for systematically determining the landmark worthiness of sites based on individual merits, the same law also required that the commission's fact-based designation decisions be approved by a political entity, originally New York City's Board of Estimate and today the city council. In addition, the mayor has essential roles to play in that process—appointing the Landmarks Preservation Commission, naming its chair, and exercising the ability to veto council action on designations, subject to override by a two-thirds vote of the council. The law itself introduced political dynamics into the formal process and, in so doing, institutionalized the need for citizen advocacy.

Preservationists have no choice but to know their politics as well as they know their pilasters!

The advocacy behavior Goldstone found so disagreeable has been called on countless times to support the Landmarks Commission and its decisions. In recent years, the city council has become an increasingly important and active player in the landmark designation process.[32] So has the mayor. In swearing in Harmon Goldstone in 1968, Mayor Lindsay was quoted as saying: "I don't interfere with the designation of landmarks any more than I do with teachers and policemen. But when in any doubt on landmarks, I say, 'designate.'"[33] Times have changed. With an increasingly powerful real estate industry, astronomical property values, and memories of pre-Landmark Law days largely faded, mayoral support for preservation cannot be assumed.[34] The need for a vocal and visible preservation constituency is just as real today as in was in the 1950s and 1960s.

Advocacy has also played a key role in defending the law from those who would destroy it. Time and again, whether it be the threat to Grand Central Terminal in the 1970s or the battle over St. Bartholomew's Church in the 1980s, preservation advocacy has played a critical role in gaining the attention of the press. Over the years, the bright light of such publicity has helped make evident to politicians and jurists alike the fact that the values of historic preservation have been widely embraced by our society. The need for such reminders, however, remains constant.

■ ■ ■ ■ ■ ■ ■ ■

FIGURE 13.8 With the passage of the Landmarks Law, Harmon Goldstone hoped that the day of preservation "organized torchlight processions" was over. He failed to recognize that ongoing advocacy would be needed to support and encourage the ongoing work of the Landmarks Preservation Commission. Seen here in January of 1984, the author, right, holding the bag, helps organize the Municipal Art Society's candlelight vigil to save St. Bartholomew's Church, 44th Street and Park Avenue.

Events leading to the passage of the law and those following it make it clear that citizen advocacy is deeply imbedded in the preservation movement. A historical perspective suggests it is time to rethink preservation advocacy. Grassroots advocacy has begun to enter the twenty-first century. The unsuccessful though intense and extremely sophisticated campaign to obtain a public hearing to consider the landmark designation of 2 Columbus Circle demonstrates that the torchlight processions of Harmon Goldstone's era have become more sophisticated. Email blasts, webcams, and blogs have brought preservation fully into the twenty-first century.[35]

It is the preservation advocacy of New York's established civic community that needs to be rethought in response to changing circumstances.

FIGURE 13.9 The failure to save Edward Durell Stone's 2 Columbus Circle is destined to go down as a defining event in the history of preservation in New York City. Listed on World Monuments Watch List of 100 Most Endangered Sites, the National Trust for Historic Preservation's America's 11 Most Endangered Historic Places list, and the Preservation League of New York State's Seven to Save, 2 Columbus Circle is seen here surrounded by scaffolding, captured on Landmark West!'s twenty-four-hour webcam, the "SHAME CAM," as the 2005 Thanksgiving Day Parade passes by.

For decades, an unofficial preservation code of conduct largely guided that advocacy. Since the citywide civic organizations championing the cause of preservation were invited inside government in 1961 to help create the Landmarks Law, the civic community has largely deferred to and taken its cues from the mayor's committee and then from the Landmarks Preservation Commission.

This was only natural. These governmental entities were generously populated with the leadership of the civic community. In 1965, preservationists referred to the Landmarks Preservation Commission as "an unofficial arm" of the Municipal Art Society.[36] With prominent civic leaders either on the Landmarks Preservation Commission or its staff, it was logical that the established preservation community would not only follow the agency's lead, but be extremely protective of the commission, forming a common preservation front. During the commission's first eighteen years, it had four chairs, three of whom had been prominent leaders of the Municipal Art Society. Additionally, for many years, the ranks of landmarks commissioners were heavily populated with prominent civic leaders with strong ties to preservation-minded civic and professional organizations.

Over the decades, the unofficial close working relationship between such civic organizations and the commission served preservation well. On rare occasions, the civic community would challenge the commission's leadership on a major issue.[37] If there were disagreements with the agency, they were usually kept as private as possible, fearing that criticism from the preservation community could only weaken a commission already receiving criticism from real estate developers and other traditional enemies. An informal code of preservation conduct evolved.

Circumstances have changed, but not the code of conduct. Starting in the 1990s, the number of landmark commissioners with strong personal and professional ties to preservation-minded organizations began to decrease. Additionally, the tradition of appointing landmark commission chairs from the fields of architecture, planning, or preservation came to an end.[38]

Despite such changes and growing reservations about the way the Landmarks Preservation Commission goes about its work, there remain vestiges of that old code of conduct. An institutional reluctance among preservation organizations to publicly criticize the Landmarks Preservation Commission, even when privately taking issue with it, is still a dynamic of contemporary preservation politics.[39] Though there are a variety of tactical explanations for such behavior, its continued prevalence—in the face of such changed historic circumstances—suggests it may be a subconscious reflex, conditioned by years of ingrained behavior forged decades ago under circumstances bearing little resemblance to those of today.

Should the civic sector reassert the preservation leadership role it played in pre-Landmark Law days? Do changed circumstances call for a different type of advocacy? After close to half a century, is the preservation field and the Landmarks Preservation Commission strong enough to withstand and even benefit from thoughtful critical appraisal from inside the established preservation community?

■ ■ ■ ■ ■ ■ ■

FIGURE 13.10   Preservation's rich tradition of preservation advocacy did not stop with the passage of the Landmarks Law. Here, the famous August 2, 1962 AGBANY Pennsylvania Station picket line is restaged in June of 1988 to protest proposed changes to weaken the Landmarks Law. Here two veterans of the Pennsylvania Station campaign, Ray Rubinow, right with hat, and Alice Sachs, front center, join the author, left with glasses, in the successful protest.

Edward Finch, the Municipal Art Society's counsel, wrote in June of 1965 after the passage of the law: "We have won an important legislative battle but it is not the end of the Landmark's war by any means. Vigilance is the price of preservation."[40] This is also perhaps the greatest lesson to be found in preservation's history.

The story of the Landmarks Law is a story of vigilance—its price and its reward. Knowing that Albert Bard made his signature contribution to preservation at the age of eighty-nine, after over four decades of civic engagement, should encourage us all. There are lessons to be learned from the victories and defeats on the road to the law. But, beyond valuable inspiration and instruction, the history of the law provides context and perspective, both essential for preservationists today.

One closing cautionary note. Though an awareness of preservation's past is essential for a heightened preservation consciousness, it cannot guarantee that consciousness. "I watched as Penn Station was ripped down and saw what a tragedy that was." This statement was made by the developer Donald Trump, who went on to demolish the art deco Bonwit Teller building at Fifth Avenue and 56th Street, reminding us that even the powerful lessons of preservation's past are filtered through the eyes and the heart of the beholder.[41]

Still ringing as true today as it did when issued in the 1970s is the greeting the Municipal Art Society then gave to preservation's new recruits and I now heartily offer to all who feel compelled to join the presevation cause, "Welcome to the fight."

ENDNOTES

1. The latest landmark designations figures are available on the Landmark Preservation Commission's website.

2. In Barbaralee Diamonstein-Spielvogel, *The Landmarks of New York*, she notes there are 837,844 tax lots in the city (excluding condominiums). The number of structures under the jurisdiction of the Landmarks Preservation Commission is usually cited as 24,000. Though the less than 3 percent figure is at best an imprecise measure, it does provide a larger context in which to place the city's landmarks.

3. Elliot Willensky and Norval White, *AIA Guide to New York City* (New York: Harcourt Brace Jovonovich, 1988), 863.

4. Robert A. M. Stern, David Fishman, and Jacob Tilove, *New York 2000* (New York: Monacelli Press, 2006), 778, 777–779.

5. Fred Bernstein, "105-Year Watch," Oculus, summer 2006.

6. Rolando Pumul, "Urban Gems Under Threat," *amNew York*, December 18, 2006.

7. Indications of unhappiness with the performance of the Landmarks Preservation Commission among preservationists can be found in such documents as the Committee on Governmental Operations, "Forty Years of New York City Landmarks

Preservation: An Opportunity to Review, Reflect and Reform," (New York: The Council of the City of New York, August 2005); Women's City Club Report. The creation in 2006 of the Citizens Emergency Committee to Preserve Preservation is an indication of the heightened level of concern over the direction and operation of the Landmarks Preservation Commission. Concerns about the Landmarks Preservation Commission have also been covered in the press, including Nicolai Ouroussoff, "Turning Up the Heat on a Landmarks Agency," *New York Times*, November 14, 2005.

8. "Mr. Bloomberg's Future Vision," *New York Times*, December 24, 2006.

9. Thanks to David Doheny for reminding me of this gem and for pinpointing it to William Faulkner's *Requiem for a Nun* (New York, 1952).

10. Local laws of the City of New York, Administrative Code, Title 25, Chapter 3, 25–301.

11. "Landmarks Bill Signed by Mayor," *New York Times*, April 20, 1965.

12. Wood, "An Interview with the First Chairman of the Landmarks Preservation Commission, The Late Geoffrey Platt," 24.

13. Wood, "An Interview with Harmon Goldstone," 32.

14. Dan Barry, "Historic Bungalow Camp Is Facing the Bulldozers," *New York Times*, August 14, 1998; Dan Barry, "Inquiry Delves Into Razing of S. I. Cottages in Line for Historic Status," *New York Times*, March 12, 2001; Michael Luo, "Court Hears Arguments on Suit to Stop a Church's Demolition," *New York Times*, June 14, 2006; David Scharfenberg, "Neighborhood Report: East Village; Coming Back to Fight for the Church of Their Ancestors," *New York Times*, June 18, 2006; Michael Luo, "Demolition Starts at Historic Catholic Church in East Village," *New York Times*, July 28, 2006.

15. Michael Clancy, "A Bittersweet Day; Iconic Red Hook Sugar Refinery Faces Demolition," *amNew York*, December 8–10, 2006; "Three Small Houses Linked to the Abolition of Slaver: Destroyed for the Downtown Brooklyn Plan," *Village Views* 10, no. 1 (2006), 3–34; Diamonstein-Spielvogel, 23.

16. Ned Kaufman, "The Battle to Protect Sites of Community History in New York: What Happens When the Community Becomes the Site?" (Address, VIII Congreso Internacional de Rehabilitacion del Patrimonio Arquitectonico y Edificacion Centro Internacional para la Conservacion del Patrimonnio, Argentina, Buenos Aires, September 2006).

17. The National Trust for Historic Preservation has helped focus national attention on the teardown "epidemic." In addition to listing "Teardowns in Historic Neighborhoods" on their 2002 list of America's 11 Most Endangered Historic Places, the trust also tracks teardowns on their website.

18. Ned Kaufman, *History Happened Here: A Plan for Saving New York City's Historically and Culturally Significant Sites* (New York: Municipal Art Society, 1996), 47.

19. "The partial destruction of the Audubon Ballroom was followed by the loss of the Dvorak House and of Pier 54, the last of the great Cunard piers. The destruction of portions of the African Burial Ground, and the controversies over the retention of the Naumburg Bandshell in Central Park and, more recently, of the Children's Zoo made it clear that a great many people were responding with passion to the claims of historic sites." Kaufman, *History Happened Here: A Plan for Saving New York City's Historically and Culturally Significant Sites*, 1; Ned Kaufman, "Historic Places and the Diversity Deficit in Heritage Conservation," CRM: *The Journal of Heritage Stewardship* 1, no. 2 (Summer 2004): 68–69.

20. Kaufman, *History Happened Here*, 35.

21. "About Place Matters: Mission and History," Place Matters, www.placematters.net/flash/about.htm (accessed November 24, 2006).

22. The National Trust devoted an issue of its forum journal to the subject. "Preservationists Debate the Recent Past," *forum journal*, (Fall 2005): 20, no. 1.

23. Stern, *New York 2000*, 777–779; Tom Wolfe, "The (Naked) City and the Undead," *New York Times*, November 26, 2006; Robin Pogrebin, "In Preservation Wars, A Focus on Midcentury," *New York Times*, March 4, 2005; Francis Morrone, "The Rise and Fall of a Modernist Gem," *New York Sun*, September 25, 2006.

24. Emory Lewis, "S.O.S. for New Yorkers: Save Our Landmarks," *Cue*, March 13, 1965.

25. Robert A. M. Stern, *New York 2000*, 153–157.

26. Ned Kaufman, email to author, December 14, 2006.

27. Ned Kaufman has done some interesting thinking on a national level about the future of preservation, including the use of new legal tools. Ned Kaufman, "Moving Forward: Futures for a Preservation Movement" in *Giving Preservation a History*, Max Page and Randall Mason, eds., 313–328.

28. Among these are Vicki Weiner, preservation specialist, Pratt Center for Community Development; preservation consultant Ned Kaufman, and Laura Hansen, program officer at the J. M. Kaplan Fund.

29. Roberta Brandes Gratz, then a reporter for the *New York Post*, wrote a series of articles in 1973 that helped make the case for the proposed amendments. Among them are: "Landmark Law—A City Tragedy," January 8, 1973; "Is There a 'Catch-22' in the Landmark Law?" January 9, 1973; "Trying to Save a Bit of Brooklyn's Past," January 10, 1973; "Saving the Ansonia: An Uphill Battle," January 11, 1973; and "Landmarks: A Rating after 10 Years," January 12, 1973.

30. Kelli Whitlock Burton and Alexis Raymond, "Class Acts," *Kenyon College Alumni Bulletin*, fall 2006, 29.

31. Wood, "An Interview with Harmon Goldstone," 37.

32. Diamonstein-Spielvogel, 19–21.

33. Charles G. Bennett, "First Paid Head of Landmarks Group is Sworn In," *New York Times*, October, 22, 1968.

34. Tom Wolfe, "The (Naked) City and the Undead," *New York Times*, November 26, 2006.

35. Nicolai Ouroussoff, "Turning Up the Heat on a Landmark Agency," *New York Times*, November 14, 2005.

36. "Minutes of the Landmarks Meeting," January 20, 1965 at the Architectural League, chaired by Giorgio Cavaglieri, Municipal Art Society.

37. One such example is the work of the Historic City Committee leading to its report: New York: The Historic City, February 6, 1989.

38. Nicolai Ouroussoff, "Turning Up the Heat on a Landmarks Agency," *New York Times*, November 14, 2005; Tom Wolfe, "The (Naked) City and the Undead," *New York Times*, November 26, 2006.

39. In 2003, the Municipal Art Society's staff prepared "New York City's Landmarks Preservation Commission: Meeting the Challenges of the 21st Century," a critical appraisal of the problems facing the Landmarks Preservation Commission. The society asks that the document be described as "an internal memorandum prepared by a then-employee of the Municipal Art Society but never approved or released by MAS." The society privately shared the document with the commission but did not make it public.

40. Edward R. Finch, Jr., "News of the Municipal Art Society," June 1965.
41. "The Short Answer: An Exchange with Donald Trump," *Preservation*, July/August, 2006, 18; Stern, *New York 2000*, 548–549.

SELECTED BIBLIOGRAPHY

ARCHIVES

American Scenic and Historic Preservation Society Records, The New York Public Library

Albert Bard Archive, New York Preservation Archive Project

Albert S. Bard Papers, Manuscripts and Archives Division, The New York Public Library, Astor, Lenox and Tilden Foundations

Brooklyn Heights Association Archive

Century Association Archives Foundation

Richard S. Childs Papers, Rare Book & Manuscript Library, Columbia University

Fine Arts Federation of New York Records, Archives of American Art

Harmon Hendricks Goldstone Papers, The New York Historical Society

Greenwich Village Society for Historic Preservation Archive

Talbot F. Hamlin Collection, Avery Architectural & Fine Arts Library, Columbia University

Charles B. Hosmer Collection, National Trust for Historic Preservation Library Collection and Archives, Special Collections, University of Maryland at College Park Libraries

Ely Jacques Kahn Papers, Avery Architectural & Fine Arts Library, Columbia University

MTA Bridges and Tunnels Special Archive

Municipal Art Society of New York Records, Archives of American Art

National Trust for Historic Preservation Library Collection and Archives, Special Collections, University of Maryland at College Park Libraries

New York Preservation Archive Project

Otis Pratt Pearsall Papers, New York Preservation Archive Project

Records of the National Trust for Historic Preservation, National Archives at College Park, Maryland

New York City Department of Parks and Recreation

NYC Municipal Archives

James Grote Van Derpool Papers, Avery Architectural and Fine Arts Library, Columbia University

Professional Papers of Robert C. Weinberg, Long Island University

Anthony C. Wood Archive

BOOKS AND ARTICLES

Abbott, Berenice, and Henry Wysham Lanier. *Greenwich Village Today & Yesterday.* New York: Harper & Brothers, 1949.

Ballon, Hilary. *New York's Pennsylvania Stations.* New York: W.W. Norton, 2002.

Ballon, Hilary, and Kenneth T. Jackson, eds. *Robert Moses and the Modern City: The Transformation of New York.* New York: W.W. Norton, 2007.

Bard, Albert S. "Aesthetics and the Police Power." *The American Journal of Economics and Sociology* 15, 3 (April 1956): 265–275.

Blake, Peter. *God's Own Junkyard.* New York: Holt, Rhinehart and Winston, 1964.

Bogart, Michelle. *The Politics of Urban Beauty: New York and Its Art Commission.* Chicago: University of Chicago Press, 2006.

Burnham, Alan. *New York Landmarks.* Middletown, CT: Wesleyan University Press, 1963.

Capote, Truman. *A House on the Heights.* New York: The Little Bookroom, 2001.

Caro, Robert A. *The Power Broker: Robert Moses and the Fall of New York.* New York: Random House, 1975.

Dana, Nathalie. *1892–1967 The Municipal Art Society: Seventy-Five Years of Service to New York.* New York: Municipal Art Society.

Diamonstein-Spielvogel, Barbaralee. *The Landmarks of New York.* New York: Monacelli Press, 2005.

Diehl, Lorraine B. *The Late, Great Pennsylvania Station.* New York: Stephen Greene Press, 1987.

Doheny, David. *David Finley: Quiet Force for America's Arts.* Washington, D.C.: National Trust for Historic Preservation, 2006.

Dolkart, Andrew. *Guide to New York City Landmarks.* Washington, D.C.: Preservation Press, 1992.

Dolkart, Andrew. *Touring the Upper East Side.* New York: New York Landmarks Conservancy, 1995.

Elkind, Charlotte W. "The Brooklyn Heights Association," paper prepared for an M.A. in history, New York University, 1988.

Fagin, Henry, and Robert C. Weinberg, eds. *Planning and Community Appearance.* New York: Regional Plan Association, 1958.

Fein, Albert, and Elliott S. M. Gatner, eds. *A Guide to the Professional Papers of Robert C. Weinberg.* New York: Department of Urban Studies, Long Island University, 1984.

Folpe, Emily Kies. *It Happened on Washington Square.* Baltimore: Johns Hopkins University Press, 2002.

Fosdick, Raymond B. *A Report on an Investigation of Billboard Advertising in the City of New York.* New York: City of New York, Office of the Commissioner of Accounts, 1912.

Gilmartin, Gregory F. *Shaping the City: New York and the Municipal Art Society.* New York: Clarkson Potter, 1995.

Goldstone, Harmon. "The Future of the Past." *Village Views* 4, no. 3 (Summer 1987): 10–16.

Gray, Christopher. *Fifth Avenue, 1911 from Start to Finish.* New York: Dover, 1994.

Greenwald, Lisa. *History of the J.M. Kaplan Fund.* Unpublished monograph: 2004.

Gudis, Catherine. *Buyways: Billboards, Automobiles, and the American Landscape.* New York: Routledge, 2004.

Halberstam, David. *The Fifties.* New York: Ballantine, 1993.

Hall, Edward Hagaman. "The Poster Nuisance/An Argument Against the Abuses of Outdoor Advertising." *Annual Report*. American Scenic and Historic Preservation Society, 1905.

Hiss, Tony. *The View from Alger's Window*. New York: Knopf, 1999.

Holden, Arthur Cort. *Planning Recommendations for the Washington Square Area*. New York: Washington Square Association, 1946.

Hone, Philip. *The Diary of Philip Hone, 1828–1851*. New York: Dodd, Mead and Company, 1927.

Hosmer, Charles B. Jr. *Presence of the Past*. New York: G.P. Putnam's Sons, 1965.

Hosmer, Charles B. Jr. *Preservation Comes of Age: From Williamsburg to the National Trust 1926–1949*. Charlottesville, VA: University Press of Virginia, 1981.

Hurwitz, Rudie. "Unsung Urbanist: Robert C. Weinberg, New Yorker Behind the Scenes." New York Preservation Archive Project. http://www.nypap.org/public_programs/ UnsungUrbanistRobertCWeinbergNewYorkerBehindtheScenes.htm.

Huxtable, Ada Louise. *Four Walking Tours of Modern Architecture in New York City*. New York: Doubleday, 1961.

Jackson, Huson. *A Guide to New York Architecture 1650–1952*. New York: Reinhold, 1952.

Jackson, Kenneth T., ed. *The Encyclopedia of New York City*. New Haven: Yale University Press, 1995.

Kaufman, Ned. "Historic Places and the Diversity Deficit in Heritage Conservation," *CRM: The Journal of Heritage Stewardship* 1, no. 2 (Summer 2004): 68–85.

Kaufman, Ned. *History Happened Here: A Plan for Saving New York City's Historically and Culturally Significant Sites*. New York: Municipal Art Society, 1996.

Ketchum, Morris, Jr. *Blazing a Trail*. New York: Vantage, 1982.

Kouwenhoven, John A. *The Columbia Historical Portrait of New York*. New York: Harper and Row, 1972.

Kramer, Jane. *Off Washington Square*. New York: Duell, Sloan and Pearce, 1963.

Kroessler, Jeffrey A. *New York Year by Year*. New York: New York Universitiy Press, 2002.

Lancaster, Clay. *Old Brooklyn Heights: New York's First Suburb*, 2nd ed. New York: Dover, 1979.

Langstaff, B. Meredith. *Brooklyn Heights Yesterday Today Tomorrow*. New York: Brooklyn Heights Association, 1937.

Landmarks Preservation Commission of the City of New York. *Brooklyn Heights Historic District Designation Report*. New York, 1965.

Landmarks Preservation Commission of the City of New York. *Greenwich Village Historic District Designation Report*. New York, 1969.

Makielski, Stanislaw, J. *The Politics of Zoning: The New York Experience*. New York: Columbia University Press, 1966.

Martin, George. *CCB: The Life and Century of Charles C. Burlingham, New York's First Citizen, 1858–1959*. New York: Hill and Wang, 2005.

Mason, Randall F. "Memory Infrastructure: Preservation, 'Improvement,' and Landscape in New York City, 1898–1925." Unpublished dissertation, Columbia University, 1999.

McNickle, Chris. *To Be Mayor of New York*. New York: Columbia University Press, 1993.

Ment, David. *Building Blocks of Brooklyn*. Brooklyn, NY: Brooklyn Educational & Cultural Alliance, 1979.

Ment, David. *The Shaping of a City. Brooklyn, NY.* Brooklyn Educational & Cultural Alliance, 1979.

Miller, Terry. *Greenwich Village and How It Got That Way.* New York: Crown, 1990.

Moore, Peter. *The Destruction of Penn Station.* New York: Distributed Art, 2000.

Morrison, Jacob H. *Historic Preservation Law.* Washington, DC: National Trust for Historic Preservation, 1965.

Moses, Robert. *Public Works: A Dangerous Trade.* New York: McGraw-Hill, 1970.

Municipal Art Society, *New York Landmarks: An Index of Architecturally Notable Structures in New York City.* New York: The Municipal Art Society, 1957.

Murtagh, William J. *Keeping Time: The History and Theory of Preservation in America.* New York: Sterling, 1990.

Neville, Christopher. "Building and Rebuilding New York: The Radio Urbanism of Robert C. Weinberg, 1966–1971." New York Preservation Archive Project. http://www.nypap.org/public_programs/WeinbergPublication.html.

New York, City of. *Report of the Mayor's Billboard Advertising Commission of the City of New York.* New York: City of New York, August 1, 1913.

New York Community Trust. *The Heritage of New York.* New York: Fordham University Press, 1970.

Page, Max. *The Creative Destruction of Manhattan 1900–1940.* Chicago: University of Chicago Press, 1999.

Page, Max and Randall Mason, eds. *Giving Preservation a History.* New York: Routledge, 2004.

Patterson, James T. *Grand Expectations: The United States, 1945–1974.* Oxford: Oxford University Press, 1996.

Patterson, Jerry E. *Fifth Avenue: The Best Address.* New York: Rizzoli, 1998.

Pearsall, Otis Pratt. "Otis Pratt Pearsall's Reminiscences of the Nine-Year Effort to Designate Brooklyn Heights as New York City's First Historic District and its First Limited Height District." *Village Views* 7, no. 2 (1995).

Plosky, Eric J. "The Fall and Rise of Pennsylvania Station: Changing Attitudes toward Historic Preservation in New York City." Master's thesis, Massachusetts Institute of Technology, February 2000.

Sayre, Wallace S., and Herbert Kaufman. *Governing New York City: Politics in the Metropolis.* New York: Russell Sage Foundation, 1960.

Shanor, Rebecca. *The City that Never Was.* New York: Penguin, 1988.

Silver, Nathan. *Lost New York.* New York: Shocken Books, 1971.

Stayton, Kevin. *Dutch by Design; Tradition and Change in Two Historic Brooklyn Houses: The Schenck Houses at the Brooklyn Museum.* New York: Brooklyn Museum in association with Phaidon Universe, 1990.

Stern, Isaac with Chaim Potok. *My First 79 Years.* Cambridge, MA: Da Capo Press, 2000.

Stern, Robert A. M., Thomas Mellins, and David Fishman. *New York 1880.* New York: Monacelli Press, 1999.

———. *New York 1960.* New York: Monacelli Press, 1995.

Stern, Robert A. M., David Fishman, and Jacob Tilove. *New York 2000.* New York: Monacelli Press, 2006.

Stipe, Robert E., ed. *A Richer Heritage.* Chapel Hill, NC: University of North Carolina Press, 2003.

Tift, Susan, and Alex S. Jones. *The Trust.* New York: Little, Brown, 1999.

Wetzsteon, Ross. *Republic of Dreams Greenwich Village: The American Bohemia, 1910–1960*. New York: Simon and Schuster, 2002.

Willensky, Elliot and Norval White. *AIA Guide to New York City*. New York: Harcourt Brace Jovanovich, 1988.

Wolfe, Thomas. *You Can't Go Home Again*. New York: Harper Perennial Classics, 1998.

Wood, Anthony C. "At Dawn We Slept: Pearl Harbor and Preservation in New York City." *New York Chronicle* 2, no. 1 (Winter, 1999): 10–12.

Wood, Anthony C. "Celebrating Preservation's Story: 'It's your memory. It's our history. It's worth saving." *forum journal* 20, no. 2 (Winter 2006): 45–52.

Wood, Anthony C. "Pioneers of Preservation: An Interview with the First Chairman of the Landmarks Preservation Commission, The Late Geoffrey Platt." *Village Views* 4, no. 1 (Winter 1987): 7–37.

Wood, Anthony C. "Pioneers of Preservation: Brooklyn Heights and the Landmarks Law: An Interview with Otis Pratt Pearsall." *Village Views* 7, no. 2 (1995): 29–48.

Wood, Anthony C. "Pioneers of Preservation: Part II: An Interview with Harmon Goldstone." *Village Views* 4, no. 3 (Summer 1987): 17–42.

Wood, Anthony C. "Pioneers of Preservation: Part III: Preservation's Scholarly Roots: Talbot Hamlin and the Avery Library; An Interview with Commissioner Adolf Placzek." *Village Views* 4, no. 4 (Fall 1987): 3–37.

■　■　■　■　■　■

FIGURE CREDITS

CHAPTER 1

FIGURE 1.1   Image appeared in *The Heritage of New York*, 1970, Community Funds, Inc. Image courtesy of the New York Community Trust. With permission.

FIGURE 1.2   *Park East*, newspaper, vol. 1, no. 38, Thursday, October 1, 1964, front page, negative number 78743d. Collection of The New-York Historical Society. With permission.

FIGURE 1.3   The Queens Borough Public Library, Long Island Division, *New York Herald-Tribune* Photograph Collection. Image courtesy of the IEEE History Center. With permission.

FIGURE 1.4   Image courtesy of the Anthony C. Wood Archive.

FIGURE 1.5   David L. Hirsch. With permission.

FIGURE 1.6   Culver Pictures, Inc. With permission.

FIGURE 1.7   Chi Psi Fraternity. With permission.

FIGURE 1.8   Up Dumaine Street along 500 block, negative by Charles L. Franck Photographers. Image courtesy of The Historic New Orleans Collection. With permission.

FIGURE 1.9   John Tresilian/*New York Daily News*. With permission.

FIGURE 1.10   Image courtesy of the Anthony C. Wood Archive.

FIGURE 1.11   Image courtesy of Michael Miscione.

CHAPTER 2

FIGURE 2.1   Chi Psi Fraternity. With permission.

FIGURE 2.2   Image courtesy of the Anthony C. Wood Archive.

FIGURE 2.3   Image courtesy of the Anthony C. Wood Archive.

FIGURE 2.4   Billboards on Fifth Avenue between 89th and 90th Streets, from the Report of the Mayor's Billboard Advertising Commission, 1913. Courtesy NYC Municipal Archives. With permission.

FIGURE 2.5   Picture Collection, The Branch Libraries, The New York Public Library, Astor, Lenox and Tilden Foundations. Anonymous. City Hall, New York. 1913. Sepia photograph. With permission.

FIGURE 2.6   Photograph courtesy Peabody Essex Museum. PEM Negative #3132, St. John's Exterior by Frank Cousins.

FIGURE 2.7   Photograph courtesy Peabody Essex Museum. PEM Negative #2581, Gracie House, East River Park by Frank Cousins. With permission.

CHAPTER 3

FIGURE 3.1   Image courtesy of the Anthony C. Wood Archive.

FIGURE 3.2   Courtesy MTA Bridges and Tunnels Special Archive. With permission.

FIGURE 3.3   *New York Times*/Redux. Image courtesy of the Collection of The New-York Historical Society, negative number 79508d. With permission.

FIGURE 3.4   The Queens Borough Public Library, Long Island Division, *New York Herald-Tribune* Photograph Collection. Image located in the American Newspaper Repository Collection at the Rare Book, Manuscript, and Special Collections Library, Duke University. With permission.

FIGURE 3.5   Courtesy of Charles Burlingham Jr. With permission.

FIGURE 3.6   The Queens Borough Public Library, Long Island Division, *New York Herald-Tribune* Photograph Collection. Image located in the American Newspaper Repository Collection at the Rare Book, Manuscript, and Special Collections Library, Duke University. With permission.

FIGURE 3.7   Albert S. Bard Papers, Manuscripts and Archives Division, The New York Public Library, Astor, Lenox and Tilden Foundations. With permission.

FIGURE 3.8   Aquarium exterior, Battery Park main entrance, New York City, from the WPA Collection. Courtesy NYC Municipal Archives. With permission.

FIGURE 3.9   American Scenic and Historic Preservation Society, Manuscripts and Archives Division, The New York Public Library, Astor, Lenox and Tilden Foundations. With permission.

FIGURE 3.10   Worsinger Photos/New York City Parks Photo Archive. Negative #40001-27, Battery Park Bulkhead Pier A series, looking south from 3rd Floor of Pier A, with progress of Aquarium demolition at left, Battery Park, Manhattan, September 27, 1946. With permission.

FIGURE 3.11   Alajos L. Schuszler/New York City Parks Photo Archive. Negative #3080, Johannes Schenck House (Dutch-style farmhouse, construction 1686–1765), view of east, Highland Park, Brooklyn, May 8, 1934. With permission.

FIGURE 3.12   Avery Architectural and Fine Arts Library, Columbia University. With permission.

CHAPTER 4

FIGURE 4.1   The Ritz-Carlton Hotel New York/Byron, NY, Library of Congress, LC-USZ62-116039.

FIGURE 4.2   Main gate from the exterior, Aquarium and Castle Clinton, Battery Park, New York, photograph, negative number 30367. Collection of The New-York Historical Society. Image courtesy of the National Park Service. With permission.

FIGURE 4.3   Image courtesy of the National Trust for Historic Preservation Library Collection, Special Collections, University of Maryland Libraries.

FIGURE 4.4   Photography collection, Miriam and Ira D. Wallach Division of Art, Prints and Photographs, The New York Public Library, Astor, Lenox and Tilden Foundations. Berenice Abbott. Rockefeller Center: Collegiate Church of St. Nicholas in foreground, Fifth Avenue and 48th Street, Manhattan. December 08, 1936. Gelatin silver print. With permission.

FIGURE 4.5   *New York Times*/Redux. With permission.

FIGURE 4.6   Milstein Division of United States History, Local History and Genealogy, The New York Public Library, Astor, Lenox and Tilden Foundations. Welles & Co. "Washington Arch—No. 12 Apartment house, West 8th St." *Fifth Avenue, New York, from start to finish.* 1911. Halftone photomechanical print. With permission.

FIGURE 4.7   Collection of the Museum of the City of New York. Beecher Ogden, Washington Square North, Corner of Fifth Avenue, January 19, 1951. With permission.

CHAPTER 5

FIGURE 5.1   Albert S. Bard Papers, Manuscripts and Archives Division, The New York Public Library, Astor, Lenox and Tilden Foundations. With permission.

FIGURE 5.2   Down Royal Street from 700 block corner St. Ann Street, ca. 1940, negative by Charles L. Franck Photographers. Image courtesy of The Historic New Orleans Collection. With permission.

FIGURE 5.3   Brooklyn Public Library, Brooklyn Collection. With permission.

FIGURE 5.4   Detroit Publishing Company Photograph Collection, Library of Congress.

FIGURE 5.5   Talbot Hamlin at work; with permission of the University Archives, Columbia University in the City of New York. With permission.

FIGURE 5.6   University Archives. Department of Rare Books and Special Collections. Princeton University Library. With permission.

FIGURE 5.7   Professor James Grote Van Derpool examines the Renwick collection; with permission of the University Archives, Columbia University in the City of New York. With permission.

FIGURE 5.8   Berenice Abbott/Commerce Graphics Ltd, Inc., NYC. Image courtesy of the Milstein Division of United States History, Local History and Genealogy, The New York Public Library, Astor, Lenox and Tilden Foundations. With permission.

FIGURE 5.9   Queens Historical Society. With permission.

FIGURE 5.10   Pieter Claesen Wyckoff House with Caretaker Edith Schwenke, 1963. Image courtesy of the Wyckoff House & Association. With permission.

CHAPTER 6

FIGURE 6.1   Chi Psi Fraternity. With permission.

FIGURE 6.2   Long Island University Archives. With permission.

FIGURE 6.3   Milstein Division of United States History, Local History and Genealogy, The New York Public Library, Astor, Lenox and Tilden Foundations. Anonymous. "42nd Street (East)—Vanderbilt Avenue." *Photographic views of New York City, 1870s–1970s, Supplement.* With permission.

FIGURE 6.4   Image courtesy of *The Villager* newspaper. April 6, 1961. With permission.

FIGURE 6.5   *New York Times*/Redux. With permission.

FIGURE 6.6   *New York Times*/Redux. With permission.

FIGURE 6.7   Front cover of *New York Landmarks*, 1957, Municipal Art Society of New York.

FIGURE 6.8   Image appeared in *The Heritage of New York*, 1970, Community Funds, Inc. Image courtesy of the New York Community Trust. With permission.

CHAPTER 7

FIGURE 7.1   Berenice Abbott/Commerce Graphics Ltd, Inc., NYC. With permission.

FIGURE 7.2   *New York Times*/Redux. With permission.

FIGURE 7.3   *New York Times*/Redux. With permission.

FIGURE 7.4   *New York Times*/Redux. With permission.

FIGURE 7.5   Copyright 1958, *Village Voice* Media, Inc. Reprinted with the permission of The *Village Voice*. Image courtesy of General Research Division, The New York Public Library, Astor, Lenox and Tilden Foundations.

FIGURE 7.6   Cartoon by Joseph Papin. Image courtesy of *The Villager* newspaper. November 6, 1958. With permission.

FIGURE 7.7   Copyright 1958, *Village Voice* Media, Inc. Reprinted with the permission of The *Village Voice*. Image courtesy of General Research Division, The New York Public Library, Astor, Lenox and Tilden Foundations.

FIGURE 7.8   Copyright 1958, *Village Voice* Media, Inc. Reprinted with the permission of The *Village Voice*. Image courtesy of General Research Division, The New York Public Library, Astor, Lenox and Tilden Foundations.

FIGURE 7.9   Photograph by Beth Bianculli. Image courtesy of *The Villager* newspaper. November 4, 1998. With permission.

CHAPTER 8

FIGURE 8.1   Culver Pictures, Inc. With permission.

FIGURE 8.2   The Brooklyn Historical Society. With permission.

FIGURE 8.3   Photo by Edmund V. Gillon, Jr. Reproduced by permission of the publisher from Clay Lancaster, *Old Brooklyn Heights: New York's First Suburb*, 2nd ed. New York: Dover Publications, 1979, 86. With permission.

FIGURE 8.4   Courtesy of Otis and Nancy Pearsall. With permission.

FIGURE 8.5   The Brooklyn Historical Society. With permission.

FIGURE 8.6   Photo by Carroll Cline, April 7, 1959. Image courtesy of the Warwick Foundation. With permission.

CHAPTER 9

FIGURE 9.1   *New York Times*/Redux. With permission.

FIGURE 9.2   Copyright 1965, *Village Voice* Media, Inc. Reprinted with the permission of The *Village Voice*. Image courtesy of General Research Division, The New York Public Library, Astor, Lenox and Tilden Foundations.

FIGURE 9.3   Chi Psi Fraternity. With permission.
FIGURE 9.4   Photograph by John Minutoli. Image courtesy of *The Villager* newspaper. June 30, 1960. With permission.
FIGURE 9.5   *New York Daily News*. With permission.
FIGURE 9.6   Photograph by C. Binkins, August 11, 1966. Image courtesy of the Warwick Foundation. With permission.

CHAPTER 10

FIGURE 10.1   William C. Eckenberg/*New York Times*/Redux. With permission.
FIGURE 10.2   Courtesy MTA Bridges and Tunnels Special Archive. With permission.
FIGURE 10.3   Newl Boenzi/ *New York Times*/Redux. With permission.
FIGURE 10.4   Private Collection. With permission.
FIGURE 10.5   Picture Collection, The Branch Libraries, The New York Public Library, Astor, Lenox and Tilden Foundations. Anonymous. Façade, Depew Place, Grand Central Terminal, New York, 1913. Photograph. With permission.
FIGURE 10.6   Photograph by Dan Miller. Image courtesy of *The Villager* newspaper. April 6, 1961. With permission.

CHAPTER 11

FIGURE 11.1   Avery Architectural and Fine Arts Library, Columbia University. With permission.
FIGURE 11.2   Berenice Abbott/Commerce Graphics Ltd, Inc., NYC. With permission.
FIGURE 11.3   Image courtesy of Gordon Hyatt. With permission.
FIGURE 11.4   Photograph by Garth Huxtable. With permission.
FIGURE 11.5   From the Harmon H. Goldstone papers, Manuscript Collection, negative number 79462d. Collection of The New-York Historical Society. With permission.
FIGURE 11.6   American Scenic and Historic Preservation Society, Manuscripts and Archives Division, The New York Public Library, Astor, Lenox and Tilden Foundations. With permission.
FIGURE 11.7   Copyright 1962, *Village Voice* Media, Inc. Reprinted with the permission of The *Village Voice*. Image courtesy of General Research Division, The New York Public Library, Astor, Lenox and Tilden Foundations.
FIGURE 11.8   Norman McGrath Photographer, Inc. With permission.
FIGURE 11.9   Photo by Peter Moore © Est. of Peter Moore/VAGA, NYC from *The Destruction of Penn Station* (D.A.P., 2000.) With permission.
FIGURE 11.10   Photo by Peter Moore © Est. of Peter Moore/VAGA, NYC from *The Destruction of Penn Station* (D.A.P., 2000.) With permission.
FIGURE 11.11   *The New Yorker Collection*, 1963, Alan Dunn from cartoonbank.com. All rights reserved. With permission.
FIGURE 11.12   Photograph by Steven Tucker. Image courtesy of The New York Preservation Archive Project. With permission.
FIGURE 11.13   Chi Psi Fraternity. With permission.

CHAPTER 12

FIGURE 12.1	The Brooklyn Historical Society. With permission.
FIGURE 12.2	Front cover of *New York Landmarks,* edited by Alan Burnham, 1963, Wesleyan University Press.
FIGURE 12.3	Photograph by Micki Wolter. Image courtesy of *The Villager* newspaper. July 25, 1963. With permission.
FIGURE 12.4	Charles Payne/*New York Daily News*. With permission.
FIGURE 12.5	Photograph by Arthur Lind. Image courtesy of Margot Gayle.
FIGURE 12.6	Samuel H. Gottscho, Central Park Looking Toward 59th Street, 1932, Museum of the City of New York, The Gottscho-Schleisner Collection, 34.114.18. With permission.
FIGURE 12.7	The Queens Borough Public Library, Long Island Division, *New York Herald-Tribune* Photograph Collection. With permission.
FIGURE 12.8	Don Hogan Charles/*New York Times*/Redux. With permission.
FIGURE 12.9	The New York City Landmarks Preservation Commission. With permission.
FIGURE 12.10	Image courtesy of the IEEE History Center. With permission.
FIGURE 12.11	Image appeared in *The Heritage of New York,* 1970, Community Funds, Inc. Image courtesy of the New York Community Trust. With permission.
FIGURE 12.12	Image courtesy of *The Villager* newspaper. March 11, 1965. With permission.
FIGURE 12.13	Photograph by Deborah Jones. Image courtesy of *The Villager* newspaper. March 11, 1965. With permission.
FIGURE 12.14	Image courtesy of Margot Gayle. With permission.

CHAPTER 13

FIGURE 13.1	Photograph by Frank W. Kroha. Image courtesy of the National Park Service.
FIGURE 13.2	Image courtesy of the Anthony C. Wood Archive.
FIGURE 13.3	Harry Hamburg/*New York Daily News*.
FIGURE 13.4	Photograph by Rose Morse, 1974.
FIGURE 13.5	Image courtesy of Linda C. Jones.
FIGURE 13.6	Image courtesy of James Higgins.
FIGURE 13.7	Image courtesy of Richard A. George.
FIGURE 13.8	Photograph by Rhoda Galyn.
FIGURE 13.9	Image courtesy of Landmark West!
FIGURE 13.10	Image courtesy of Steven Tucker.

Index